The Rough

Cairo and the Pyramids

written and researched by
Dan Richardson and Daniel Jacobs

ROUGH
GUIDES

www.roughguides.com

Contents

Islamic architecture colour section following p.112

The pharaohs colour section following p.240

Cairo Marriott **Colour maps** following p.296

◄◄ View over the city from the Cairo Tower ◄ Khan el-Khalili Bazaar

Introduction to

Cairo and the Pyramids

Cairo, the Islamic world's greatest city, is a teeming and chaotic megalopolis that draws you in further and further as you get to know it. At its heart lies the fabled Islamic city of a thousand minarets, crowded and compelling, its bazaars spilling over with spices, perfumes and fine fabrics, its mosques steeped in the architecture of a bygone golden age. The early twentieth-century downtown area, elegantly modern by comparison, is centred on famous Tahrir Square, where the Egyptian Museum houses treasures from five millennia of history. And at the city's limits, the Pyramids, planted with four-square solidity in the desert, have been wonders of the world since ancient times, when they themselves were ancient already; to this day they remain one of the world's absolute must-sees, a suitable climax of any visit to this alluring city.

Egyptians have two names for the city, one ancient and popular, the other Islamic and official. The first is **Masr**, meaning both the capital and the land of Egypt – "Egypt City" – the great metropolis that dominates and embodies a nation rooted in pharaonic civilization. But whereas Masr is timeless, the city's other name, **al-Qahira** (The Conqueror), is linked to an event: the Fatimid conquest of 969 that made this the capital of an Islamic empire covering North Africa, Syria, and even (for a time) Mecca. But although it gives us our English name for the city, the term Al-Qahira is rarely used for it in everyday speech in Egypt.

Both of the city's names and identities still resonate, and they are symbolized by two dramatic **landmarks**: the **Pyramids of Giza** at the edge of the Western Desert and the great **Mosque of Mohammed Ali** – the modernizer of Islamic Egypt – which broods atop the Citadel. Between these two monuments sprawls a vast city, the colour of sand and ashes, spanning diverse worlds and epochs, and encompassing great joy, great riches and gross inequities.

Cairo has been the biggest city in the Middle East ever since the Mongols wasted Baghdad in 1258. Acknowledged as *umm dunya* or "**Mother of the World**" by medieval Arabs, and as Great Cairo by nineteenth-century Europeans, it has been a fulcrum of power in the Arab world from the Crusades to the present day. It is a city, as Welsh travel writer Jan Morris put it, "almost overwhelmed by its own fertility", with a **population** estimated at over seventeen million, and swollen by a further million commuters from the Delta and a thousand new migrants every day. Many of its inhabitants live in poverty, with forty percent of households in some parts of town having no running water and over half lacking sewers, while an estimated half a million people occupy squatted cemeteries – the famous **Cities of the Dead**. But it is not just the sheer size of the population which gives Cairo its weight in the world. It is also one of the most important centres of Islamic learning, and the jurists of its thousand-year-old Al-Azhar Mosque remain the ultimate religious authority for millions of Sunni Muslims worldwide, from Jakarta to Birmingham.

Yet for all its teeming crowds, Cairo is an amazingly safe and gentle place. This is not so much due to the massive police presence on its streets as to the **social rituals** that lubricate the rubbing of shoulders that is inevitable in such

Craftsman in the Tentmakers' Bazaar

a densely populated metropolis. When tempers do rise, a crowd will gather, restraining both parties, sympathizing with their grievances, and finally urging "*Maalesh, maalesh*" (Never mind, never mind). This is a city where people look out for each other, and where everyday life is sweetened by flowery gestures and salutations, and large amounts of well-sugared tea. Even misfortune evokes thanks for Allah's dispensation (after all, things could be worse), and even the poorest can be respected for piety, while inside the city's mosques and churches, millionaire and beggar kneel side by side, all equal in the sight of God.

What this means in practical terms for a foreigner visiting the city is that its people are friendly, hospitable and generally kind-hearted. "Welcome to Egypt!" people often shout on the streets, and they mean it. Even so, it is hard not to be a little overwhelmed, at first, by the city's size and density.

Feluccas on the Nile, at night

Flowing through this huge metropolis from south to north is the Nile, the world's longest river. The eastern side is Cairo proper, the west, strictly speaking, is its own city, Giza. Along each waterfront is a **Corniche** (embankment), and between the two sides are **islands** such as Gezira and Roda. The **downtown** area, formerly marshland outside the city walls, bears the stamp of Western planning; it's the labyrinthine area of Islamic Cairo, east of downtown, that really gives the feel of a true Middle Eastern city. On the other side of this spread the eerie **Cities of the Dead** – the Northern and Southern cemeteries – and beyond them rise the **Muqqatam Hills**, a barrier throughout history against Cairo's further eastward spread.

What to see

The **Pyramids**, obviously, are Cairo's big, big attraction, rising out of the desert west of town like huge fossilized artefacts from a lost civilization. Aside from the famous **Sphinx** and **Pyramids of Giza**, there's their prototype, **Zoser's Step Pyramid**, with its elegant funerary temple at **Saqqara**, and a less known, less visited but no less fascinating group of pyramids at **Dahshur**. Even then, the stock of pyramids is not exhausted, with more, should you wish to venture further, at **Abu Sir**, **Maidum** and **Lisht**.

In town, the ancient artefacts continue in the **Egyptian Antiquities Museum**, a dusty, cavernous collection containing some of the world's most stunning treasures, including Tutankhamun's solid-gold funeral mask and the mummies of pharaohs including Ramses II.

Undoubtedly too, you'll want to explore the city's old quarters: **Old Cairo** (Masr al-Qadima in Arabic – Old Masr), with its ancient churches and synagogue, not to mention the fascinating **Coptic Museum**; and **Islamic Cairo** (al-Qahira al-Qadima in Arabic – Old al-Qahira), the medieval heart of the "City of a Thousand Minarets", whose frenetic bazaars, elegant Mamluk mosques and imposing city gates draw you back again and again into their vortex of sights, sounds and smells.

▶ Courtyard of the Al-Azhar Mosque

At the Islamic city's southern end, Saladin's huge and imposing **Citadel** contains its own mosques, museums and historical sites, offering impressive views and enough to entertain you for the best part of a day. The nearby **Cities of the Dead** are more than just mere cemeteries, rather whole suburbs in their own right, where the huge mausoleums double as houses of prayer, while many of the smaller ones have become family homes.

The modern city, too, has attractions to seek out. Its elegant *fin-de-siècle* boulevards and glitzy shops contain the **Abdin Palace**, home of Egypt's presidents, and formerly its royal family, whose treasures you can visit in its museum. In the Nile itself, the tranquil island of **Zamalek** offers a more relaxed and urbane pace of life, while **Roda Island** holds the superb **Manial Palace** and a museum dedicated to singer Umm Kalthoum. To the north of the modern city centre, the early twentieth-century suburb of **Heliopolis** is full of neo-Moorish and Art Deco houses, including Baron Empain's outrageous Indian-style palace. Not far away, the sprawling modern neighbourhood of **Medinet Nasr** holds the tomb of murdered president Anwar Sadat, and the October War Panorama, a bizarre Maoist-style monument to Egypt's 1973 war with Israel.

Within easy reach of Cairo are even more attractions, including the enigmatic **Collapsed Pyramid** at Maidum, the camel market at **Birqesh**, and the desert monasteries at **Wadi Natrun**, all of which make excellent day-trips. The urbane seaside city of **Alexandria**, with its amazing Greco-Roman heritage and its air of old-fashioned gentility, can also be seen in a day, though it's worth staying for longer if you can.

Sheeshas

All over town, you'll see men in cafés chugging away on hookah pipes, known as *sheeshas*, where the smoke from the tobacco is drawn through water in a glass vessel. Though the traditional *ma'azil* tobacco is pretty rough, the water is an efficient filter, as you'll see from the state of it after use. *Ma'azil* is also now giving way to sweeter, fruit-flavoured tobaccos, and these are giving the *sheesha* a new lease in life, as the young – and even some women – are now joining in what was becoming just an old man's habit.

The origin of the *sheesha* is mysterious. The name is Persian for "glass", a reference to the vessel, which would appear to indicate that the pipe came to the Arab world from Iran. The *sheesha* must have predated the introduction of tobacco, as there were sophisticated water-pipes in Iran almost as soon as that pernicious weed arrived. Tobacco historian Alfred Dunhill suggested in the 1950s that it started out in East Africa as a cannabis pipe (Iran had longstanding trade links with that region), and archeological finds in Ethiopia have since proved him right.

When to go

Early spring (February and March) and autumn (October and November) are the best **times to visit**, when temperatures are warm, but not too hot. In summer, Cairo can be roasting, with city grime and desert dust conspiring to glue themselves to sweaty skin; winters can be surprisingly cold, especially at night. Rain is sparse throughout the year, and almost never heavy. April and late November see hot sirocco winds from the Sahara blowing sand across the city. In May and June the heat is still tolerable, but from July to September it is ferociously hot, though this does have the effect of reducing the crowds at monuments such as the Giza Pyramids and the Egyptian Museum. Autumn has the edge over spring in this respect, with fewer visitors in October and November than there are in March and April, particularly during Easter.

Climate and crowds aside, the **Islamic calendar** and its associated festivals can have an effect on your travel. The most important factor is Ramadan, the month of daytime fasting, which can be problematic for eating and transport, though the festive evenings do much to compensate. See p.217 for more background on Ramadan, and for details of its timing.

Cairo climate

	Jan	Feb	Mar	Apr	May	Jun	Jul	Aug	Sep	Oct	Nov	Dec
Average daily temperature												
Max (°F/°C)	66/19	70/21	75/24	82/28	90/32	95/35	95/35	95/35	91/33	86/30	79/16	70/21
Min (°F/°C)	48/9	48/9	54/12	57/14	64/18	68/20	72/22	72/22	68/20	64/18	57/14	50/10
Average monthly rainfall												
mm	4	4	3	1	2	0.5	0	0	0.5	1	3	7

19

things not to miss

Unless you're in town for a while, it's not possible to see everything Cairo has to offer in one trip. What follows is a selective taste of the city-state's highlights – the most fascinating architecture, best museums and most captivating events. They're all arranged in five colour-coded categories so you can find the very best things to see, do and experience. All highlights have a page reference to take you straight into the Guide, where you can find out more.

01 **The Sphinx and Pyramids of Giza** Page **153** • The world's most famous monuments have inspired scholarly and crackpot speculations for centuries.

02 The Egyptian Museum Page **53** • This amazing collection – which includes Tutankhamun's treasures, monumental statues from the Old Kingdom and the Amarna era, and a dozen royal mummies – is among the world's very best museums.

03 Whirling dervishes Page **206** • The dance used by Sufi dervishes to induce a trance-like ecstasy is also a colourful spectacle performed for tourists twice a week free of charge at the Wikala of al-Ghuri.

04 Khan el Khalili Page **77** • Haggle like mad for souvenirs, clothes, glassware, perfumes, jewellery or bric-a-brac in the Middle East's busiest and most bustling bazaar.

05 Sheesha Page **8** •
The traditional Middle Eastern smoke, a hubble-bubble water-pipe, can now be sampled with milder fruit-flavoured tobaccos as well as the traditional, molasses-flavoured ma'azil.

06 Ibn Tulun Mosque Page **105** • Quite unlike any of Cairo's other mosques, this huge enclosure, with its spiral minaret, once held the city's entire population for Friday prayers.

07 Juice bars Page **199** • On almost every street corner, you can quench your thirst with whatever's in season, from freshly pressed oranges and mangoes to strawberries and sugar cane.

09 **Moulids** Page **215** • If you can catch one, do make the effort to join in with these extremely traditional popular religious celebrations, with their fairground-type sideshows, Sufi chanting and colourful processions.

08 **Mezze** Page **189** • Consisting of an array of delicious small dishes, from salads and dips to cheese and falafel, mezze is a highlight of local cuisine, and particularly good for vegetarians.

10 **Mamluke architecture** See *Islamic architecture* **colour section** • With their stripy *ablaq* stonework, geometrically decorated domes and bizarre stalactite-like *murqanas*, the buildings endowed by the Mamlukes characterize Islamic Cairo.

11 **The Citadel** Page **100** • Looming imposingly over the city, Salah al-Din's craggy bastion is dominated by the needle-like Turkish-style minarets of Mohammed Ali's nineteenth-century mosque.

12 **Dahshur Pyramids** Page **175** • Less famous than the Giza pyramids but no less interesting, and far less crowded. The Bent Pyramid, resting place of Snofru, has a distinctive angled top.

13 The Coptic Museum

Page **118** • This fascinating museum tells the history of Egypt's ancient Christian community in manuscripts, monuments, stonework and frescos from the flight of the Holy Family through to the present day.

14 Alexandria
Page **235** • With its dazzling new library, and the chance to dive into the ruins of Cleopatra's Palace and the Pharos Lighthouse, this Mediterranean port city founded by Alexander the Great makes a great day-trip from Cairo.

15 Tea in Fishawi's
Page **198** • Open round the clock, this venerable teahouse in the heart of Khan el Khalili is the place to sink a cuppa in Cairo.

16 **Palace Walk** Page **79** • The very heart of Islamic Cairo, the street known as Bayn al-Qasrayn once ran between two Fatimid palaces, and now runs between the city's finest medieval prayer complexes.

18 **The October War Panorama** Page **144** • Over-the-top Maoist kitsch at this recreation of the 1973 October War, which Egyptians are still convinced they won.

19 **Bellydancing** Page **205** • The centuries-old tradition of *raqs sharqi* (oriental dance) is best seen at Cairo's five-star hotels and floating restaurants, where the top dancers and musicians perform.

17 **The Step Pyramid** Page **165** • The prototype upon which all the later pyramids are modelled, Zoser's Step Pyramid sits amid a host of intriguing ancient tombs.

Basics

Basics

Getting there

Cairo has direct scheduled flights from London and New York, and can be easily reached on an indirect flight from most British, Irish, North American and Australasian airports. The best air fares are available in low season, November through March, excluding Christmas and New Year, which counts as high season along with June, July and August. Flights at weekends can cost more than on weekdays; prices quoted below are for the cheapest round-trip midweek, including tax. Many have restrictions such as fixed dates, and may require advance booking.

Flights from the UK and Ireland

EgyptAir (◉www.egyptair.com.eg), British Airways (◉www.ba.com) and BMI (◉www.flybmi.com) have scheduled flights to **Cairo** from **London** Heathrow (5hr). Several airlines also have **indirect flights** from London, and BA, BMI, KLM (◉www.klm.com), Air France (◉www.airfrance.com) and Lufthansa (◉www.lufthansa.com) also offer indirect flights from a number of other British and Irish airports. Flights can cost as little as £285 return in low season if you shop around online, or around £360 in high season.

From **Ireland**, you can either make your own way to London and fly from there, or take an indirect flight, changing planes in Britain or Europe. Fares start at around €400 off-season, or around €550 in high season.

Flights from the US and Canada

From the **US**, EgyptAir (◉www.egyptair.com.eg) and Delta (◉www.delta.com) fly direct to Cairo from New York (11hr), and several European and Middle Eastern airlines offer indirect flights from a range of departure points, though New York still offers the biggest choice of airlines. West Coast flights are routed via the airlines' hub cities, so check that you won't have to wait overnight for your onward connection. You should be able to pick up a round-trip ticket for as little as $800 out of New York in low season, $925 in high season. Flying from the West Coast, expect to pay $1020 in low season, $1035 in high season.

From **Canada** there are direct flights to Cairo out of Montreal twice weekly in summer with EgyptAir, who also offer through tickets from other cities via New York in conjunction with local airlines. Otherwise, European carriers such as BA (◉www.ba.com) and Air France (◉www.airfrance.com) fly via London or Paris from Toronto, Montreal or Vancouver, while Air Canada (◉www.aircanada.com) offers through tickets from most Canadian airports in combination with Lufthansa (◉www.lufthansa.com). Low-/high-season fares start at around Can$1100/1350 from Montreal or Toronto, Can$1250/1900 from Vancouver.

Flights from Australia, New Zealand and South Africa

A number of European, Middle Eastern and Asian carriers offer indirect flights to Cairo from **Australia** and **New Zealand**, changing planes at their hub airports. Fares start at around Aus$2050 in low season, or Aus$2850 in high season from Australia, and around NZ$2850 year-round from New Zealand. Emirates (◉www.emirates.com) and Etihad (◉www.etihadairways.com) are usually the cheapest and most convenient airlines.

From **South Africa**, there are direct Cairo flights from Johannesburg with EgyptAir (◉www.egyptair.com.eg); South African Airways (◉www.flysaa.com) codeshare these flights, offering through tickets from most South African airports. Otherwise, you can take an indirect flight with an East African airline such as Kenya Airways (◉www.kenya-airways.com) or Ethiopian Airlines

Six steps to a better kind of travel

At Rough Guides we are passionately committed to travel. We feel strongly that only through travelling do we truly come to understand the world we live in and the people we share it with – plus tourism has brought a great deal of **benefit** to developing economies around the world over the last few decades. But the extraordinary growth in tourism has also damaged some places irreparably, and of course **climate change** is exacerbated by most forms of transport, especially flying. This means that now more than ever it's important to **travel thoughtfully** and **responsibly**, with respect for the cultures you're visiting – not only to derive the most benefit from your trip but also to preserve the best bits of the planet for everyone to enjoy. At Rough Guides we feel there are six main areas in which you can make a difference:

- Consider what you're contributing to the **local economy**, and how much the services you use do the same, whether it's through employing local workers and guides or sourcing locally grown produce and local services.
- Consider the **environment** on holiday as well as at home. Water is scarce in many developing destinations, and the biodiversity of local flora and fauna can be adversely affected by tourism. Try to patronize businesses that take account of this.
- Travel with a purpose, not just to tick off experiences. Consider **spending longer** in a place, and getting to know it and its people.
- Give thought to how often you **fly**. Try to avoid short hops by air and more harmful night flights.
- Consider **alternatives to flying**, travelling instead by bus, train, boat and even by bike or on foot where possible.
- Make your trips "**climate neutral**" via a reputable carbon-offset scheme. All Rough Guide flights are offset, and every year we donate money to a variety of charities devoted to combating the effects of climate change.

(⊛www.ethiopianairlines.com), or with a Middle Eastern airline such as Emirates or Gulf Air (⊛www.gulfair.com). Most serve only Johannesburg, but Emirates also flies from Cape Town and Durban. Fares start at around R5600 in low-season, R7150 in high season.

By land and sea from Israel, Palestine and Cyprus

Mazada Tours (141 Rehov Ibn Gvirol, Tel Aviv ☏03/544 4544; 15 Jaffa Road, West Jerusalem ☏02/623 5777; ⊛www.mazada.co.il) runs **buses to Cairo** twice weekly (Sunday and Thursday) from both **Tel Aviv** and **Jerusalem**. One-way tickets are US$95 (plus border taxes totaling US$55), return tickets US$110 (plus US$55). It's best to book (and confirm return journeys) at least three days in advance. The company can apply for a visa for you on request, but the Egyptian embassy is just around the corner

from its Tel Aviv office (see above for the address), and it is cheaper to do it yourself.

It is also possible to reach Cairo from Israel (but not usually from the Gaza Strip) using local buses or **service taxis**. All traffic between Israel and Egypt crosses the border at **Taba** near Eilat (open 24/7 except Eid el-Adha and Yom Kippur). Entering Egypt via Taba, you're subject to an Israeli departure tax of US$25 (NIS94.50; NIS4.50 less if you pay in advance at the main post office in Eilat, Tel Aviv, West Jerusalem, Haifa or Beersheba rather than at the border) and an Egyptian entry tax of £E75 (US$15). There are three direct daily buses from Taba, taking some ten hours to reach Cairo. The **Rafah** border crossing between Gaza and Egypt is only intermittently open. The Israel Airports Authority keep some current information about the Taba border crossing on their website at ⊛www.iaa.gov.il/Rashat/en-US/Borders/Taba.

The passenger **ferry** from **Limassol** (Cyprus) to Port Said (Egypt), with some services calling at **Haifa** (Israel), has often been suspended, but was running at last check, approximately weekly over the summer. For details contact Varianos Travel, 8C Pantelides Avenue, PO Box 22107, 1517 Nicosia, Cyprus ☎+357/2268 0500, ⊚www .varianostravel.com/Cruises/ferry_service.htm. The ferry does not carry vehicles. The fare is €200–250 in a shared cabin depending on the season (regardless of whether you board in Limassol or Haifa), and takes 16hr 30min direct, or 38hr via Haifa (where it stops for 14hr). From Port Said, it's an easy bus ride to Cairo (half-hourly through the day; 3hr), or you can take a train (4 daily; 4hr).

By land and sea from Jordan and Syria

Direct **buses** make the 21-hour journey **from Amman** to Cairo via Aqaba–Nuweiba, but they are neither pleasant nor economical, and unless speed is of the essence, it's better to break the journey at Aqaba or in Sinai. JETT, on King Hussein Street (☎06/566 4146, ⊚www.jett.com.jo), 900m north from Abdali station, have two weekly departures (JD75 one-way, plus JD6 border tax). Afana, next door to JETT and at Abdali station (☎06/568 1560), runs weekly buses for the same price. Some buses arrive at Cairo's Sinai bus terminal; others at Almaza terminal (see p.24).

From Aqaba, the quickest route to Cairo is by land via Eilat in Israel, using local buses (see below). Disincentives are the Taba border stamp (which shows that you've been to Israel, and therefore bans you from travel to Syria, Lebanon, Sudan or Libya), and the hefty exit and entry taxes (totalling around US$46) payable at Eilat and Taba. Alternatively, there are **ferries** to Nuweiba in Sinai operated by the Arab Bridge Maritime Co. (⊚www .abmaritime.com.jo): a fast service (2 daily; 1hr; $70); and a notoriously unpunctual slow one (daily; 3hr 30min; $60); both will take vehicles. You can buy tickets from the company's offices in Amman (beside the Royal Jordanian building just off 7th Circle; ☎06/585 9554) or Aqaba (downtown near the *China* restaurant; ☎03/209 3237), from agents in Aqaba, or up to an hour before departure at the passenger terminal itself,

6km south of Aqaba (☎03/201 3236). The terminal is served by local buses from Aqaba's fort (heading towards the Saudi border at Durra), and a taxi will cost around JD4. You pay a JD6 exit tax when boarding the ferry.

There are three daily buses to Cairo (Sinai terminal and Cairo Gateway) from **Taba** (10hr) and **Nuweiba** (9hr) in Sinai. You might even (especially arriving by ferry) find a service taxi from Nuweiba to Suez, from where there is plenty of transport (service taxis and half-hourly buses) for the three-hour journey to Cairo.

Agents and operators

Ancient World Tours UK ☎020/7917 9494, ⊚www.ancient.co.uk. In-depth archeological and historical tours led by experts, including exclusive access to the Pyramid of Unas at Saqqara and other sites otherwise off-limits to tourists.

Discover Egypt UK ☎0844/880 0462, ⊚www .discoveregypt.co.uk. Packages featuring stays at five-star Cairo hotels.

North South Travel UK ☎01245/608 291, ⊚www.northsouthtravel.co.uk. Friendly, competitive travel agency, offering discounted fares worldwide. Profits are used to support projects in the developing world, especially the promotion of sustainable tourism.

Soliman Travel UK ☎020/7244 6855, ⊚www .solimantravel.co.uk. One of the longest-established UK-based Egypt tour operators, with charter flights and a large range of packages and tailor-made holidays, mainly in five-star accommodation.

STA Travel Australia ☎134 782, ⊚www.statravel .com.au; New Zealand ☎0800/474400, ⊚www .statravel.co.nz; South Africa ☎0861/781 781, ⊚www.statravel.co.za; UK ☎0871/230 0040, ⊚www.statravel.co.uk; US ☎1-800/781-4040, ⊚www.statravel.com. Specialists in independent travel; also student IDs, travel insurance, and more. Good discounts for students and under-26s.

Trailfinders Australia ☎1300/780 212, ⊚www .trailfinders.com; UK ☎0845/058 5858, Ireland ☎01/677 7888. One of the best-informed and most efficient agents for independent travellers.

Travel Cuts Canada ☎1-866/246-9762; US ☎1-800/592-2887, ⊚www.travelcuts.com. Canadian youth and student travel firm.

USIT Republic of Ireland ☎01/602 1906; Northern Ireland ☎028/9032 7111, ⊚www.usit.ie. Ireland's main student and youth travel specialists.

Ya'lla Tours US ☎1-800/644-1595, ⊚www.yalla tours.com. Egypt and Middle East package specialists offering four-night breaks in Cairo, with optional add-ons to Alexandria, the Fayoum or Mount Sinai.

Arrival

Setting foot in a new city can be daunting at the best of times, and in Cairo you have to contend with touts and hustlers at the airport (and sometimes at bus stations) trying to con new arrivals into taking an overpriced second-rate hotel (see box below). Even taxi drivers who aren't in on this game may well try to overcharge you. Obviously it's worth trying to avoid these things, but they aren't the end of the world – sometimes it's easiest to just get in a taxi and not bother to argue, even if you know you're paying over the odds. Alternatively, some hotels and hostels will arrange a taxi pick-up if requested.

By air

Cairo International Airport (ⓦwww.cairo-airport.com) is situated about 15km northeast of the city centre, beyond the suburb of Heliopolis. It has three terminals, the third being roughly 3km from the other two. **Terminal 1** is known as the old airport, but having been refurbished, is actually more modern than **Terminal 2**, which is closed for renovation until 2013. **Terminal 3** is used by EgyptAir and other Star Alliance airlines (such as Lufthansa). You'll find 24-hour currency exchange, ATMs and tourist offices at both terminals. Should you discover that your baggage has gone missing en route, do *not* leave the airport without filing a report or you will never be able to reclaim it once it arrives.

Commission rackets

Newly arrived tourists need to be aware of **commission rackets**, whereby hotels and shops pay a commission to guides, taxi drivers and street touts to bring them customers – the commission being added to the customer's bill. Taxi drivers and touts can go to amazing lengths to lure tourists into such places.

As soon as you arrive at **Cairo airport**, even before customs, you may be approached by "travel agents" wearing official badges with their photo, on which the only thing written in English is the words "Ministry of Tourism". This doesn't mean that they work for the ministry, merely that they have a licence to operate in the airport. They may try to dissuade you from going to the hotel you had in mind (by saying it's closed or no good), and may even appear to call the hotel to check if there is a room. Don't believe it if a voice on the other end of the phone says, "sorry, we are full".

Likewise, don't believe similar stories from **taxi drivers** (especially those who accost you before you leave the airport) or any "friendly" stranger who gets talking to you on the bus into town. If a driver tells you that the hotel you want has closed, take another taxi or, if you are already on your way into town, ask to be dropped off at Midan Tahrir or on Sharia Talaat Harb and walk the rest of the way, or simply demand to be taken to the "closed" hotel you asked for anyway. **Touts** may also approach you on the street or hang around downstairs below popular hotels, and even claim to be the manager (genuine hotel managers and receptionists do not hang around on the stairs to warn potential customers that they are full).

Other commission rackets affect tours. Sightseeing tours, for example, may spend most of their time at commission-paying **shops** (sometimes billed as "museums") rather than tourist sights, and tours sold at hotel reception desks are among the worst offenders. The best advice is not to buy a tour except from a reputable operator, or following a personal recommendation from somebody who's already been on it.

For more on street touts, see p.32.

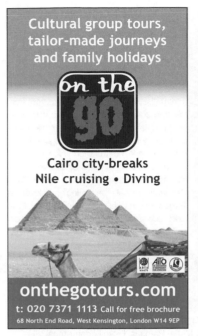

Emerging from customs, you'll be waylaid by taxi drivers who'll swear that they're the only way of **getting into town**. In fact this isn't so, but you might prefer going by **taxi** anyway. Airport cab drivers will probably demand at least £E60; to get a taxi into town for £E30–40, head out beyond the airport car park and pick up a taxi outside its precincts (airport taxis add a surcharge as they pay a fee to enter the airport premises). Many hotels and hostels can arrange a driver to meet you for around £E85, or you can book in advance with a firm such as Blue Cab (☎02/3760 9717, ⓦwww.thebluecab.com; around £E90 to central Cairo). The Cairo Airport Shuttle (☎19970, ⓦwww.cairoshuttlebus.com; £E100 to central Cairo) offer transfers using a/c minibuses which can accommodate up to seven people; they have desks in every arrivals hall, and may possibly offer a reduced rate if you are prepared to share. There's also a **limousine taxi service** with a desk in the arrivals halls; prices are fixed and posted, though higher than regular taxi rates (a limo into central Cairo will cost around £E150).

Public **buses** and **minibuses** into town leave from the forecourt outside Terminal 1.

The most comfortable of the bus services is the a/c bus #356 (£E2), which stops at Terminal 2 before continuing to Midan Ramses and Abdel Mouneem Riyad terminal by Midan Tahrir in downtown Cairo. This service runs from about 7am to 11pm, as does minibus #27 (£E2), which follows the same route. After hours, you can use bus #400 (50pt), which plies the same route round the clock, though it is less comfortable and takes longer to get downtown – over an hour in rush hour, about forty minutes at night. Bus #948 also runs 24/7, to Midan Ataba, on the eastern edge of downtown. None of these buses serves Terminal 3, but the terminals are connected to each other by a free 24hr EgyptAir **shuttle bus**, and a **monorail train** connecting all three terminals is expected to come into operation in 2011.

By bus

Most buses from Jordan and Sinai arrive at the old **Sinai Terminal** (aka Abbassiya Station), 4km from the centre. Taxis outside grossly overcharge newcomers (the proper fare into town is £E5–8); if you want to take a cab, cross the street outside the terminal

(Sharia Ramses) and hail one that's passing, or catch a bus or minibus from the bus stop 100m to your right once you've crossed the road – buses #28, #310 and #710, and minibuses #1 and #998 serve Midan Ramses; buses #27 and #998 and minibus #30 serve both Midan Ramses and Midan Tahrir. By turning left outside the terminal and walking 300m on, past the flyover, to the hospital, you'll have an even wider choice of buses and minibuses to Ramses, Tahrir and Ataba. Tickets on the buses and minibuses plying these routes cost 25pt–£E1. It shouldn't take you more than twenty minutes to get into town.

Coming from Jordan on a Superjet bus, you'll arrive at the **Almaza Terminal**, at the back end of Heliopolis. A taxi into town from

here costs £E15–20 and should take around half an hour, but the terminal is also served by bus #15 to Midan Ataba and Midan Ramses, or minibus #39 to Ramses and Tahrir, taking around 45 minutes. Alternatively, 300m north of the terminal along Sharia Abu Bakr al-Siddiq, under the flyover, you can pick up a tram (the Heliopolis Metro; see p.145) from the stop across the tracks and to your right, which goes direct to Midan Ramses: make sure you get the right tram, though – it's the long green one, not the short yellow one.

Superjet services from Sinai, Alexandria, Hurghada and Luxor terminate at the **Cairo Gateway** terminal – better known to locals as **Turgoman** – in Bulaq (see map, pp.50–51). To reach downtown Cairo from here, the simplest option is to take a taxi (around £E3 to Midan

Leaving Cairo

By air

Terminal 1, the "old airport" (*al-mataar al-qadima*) can be reached by bus, minibus or taxi (£E50 is the going rate, though drivers may demand more). Air-conditioned bus #356, minibus #27 and 24-hour bus #400, all run from Abdel Mouneem Riyad terminal (in front of the *Ramses Hilton*) and Midan Ramses. From Midan Ataba there's the 24-hour bus #948. During rush hour, and especially by bus, the journey can take well over an hour, so always allow plenty of time. From Terminal 1, there is a free shuttle to Terminal 3.

For **airport information** call ☎02/2265-5000 (Terminal 1), or ☎02/2266-2505 (Terminal 3), or check ⓦwww.cairo-airport.com.

By bus

Intercity and international bus services depart from four main terminals: **Cairo Gateway** (aka Turgoman; for most Egyptian destinations, especially the Canal cities), **Aboud** (mostly to Alexandria, the Delta, Middle and Upper Egypt; some of those serving the Delta may also be picked up from Sharia Orabi near Ramses Station), and **Sinai Terminal** (aka Abbassiya Terminal; for services to Sinai). Some services (particularly Superjet buses to the Canal cities, as well as international services to Jordan and Libya) leave from, or call at, **Almaza Terminal** in Heliopolis (see above). Those going to Alexandria call there, but start more conveniently on Sharia al-Galaa near the *Ramses Hilton*, with El Gouna buses to Hurghada and Sharm el-Sheikh based just a few doors down from them.

Some destinations may be served by buses from more than one departure point, notably Alexandria (Aboud, Turgoman, Almaza and the *Ramses Hilton*), Hurghada (Cairo Gateway, Aboud and *Ramses Hilton*), Sharm el-Sheikh and Dahab (Sinai and Cairo Gateway). For further details on these terminals, see p.23 and above.

Buses to **Tel Aviv** and **Jerusalem** depart from the *Cairo Sheraton* in Dokki (see map, pp.132–133), currently on Thursday and Sunday mornings. For tickets and information, contact Misr Travel at the *Pyramisa Hotel*, 60 Sharia el-Giza (see map, pp.132–133; ☎02/3335-5470).

By service taxi

If you don't mind a slightly cramped and definitely hair-raising journey, **service taxis** (*servees*), whether Peugeots, microbuses or minibuses, are usually the fastest way

Ramses, £E4–5 to Midan Tahrir), though it's also possible to walk (10–15min to Midan Ramses; 20–30min to Midan Tahrir): turn right out of the front, then left at the next junction (by a mosque), along Sharia al-Sahafa to the end; cross Sharia al-Galaa (under the flyover), then head right and take the next left (26th July Street), and Sharia Talaat Harb is 250m ahead. For Midan Ramses, turn left when you come out of the terminal, continue on to the flyover (Sharia Shanan), then turn right and right again up Sharia al-Galaa. Other bus services from Alexandria and the Delta and Upper Egypt arrive at **Aboud Terminal** in Shubra. By far the easiest way into town from here is to climb up the steps to the main road where microbus service taxis await to take you straight to Sharia Orabi by Ramses train station (see map, p.69), which will take about fifteen minutes.

By train

All **trains** into Cairo stop at **Ramses Station** (see map, p.69), which has a tourist office by the main entrance, and a **left luggage** office by platform 1 (open 24/7 and charging £E2.50 per item per day). There are hotels nearby, but most visitors prefer to head downtown. You can do this by metro (Mubarak Station is beneath Midan Ramses), taxi (£E5–8), or on a bus along Sharia Ramses. Alternatively, it's a ten- to fifteen-minute walk down Sharia Ramses, taking a left at Sharia Emad el-Din or Sharia Orabi, into the main downtown area, where most of the budget hotels are located.

to reach a host of destinations. Their biggest advantage is that they leave as soon as they're full; just turn up, and you'll probably be away in 15min (morning and late afternoon are prime times). Fares generally work out 20–30 percent above the bus fare, though they are occasionally cheaper. Drivers are unlikely to overcharge you, but watch what Egyptians pay and you can hardly go wrong.

For **Alexandria and the Delta**, the best place to pick up a service taxi is Aboud Terminal (see above). Service taxis for **Suez** and **Ismailiya** leave from Sharia Orabi near Ramses Station (see map, p.69). For **Fayoum**, the best place to pick up a service taxi is at Midan Giza (served by transport to the Pyramids; see boxes on p.28 and p.29), though you can get them from Sharia Orabi near Ramses station (see map p.69). Service taxis to the Fayoum also leave from a depot opposite El Mouneeb bus station.

International service taxis to **Libya**, run by Wikala Suessi on Midan Opera (⊕02/2395-4480; see map, pp.50–51), leave daily around 8pm bound for Benghazi and Tripoli. It's wise to book your place a day or two ahead if possible.

By train

Most trains depart from **Ramses Station** (Mahatat Ramses), just north of the city centre on Midan Ramses, but for some southbound services, you may have to board at **Giza Station**, which can be reached from downtown by taxi (£E10–15) or metro.

In Ramses Station, tickets for air-conditioned services to Alexandria, the Delta and Canal Zone are sold at the far end of the main hall, when you enter from Midan Ramses, but if you want to use a slow, non-a/c train, you'll find the ticket office outside, through the doorway to the left of the a/c ticket office.

Foreigners travelling to Upper Egypt are only allowed to use certain services, most of which depart from Giza, though tickets can be bought at Ramses.

Timetables are not available in leaflet or booklet form, but can be checked online at ⊛www.egyptrail.gov.eg, though the trains listed don't include "ordinary" (3rd and non-air-conditioned 2nd class) services. A full list of train times, in Arabic only, can be downloaded as a PDF from the website, and is posted up at various points around the station, most prominently by the round **information kiosk** (⊕02/2575-3555) opposite platform 4. Staff here should in theory be able to advise on departures, schedules and any problems you may have with ticket buying, but you may need to fall back on the tourist office (see p.45).

By service taxi

Arriving from the Canal cities of Suez or Ismailiya by **service taxi**, you'll probably end up at **Sharia Orabi**, close to Ramses Station (see map, p.69); transport from the Delta usually winds up at the **Aboud Terminal** (see "By bus", p.25), but occasionally at Ramses Station. Service taxis from the Fayoum terminate at **El Moneeb Terminal** in Giza, under a flyover 300m north of El-Monib metro station. The metro offers a quick and easy way into town from here; a taxi will cost £E15–20; or there are buses (#987 to Ramses or #107 to Ataba).

International service taxis from Libya arrive at Midan Opera, on the east side of the downtown area, and very close to most downtown hotels.

City transport

Getting around Cairo is relatively straightforward; Midan Tahrir is the main transport hub, with several other central terminals connecting up the city. The metro is simple to use, and taxis are inexpensive. Familiarize yourself with Arabic numerals (see p.278) and you can also use buses and minibuses, which reach most parts of the city. You may as well resign yourself to the fact that Cairenes drive like participants in the Paris–Dakar Rally, but accidents are surprisingly rare, all things considered. The streets are busy from 8am to midnight, and, unless you enjoy sweltering in traffic jams, it's best to try and avoid travelling by road during rush hours (7–10am & 4–7pm).

Walking

One advantage of Cairo's density is that many places of interest are within walking distance of Midan Tahrir or other transport inter-changes. You can walk across downtown Cairo from Tahrir to Midan Ataba in fifteen to thirty minutes; the same again brings you to Khan el-Khalili in the heart of Islamic Cairo. This fascinating medieval quarter can really only be explored on foot, starting from Khan el-Khalili or the Citadel.

Arguably, walking is the best way to experience the city's pulsating **streetlife**. Though pavements are congested with vendors and pedestrians, they weave gracefully around each other, seldom jostling. The commonest irritants are rubbish, noxious fumes and puddles, uneven pavements and gaping drains; in poorer quarters, the last two may not even exist.

At all times, **crossing the road** takes boldness. Drivers will slow down to give people time to dart across, but be decisive and don't dither. A prolonged horn burst indicates that the driver can't or won't stop. Remember that motorists obey police signals rather than traffic lights, which were only installed in the 1980s and have still to acquire credibility.

Taxis

The commonest type of **taxi** is the old-style **black-and-white** four-seater, which in peak hours may carry passengers collectively, picking up extra passengers en route. They do not have working meters and most drivers will overcharge you mercilessly if they think you don't know the price, so you need to know it before you get in, and pay the money with confidence when you get out (they'll let you know if it isn't enough, but they'll always ask for more if you look doubtful). Cairenes normally pay a £E3 minimum, £E5–8 for a downtown hop (for example, Midan Tahrir to Al-Azhar, Zamalek or Mohandiseen), and more if heading further out, especially to a prosperous area (for example £E15–20 to Heliopolis or the Pyramids). Drivers may expect more late at night.

Though foreigners can get away with local rates, cabbies expect you to pay over the odds, especially if you are well dressed or staying in an expensive hotel: say £E5 minimum, £E8–12 across downtown or the Nile, and £E20–25 further out. The airport and the Pyramids are special cases (see p.24 and p.154). Drivers who wait outside upmarket hotels and tourist sites, or call out to tourists in the street, do so with the intention of overcharging – always hail a taxi yourself rather than taking one which hails you.

If all this sounds like a hassle, fear not: new on the scene are **white cabs**, which also take four passengers, and work on a meter. These cost £E2.50 to get in, plus £E1.25 per kilometre and £E10 per hour waiting time. Because the rate is fixed, they generally work out cheaper than black and white cabs, and are certainly a lot more convenient. If you feel like tipping the driver you can do so, but it isn't expected. And if the driver starts giving you any nonsense about the meter not working, just get out and hail another cab. While metered cabs could inflate your fare by taking you round the houses, this isn't common. Meters show distance travelled as well as the fare, and should rise in 25pt increments every 200m; it isn't unknown for drivers to fiddle the meter to rise in 60pt increments, but you'll be able to see it if they do, and getting caught means big trouble for them.

The third type are **yellow cabs**, which can be hailed in the street, but are more commonly called by phone. They also use a meter, but are slightly more expensive than white taxis, with a flagfall of £E3.50. Two firms operate yellow cabs: City Cab (℡16516) and Cairo International Taxi (℡19155, ⊛www.citaxi .com), but they tend to arrive either very early, or late, often phoning several times en route to ask for directions to where you are, so they generally aren't worth bothering with.

Finally, there are **limousines**, usually Mercedes or Peugeot 406s, operated by firms such as Limousine Misr Travel (℡02/2269-5675) and Target Limousine (℡02/3377-2666). They are stationed at five-star hotels and at the airport, with fixed fares (£E66 from the airport to downtown, for example), and are rentable by the day as well as for set routes. A limo for the day (12hr and 100km) costs around £E500.

Service taxis

Collective **service taxis** (known as *servees*) are usually **microbuses** seating a dozen people, sometimes also called *meecros* or *arrabeya bin nafar*. They run on fixed routes (see box below) and leave when full, but can be flagged down anywhere if there is space aboard. **Fares** range from 50pt to £E1 per person, according to the distance travelled. They are especially useful for longer-distance journeys such as from town to the Pyramids. Their main terminals are at **Abdel Mouneem Riyad** (behind the Egyptian Museum and in front of the *Ramses Hilton* hotel), and behind and around **Ramses Station**. For Saqqara and Dahshur, they leave from a street off Maryotteya Canal near its junction with Pyramids Road (down the east bank of the canal and first left), the junction itself being easily reached on a Pyramids-bound service taxi from Ramses or Abdel Mouneem Riyad.

Useful service taxi routes

Abdel Mouneem Riyad (behind the Museum of Egyptian Antiquities) to the Pyramids (*Al-Aharam*), Sharia Faisal (near the Pyramids), Midan Giza, Mohandiseen, Bulaq, Bulaq al-Dakrour, Imbaba, Ma'adi and Helwan. Also to Qanatir (Fri & Sat only).

Ramses Ahmed Helmi, behind Ramses Station, to Abbassiya, Medinet Nasr, al-Basatin, Ma'adi and Helwan; Sharia al-Gala to Aboud terminal; Sharia Orabi to Midan Giza and the Pyramids; al-Fath Mosque to Midan Ataba.

Midan Giza (at the eastern end of Pyramids Road, and around 1km west of El-Giza bridge) to Ramses, the Pyramids and Badrasheen (for Saqqara).

Maryotteya Canal Pyramids Road to Tahrir, Ramses and sometimes Ataba; west bank of canal to Abu Sir and Saqqara, usually changing at the latter for Dahshur.

Buses

Cairo's **buses** mainly operate from 5.30am to 12.30am daily (6.30am–6.30pm & 7.30pm–2am during Ramadan). Fares are cheap enough to be affordable for everyone, so buses are usually full and overflow during rush hour, when passengers hang from doorways. Though many foreigners are deterred from using buses by the crush, not to mention the risk of pickpockets and gropers, there's no denying that the network reaches virtually everywhere. Because buses tend to make slow progress against the traffic, however, service-taxi microbuses are generally a better option, where available, though there are **air-conditioned buses** on some routes to prosperous suburbs such as Heliopolis and Medinet Nasr, and to tourist sights such as the Pyramids.

Buses should have **route numbers** in Arabic numerals on the front, side and back. Those with a slash through the number (represented in this guide as, for example, #13) may follow different routes from buses with the same number unslashed; some route numbers even have two slashes. **Bus stops** are not always clearly signposted (look for metal shelters, plaques on lampposts or crowds waiting), and buses often just slow down instead of halting, compelling passengers to board and disembark on the run. Some bus stops (at the time of writing, only on the west bank of the river, in and around Mohandiseen) have route information posted, but this is in Arabic only.

Most buses start from (or pass through) at least one of the main city-centre nuclei at Midan Tahrir, Abdel Mouneem Riyad terminal (behind the Egyptian Museum), Midan Ramses or Midan Ataba. At each of these locations, there are several bus stops, and where exactly you pick up your bus will depend on which direction it is going in and

whether it starts there or is simply passing through. If possible, ask the conductor "*Rayih*...?" (Are you going to...?) to make sure.

Except at terminals, you are supposed to enter through the rear door (often removed to facilitate access) and exit from the front. Conductors sell **tickets** (the flat fare on most routes is 50pt–£E1, or £E2 on air-conditioned buses) from behind a crush-bar by the rear door. The front of the bus is usually less crowded, so it's worth squeezing your way forwards; start edging towards the exit well before your destination.

Minibuses

Minibuses run along many of the bus routes, with privately run green minibuses running on

---

Useful bus routes

Abdel Mouneem Riyad and Midan Ramses to: Airport #356, #400 (24hr), minibus #27; Abbassiya and Heliopolis (Midan Roxi) #400, #400/, #500, minibus #27.

Abdel Mouneem Riyad to: Citadel (Bab Gabal) #951, minibus #105; Midan Salah el-Din #456, #955, minibus 35; Saiyida Zeinab and Ibn Tulun Mosque #72//, #102, #160; Immam al-Shafi'i minibus #154; Manashi #214; Muqattam Hills #951; Pyramids #30, #355, #357, #900; Qanatir #210; Sphinx #997.

new routes. Besides making better headway through traffic and actually halting at stops (usually the same stops as used by ordinary buses), minibuses are far more comfortable than ordinary buses and never crowded, as standing is not permitted. Tickets (25pt–£E1) are bought from the driver. Minibuses should not be confused with service taxis (usually smaller microbuses, see p.28). There are minibus **terminals** alongside the big bus stations in Midan Tahrir (by the *Nile Hilton* and near Arab League/Omar Makram Mosque) and Midan Ataba.

The metro

Cairo's **metro** works like nothing else in the city – it's clean and efficient, with a well-enforced ban on littering and smoking. Trains run every few minutes from 5.30am to midnight; outside of the rush hours they're no more overcrowded than in other cities around the world. The front carriage of each train is reserved for women, which is worth keeping in mind if you're a lone female traveller.

Stations are signposted with a large "M"; signs and route maps appear in Arabic and English. **Tickets** are purchased in the station (£E1 flat fare, 50pt during Ramadan); twin sets of booths cater for passengers heading in opposite directions, sometimes with separate queues for either sex. Hang on to your ticket to get through the automatic barriers at the other end. Travelling without a ticket will result in a E£50 fine.

Line One connects the northeastern suburb of **El-Marg** with the southern industrial district of **Helwan** (via Mubarak, Sadat, Saad Zaghoul, Saiyida Zeinab, Mar

Girgis and Maadi), with Line Two running from **Shubra** in the north to **El Monib** (via Mubarak, Ataba, Sadat, Opera and Giza). The newest stations on Line Two (those at the southern end) are wheelchair accessible, but stations on Line One are not. Line Three is now under construction, and should eventually run from the airport via the city centre (Ataba and Nasser) to Zamalek and Mohandiseen. In theory, the first section of the line, from Ataba to Abbassiya, should open in October 2011, with the rest of the line opening in sections over the next few years, but the extension to the airport won't be finished until at least 2019.

Trams

As the metro and minibus systems expand, Cairo's original **tram network** (built in colonial times) is being phased out. The Heliopolis tram system remains in use throughout that area (see p.145), but all the other lines into town have been withdrawn, though a few suburban lines still run. Like buses, the trams are cheap (25–50pt) and battered, sometimes with standing room only; their Arabic route numbers are posted above the driver's cab.

River taxis

River taxis (aka waterbuses) leave from the Maspero Dock outside the Television Building, 600m north of the Museum of Egyptian Antiquities (see map, pp.50–51). Boats run every hour from 7am to El Gama'a Bridge in Giza. You can buy tickets (£E1) at the dock. On Fridays and Sundays, they also run up to the Nile barrages at Qanatir (£E5 each way; see p.230).

Useful metro stations

From a tourist's standpoint, there are six crucial stations:

Mubarak, beneath Midan Ramses, for Ramses Station.

Nasser, two stops on, leads onto 26th July Street near the top end of Talaat Harb (take the High Court exit).

Sadat, the most used (and useful) station, is set beneath Midan Tahrir, and doubles as a pedestrian underpass.

Saiyida Zeinab, two stops beyond Sadat, lies midway between the Saiyida Zeinab quarter and the northern end of Roda Island.

Mari Girgis is the best stop for Coptic Cairo and Amr's Mosque.

Opera (Gezira) is by the Opera Complex in south Gezira.

Driving

The only thing scarier than **driving in Cairo** is cycling, which is tantamount to suicide. Dashes, crawls and finely judged evasions are the order of the day; donkey carts and jaywalkers trust in motorists' swift reactions. Minor dents are often settled by on-the-spot payoffs, but should injury occur, it's wise to involve a cop right away. Multi-storey car parks, such as the one on Midan Ataba, are ignored as motorists park bumper-to-bumper along every kerb, leaving their handbrakes off so vehicles can be shifted by the local *minaidy* (street parking attendant), whom they tip £E1 or so. Given all this, it's no surprise that few foreigners drive in Cairo. **Renting a car** with a driver costs around $20 a day more than doing the driving yourself; rental firms include European (☏02/1661-1027) and Hertz (☏02/2265-2430).

Culture and etiquette

While some people who approach you in Cairo are on the make (see box, p.22), when Egyptians say "Welcome to Egypt!" they generally mean it – don't assume that everyone who approaches you expects to profit from the encounter. Too many tourists do, and end up making little contact with the country's extraordinarily friendly people. It doesn't take much effort to avoid cultural pitfalls and turn local etiquette to your advantage, if you keep in mind Egyptian customs and sexual morality.

Behaviour and **attitude** on your part are important. If some Egyptians treat tourists with contempt, it has much to do with the way the latter behave. It helps everyone if you can avoid rudeness or aggressive behaviour in response to insistent offers or demands. On another tack entirely, intimate behaviour in public (kissing and cuddling) is a no-no, and even holding hands is disapproved of.

Be aware, too, of the importance of **dress**: shorts and miniskirts are regarded as indecent, and shirts should cover your shoulders. Many tourists ignore these conventions, unaware of how it demeans them in the eyes of the Egyptians. Women wearing halter-necks, skimpy T-shirts, miniskirts and the like will attract gropers, and the disapproval of both sexes. If you're visiting a mosque, you're expected to be "modestly" dressed (men should cover their arms to below the shoulder and their legs to below the knee, women should be covered from their neck to the wrist and ankle). It's also obligatory to remove shoes (or don overshoes). When **invited to a home**, it's normal to take your shoes off before entering the reception rooms. It is customary to take a gift: sweet pastries from a shop such as El Abd or La Poire (see p.199) will always go down well.

One important thing to be aware of in Egypt is the different functions of the two hands. Whether you are right- or left-handed, the **left hand** is used for "unclean" functions, most importantly wiping your bottom, but also doing things like putting on and taking off shoes. This means that it is considered unhygienic to eat with your left hand. You can hold things like bread in your left hand in order to tear a piece off with your right hand, but you should never put food into your mouth with your left hand, or put it into the bowl when eating communally.

Egyptians are likely to feel very strongly about certain subjects – Palestine, Israel and Islam, for instance – and these should be treated diplomatically if they come up in **conversation**. Some Egyptians are keen to discuss them, others not, but carelessly expressed opinions, and particularly open contempt for religion, can cause serious offence.

Tipping and baksheesh

As a presumed-rich *khawaga* (the Egyptian term for a foreigner), you will be expected to be liberal with **baksheesh**, which can be divided into three main varieties. The most common is **tipping**: a small reward for a small service, which can encompass anything from being waited on to someone unlocking a tomb or museum room at one of the ancient sites. The sums involved are often paltry, but try to strike a balance between defending your own wallet and acquiescing gracefully when appropriate. There's little point in offending people over what are trifling sums for a Western tourist but often an important part of people's livelihood in a country where most people earn less than £50/$82 a month.

Typical tips might be £E1–2 for looking after your shoes while you visit a mosque (though congregants don't usually tip for this), or £E5–10 to a custodian for opening up a door to let you enter a building or climb a minaret. In restaurants, you do not usually leave a percentage of the bill: typical tips (regardless of whether the bill claims to include "service") are as little as 50pt in an ultra-cheap place such as a *kushari* joint, £E2 in a typical cheap restaurant, or £E5 in a smarter establishment. Customers also usually give tips of 50pt–£E1 per person in a café, and sometimes 25pt in a juice bar.

A more expensive and common type of baksheesh is for rewarding the **bending of rules** – many of which seem to have been designed for just that purpose. Examples might include letting you into an archeological site after hours (or into a vaguely restricted area), finding you a sleeper on a train when the carriages are "full", and so on. This should not be confused with bribery, which is a more serious business with its own etiquette and risks – best not entered into.

The last kind of baksheesh is simply **alms-giving**. For Egyptians, giving money and goods to the needy is a natural act – and a requirement of Islam. The disabled are traditional recipients of such gifts, and it seems right to join locals in giving out small change.

Children, however, are a different case, pressing their demands only on tourists. If someone offers some genuine help and asks for an *alum* (pen), it seems fair enough, but to yield to every request encourages a cycle of dependency that Egypt could do without.

Since most Egyptian money is paper, often in the form of well-used banknotes that can be fiddly to separate out, it can make life easier to keep small bills in a separate "baksheesh pocket" specifically for the purpose. If giving baksheesh in foreign currency, give notes rather than coins (which can't be exchanged for Egyptian currency).

Hustlers

Hustling is a necessity for millions of Egyptians – cadging money for errands or knowing a "cousin" who can sort things out. The full-time *khirtiyya* who focus on tourists will latch on to you as soon as you arrive at the airport, hail you on the street like an old friend ("Hey! Remember me?"), or say anything to grab your attention ("You've dropped your wallet"). If they don't already know, they'll try to discover where you're staying, what your plans are, and pester you regularly.

It's easy for tourists to get fed up with being hassled and react with fury to any approach from strangers – even a sincere "Welcome to Egypt". Try to keep your cool and respond politely; intoning *shukran* (literally "thanks" – the "no" is implied) with your hand on your heart, while briskly moving on, is an effective way of dissuading most street peddlers. If necessary, escalate to a gruff *khalas* ("Enough!") and if that doesn't suffice, bawling *shorta* ("Police!") is sure to send any hustler packing.

Women travellers

Egyptian society is sexually restrictive: women are expected to be virgins when they marry, and few men can afford to wed before their thirties. With extra-marital sex so frowned upon (it is illegal for an unmarried man and woman to share a room unless they are close relatives, though this isn't enforced against foreign couples), sexual frustration is common and **sexual harassment** is rife: according to one survey, 98 percent of foreign women visitors and 83 percent of Egyptian women have experienced it. The perception that women tourists are "easy" is reinforced by the fact that many do a range of things that no respectable Egyptian woman would: dressing "immodestly", showing shoulders and cleavage; sharing rooms with men to whom they are not married; drinking alcohol in bars or restaurants; smoking in public; even travelling alone on public transport, without a relative as an escort. While well-educated Egyptians familiar with Western culture can take these in their stride, less sophisticated ones are liable to assume the worst.

Without compromising your freedom too greatly, there are a few steps you can take to reduce harassment. Most important and obvious is **dress**: loose opaque clothes that cover all "immodest" areas (thighs, upper arms, chest) and hide your contours are a big help, and essential if you are travelling alone or in rural areas (where covering long hair is also advisable). On public transport (buses, trains, service taxis), try to sit with other women – who may often invite you to do so. On the metro there are carriages reserved for women. If you're travelling with a man, wearing a wedding ring confers respectability, and asserting that you're married is better than admitting to being "just friends".

Looking confident and knowing where you're going is a major help in avoiding hassle. It's also a good idea to avoid making eye contact with Egyptian men (some women wear sunglasses for the purpose), and it is best to err on the side of standoffishness, as even a friendly smile may be taken as a come-on. Problems – most commonly hissing or groping – tend to be commonest in the downtown area.

Your reaction to **harassment** is down to you. Some women find that verbal hassle is best ignored, while others may prefer to use an Egyptian brush-off like *khalas* ("Finished") or *uskut* ("Be quiet"). If you get groped, the best response is to yell *aram!* ("Evil!") or *sibnee le wadi* ("Don't touch me"), which will shame any assailant in public and may attract help, or scare them away by shouting *shorta!* ("Police!")

On the positive side, spending time with **Egyptian women** can be a delight. The difficulty in getting to know women is that fewer women than men speak English, and that you won't run into women in traditional cafés. However, public transport can be a good meeting ground, as can shops. If asking directions in the street, it's always better to ask a woman than a man.

Female genital mutilation

A little-known fact about Egyptian women is that the vast majority – as many as 97 percent according to one survey – have been subjected to a horrific operation known euphemistically as "female circumcision", and more correctly as female genital mutilation (FGM). In this procedure, typically carried out on girls aged between 7 and 10, the clitoris and sometimes all or part of the inner vaginal lips are cut off to prevent the victim from enjoying sex.

Egypt has the world's highest prevalence of FGM, which is an African rather than an Islamic practice, performed by Copts as much as by Muslims. Nonetheless, spurious religious reasons are sometimes given to justify it, including two disputed *hadiths* (supposed quotations from Mohammed). In 1951, the Egyptian Fatwa Committee decreed that FGM was desirable because it curbs women's sex drive, and in 1981 the Sheikh of al-Azhar Mosque and University said that it was the duty of parents to have their daughters genitally mutilated.

The good news is that things have changed since then. FGM is now illegal – the government banned it in 1996 and again in 2007. Former first lady Susanne Mubarak has spoken out against it, and the Islamic religious authorities have issued a fatwa declaring it *haram* (forbidden). The law can be hard to enforce in rural communities, but especially in cities, and particularly Cairo, FGM is now in decline, though it remains at high levels countrywide: by the time of the 2007 ban, the percentage of teenage girls subjected to it had fallen to just over fifty percent, compared with around eighty percent in 1995.

Gay and lesbian travellers

As a result of sexual segregation, male homosexuality is relatively common in Egypt, but attitudes towards it are schizophrenic. Few Egyptians will declare themselves gay – which has connotations of femininity and weakness – and the dominant partner in gay sex may well not consider himself to be indulging in a homosexual act. Rather, as in prisons, homosexuality is tacitly accepted as an outlet for urges that can't otherwise be satisfied. Despite this, people are mindful that homosexuality is condemned in the Koran and the Bible, and the common term for gay men in Egyptian Arabic, *khawal*, has derogatory connotations.

Homosexuality is not illegal in Egypt, but that doesn't stop the authorities from persecuting gay men, and places that are well known as gay locales have become dangerous for Egyptians. The start of the clampdown was marked by a widely-reported 2001 raid on a Cairo floating discoteque in which 52 people ("the Cairo 52") were arrested, and many were sentenced to hard labour for offences such as "habitual debauchery" and "contempt of religion". Foreigners seem to be safe from arrest, but if you have a gay relationship with an Egyptian man, be aware that discretion is vital. **Lesbians** do not face this kind of state harassment, but they have never been visible in Egyptian society. As a Western woman, your chances of making contact are virtually zilch.

Online resources

Gay Egypt Ⓦ www.gayegypt.com. Practical advice and contacts, but don't log onto it within Egypt, as the Security Police not only monitor the site but may also take an interest in computers that access it.
Globalgayz Ⓦ www.globalgayz.com/country/Egypt /EGY. Their Egypt page has articles about the current situation facing gays in Egypt.
International Gay and Lesbian Human Rights Commission Ⓦ www.iglhrc.org. Posts information about civil rights for gay people in Egypt.

The media

The Egyptian press encompasses a range of daily papers and magazines, published in Arabic, English or French. All are fairly heavily censored, as are terrestrial TV channels.

The **English-language** *Egyptian Gazette* (on Saturday, the *Egyptian Mail*) carries agency reports, articles on Middle Eastern affairs and tourist features, but it's pretty lightweight and you can read the whole thing in a few minutes flat. The same applies to the *Egypt Daily News* (Ⓦ www.thedailynewsegypt .com), though it's more independent and has more foreign news. The English weekly edition of *Al-Ahram* has interesting opinion pieces on politics and international affairs.

In fact, as a daily **Arabic paper**, *Al-Ahram* ("The Pyramids"), founded in 1875, is Egypt's oldest newspaper, but it invariably reflects government opinion, as do *Al-Akhbar* and *Al-Gomhouriya*. Other Arabic dailies include the conservative *Al-Wafd* ("The Delegation"), the socialist *Al-Ahaly* ("The Nation") and *Al-Da'wa* ("The Call"), the journal of the Muslim Brotherhood.

Various British, US, French and German newspapers are available in Cairo, as are *Newsweek* and *Time*.

TV

Many Egyptians prefer satellite television to state-controlled terrestrial channels. Arab music channels with "sexy dancing", or news from Al-Jazeera or Al-Arabiya, are staple viewing in coffeehouses. Foreigners may be shocked by their reportage (far gorier than anything broadcast by Western channels), yet bored by national TV channels, whose programming is heavy on local football matches, Koranic recitations, and chat shows. **Nile TV** has English subtitles on most programmes, most notably classic old Egyptian movies, plus news in English and French. **Channels 1 and 2** often screen American films (generally after 10pm, or between midnight and 4.30am during Ramadan). It's not worth paying extra for a TV set in your hotel room unless it receives cable or satellite TV – and even then, chances are that half the channels will be Turkish or Kuwaiti. You might, however, get BBC World, CNN, Star Plus, Prime Sports or EuroNews. Daily TV **schedules** appear in the *Egyptian*

Gazette, whose Monday edition lists all the movies for the forthcoming week.

Radio

With a short-wave radio you can pick up the **BBC World Service** (www.bbc.co.uk /worldservice), **Voice of America** (www .voa.gov) and other broadcasters; check their websites for frequencies. You should also be able to pick up the BBC on 1323kHz MW.

Cairo has two privately run music stations which are worth a listen: Nogoum Radio (100.6FM) and Radio Misr (88.7FM) play mainly Arabic pop music, while Nile FM (104.2FM) plays Western pop. In addition, the state-owned Music Programme (98.8FM) plays folk and classical music, while the European Programme (95.4FM) has the news in English at 7.30am, 2.30pm and 8pm daily.

Travel essentials

Costs

Cairo is one of the most inexpensive cities in the world, and so long as you avoid luxury hotels and tourist-only services, costs for food, accommodation and transport are extremely low.

If you really want to spend the absolute minimum, it is possible to get by on £20/$33 a day by staying in a cheap hotel and living on a diet of *falafel* and *kushari*, but it seems silly to scrimp here when paying a just little extra will buy you so much more. On £40/$66 a day, you can eat well and stay in a two- or even three-star hotel. If you want to stay in tip-top accommodation, you could be paying upwards of £100/$165 a night, but even if you travel everywhere by taxi and eat in the very best restaurants, you'll be hard put to add more than £30/$50 a day to that figure.

Although Cairo is generally fairly cheap, there are some hidden costs that can bump up your daily budget. Most restaurant and hotel bills are liable to a **service charge**, plus local

taxes, which increase the final cost by 17–25 percent (unless already included in the price). Entry for the Pyramids and other monuments typically costs £E15 to £E50, though holders of ISIC student cards usually get a discount of at least a third. The custodians of tombs, temples and the medieval mosques of Islamic Cairo also expect to be tipped.

Egyptian inflation is currently running at around fifteen percent. Prices for luxury goods and services (i.e. most things in the private sector) rise faster than for public transport, petrol and basic foodstuffs, the costs of which are held down by subsidies that the government dare not abolish.

Student discounts

Full-time students are eligible for the **International Student Identity Card** (ISIC), which entitles to you to a fifty-percent discount on most of Cairo's museums and sites, including the Pyramids, and a thirty-percent discount on rail fares. To obtain the card, you will need to provide a valid student ID card or proof of student status. ISICs can be bought at home (see ⓦwww.istc.org for details of outlets) or for £E80 at the Egyptian Student Travel Services at 23 Sharia el-Manial, on Roda Island in Cairo (☏02/2363-7251, ⓦwww .estsegypt.com; Sat–Thurs 8am–6pm, Fri 9am–4pm); you can get there on foot from the El-Malek el-Saleh metro. An alternative available to anyone under 26 is the **International Youth Travel Card**, and teachers qualify for the **International Teacher Identity Card**, both at the same price, from the same places, and offering similar discounts.

Crime and security

While relatively few in number, **pickpockets** are skilled and concentrate on tourists. To play safe, keep your valuables in a money belt or a pouch under your shirt (leather or cotton materials are preferable to nylon, which can irritate in the heat). Cheap hotels often have poor security, though at most places you can deposit valuables at the reception (always get a receipt for cash). If you are **driving**, it goes without saying that you shouldn't leave anything you cannot afford to lose visible or accessible in your car.

To reduce the risk of petty squabbles or misunderstandings developing, always **respect local customs**; see p.31 for more.

Terrorism

Since the 1990s, Egypt's image as a safe country to visit has been shattered by sporadic waves of terrorism. Though the Islamist insurgency in Middle Egypt was crushed in the 1990s, bomb attacks in Cairo and Sinai still occur (two in Cairo in 2009, for example). There are armed police and often metal-detecting arches at tourist sites, stations and upmarket hotels, and plain-clothes agents in bars and bazaars. Along the Nile Valley, foreigners travelling by rail can only use services designated for tourists, which have plainclothes guards riding shotgun. Tourist buses between Cairo and Israel, and from Aswan to Abu Simbel, travel in a **convoy** with a police escort.

Of course the vast majority of tourists spend their stay in Egypt without encountering any

kind of terrorist incident, and most parts of the country have never had one. Insofar as any danger can be predicted, visitors should check government travel advisory websites before leaving home (ⓦwww.fco.gov.uk /travel in Britain; ⓦwww.foreignaffairs.gov .ie in Ireland; ⓦwww.travel.state.gov in the US; ⓦwww.voyage.gc.ca in Canada; ⓦwww .smartraveller.gov.au in Australia).

The police

Egypt has a plethora of police forces (collectively dubbed *shorta*) whose high profile in Cairo (which has more cops per thousand citizens than any other capital in the world) strikes first-time visitors as a sign of recent trouble, although it has actually been the rule since the 1960s. Whereas ordinary Egyptians fear police brutality, foreign visitors are usually treated with kid gloves and given the benefit of the doubt unless drugs or espionage are suspected.

If you've got a problem or need to report a crime, always go to the **Tourist and Antiquities Police** (☏126). Found at tourist sites, museums, airports, stations and ports, they are supposedly trained to help tourists in distress, and should speak a foreign language (usually English). Ordinary ranks wear the regular khaki police uniform with a "Tourist Police" armband. The more senior the officer, the better the chance they'll speak English.

The **Central Security** force (dressed all in black and armed with Kalashnikovs) guard embassies, banks and highways. Though normally genial enough, this largely conscript force will shift rapidly from tear gas to live rounds when ordered to crush demonstrations, strikes or civil unrest. Ordinarily, though, they are nothing to worry about. To guard vital utilities, there are also Electricity, Airport and **River Police** forces.

All the different police forces deploy **plainclothes agents** who hang around near government buildings and crowded places, dressed as vendors or in the *galabiyya* robe traditionally worn by working-class Egyptians – hence their nickname, the "Galabiyya Police". In hotels or bars, you might be disconcerted to find yourself chatting with a guy who suddenly announces that he's a cop. There are a lot of them around.

Drugs

Egypt has its own **bango** (marijuana) industry, based in Sinai, whose output is supplemented by **hashish** from Morocco and Lebanon. Despite a tradition of use stretching back to the thirteenth century, Egypt was one of the first countries in modern times to ban cannabis: possession merits a severe prison sentence and a heavy fine (plus legal costs), while trafficking is punishable by up to 25 years' hard labour, or even execution. Middle Egypt also produces a certain amount of **opium** (*affium*), though it's rarely seen in Cairo. Until the 1980s, these were the only drugs seen in Egypt, and under Sadat – widely believed to have been a keen hashish smoker – their use was tolerated, and hashish could be bought quite openly, especially in neighbourhoods such as Butneya. When Sadat was assassinated however, the government immediately clamped down on cannabis, and heroin soon appeared on the streets instead, becoming quite a problem in some parts of town, notably the area around the southern cemetery.

As a foreigner, the best you can expect if caught with illegal drugs is immediate deportation and a ban from ever visiting Egypt again. You may be able to buy your way out of trouble, but this should be negotiated discreetly and as soon as possible, while the minimum number of cops are involved: once you're at the police station, it will be a lot more difficult. Needless to say, your embassy will be unsympathetic. The best advice is to steer clear of all illegal drugs while in the country.

One legal drug that may be of interest to some people is yohimbine, related chemically to LSD, but actually a stimulant and aphrodisiac rather than a hallucinogen. It is sold over the counter in pharmacies under the brand name Yohimbex.

Electricity

The current in Egypt is 220V, 50Hz. North American travellers with appliances designed for 110V should bring a converter. Most sockets are for two-pin round-pronged plugs (as in Continental Europe), so you may need an adapter.

Entry requirements

All visitors to Egypt must hold passports that are valid for at least six months beyond the proposed date of entry to the country. Citizens of most countries must also obtain tourist visas.

Most nationalities, including British, Irish, Americans, Canadians, Australians, New Zealanders and all EU citizens, can also obtain visas on arrival at Cairo airport. The process is generally painless and cheaper than getting one through an embassy or consulate (see list, p.38) in advance, but visas issued at the airport are valid for one month only, whereas embassies issue single-visit and multiple-entry visas entitling you to stay in Egypt for three months (the latter allow you to go in and out of the country three times within this period). Visas are *not* available at overland border crossings or sea ports.

Visa applications can be made in person or by post. If applying in person, turn up early in the day. Postal applications take between seven working days and six weeks to process. Don't be misled by statements on the application form indicating "valid for six months"; this simply means that the visa must be used within six months of the date of issue. When returning the form, you need to include a registered or recorded SAE, your passport, one photo, and a postal or money order (not a personal cheque).

Getting a standard visa on arrival costs US$17, irrespective of your nationality. The cost of getting a visa in advance of your trip varies according to your nationality, and from place to place. Some consulates may demand that you pay in US dollars instead of local currency, or ask you to supply extra photos.

Visa extensions

Tourists who **overstay** their visa are allowed a fifteen-day period of grace in which to renew it or leave the country. After this, they're fined £E140 unless they can present a letter of apology from their embassy (which may well cost more).

Visa **extensions** cost around £E12, and are obtainable from the Mugamma (see p.52) in Midan Tahrir (daily except Fri 8am–2pm). For a tourist visa extension, go to windows

#13–14 of the immigration section on the first floor (these numbers may change so check at the information desk on the landing) – accessed via entrance 4 on the same floor, and down the corridor to the end – and pick up a form. You need to provide a passport photo plus a photocopy of the pages in your passport bearing your personal details and your Egyptian visa – there are copying facilities on the ground floor. Take your form to window #43 to get a stamp (£E11.10), then back to window #13 or #14 where your new visa will be issued. This may be done the same day or the next, or could take longer depending on your nationality and the length of stay requested. A re-entry visa will cost £E51.10 (£E61.10 for two re-entries). Display patience and good humour when dealing with the Mugamma; only stage a tantrum or nervous breakdown as a last resort.

Duty-free

Duty-free allowances for Egypt are one litre of alcoholic liquor, 200 cigarettes or 25 cigars or 200g of tobacco, one litre of perfume or eau de cologne, plus up to £E500-worth of gifts. Foreigners can also buy up to three litres of imported spirits (or two bottles of spirits plus a two-dozen-can carton of beer) at **duty-free** prices within 24 hours of arrival in Egypt, either at the airport, or cheaper, at the Egypt Free Store at 106 Arab League Street in Mohandiseen (☎02/3760-9818), with branches at 17 Sharia el-Gumhoriyya (☎02/2391-5134) and in the *Cairo Sheraton* hotel in Dokki (☎02/3748-9059); bring your passport, as you'll need to get a stamp saying what you've bought. There is a black market for duty-free booze (especially Johnny Walker Black Label), but under no circumstances should you allow a stranger to be involved in the transaction inside the shop as they may collude with staff to defraud you (adding items for which you are charged duty when leaving the country).

Egyptian embassies and consulates abroad

Links to the web pages of Egyptian embassies and consulates worldwide can be found at ⊕www.mfa.gov.eg (choose English and click on "Sites of Egyptian Missions").

Australia 1 Darwin Ave, Yarralumla, ACT 2600 ☎02/6273 4437, ⊜egyembassy@bigpond.com; Level 3, 241 Commonwealth St, Surry Hills, NSW 2010 ☎02/9281 4844; Level 9, 124 Exhibition St, Melbourne, Vic 3000 ☎03/9654 8634. Visa application forms are available at ⊕www.egypt.org.au.
Canada 454 Laurier Ave E, Ottawa, ON K1N 6R3 ☎613/234 4931, ⊜egyptemb@sympatico.ca; 1000 Rue de la Gauchetière Ouest, Suite 3320, Montreal, PQ H3B 4W5 ☎514/866 8455, ⊕www.egyptianconsulatemontreal.org.
Ireland 12 Clyde Rd, Ballsbridge, Dublin 4 ☎01/660 6566, ⊕www.embegyptireland.ie.
New Zealand c/o the embassy in Australia.
South Africa 270 Bourke St, Muckleneuk, Pretoria ☎012/343 1590 or 91, ⊜egyptemb@global.co.za.
UK 2 Lowndes St, London SW1X 9ET ☎020/7235 9777, ⊕www.egyptianconsulate.co.uk.
USA 3521 International Court NW, Washington DC 20008 ☎202/895-5400, ⊕www.egyptembassy.us; 1110 2nd Ave, Suite 201, New York, NY 10022 ☎212/759-7120 to 22, ⊕www.egyptnyc.net; 3001 Pacific Ave, San Francisco, CA 94115–1013 ☎415/346-7352, ⊕www.egy2000.com; 500 N Michigan Ave, Suite 1900, Chicago, IL 60611 ☎312/828-9162 to 4; 1990 Post Oak Blvd, Suite 2180, Houston, TX 77056 ☎713/961-4915 or 6.

Foreign embassies and consulates in Cairo

Australia 11th floor, World Trade Centre, 1191 Corniche el-Nil, Bulaq, 200m north of the 26th July Bridge ☎02/2575-0444, ⊕www.egypt.embassy.gov.au.
Canada 26 Sharia Kamel el-Shenawi, Garden City ☎02/2791-8700, ⊕www.canadainternational.gc.ca/egypt-egypte.
Ireland 22 Sharia Hassan Assem, Zamalek ☎02/2735-8264, ⊕www.embassyofireland.org.eg.
New Zealand 8th floor, North Tower, Nile City Towers, 2005C Corniche El Nil, Rod el-Farag ☎02/2461-6000, ⊕www.nzembassy.com/egypt.
South Africa 6th floor, 55 Rd 18, Ma'adi ☎02/2359-4365, ⊜cairo.embassy@foreign.gov.za.
UK 7 Sharia Ahmed Ragheb, Garden City ☎02/2791 6133, ⊕ukinegypt.fco.gov.uk.
USA 5 Sharia Amerika Latina, Garden City ☎02/2797-3300, ⊕cairo.usembassy.gov.

Health

Most visitors to Cairo will experience nothing worse than perhaps an upset stomach, and a change of diet and climate accounts for most visitors' health problems. Some people adapt quickly, others take longer, especially children and older people. If you're only here for a few days, it makes sense to be cautious with what you eat, but for longer-staying visitors it isn't worth being too finicky, and an upset stomach every now and then is the just the price you have to pay while acclimatizing to local germs.

Unless you're coming from an area where yellow fever is endemic (in practice this means countries in sub-Saharan Africa), there are no compulsory **inoculations** for Egypt, though you should always be up to date with polio and tetanus.

The emergency number for an **ambulance** is ☏123. The ambulance will take you for free to whatever hospital is the nearest, or to one of your choice for £E100.

Water

Tap water in Cairo is heavily chlorinated and mostly safe to drink, but is unpalatable and rough on tender stomachs. Consequently, most tourists stick to bottled mineral water, which is widely available and tastes better (genuine Egyptian mineral water brands such as Baraka or Siwa are better than the filtered tap water marketed in bottles by foreign multinationals). However, excessive fear of tap water is unjustified and hard to sustain in practice if you're here for long.

Heat and dust

Many visitors experience problems with Cairo's heat and dust, particularly in summer and in the middle of the day. Wearing a hat can help, as do loose-fitting clothes (preferably not synthetic fabrics), and a high-factor sunscreen to protect your face from sunburn. Because sweat evaporates immediately in the dry atmosphere, you can easily become dehydrated without realizing it. Dehydration is exacerbated by both alcohol and caffeine, so drink plenty of other fluids – fruit juice, for example, which is rarely hard to find.

Less seriously, visitors may suffer from **prickly heat**, an itchy rash caused by excessive perspiration trapped beneath the skin. Loose clothing and frequent bathing can help reduce it.

Dust and grit in the atmosphere can irritate your eyes. Contact-lens users may find switching to glasses helps. If ordinary eye drops don't help, try antihistamine decongestant eye drops such as Vernacel, Vascon-A or Optihist. Persistent irritation may indicate trachoma, a contagious infection which is easily cured by antibiotics at an early stage, but eventually causes blindness if left untreated. Dust can also inflame sinuses. Covering your nose and mouth with a scarf helps prevent this; Olbas oil or a nasal decongestant spray can relieve symptoms.

Digestive complaints

Almost every visitor to Egypt gets **diarrhoea** at some stage. Rare meat and raw shellfish top the danger list, which descends via creamy sauces down to salads, juices, raw fruit and vegetables. Visitors who insist on washing everything (and cleaning their teeth) in mineral water are overreacting. Just use common sense, and accustom your stomach gradually to Egyptian cooking. Asking for dishes to be served very hot (*sukhna awi*) will reduce the risk of catching anything.

If you have diarrhoea, the best initial treatment is to simply adapt your diet, eating plain boiled rice and vegetables, while avoiding greasy or spicy food, caffeine, alcohol, and most fruit and dairy products (although some say that bananas and prickly pears can help, while yoghurt provides a form of protein that your body can easily absorb). Most importantly, keep your bodily fluids topped up by drinking plenty of bottled water. Especially if children are affected, you may also want to add rehydration salts (brands include Rehydran) to the water, or failing that, half a teaspoon of salt and eight of sugar in a litre of water will help the body to absorb the fluid more efficiently.

Drugs like Imodium or Lomotil can plug you up, but undermine your body's efforts to rid itself of infection. Avoid Enterovioform, which is still available in Egypt despite being suspected of damaging the optic nerve. Antinal (nifuroxazide) is widely prescribed against diarrhoea in Egypt, and available over the counter in pharmacies. Note that having diarrhoea may make orally administered drugs (such as contraceptive pills) less effective, as they can pass straight through you without being absorbed.

If symptoms persist longer than a few days, or if you develop a fever or pass blood in your faeces, get medical help immediately, since acute diarrhoea can also be a symptom of dysentery, cholera or **typhoid.**

Mosquitos

Though there is no malaria in Cairo, **mosquitoes** are a nuisance, ubiquitous in summer and never entirely absent. Fans, mosquito coils, repellent and plug-in vaporizers (sold at pharmacies) all help. A lot of Egyptians use citronella oil, obtainable from many pharmacies, as a repellent, but tests have shown it to be less effective (and to require more frequent applications) than repellents containing DEET (diethyltoluamide), which are the ones recommended by medical authorities. Xgnat skin gel is an effective natural alternative. Don't forget to put repellent on your feet and ankles if they are uncovered when you go out in the evening. The best guarantee of a bite-less night's sleep is to bring a mosquito net.

Healthcare

Egyptian **pharmacists** are well trained, usually speak English and can dispense a wide range of drugs, including many normally on prescription. If necessary, they can usually recommend a doctor – sometimes on the premises.

Private **doctors** are just as common as pharmacies, and most speak English or French. They charge for consultations: expect to pay about £E100 a session, which doesn't include drugs, but should cover a follow-up visit.

If you get seriously ill, **hospitals** (*mustashfa*) that are privately run are generally preferable to public-sector ones. Private hospitals usually require a cash deposit of at least £E150 (it can go as high as £E1500) to cover the cost of treatment, and often require payment on the spot; you will then have to claim it back from your insurance provider. Despite several good hospitals, Cairo is not a place to fall seriously ill in; in particular, if you need surgery, it's best to get back home for it if you can.

24-hour Pharmacies

In cases of emergency, these pharmacies will also deliver medicines.

Abdallah 2 Sharia Tahar Hussein, Zamalek ☎ 02/2738-1988 (see map, pp.132–133).
Al-Esa'af 27 26th July St (at the junction with Sharia Ramses) ☎ 02/2574-3369 (see map, pp.50–51).
Atalla 13 Sharia Sherif (at the junction with Sharia Rushdi) ☎ 02/2393-9029 (see map, pp.50–51).
El-Ezaby in Ramses station ☎ 02/2575-6272.

Hospitals

Anglo-American Hospital 3 Sharia Hadiqet El Zohreya by Cairo Tower, Gezira ☎ 02/2735-6162 or 3 or 5.
Al-Salam International Hospital Corniche el-Nil, Ma'adi ☎ 02/2524-0250 or 0077.
Cairo Medical Centre Sharia al-Ansari (just off Sharia Higaz by Midan Roxi), Heliopolis ☎ 02/2450-9800.

Doctors

Dr Magdi Francis, 20 Sharia Mossadek, Dokki ☎ 02/3749-0818.
Dr Moustafa Chakankiry, Jedda Tower, 17 Sharia Ismail Mohammed, Zamalek ☎ 02/2739-4625.

Dentists

Dr Avedis Djeghalian, 6 Sharia Abdel Hamid Said ☎ 02/2577-7909.
Dr Samih Barsoum, 7 26th July St (at Sharia Emad el-Din) ☎ 02/2589-8303.

Insurance

Travel insurance is vital in case of accident or serious illness, and handy in case of theft or loss of belongings. The only exception is if you are covered by a private health insurance scheme from home, but always check before travelling. If you need to make a claim, you should keep receipts for medicines and medical treatment, and in the event you have anything stolen, you must obtain an official theft report from the police (called a *mahdar*). You may also be required to provide proof that you owned the items that were stolen, in the form of shop receipts or a credit-card statement recording the purchase.

Internet access

It's easy to access the internet in Cairo. On top of the numerous **internet cafés**, there

Rough Guides travel insurance

Rough Guides has teamed up with WorldNomads.com to offer great **travel insurance** deals. Policies are available to residents of over 150 countries, with cover for a wide range of **adventure sports**, 24hr emergency assistance, high levels of medical and evacuation cover and a stream of **travel safety information**. Roughguides.com users can take advantage of their policies online 24/7, from anywhere in the world – even if you're already travelling. And since plans often change when you're on the road, you can extend your policy and even claim online. Roughguides.com users who buy travel insurance with WorldNomads.com can also leave a positive footprint and donate to a community development project. For more information go to ⓦ**www .roughguides.com/shop**.

are one or two cafés (such as *Café Tabasco* in Zamalek, see p.198) and hotels (such as the *Berlin*, see p.183) with free **wi-fi**, where you can get on line for free if you have an internet-enabled laptop, though of course your connection will not be secure (so don't type in credit card numbers, for example).

Internet cafés

Café Paris in the Bustan Centre, Sharia Bustan (daily 8am–10pm; £E6/hr).
Concord Net Sharia Mohammed Mahmoud, between Sharia Falaky and Sharia Mansour (daily 9am–2am; £E4/hr).
Five Stars 3 Sharia Talaat Harb (daily 9am–midnight; £E5/hr).
Hany 16 Abdel Khaliq Sarwat (daily 10.30am–8pm; £E2/hr).
Inter Club in the passage by 12 Sharia Talaat Harb (by Estoril restaurant; Sat–Thurs 9am–midnight, Fri 4.30pm–midnight; £E5/hr).
Zamalek Center 25 Sharia Ismail Mohammed, Zamalek (daily 8am–midnight; £E5/hr).

Laundry

Wherever you are staying, there will either be an in-house laundry (*mahwagi*) or one close by to call on, charging piece rates. One or two budget hotels allow guests to use their washing machine for a small charge, or gratis. You can buy washing powder at most pharmacies.

Libraries and cultural centres

American Research Center in Egypt 1st floor, 2 Midan Simon Bolivar, Garden City (☎02/2794-8239, ⓦwww.arce.org) has lectures on Egyptology and Islamic art.

Egyptian Centre for International Cultural Cooperation (ECIC) 11 Sharia Shagar al-Durr, Zamalek (☎02/2736-5419, ⓔegycenter2008 @yahoo.com; daily except Fri 9am–2.40pm); organizes exhibitions, recitals and occasional tours.
Maulana Azad Centre for Indian Culture by 23 Sharia Talaat Harb (☎02/2393-3396; Sun–Thurs 10.30am–5.30pm), has a library (borrowing for members only), and also offers yoga classes.
Netherlands–Flemish Institute 1 Sharia Mahmoud Azmi, Zamalek (☎02/2738-2522, ⓦwww.institutes.leiden.edu/nvic), runs lectures in English about Egypt (Sept–June Thurs 6pm).

Mail

Airmail **letters** from Egypt generally take a week to ten days to reach Britain or Ireland, two to three weeks to North America or Australasia. It speeds up the delivery if you get someone to write the name of the country in Arabic. As a rule, around fifteen percent of correspondence (in either direction) never arrives; letters containing photos or other items are especially prone to go astray.

Airmail (*bareed gawwi*) stamps can be purchased at post offices, hotel shops and postcard stands, which may charge a few extra piastres on top of the stamp's official price (£E2.50 for a postcard/letter to anywhere in the world). Registered mail, costing £E10 extra, can be sent from any post office.

The central **post office** is on Midan Ataba (daily except Fri 8am–9pm, Ramadan 9am–2pm), with branches (daily except Fri 8am–6pm, Ramadan 9am–3pm) citywide, including on Sharia Tahrir by Midan Falaki, on Sharia Ramses by the junction with 26th July Street, and in Ramses station.

Poste restante (general delivery) is in Sharia al-Bedak, round the corner from the main entrance to Ataba post office, on the west side of the building – enter the last door, signposted "Private boxes", and ask at counter #10 (Sun–Thurs 8am–9pm, Ramadan 9am–2pm; bring your passport). Mail should be addressed to you, with surname in capitals and underlined, at Poste Restante, Post Office Ataba, 11511 Cairo. Letters are held for a month, often filed under the wrong name.

Parcels can only be mailed abroad from the Ramses Square post office, round the back (the north side of the building), in an office marked "Foreign Parcels Office" (daily except Fri 8am–4pm). To send a parcel, take it unsealed for inspection, and wrap it on the premises. To receive a parcel, go to the main entrance (east side) of the same building, fourth floor. For **Express Mail**, EMS (daily 24hr), opposite the west side of Ataba post office in Sharia al-Bedak, promises worldwide delivery in three to four working days. Private firms (faster but more expensive) include DHL, 38 Abdel Khaliq Sarwat (☎02/3308-6330), with branches citywide, and UPS, c/o Maadi Express Center, 8 Road 78, Ma'adi (☎02/2981-5099 or 5328).

Maps, addresses and directions

If you can find a copy, the *New Handy Map of Cairo* is generally the best **map** of the city, and Cairo City Key's *Detailed Map of Greater Cairo* comes second, but these were unavailable at last check so your choice is between the Cairo Engineering and Manufacturing Company's *Cairo Tourist Map*, which extends out to Heliopolis, and Lehnert & Landrock's map of the same name, which is better for downtown. Geodia's *Cairo City Map*, on laminated paper, is a lot less detailed. A free map with advertisements can occasionally be found at upmarket hotels, containing reasonable plans of Heliopolis, Ma'adi, Mohandiseen, Zamalek and the downtown area. Of more use for longer stays are the American University in Cairo's (AUC) *Cairo: The Practical Guide Maps* (£E50), which contains a useful set of maps, and the *Cairo City Key* (£E60). The best place to buy maps is at a bookshop such as Lehnert & Landrock (44 Sharia Sherif) or Shorouk (1 Midan Talaat Harb), but Buccellati, at Sharia Qasr el-Nil with Sharia Mohammed Farid, may have maps that other places don't stock.

Don't expect Cairenes themselves to relate to maps; they comprehend their city differently. Also be aware when asking **directions** that people are unlikely to admit they don't know where something is, and will make up some directions instead; for that reason it's always best to ask more than one person.

Street names are posted in English (or French) and Arabic in central Cairo and Zamalek, almost everywhere else in Arabic only, or not at all. The same goes for numbers, rendered in Western and Arabic numerals (see p.278), or just the latter; a single number may denote a whole block with several entrance passageways – something to remember when you're following up addresses.

El Houssein or al-Husain

While scholars may transliterate Arabic into English using complicated systems of dots, lines and accents above and below letters, out on the street there's no standard system for transcribing Arabic script into Roman, so you're sure to find that the spellings we've used for Arabic words in this book don't always match the versions you'll see elsewhere. Maps and street signs are the biggest sources of confusion, so we've generally gone for whatever's the most commonly used spelling on the spot. That said, it's not unusual to find one spelling posted at one end of a street, with another at the opposite end. The definite article ("the"), in Arabic attached to the word it defines, is reproduced in several forms (al-, el-, and, if elided with the next letter, as it often is, even en- or ash-), and letters that have no English equivalent may be left out or represented by apostrophes. For an introduction to Egyptian Arabic, see p.275.

Money

Egypt's basic unit of **currency** is the **Egyptian pound** (called a *ginay* in Arabic, and written £E or LE), divided into 100 piastres ('*urush*, singular '*irsh*). At the time of writing, exchange rates were around £E9.26 to the pound sterling, £E5.83 to the US dollar, and £E7.98 to the euro.

Egyptian **banknotes** bear Arabic numerals on one side, Western numerals on the other, and come in denominations of 25pt, 50pt, £E1, £E5, £E10, £E20, £E50, £E100 and £E200. Coins for 25pt, 50pt and £E1 are common, and you may also come across coins of 5pt, 10pt and 20pt.

Some banknotes are so ragged that merchants refuse them, but some vendors won't accept high-denomination notes (£E20 upwards) due to a shortage of change, so try to hoard coins and small-value notes for tips, fares and small purchases.

Carrying your money

The easiest way to access your money in Cairo is with **plastic**, though it's a good idea to also have some back-up in the form of cash or travellers' cheques. Using a Visa, MasterCard, Plus or Cirrus card, you can draw cash using ATMs. By using ATMs you get trade exchange rates, which are somewhat better than those charged by banks for changing cash, but your card issuer may well add a foreign transaction fee, sometimes as much as five percent. There is a daily limit on ATM cash withdrawals, usually £E4000. If you use a credit card rather than a debit card, note also that all cash advances and ATM withdrawals obtained are treated as loans, with interest accruing daily from the date of withdrawal.

It's wise to make sure your card is in good condition and, before you leave home, make sure that the card and PIN will work overseas. Where there is no ATM, cash advances on Visa and MasterCard can be obtained at most branches of the Banque Misr on the same basis.

Credit cards are accepted for payment at major hotels, top-flight restaurants, some shops and airline offices, but virtually nowhere else. American Express, MasterCard and Visa are the likeliest to be accepted.

Arriving by air, you should have no trouble changing money as airport banks are open around the clock. It is illegal to import or export more than £E5000 in local currency.

Banks and ATMs

There are plenty of **ATMs** that accept foreign cards, especially around Sharia Talaat Harb, but also in Zamalek, Mohandiseen and Dokki. Changing cash or travellers' cheques is usually quick and easy at the 24hr Bank Misr exchange bureaux in the *Nile Hotel*, the *Ramses Hilton* and the *Shepheard*.

Alternatively there are **Forex bureaux** (money changers) dotted around town, which usually give better rates than banks, with a lot less queuing and messing around. Forex bureaux in central Cairo include a couple on Abdel Khalek Sarwat east of Sharia Talaat Harb, a handful around the junction of Sharia Qasr el-Nil and Sharia Mohammed Farid, and another group on the corner of Sharia el-Gumhoriyya with Midan Opera, which are your best bet for changing currencies such as Israeli shekels or Sudanese pounds. You can also change money at Thomas Cook (17 Sharia Bassiouni ☏02/2576 6982; daily 8am–5pm; full branch list at ⓦwww .thomascookegypt.com/our_branches.aspx) or American Express (15 Sharia Qasr el-Nil; daily except Fri 9am–4pm; Ramadan 9am–2.30pm).

For **international transfers**, MoneyGram's agents in Cairo include Sphinx Trading at 2 Sharia Sherif, and Piraeus Bank at 9 Sharia Adly; Western Union's agents are International Business Associates (at 1079 Corniche el-Nil in Garden City or downtown at 4 Sharia Hassan Basha al-Memmary off Sharia Bassiouni) and branches of the Arab African International Bank (downtown at 44 Sharia Abdel Khaliq Sarwat, or 54d Sharia el-Gumhorriya at Sharia Alfi Bey).

Opening hours and public holidays

Offices tend to open Sunday to Thursday from 8.30am to 5pm. Shops are usually open from around 10am to around 8pm, sometimes later, with small places often closing briefly for prayers, especially Friday lunchtime between around noon and 3pm, but most shops take their day off on Sunday.

During **Ramadan**, all these hours go haywire. Since everybody who keeps the fast will want to eat immediately when it ends at sunset, most places close early to allow this, and may open early to compensate. Offices may open 7am–4pm, shops may simply close to break the fast, reopening afterwards, while banks open 9.30am to 1.30pm. Ramadan opening times are given, where available, throughout the text.

Public holidays include Eid el-Adha, Ras el-Sana el-Hegira, the Moulid el-Nabi and Eid el-Fitr, all dated on the Islamic calendar (see p.216). Others, following the Gregorian calendar, are: Coptic Christmas (Jan 7), Sinai Liberation Day (April 25), Labour Day (May 1), Evacuation Day (June 18), Revolution Day (July 23), Flooding of the Nile (Aug 15), Armed Forces Day (Oct 6), Suez Liberation Day (Oct 23), and Victory Day (Dec 23). Sham al-Nassim falls according to the Coptic calendar (see p.218). Banks and offices close on public holidays; most shops and transport operate as usual.

Phones

Phone calls can be made, and faxes sent (at per-minute phone rates) and received (for £E1 per page), at the following telecom offices: 8 Sharia Adly (℗02/2239-7580); Sharia Alfi Bey by the *Windsor Hotel* (℗02/2589-7635); Sharia Ramses, opposite Sharia Tawfiqia (no fax service at last check); 13 Midan Tahrir; Midan Ataba by the National Theatre (℗02/2578-0979). All are open 24hr. Phone rates are around twenty percent cheaper at night (8pm–8am). The phone offices will inform you of your fax's arrival if your name and phone number are at the top of the page, as will EMS (see p.42), where you can also send and receive faxes.

You can buy a card at grocers or kiosks to use in public phones on the street. Cards such as Egypt Telecom's Marhaba card, with a scratch-off panel covering a PIN, can be used from private phones by dialling a toll-free number, then the PIN on the card, and finally the number you wish to call. They usually work out cheaper than ordinary phonecards, and are available from the same places, but they generally don't work from public phones.

Mobile phones

If you want to use your mobile phone while in Cairo, you'll need to check with your phone provider whether it will work in Egypt and what the charges are. A US cellphone must be GSM/triband to work in Egypt.

If you're planning to use your phone a lot in Egypt, especially for local calls, it's worth getting a SIM card from one of the Egyptian providers, Mobinil (prefix ☎012) and Vodafone (☎010), both of which have retailers all over town. A typical deal gives you a SIM card for around £E100, including

International calls

Omit the initial zero from the area code when dialling Egypt, the UK, Ireland, Australia, New Zealand or South Africa.

	From Egypt	To Egypt
UK	☎00 44	☎00 20
Ireland	☎00 353	☎00 20
US and Canada	☎001	☎011 20
Australia	☎00 61	☎0011 20
New Zealand	☎00 64	☎00 20
South Africa	☎00 27	☎09 20

Emergencies and information
Ambulance	☎123
Police	☎122
Tourist police	☎126
Fire brigade	☎180
Directory enquiries	☎140 or 141
International operator	☎120

£E70 of free calls. Top-up cards are available in denominations from £E10 to £E200.

Time

Egypt is on GMT+2, which means that in principle it is two hours ahead of the UK, seven hours ahead of the US East Coast (EST), eleven hours ahead of the US West Coast (PST), six hours behind Western Australia, eight hours behind eastern Australia and ten hours behind New Zealand. Daylight Saving Time at home or in Egypt may vary those differences. Egypt's clocks move forward for daylight saving on the last Friday in April and back again on the last Friday in September.

Tourist information

The Egyptian Tourism Authority (ⓦwww .egypt.travel) has a downtown **tourist office** at 5 Sharia Adly (daily 9am–6pm, Ramadan and public holidays 9am–3pm; ☎02/2391-3454), where staff are not very well informed, but may be able to answer simple queries. There are also 24-hour tourist offices at all the airport terminals and offices at Ramses Station (daily 9am–8pm; ☎02/2579-0767), Giza train station (daily 9am–2pm & 5–9pm; ☎02/3570-2233), the Giza Pyramids (daily 8.30am–5pm; ☎02/3383-8823) and Souk Fustat (supposedly open daily 8.30am–9pm, but in practice often closed for no apparent reason; ☎02/2532-5269).

Egyptian tourist offices abroad

Canada 2020 University St, Suite 2260, Montreal, PQ H3A 2A5 ☎1-514/861-8071, ⓔinfo .ca@egypt.travel.
UK 170 Piccadilly, London W1J 9EJ ☎020/7493 5283, ⓔinfo.uk@egypt.travel.
US 645 N Michigan Ave, Suite 829, Chicago, IL 60611 ☎1-312/280-4666, ⓔinfo.us@egypt.travel; 8383 Wilshire Bvd, Suite 215, Beverly Hills, Los Angeles, CA 90211 ☎1-213/653-8815, ⓔinfo .us@egypt.travel; 630 5th Ave, Suite 2305, New York, NY 10111 ☎1-212/332-2570, ⓔinfo.us @egypt.travel.

Travellers with disabilities

Disability is common in Egypt. Many conditions that would be treatable in the West, such as cataracts, cause permanent disabilities here because people can't afford the treatment, but people with disabilities are unlikely to get jobs (though there is a tradition of blind singers and preachers), so the choice is usually between staying at home, being looked after by your family, and going out on the streets to beg for alms.

For a blind or wheelchair-using tourist, the streets are full of obstacles that you will find hard going. Queuing, steep stairs, unreliable elevators, and the heat, will also make things difficult. A light, folding campstool could be invaluable if you have limited walking or standing power. In that case, it's a good idea to avoid visiting in the summer months.

For wheelchair users, the **monuments** are a mix of accessible and impossible. The Pyramids of Giza are fine to view but not enter, though the sound-and-light show is wheelchair accessible; Saqqara is difficult, being so sandy. Islamic Cairo is especially difficult, with its narrow, uneven alleys and heavy traffic, but with a car and helper, you could still see the Citadel and other major monuments. There's a lift in the Egyptian Antiquities Museum, and newer metro stations have elevator access from street level to the platforms, though none of the older ones do, which unfortunately includes all those in the city centre.

Taxis are easily affordable and quite adaptable; if you charter one for the day, the driver is certain to help you in and out, and perhaps even around the sites you visit. If you employ a guide, they may well also be prepared to help you with steps and other obstacles.

Nearly all the city's five-star hotels have wheelchair access and adapted rooms. The *El Borg Novotel*, *Four Seasons* (in both Garden City and Giza), *Ramses Hilton*, *Semiramis Intercontinental*, *Cairo Marriott*, *Conrad*, *Grand Hyatt*, *Le Meridien Pyramids*, *Mena House Oberoi* and *Sofitel* all have adapted rooms, as do the *Nile Hotel* and the *Shepheard*, but without wheel-in showers in the bathroom. Downtown budget hotels tend to have narrow entrances with steps, and small lifts with awkward doors, making access very hard.

Planning a holiday

There are **organized tours and holidays** specifically for people with disabilities, and some companies, such as Discover Egypt in the UK (see p.21), offer packages tailor-made to your specific needs. Egypt for All (ⓦwww.egyptforall.com) runs a range of tours that cover Cairo along with other parts of Egypt, but also offers tailor-made holidays to your specifications and may be able to arrange transport or equipment rental.

It's a good idea to carry spares of any clothing or equipment that might be hard to find; if there's an association at home for people with your particular disability, contact them early for more specific advice.

Working and studying in Cairo

Some foreigners make a living in Cairo, teaching English, writing for the English-language media, or even bellydancing. Getting a **work permit** involves getting a job offer, then taking evidence of this to Mogamma (see p.37) to apply. So long as the offer is for a job where foreigners rather than Egyptians are needed, it is simply then a question of jumping through the necessary bureaucratic hoops.

Private **language schools** are often on the lookout for English teachers, and the British Council (192 Corniche el-Nil, Aguza ☎19789, ⒺInformation@britishcouncil.org.eg) may be able to supply a list of schools to approach; the more reputable firms will want an EFL qualification. You may also be able to find work with the local **English-language media**: *Egypt Today* sometimes accepts articles and photos, and the *Egyptian Gazette* may need sub-editors from time to time.

For **studying**, the **American University in Cairo** (☎02/2794 2964, ⓦwww.aucegypt .edu) offers year-abroad and non-degree

programmes, a summer school and intensive Arabic courses. A full year's tuition (two semesters and summer school) costs roughly US$20,250. US citizens may apply to the Stafford Loan Program, at Office of Admissions, 420 5th Ave, 3rd Floor, New York, NY 10018-2729 (☎212/730-8800).

Foreign students may also attend one- or two-term programmes at **universities** such as Cairo (ⓦwww.cu.edu.eg), Ain Shams (ⓦnet.shams.edu.eg) and Al-Azhar (ⓦwww .azhar.edu.eg). Like the AUC's courses, these are valid for transferable credits at most American and some British universities. In the US, you can get information on exchange programmes from the Egyptian Cultural and Educational Bureau, 1303 New Hampshire Ave NW, Washington DC 20036 (☎202/296-3888, ⓦwww.eecous.net) or AmidEast, 1730 M St NW Suite 1100, Washington DC 20036–4505 (☎202/776-9600, ⓦwww.amideast.org).

Arabic lessons are offered by: International Language Institute (ILI), 4 Sharia Mahmoud Azmi, Sahafayeen (north of Mohandiseen) (☎02/3346-3087, ⓦwww.arabicegypt.com); Kalimat Language and Cultural Centre, 22 Sharia al-Koroum, behind Mohammed Mustafa Mosque, Mohandiseen (☎02/3761-8136, ⓦwww.kalimategypt.com), which was set up by former British Council teachers; AUC, 113 Sharia Qasr al-Aini (☎02/2797-6872 or 3, Ⓔsami@aucegypt.edu), which is well-respected, though its teaching methods may not be as up-to-date as at Kalimat or the ILI. ILI charges £E215 for 32 hours of tuition over four weeks in Egyptian Colloquial Arabic, and also offers Modern Standard Arabic, or a combination of both. The *Berlin Hotel* (see p.183) can also organize low-priced one-to-one tuition.

The City

The City

Central Cairo

Central Cairo encapsulates the city's febrile energy, its rampant consumerism and inequalities. Towering riverside hotels and ministries, ugly flyovers, relentless traffic and pollution almost overwhelm the faded elegance of its Art Deco and *belle époque* buildings. Yet its ambience is neither impersonal nor intimidating, not least because Cairenes revel in repartee and scandal. While much of this banter goes over the heads of non-Arabic speakers, you can't fail to notice the animation of life here, or how people create tiny oases of calm amidst the turmoil.

The **downtown** area (known locally as *Wust al-Balad*) forms a parallelogram, extending inland from **Midan Tahrir** – the site of Egypt's 2011 revolution and the world famous **Egyptian Museum** – towards the **Ezbekiya Gardens**, beyond **Bab al-Luq market** and the **Shaar HaShamayim Synagogue.** This area is packed with shops, hotels, cafés, bars and travel agencies, and most visitors use it as a base for exploring the rest of the city.

Three peripheral areas complete the centre. **Abdin** (the government district) and **Garden City** (the diplomatic quarter) both have a heavy security presence, but you shouldn't let that deter you from enjoying the kitsch **Abdin Palace Museum** nor the leafy streets of Art Deco villas that give Garden City its character; both are near Midan Tahrir.

From Midan Tahrir it's only three stops north on the metro to **Ramses Station,** north of the downtown area. Egypt's main railway terminal is useful to anyone planning a day-trip to Alexandria (see p.235), but otherwise only worth visiting to see the adjacent **Egyptian Railways Museum**.

All of these areas were laid out during the reign of Khedive Ismail (1863–79), on the flood plain beside the medieval city, which was rendered buildable-upon by drainage works. Enriched by the soaring price of cotton, Ismail could afford to splurge on realising his ambition to make Cairo a truly modern city, fit to rival Paris – with wide boulevards, grand villas, parks and an opera house constructed in record time to be ready for the inauguration of the Suez Canal in 1869.

His new Europeanized quarter (modestly named "Ismailiya") was intended to be the antithesis of the crumbling, once-magnificent medieval city beyond Midan Ataba. "To the West lies Europe, to the East the Orient," declaimed a British journalist forty years later, by which time an eighth of Cairo's inhabitants were foreign-born, outnumbering native Egyptians by three to one in the area to the west of Ataba. Not until after King Farouk was overthrown by army officers in 1952 did Egyptians claim it as their own patrimony.

In 2011, the world was transfixed by another revolution in the heart of Cairo, as vast crowds defied the regime on Midan Tahrir until President Mubarak was toppled from power on February 11. Two million Cairenes celebrated on the square – a jubilant climax to a revolution whose credo was expressed in the chant *Slimiyya!* ("Peacefully!").

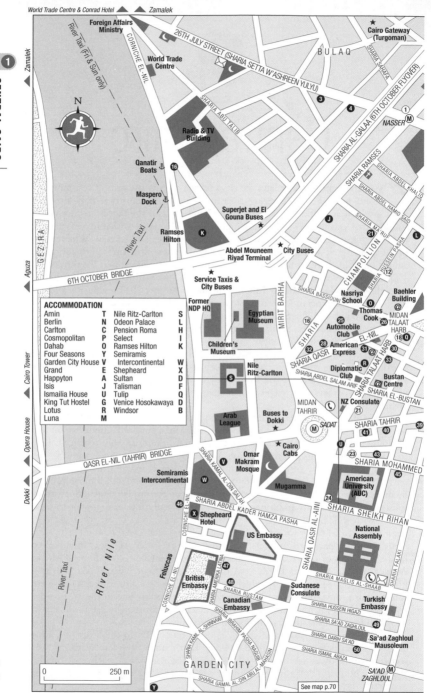

World Trade Centre & Conrad Hotel ▲ ▲ ▲ Zamalek

Foreign Affairs Ministry

River Taxi (Fri & Sun only)

Zamalek

26TH JULY STREET (SHARIA SETTA W'ASHREEN YULYU)

BULAQ

Cairo Gateway (Turgoman)

World Trade Centre

SHARIA SAFFA

SHARIA ABU TALIB

3

4

SHARIA AL-GALAA (6TH OCTOBER FLYOVER)

NASSER M 1

Radio & TV Building

SHARIA RAMSES

SHARIA ABDEL KHALIQ

Qanatir Boats 16

SHARIA MA'RUF

SHARIA ABDEL HAMID SAID

N

GEZIRA

Maspero Dock

Superjet and El Gouna Buses ★

J

SHARIA HUSSEIN PASHA

21

L

Aguza

Ramses Hilton

K

Abdel Mouneem Riyad Terminal

★ City Buses

CHAMPOLLION

12

Baehler Building

6TH OCTOBER BRIDGE

Cairo Tower

★ Service Taxis & City Buses

Former NDP HQ

Egyptian Museum

MIRIT BARHA

SHARIA BASSIOUNI

Nasriya School

SHARIA

O

Thomas Cook

MIDAN TALAAT HARB

ACCOMMODATION

Amin	T	Nile Ritz-Carlton	S
Berlin	N	Odeon Palace	L
Carlton	C	Pension Roma	H
Cosmopolitan	P	Select	I
Dahab	O	Ramses Hilton	K
Four Seasons	Y	Semiramis	
Garden City House	E	Intercontinental	W
Grand	A	Shepheard	X
Happyton	A	Sultan	D
Isis	J	Talisman	F
Ismailia House	U	Tulip	Q
King Tut Hostel	G	Venice Hosokawaya	D
Lotus	M	Windsor	B
Luna	M		

16

EL-NIL

25

Automobile Club

American Express

29

32

SHARIA QASR

31

@ 30

18 O

33

Children's Museum

Nile Ritz-Carlton

S

SHARIA ABDEL SALAM ARIF

Diplomatic Club

R

Bustan @ Centre

SHARIA EL-BUSTAN

Opera House

Arab League

MIDAN TAHRIR

Buses to Dokki

★ Cairo Cabs

M SADAT

NZ Consulate

21

SHARIA TAHRIR

41

40

39

QASR EL-NIL (TAHRIR) BRIDGE

Semiramis Intercontinental

W

V

SHARIA KAMAL AL-DIN SALAH

Omar Makram Mosque

Mugamma

U

23

43

45

SHARIA MOHAMMED

Dokki

46

X

Shepheard Hotel

SHARIA ABDEL KADER HAMZA PASHA

24

American University (AUC)

SHARIA SHEIKH RIHAN

CORNICHE EL-NIL

US Embassy

SHARIA QASR AL-AINI

National Assembly

River Taxi

47

British Embassy

48

SHARIA RUSTAM

Canadian Embassy

Sudanese Consulate

SHARIA MAGLIS AL-SHAAB

SHARIA FALAKI

Turkish Embassy

Feluccas

River Nile

SHARIA AMERIKA LATINA

SHARIA HUSSEIN HIGAZI

49

SHARIA SA'AD ZAGHLOUL

SHARIA DARIH SA'AD

Sa'ad Zaghloul Mausoleum

50

0   250 m

SHARIA KAMAL AL-SHINNAWI

SHARIA IBRAHIM PASHA NAGUIB

SHARIA GAMAL AL-DIN ABU AL-AMASIN

GARDEN CITY

Y

SHARIA ISMAIL ABAZA

See map p.70

SA'AD M ZAGHLOUL

Saiyida Zeinab

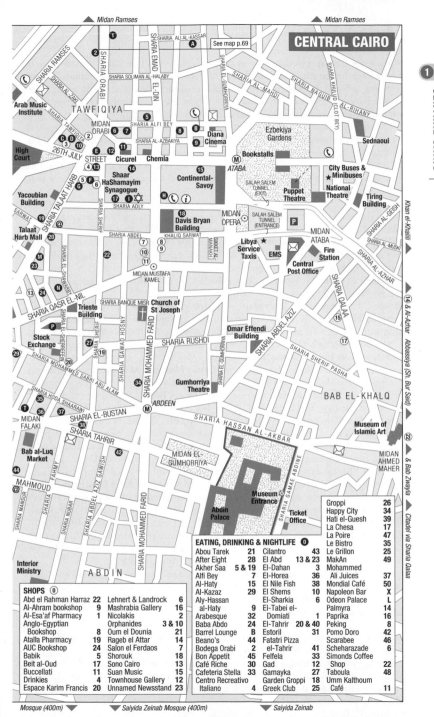

CENTRAL CAIRO

SHOPS ⓞ

Abd el Rahman Harraz	22	Lehnert & Landrock	6
Al-Ahram bookshop	9	Mashrabia Gallery	16
Al-Esa'af Pharmacy	1	Nicolakis	2
Anglo-Egyptian		Orphanides	3 & 10
Bookshop	8	Oum el Dounia	21
Atalla Pharmacy	19	Rageb el Attar	14
AUC Bookshop	24	Salon el Ferdaos	7
Babik	5	Shorouk	
Beit al-Oud	17	Sono Cairo	13
Buccellati	11	Suan Music	15
Drinkies	4	Townhouse Gallery	12
Espace Karim Francis	20	Unnamed Newsstand	23

EATING, DRINKING & NIGHTLIFE ⓞ

Abou Tarek	21	Cilantro	43
After Eight	28	El Abd	13 & 23
Akher Saa	5 & 19	El-Dahan	3
Alfi Bey	7	El-Horea	36
Al-Haty	15	El Nile Fish	38
Al-Kazaz	29	El Shems	10
Aly-Hassan		El-Sharkia	6
al-Haty	9	El-Tabei el-	
Arabesque	32	Domiati	1
Baba Abdo	24	El-Tahrir	20 & 40
Barrel Lounge	B	Estoril	31
Beano's	44	Fatatri Pizza	
Bodega Orabi	2	el-Tahrir	41
Bon Appetit	45	Felfela	33
Café Riche	30	Gad	12
Cafeteria Stella	33	Gamayka	27
Centro Recreativo		Garden Groppi	18
Italiano	4	Greek Club	25

Groppi	26
Happy City	34
Hati el-Guesh	39
La Chesa	17
La Poire	47
Le Bistro	35
Le Grillon	25
MakAn	49
Mohammed	
Ali Juices	37
Mondial Café	50
Napoleon Bar	X
Odeon Palace	L
Palmyra	14
Paprika	16
Peking	8
Pomo Doro	42
Scarabee	46
Scheharazade	6
Simonds Coffee	
Shop	22
Taboula	48
Umm Kalthoum	
Café	11

Mosque (400m) ▼   ▼ Saiyida Zeinab Mosque (400m)   ▼ Saiyida Zeinab

Midan Tahrir

Some cities have spectacular squares at their heart – but not Cairo. Instead, you'll find a huge intersection lacking any visual harmony, aptly named **Midan Tahrir** (Liberation Square). Created after the 1952 revolution on the site of Britain's Qasr el-Nil Barracks, Nasser's demolition of the building symbolically avenged the British shooting of nationalist demonstrators here in 1919.

The square's name rang hollow over decades of authoritarian rule, symbolized by the grimy concave block of the **Mugamma**, or Government Building. This Kafkaesque warren of gloomy corridors, idle bureaucrats and dejected queues was a "fraternal gift" from the Soviet Union in 1952, which sums up everything that was wrong with Nasser's Pan-Arab Socialism and the corrupt bureaucracy that stifles Egypt to this day.

On January 25, 2011, a "Day of Rage" inspired by a recent revolution in Tunisia began the protests that toppled Egypt's President Mubarak eighteen days later, and Midan Tahrir became the epicentre of a revolution that shook the Arab world. Visitors can see for themselves if the impromptu memorials and debates attesting to Egypt's fledgling democracy have outlasted the signs of battle damage on Midan Tahrir, which are only slowly being effaced.

To the east of the Mugamma – across Sharia Qasr al-Aini – the former palace built for government minister Ahmed Khairy Pasha in 1874 now houses the original campus of the **American University in Cairo** (entered from Sharia Sheikh Rihan). Responsible for publishing some of the best research on Egypt in the English language, the AUC is also a Western-style haven for wealthy Egyptian youths and US students doing a year abroad, its shady gardens and preppy ambience seeming utterly remote from everyday life in Cairo.

On the other side of the Mugamma, the **Omar Makram Mosque** is where funeral receptions for deceased VIPs are held, in brightly-coloured marquees outside. Beyond this, **Sharia Tahrir** leads past two guardian **lions** sculpted by French artist Alfred Jacquemart, and over the **Qasr el-Nil** (or Tahrir) **Bridge** to Gezira Island (see p.134) and on to Dokki (p.137) beyond the Nile. Without crossing the bridge, you can find the **Corniche el-Nil** (the road along the bank of the Nile), where, opposite today's **Shepheard Hotel**, generations of tourists once embarked on Nile cruises from Thomas Cook's landing stage, and from which the British General Gordon's ill-fated expedition to recapture Sudan set off for Khartoum in 1883.

Across Sharia Tahrir from the Omar Makram Mosque, the **Arab League Building** is a vestige of the time when Egypt was acknowledged leader of the progressive Arab cause in the 1960s and 1970s. After Sadat's controversial 1979 peace deal with Israel, the League moved its Secretariat to Tunis and most members severed relations with Egypt. Mubarak's policy of rapprochement was finally rewarded in 1992, when the League returned to Cairo with posses of limos and gun-toting bodyguards – but Egypt's influence has since been eclipsed by Saudi Arabia and Iran.

Further northlooms the **Nile Ritz-Carlton hotel**, a re-incarnation of the 1950s' *Nile Hilton* that was the acme of luxury during the Nasser and Sadat eras, but later outclassed by fancier five-star hotels. Out front is a construction site whose fencing and raw materials served as barricades and ammunition when the protesters on Midan Tahrir were bombarded by pro-regime thugs from the 6th October flyover (behind the Egyptian Museum). Pitched battles raged beneath the flyover as volunteers formed a cordon around the museum to safeguard its treasures from looters.

The Egyptian Museum is instantly recognizable by its salmon-pink Beaux Arts-style façade, while the charred high-rise between the museum and the Nile was formerly the headquarters of the ruling **National Democratic Party** (NDP) – set ablaze by protestors in 2011.

The entrances to **Sadat metro station** beneath Midan Tahrir serve as pedestrian underpasses linking the various buildings around Tahrir and the main roads leading off the square. Despite clear labelling in English, it's easy to go astray in the maze of subways and surface at the wrong location. Many Cairenes prefer to take their chances crossing by road – a nerve-wracking experience for newcomers. To watch the square over tea, try one of the Arab cafés between Talaat Harb and El-Bustan streets.

The Egyptian Museum

Downtown's star attraction is the **Egyptian Museum**, on the northern side of Midan Tahrir (daily 9am–6.45pm; Ramadan 9am–4pm; £E60, no cameras allowed; Ⓦwww.egyptianmuseum.gov.eg). Founded in 1858 by Auguste Mariette, who excavated the Serapeum at Saqqara and several major temples in Upper Egypt (and who was later buried in the museum grounds), it has long since outgrown its present building, which now scarcely provides warehouse space for 136,000 exhibits and 40,000 more items crated in the basement. A new Grand Egyptian Museum, which will house some or all the exhibits in the present one, is under construction near the pyramids of Giza (see p.160). During the chaos of the 2011 revolution, thieves abseiled down from the dome to steal or vandalize seventy artefacts (and renegade guards stripped the gift shop of jewellery), but protestors protected the invaluable collection from further harm.

A single visit of three to four hours is enough to cover the Tutankhamun exhibition and a few other **highlights**. Everyone has their favourites, but a reasonable shortlist might include, on the ground floor, the Amarna galleries (**rooms 3 and 8**), and the finest statuary from the Old, Middle and New kingdoms (**rooms 42, 32, 22 and 12**); on the upper floor, the Fayoum Portraits (**Room 14**) and model figures (**rooms 37, 32 and 27**), and, of course, the Royal Mummies (**rooms 52 and 56**) – though these cost £E100 extra. As a rule, the museum is at its most crowded from 9am to noon, and 2 till 5pm.

The water lilies growing in the pond outside the main entrance are the now-rare blue lotus, a psychoactive plant used as a drug by the Ancient Egyptians – which they are depicted using (by dipping the flowers into their wine) on several frescoes and reliefs. Also outside the museum, by the camera deposit, you'll probably be offered a **guided tour**, which generally lasts two hours (around £E50/hr, depending on your bargaining skills); the guides are extremely knowledgeable and help you to make sense of it all. Due to different systems of numbering being added at different times, some exhibits now have three different numbers, and often no other labelling (in such cases, we have given the most prominent number).

A bookshop in the foyer stocks **guidebooks**, such as the full-colour *The Egyptian Museum in Cairo – An Illustrated Guide* (Farid Atiyah Press; £E250) and the smaller *Pocket Book of the Egyptian Museum in Cairo* (Abydos Publications; £E150), both of which locate the featured exhibits by room (though not in order). Another excellent book, sold at the American University bookshop (see p.224), is the AUC's *Illustrated Guide to the Egyptian Museum* (£E150), which has a room-by-room picture index at the back to help you find what you are looking at in the text. Alternatively, you can rent an **audioguide** (£E10) from beside the souvenir shop, reached from outside the museum.

At the time of writing, a separate Children's Museum was under construction around the left-hand side of the main building, supposed to open in 2011.

Ground floor

Exhibits are arranged more or less chronologically, so that by starting at the entrance and walking in a clockwise direction round the outer galleries you'll pass

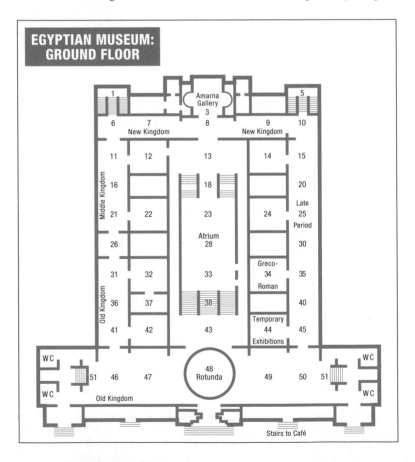

through the Old, Middle and New kingdoms, before ending up with the Late and Greco-Roman periods in the east wing. A quicker alternative is to proceed instead through the Atrium – which samples the whole era of pharaonic civilization – to the superb Amarna Gallery in the northern wing, then backtrack to cover sections that sound interesting, or instead head upstairs to Tutankhamun. Whichever approach you decide on, it's worth starting with the Atrium foyer (**Room 43**), where the dynastic saga begins.

The Rotunda and Atrium

The **Rotunda**, inside the museum entrance, kicks off with **monumental sculptures** from various eras, notably (in the four corners) three colossi of the XIX Dynasty pharaoh Ramses II and a statue of Amenhotep, son of the XVIII Dynasty royal architect Hapu (near right-hand corner). In a glass case to the left as you enter is the limestone **statue of King Zoser** (#16), installed within its *serdab* beside his Step Pyramid at Saqqara (see p.167) in the 27th century BC, and removed by archeologists 4600 years later.

The forging of dynastic rule is commemorated by a famous exhibit in **Room 43**. A decorative version of the slate palettes used to grind kohl eye make-up, the **Palette of Narmer** (#111) records the unification of the Two Lands (c.3100 BC) by a ruler called Narmer or Menes. One side of the palette depicts him wearing the White Crown of Upper Egypt, smiting an enemy with a mace, while a falcon (Horus) ensnares another prisoner and tramples the heraldic papyrus of Lower Egypt. The reverse face shows him wearing the Red Crown of Lower Egypt to inspect the slain, and ravaging a fortress as a bull; dividing these tableaux are mythical beasts with entwined necks, restrained from conflict by bearded men, an arcane symbol of his political achievement.

Three cases further on, just before the steps down into the Atrium, are fragments of two **Libyan Palettes**, the first of which (missing its top half) is beautifully carved with trains of bulls, donkeys and goats, and a grove of olive trees. A century or so older than Narmer's palette, it seems to have been made to commemorate the payment of a tribute to the Upper Egyptian ruler by the Tjemehu tribe of Libya.

Descending into **Room 33**, the Atrium proper, you'll find two black, polished **pyramidions** (pyramid capstones) from Dahshur, and several sarcophagi from the New Kingdom. Outshining those of Tuthmosis I and Queen Hatshepsut (before she became pharaoh) is the **sarcophagus of Merneptah** (#213), surmounted by a figure of the XIX Dynasty king as Osiris, protectively embraced from within by a bas-relief of the sky goddess Nut. When discovered at Tanis in 1939, Merneptah's sarcophagus actually held the coffin of Psusennes, a XXI Dynasty ruler whose gold-sheathed mummy now lies upstairs in the Jewellery Room (see p.62).

At the centre of the Atrium is a **painted floor** from **Akhenaten's** palace at **Tell el-Amarna in Middle Egypt**. It shows a river brimming with ducks and fish and framed by reeds where waterfowl and cows amble, a fine example of the lyrical naturalism of the Amarna period. For more of this revolutionary epoch in pharaonic history, head upstairs past the **colossal statues** of Akhenaten's parents, Amenophis III and Queen Tiy, with their three daughters, to Rooms 3 and 8 in the North Wing (see p.58).

At the top of the stairs into **Room 13**, off to the right of two reconstructed gateways, you'll find **Merneptah's Victory Stele** from the temple of Karnak, otherwise known as the **Israel Stele** (#134). Its name derives from the boast "Israel is crushed, it has no more seed", among a list of Merneptah's conquests – the sole known reference to Israel in all the records of Ancient Egypt. Partly on the strength of this, many believe that Merneptah, the son of Ramses II, was the pharaoh of the Exodus.

Old Kingdom Galleries

The southwest corner of the ground floor is devoted to the **Old Kingdom** (*c.*2686–2181 or 2649–2150 BC), when the III–VI dynasties ruled Egypt from Memphis and built the Pyramids. The walls of rooms 47 and 46 are lined with so-called **false doors** from various tombs – intended to allow the souls of the dead to escape confinement – and the central aisle by funerary statues of deceased VIPs, and *shabti* statuettes of servants (the custom of burying retainers alive ended with the II Dynasty).

On the north side of **Room 47**, six **wooden panels** from the tomb of **Hesy-Re** (#21) portray this senior scribe of the III Dynasty, who was also the earliest known dentist. Three slate **triads**, or triple statues, represent the III Dynasty ruler Menkaure, flanked by the goddess Hathor and a lesser provincial deity. The two alabaster **lion tables** were probably used for sacrifices or libations during the II Dynasty.

Two life-sized **statues of Senusret I** flank the entrance to **Room 46**, where case #54 displays **statuettes of Khnumhotep**, Overseer of the Wardrobe, a man evidently afflicted by Pott's disease (tuberculosis of the spine), which left him with a hunchback, a deformed head and reduced stature. Nearby, the painted limestone **funerary chamber of Desheri** from Saqqara shows the food, drink and accoutrements that Desheri anticipated enjoying in the afterlife. At the end of the hall, near the stairs, the **sculpted head** of the V Dynasty pharaoh Userfaf represents the earliest known larger-than-life statue in the world.

At the entrance to **Room 41** in the West Wing, **reliefs** from a V Dynasty tomb at Maidum (#25) depict a desert hunt and other rural activities. Another panel (#59) from a V Dynasty tomb at Saqqara shows grain being weighed out, milled and graded, glass being blown and statues carved. The women on these reliefs wear long chemises, the men loincloths or sometimes nothing (revealing them to be circumcised, according to Egyptian custom).

Room 42

This room contains some of the finest artefacts from the Old Kingdom. Its centrepiece is a superb **statue of Chephren**, the pharaoh responsible for Giza's second pyramid, his head embraced by the hawk-headed god Horus (#31). The statue comes from Chephren's valley temple at Giza (see p.159), and is carved from black diorite, whose white marbling emphasizes the sinews of his knee and clenched fist. Even more arresting is the wooden **statue of Ka-aper** (#40), to the left, an amazingly lifelike figure with an introspective gaze, which members of the digging team at Saqqara called "Sheikh al-Balad" because it so resembled their own village headman. One of the two bewigged wooden statues just beyond him may well be the same man; the other is known to represent Ka-aper's wife. Also notice the **statue of a scribe** (to the left of the doorway as you exit), poised for notation with an open scroll across his knees.

Rooms 31, 32 and 37

The walls of **Room 31** display sandstone reliefs from Wadi Maraghah, near the ancient turquoise mines of Sinai. Twin limestone **statues of Ra-Nufer** (#45 and #46) signify his dual role as Memphite high priest of Ptah and Sokar; aside from their wigs and kilts, they look virtually identical. In the same room is a lifesize **copper statue** of VI Dynasty pharaoh Pepi I (#129) from Hierakonopolis in Upper Egypt, one of a pair made by hammering sheets of copper over wooden armatures (the other, of his son Merenre, was under restoration at time of writing).

Room 32 is dominated by life-size seated **statues of Prince Rahotep and Princess Nofret** (IV Dynasty), from their *mastaba* at Maidum (see p.178). His skin is painted brick-red, hers a creamy yellow – a distinction common in Egyptian art. Nefert wears a wig and diadem and swathes herself in a diaphanous wrap; the prince is simply clad in a waist cloth. Look out for the **tableau of the dwarf Seneb and his family** (#39). Embraced by his wife, this Overseer of the Wardrobe seems contented; his naked children hold their fingers to their lips. Don't miss the vividly stylized mural known as the **Maidum Geese** (III/IV Dynasty), which depicts three different types of goose in exquisitely observed detail, nor the relief of boatmen fighting (to the right of the door as you leave the room).

In the adjoining **Room 37**, the **furniture of Queen Hetepheres** (III Dynasty) has been expertly reconstructed from heaps of gold and rotten wood. As the wife of Snofru and mother of Cheops, she was buried near her son's pyramid at Giza with a gilded sedan chair and canopied bed. Also in the room, in a cabinet of its own, is a tiny **statuette of Cheops** (#143), the only known likeness of the Great Pyramid pharaoh.

Middle Kingdom Galleries

With **Room 26** you enter the **Middle Kingdom**, when centralized authority was restored and pyramid-building resumed under the XII Dynasty (c.1991–1786 or 1985–1795 BC). The enthroned **statue of Mentuhotep Nebhepetre II** (on the right) is a relic of the previous era of civil wars, termed the First Intermediate Period; it was this pharaoh who finally ended the wars and reunited the country. Glum-faced, and endowed with hulking feet and black skin to symbolize his royal power, plus crossed arms and a curly beard to link him to Osiris, the statue was buried near his funerary shrine at Deir el-Bahri, and was discovered by Howard Carter – whose horse fell through the roof.

Equally eye-catching is the **statue** of the XII Dynasty **Queen Neferet** (mother of Amenemhat I) wearing a sheath dress and a horned-style Hathor wig, flanking the entrance to **Room 21**, where case #54 displays painted stelae and reliefs of offerings to the dead.

The statuettes at the back of **Room 22** (#92) are striking for the expressiveness of their faces, in contrast to the manic gaze of the wooden statue of Nakhti on the right-hand side of the room, but the room's main exhibit is the **burial chamber of Harhotpe** from Deir el-Bahri, covered inside with pictorial objects, charms and texts. Surrounding the chamber are ten limestone **statues of Senusret I** from his pyramid complex at Lisht, stiffly formal in contrast to his cedarwood figure in the case to the right as you enter the room (#88). The sides of these statues' thrones bear variations of the *sema-tawy* symbol of unification: Happy the Nile god, or Horus and Seth, entwining the heraldic plants of the Two Lands.

This basic imperative of statecraft might explain the unique **double statue of Amenemhat III** (#508) in **Room 16**. Personified as the Nile god bringing his people fish on trays, the dual figures may represent Upper and Lower Egypt, or the living king and his deified *ka*. Ancient Egyptians believed that a person's *ka*, or life-force, survived their death but had to be sustained by offerings of food (either genuine, or depicted in their tomb). The hieroglyph representing the *ka* was a pair of hands, such as sprout from the head of an unusual **wooden ka-statue** of the XIII Dynasty ruler **Hor** (#75), mounted on a sliding base to signify his posthumous wanderings.

New Kingdom Galleries

With **Room 11** you pass into the **New Kingdom**, an era of renewed pharaonic power and imperial expansion under the XVIII and XIX dynasties (c.1567–1200 or 1550–1186 BC). Egypt's African and Asian empires were forged by Tuthmosis III, who had long been frustrated while his unwarlike stepmother, Hatshepsut, ruled as pharaoh. The commanding stone **head of Hatshepsut** comes from one of the Osiride pillars of her great temple at Deir el-Bahri, in the Theban Necropolis across the river from Luxor.

Room 12

This room features some intriguing XVIII Dynasty artefacts. An imposing grey schist **statue of Tuthmosis III** (#62) complements a **Hathor Shrine** (#138) from Tuthmosis's ruined temple at Deir el-Bahri, containing a statue of the goddess in her bovine form, emerging reborn from a papyrus swamp. Tuthmosis stands beneath her cow's head, and is suckled as an infant in the fresco behind Hathor's statue. Off to the right, you'll see a block **statue of Senemut and Neferure** (#418), Queen Hatshepsut's vizier and daughter, whose head touches Senemut's chin; the intimacy implied by this and other statues has prompted speculation as to a familial relationship between them.

Don't overlook a section of the Deir el-Bahri "**Punt relief**" (#130, in the second niche on the left), showing the Queen of Punt, whose grossly swollen body suggests that she may have suffered from elephantiasis. Hatshepsut personally led the depicted Egyptian expedition to the fabled land of Punt (recently identified as straddling the territory of modern-day Ethiopia and Eritrea), returning with myrrh trees, pygmies, and other exotica.

To the right of the Punt relief stands a grey granite **statue of Khonsu**, the moon-god, son of Amun and Mut (three deities collectively known as the Theban Triad, whose cult-temple was at Karnak, near Luxor), portrayed with a sidelock denoting youth and a face thought to be that of the boy pharaoh Tutankhamun. Flanking this and the Punt relief are two **seated statues of Amenhotep**, one showing him as a young scribe of humble birth (#6014) and the other as an octogenarian priest (#98), honoured for his direction of massive works like the Colossi of Memnon in the Theban Necropolis.

Rooms 6, 7, 8 and 10

Before turning the corner into the North Wing, you'll encounter in **Room 6** two **lion-headed statues of Sekhmet**, the goddess who personified the destructive power of the sun-god Re, from her temple at Karnak. A **sphinx** with the head of Queen Hatshepsut greets visitors to **Room 7**, where the first set of bas-reliefs on the southern wall come from the **Tomb of Maya** at Saqqara, which was uncovered in the nineteenth century but subsequently lost until its rediscovery in 1986. **Room 8** is largely an overflow for the Amarna Gallery (see below), but also contains a monumental **dyad of Amun and Mut**, smashed to bits by medieval limestone quarrymen and lovingly pieced together from fragments long lost in the vaults of the Egyptian Museum and at Karnak, where it originally stood.

To the left of the stairs in **Room 10**, note the painted **relief** on a block from Ramses II's temple at Memphis, which shows him subjugating Egypt's foes. In a motif repeated on dozens of temple pylons, the king grabs the hair of a Libyan, Nubian and Syrian, and wields an axe. The room is dominated by a **statue of Ramses II and Haroun**, embodying an elaborate pun. Haroun was a Levantine sun-god whom the Ancient Egyptians regarded as an avatar of their own solar deity Re (or Ra); shown here protecting the child (*mes*) king, who holds in his left hand the heraldic sedge plant (*su*) – thereby combining the syllables *Ra-mes-su*, to form the pharaoh's name.

From Room 10 you can follow the New Kingdom into the East Wing (covered on opposite), or climb the stairs to the Tutankhamun galleries on the upper floor.

The Amarna Gallery

Room 3 and much of the adjoining **Room 8** focus on the **Amarna period,** a break with centuries of tradition which barely outlasted the reign of Pharaoh Akhenaten (c.1379–1362 or 1352–1336 BC) and Queen Nefertiti. Rejecting Amun and the other deities of Thebes, they decreed the supremacy of a single god, the Aten, built a new capital at Tell el-Amarna in Middle Egypt to escape the old bureaucracy, and left enigmatic works of art that still provoke a reaction. Some have suggested that the religion of the ancient Israelites – and hence Judaism, Christianity and Islam – was derived from the monotheistic cult instituted by Akhenaten.

In the centre of Room 3 is Akhenaten's carnelian-, gold- and glass-inlaid **coffin**, the upper half displayed alongside the gilding from the bottom part of the coffin. This gilding disappeared from the museum at some time between 1915 and 1931, but resurfaced in Switzerland in the 1970s. It has now been restored and mounted on a Plexiglas cast in the presumed shape of the original coffin.

Staring down from the walls of **Room 3** are four **colossi of Akhenaten**, whose attenuated skull and face, flaring lips and nostrils, rounded thighs and belly are suggestive of a hermaphrodite or a primeval earth goddess (the single naked statue entirely lacks genitalia). Because these characteristics are carried over to the figures of his wife and daughters on certain **stelae,** statuettes and tomb reliefs, it has been argued that the Amarna style pandered to some physical abnormality in Akhenaten (or the royal family) – though others retort that the famous head of Nefertiti, in Berlin, proves that it was just a stylistic device.

Another feature of Amarna art was its note of intimacy: a **statuette** in Room 8 (case #162) portrays Akhenaten kissing their eldest daughter, Meritaten, and **stelae** show Nefertiti cradling her sisters. For the first time in Egyptian art, breakfast was depicted. The Amarna focus on this world rather than the afterlife infused traditional subjects with new vitality – witness the freer brush strokes on the fragments of a **marsh scene**, displayed around the walls of Room 8. A case on the south side of Room 8 contains some of the **Amarna Letters** (others are in London and Berlin), recording pleas for troops to aid the pharaoh's vassals in Palestine. Originally baked into earthen "envelopes" for delivery, these cuneiform tablets were stored in the archives at Tell el-Amarna. A looted statuette of Akhenaten holding an offerings table was recovered from a rubbish bin near the museum after the 2011 revolution.

The East Wing

As an inducement to follow the New Kingdom into the East Wing, **Room 15** starts with a sexy statue of Ramses II's daughter and consort Merytamun (facing Ramses' statue in Room 10). The centrepiece of **Room 14** is a pink granite triple statue of Ramses III being crowned by Horus and Seth, representing order and chaos respectively. Of the diverse statues of deities in **Room 24**, the most striking by far is that of **Tawaret** (or Tweri), the pregnant hippopotamus-goddess of childbirth. Sleekly carved from black slate, the statue was found in a sealed shrine at Karnak, which is why it is so well preserved.

Waning with the XX Dynasty and expiring with the XXI, the New Kingdom was followed by the so-called **Late Period** of mostly foreign rulers. From this era, in **Room 30**, comes an alabaster **statue of Amenirdis**, whom the pharaoh made divine votaress of Amun to watch over the Theban priesthood. Dressed as a New Kingdom queen, Amenirdis wears a falcon headdress crowned with *uraei*, originally topped by a Hathor crown bearing a solar disc and horns.

Rooms 34 and **35** cover the **Greco-Roman Period** (332 BC onwards), when Classical art engaged with Ancient Egyptian symbolism. Confronting visitors entering Room 34 is a coiled serpent, poised to strike; a strikingly youthful alabaster **head of Alexander the Great** can be seen nearby in case D. The meld of Egyptian and Greco-Roman styles is typified by the bizarre statues and sarcophagi down the corridor in **Room 49**, especially the **statue of a Ptolemaic king** (possibly Alexander II) at the threshold of the room. **Room 44**, on your way, hosts **temporary exhibitions**, which are often quite impressive and better labelled than any other section of the museum.

Upper floor

The upper floor is dominated by the Tutankhamun galleries, which occupy the best part of two wings. The other top highlights are the Jewellery Rooms, the Mummy Rooms and the Fayoum Portraits. Tutankhamun's treasures are best seen together before returning to look at the neighbouring rooms and the rest of the upper floor.

Tutankhamun Galleries

The funerary impedimenta of the boy-king **Tutankhamun** numbers 1700 items and fills a dozen rooms. Given the brevity of his reign (1361–1352 or 1336–1327 BC) and the small dimensions of his tomb in the Valley of the Kings, the mind boggles at the treasure that must have been stashed with great pharaohs like Ramses II or Seti I. Tutankhamun merely fronted the Theban counter-revolution that effaced Akhenaten's Amarna cult, and restored the god Amun and his priesthood to their former primacy – though the influence of Amarna is still apparent in some of the **exhibits**. Many visitors make a beeline for the Tut's gold and the Jewellery rooms (2, 3 and 4, which close fifteen minutes early), ignoring other artefacts from Tutankamun's tomb.

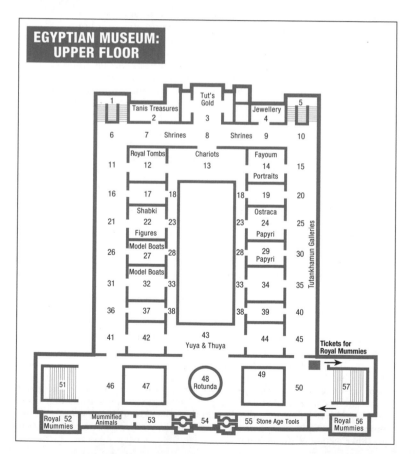

When Howard Carter's team penetrated the sealed corridor of the tomb in 1922, they found an antechamber, stuffed with caskets and detritus, that had been ransacked by robbers, and two life-size **ka-statues of Tutankhamun** (flanking the doorway to **Room 45**), whose black skin symbolized his rebirth. Just beyond are several smaller golden **statues** (mostly portraying Tut hunting with a harpoon) and ceremonial **shields**.

Rooms 35, 30 and 25

Room 35 is dominated by a **gilded throne** with winged-serpent arms and clawed feet (#179). Its seat back shows the royal couple relaxing in the rays of the Aten, their names given in the Amarna form – dating it to the time when Tutankhamun still observed the Amarna heresy. Tut's clothes were stored in the magnificent "**Painted Chest**", whose lid depicts him hunting ostriches and devastating ranks of Syrians in his war chariot; the end panels show him trampling other foes in the guise of the sphinx. You'll also see an ebony and ivory **gaming set** for playing *senet*, a game similar to draughts or checkers (#189), and a host of small **shabti figures** to fulfil any tasks the gods might set him. The plethora of **walking sticks** (#27) found in his tomb has led some Egyptologists to conclude that Tut suffered from a genetic disorder that affected his bones.

Room 30 features a case (#187) of elaborate "**Prisoners' Canes**", whose ebony- and ivory-inlaid figures symbolize the unity of north and south. A bust of the boy king emerging from a lotus (#118) shows the continued influence of the Amarna artistic style during Tutankhamun's reign. The "**ecclesiastical throne**" (#181) in **Room 25** is a prototype for Episcopal thrones of the Christian Church, its seat back exquisitely inlaid with ebony and gold. More typical of pharaonic design are the wooden Heb-Sed throne and footstools. Beyond is a collection of alabaster **perfume bottles** carved in the form of animals or deities (#61 and #90).

Rooms 7–10 and 13

Rooms 9 and 10 house **gilded beds** dedicated to the gods whose animal forms are carved on their bedposts. Beyond these is a **shrine of Anubis** (#185), carried in the pharaoh's cortege: the protector of the dead depicted as a vigilant jackal with gilded ears and silver claws. Next along, the four alabaster **canopic jars** in an alabaster chest (#176) contained the pharaoh's viscera; the chest itself was contained in the next exhibit, a golden **canopic chest** protected by statues of the goddesses Isis, Nephthys, Selket and Neith (#177). Ranged along **rooms 7 and 8** are four boxy **gilded shrines**, which fitted one inside another like Russian dolls, enclosing Tutankhamun's sarcophagus.

In contrast to the warlike figures of Tutankhamun elsewhere in the gallery, the lid of the "**Inlaid Chest**" (#188) in **Room 13** (where the yellow artificial light does it no justice) shows a gentle, Amarna-style vignette of Ankhesenamun (daughter of Nefertiti and Akhenaten) offering lotus, papyrus and mandrake to her husband, framed by poppies, pomegranates and cornflowers. Nearer the Atrium are two wooden **chariots**, found in the antechamber of Tutankhamun's tomb. Intended for state occasions, their gilded stucco reliefs show Asiatics and Nubians in bondage; pharaonic war chariots were lighter and stronger.

Tutankhamun's gold

The top attraction of all, **Tutankhamun's gold**, is in the always packed-out **Room 3**, though some of it may be on tour abroad. Assuming it's in Cairo, the centrepiece is his haunting **funerary mask**, wearing a headdress inlaid with lapis lazuli, quartz and obsidian. The middle and innermost layers of his mummiform **coffin**, adorned with the same materials, show the boy king with his hands clasped in the Osiride position, protected by the cloisonné feathers of Wadjet, Nekhbet, Isis and Nephthys. On Tutankhamun's mummy (which remains in his tomb at the Valley of the Kings) were placed scores of **amulets**, a cloisonné **corselet** spangled with glass and carnelian, gem-encrusted **pectorals** and a pair of golden **sandals** – all displayed here.

The Jewellery Rooms

Flanking Tutankhamun's gold in Room 3, the two **Jewellery Rooms** are almost as breathtaking – though many exhibits are poorly captioned and often on tour abroad. Bearing that in mind, you may or may not find in **Room 4** a VI Dynasty golden **head of a falcon** (once attached to a copper body) from Hierakonopolis in Upper Egypt; a gold collar and diadem from the **Treasure of Dush** found in Kharga Oasis in 1989; the **crown and necklaces of Princess Khnumyt** and the **diadem and pectorals of Princess Sat-Hathor from El-Lahun**. The **amethyst necklace of Mereret**, another XII Dynasty princess, was found at Dahshur, while the ceremonial **axe of Ahmosis** (founder of the XVIII Dynasty), was buried in the tomb of his mother, Queen Ahhotep. From the same cache (discovered by the museum's founder, Mariette, in 1859) came some stunning **gold collars** and the bizarre **golden flies** of the Order of Valour – bug-eyed decorations for bravery.

Displayed in **Room 2**, the **Treasure of Tanis** comes from the XXI–XXII Dynasty, when northern Egypt was ruled from the Delta. Of the three royal caches unearthed by French Egyptologist Pierre Montet in 1939, the richest was that of Psusennes I, whose electrum coffin was found inside the sarcophagus of Merneptah (which is downstairs in Room 33). The other, hawk-headed silver coffin belonged to the XII Dynasty pharaoh Shoshenk.

The Mummy Rooms

The original **Mummy Room** was closed in 1981 by President Sadat because the exhibition of human remains offended religious sensibilities, but this gave the museum and the Getty Institute an opportunity to restore the badly decomposed **royal mummies**. The results of their work are now displayed in **rooms 56 and 52**, which close at 6pm and require a separate ticket (£E100), sold in Room 50. In deference to the deceased, no guiding is allowed, and the hum of *sotto voce* chatter is only broken by the attendant calling "Silence, please!".

The eleven mummies displayed include those of some of the most famous pharaohs, such as the great conquerors of the XIX Dynasty, Seti I and his son Ramses II, the latter looking rather slighter in the flesh than the massive statues of him at Memphis and elsewhere. Most of them seem remarkably peaceful – Tuthmosis II and Tuthmosis IV could almost be sleeping – and many still have hair. The mummies were found in a spare chamber in the tomb of Amenophis II in the Valley of the Kings, and in a cache at nearby Deir el-Bahri, where they had been reburied during the XXI Dynasty to protect them from grave robbers. Two mummies in the museum were reportedly decapitated by looters during the 2011 revolution.

Mummification

Mummification techniques evolved over millennia, reaching their zenith by the **New Kingdom**, when embalmers offered three levels of mummification. The deluxe version entailed removing the brain (which was discarded) and the viscera (which were preserved in canopic jars), dehydrating the cadaver in natron salts for about forty days, and packing it to reproduce lifelike contours. For a graphic demonstration of the hollowness of a mummy, take a look up Ramses V's right nostril – from this angle you'll be able to see straight out through the hole in his skull.

Even if you decide not to view the royal mummies, the **mummified animals** in **Room 53** can be seen at no extra cost. Drawn from necropolises across Egypt, they evince the diversity of animal cults in ancient times, when devotees embalmed everything from crocodiles to birds and fish. Here too you'll find a series of **panels** from the Sun Temple of Userkaf at Saqqara, the first known example of natural scenes being used as decoration within a royal edifice: a pied kingfisher, purple gallinule and sacred ibis are clearly recognizable.

Other galleries

To view the other galleries in approximate chronological order you should start at Room 43 (overlooking the Atrium) and proceed in a clockwise direction, as on the ground floor. However, since most visitors wander in from Tut's galleries, we've described them from that standpoint. Not every room is covered.

West Wing

Mummies were buried with **"Heart Scarabs"** placed upon their throats, bearing a spell that implored the deceased's heart not to bear witness against him during the Judgement of Osiris – a collection of which is featured in **Room 6** (Case B).

Room 12's hoard of objects from **XVIII Dynasty royal tombs** includes priestly wigs and wig boxes (Case L), a libation table flanked by two leopards from the funerary cache of Amenophis II (#3842), and part of the chariot of Tuthmosis IV (#4113). Scarcely less grand are the **contents of private tombs** in **Room 17**, such as that of Sennedjem, from the Workmen's Village near the Valley of the Kings. With skills honed on royal tombs, Sennedjem carved himself a stylish vault, whose door (#215) depicts him playing *senet* (see p.61). The beautiful gold-painted sarcophagus of his son Khonsu (#216) carries a design showing the lions of Today and Yesterday supporting the rising sun, while Anubis embalms his mummy under the protection of Isis and Nephthys.

Several rooms off the corridor display delightful **Middle Kingdom models**, starting in **Room 27**. From Meketre's tomb at Thebes come tableaux of peasants netting fish from reed boats (#75), a model of his house (#78), and cattle being driven past an estate-owner for counting (#76). In **Room 32**, compare the fully crewed model boats in Case F with the unmanned solar barques for voyaging through eternity (cases B, C, D and E). Model-soldier buffs will delight in the phalanxes of Egyptian spearmen (#73) from the tomb of Prince Mesehti at Assyut, in **Room 37**; a set of Nubian archers damaged by looters in 2011 should go back on display eventually.

East Wing

Approached from the north, the inner East Wing begins with **Room 14**, exhibiting the superbly lifelike **"Fayoum Portraits"** found by British Egyptologist Flinders Petrie at Hawara in the Fayoum region. Painted in encaustic (pigments mixed into molten wax) while their sitters were alive, such portraits were glued onto Greco-Roman mummies (100–250 AD) across the Roman world but mostly only preserved in the hot, dry climate of Egypt. Their level of realism was not matched in Europe until the Renaissance.

The diversity of Egypt's pantheon by the late pagan era is suggested by the **statues of deities** in **Room 19**. The tiny statuettes are worth a closer look, especially those of the pregnant hippo goddess Taweret (Case C), Harpocrates (Horus as a child), Ibis-headed Thoth and the dwarf god Ptah-Soker (all in Case E). In Case V, notice the gold and silver effigy of Horus – apparently the case for a mummified hawk – and a winged scarab inlaid with lapis lazuli, feldspar and jasper.

Don't overlook the **ostraca and papyri** in the following rooms. Ostraca were limestone flakes or potsherds, on which were scratched sketches or ephemeral writing; papyrus was used for finished artwork and **manuscripts**. **Room 24** features the funerary texts known as the **Book of the Dead** (depicting the Judgement of Osiris) and the **Book of Amduat**, which appear on the walls of tombs. **Room 29** contains the *Satirical Papyrus* (#232 in Cabinet 9), showing mice being served by cats – an inversion of the natural order, symbolising Egypt's submission to foreign rulers under the Hyksos (Palestinian) XV Dynasty. Another curio is the child-birthing seat in Case S of **Room 33**, which suggests that the Ancient Egyptians were knowledge-able about obstetrics even though their pregnancy test (whether women's urine would cause emmer-wheat seeds to germinate) was only forty percent accurate.

South Wing

This wing is often overlooked by visitors, but contains some notable minor treasures. By the stairway in **Room 50** stands the cubic **leather funerary tent** of an XXI Dynasty queen, decorated in red-and-green checkered squares. **Room 43** houses objects from the **tomb of Yuya and Thuya**, who, as parents of Queen Tiy (wife of Amenophis III), were buried in the Valley of the Kings; their tomb was found intact in the late nineteenth century. The finest objects from it are the two mummiform coffins, Thuya's gilded funeral mask, and statuettes of the couple. To the left of the entrance to Room 42 is a panel of blue **faïence tiles** from Zoser's burial hall at Saqqara (see p.166).

The adjacent **Room 48** contains a display case (#155) featuring a stone head of Akhenaten's mother Queen Tiy that prefigures the Amarna style; a beautiful, lifelike wooden statuette of a Nubian woman with braided hair (perhaps Tiy herself); and statues of **"dancing dwarves"** (thought to be equatorial Forest People, or "Pygmies"), whom several XVIII Dynasty pharaohs cherished as pets. Nearby, another case (#82) holds a striking bright blue faïence hippopotamus.

Downtown

To encourage the rapid development of the European quarter in the 1860s, land was given to whoever would spend at least £2000 sterling on building a villa within eighteen months. Within a generation or two these had mostly been replaced by multi-storey apartment blocks, such was the demand for accommodation; from the 1960s onwards, their flat rooftops were colonised by rural migrants, forming a whole new "city" high above the downtown streets. The chief legacy of Cairo's *belle époque* is the street plan based on Haussmann's Paris, with avenues crossing at circular intersections, side-passages with shops at street level, and offices or apartments above. Their lobbies and stairwells are the domain of the *bowab* or gate-keeper – a perennial figure in intrigues and romances – whose cruder counterparts are the *minairdy*, or car-hop, who handles parking in the congested streets, and the *khirtiya*, or hustlers, who prey on tourists, undeterred by the Kalashnikov-toting police and Central Security troops on every other corner.

Talaat Harb and around

Downtown's main boulevard, **Sharia Talaat Harb**, is still widely known as "Soliman Pasha" after the French mercenary and Muslim-convert ennobled for his services to Egypt's nineteenth-century autocrat, Mohammed Ali. In colonial times

Soliman Pasha was lined with sidewalk cafés and bars; Egyptians in native dress were ejected by the police to maintain its "European" character. Today, Cairenes of all classes come here to window-shop or gawp at the lurid cinema hoardings, and peddlers have laid claim to the sidewalks, yet the street is still decorated at Christmas time for the benefit of foreign tourists.

Heading up Talaat Harb from Midan Tahrir, it's easy to overlook the domed **Diplomatic Club** on the corner of Sharia Abdel Salam Arif. Before it was commandeered by Nasser for the use of senior army officers this was the famous Mohammed Ali Club, founded in 1908 as an alternative to the racially-exclusive Gezira Sporting Club, for Egyptian pashas and beys to mix business with pleasure. You needn't be a VIP to enjoy the **Café Riche** (no.17), a tastefully nostalgic restaurant and bar (see p.201), where the Free Officers supposedly plotted their overthrow of Egypt's monarchy in 1952 and Saddam Hussein imbibed revolutionary Pan-Arabism as a law student.

Soon afterwards, the street meets Sharia Qasr el-Nil at **Midan Talaat Harb** – a French-style roundabout that's also named after the nationalist financier Talaat Harb (1876–1941), whose **statue** sports an Ottoman fez and a European tailcoat, symbolizing the contradictions of the colonial era; he founded the Banque Misr (Bank of Egypt) in 1920 to break the stranglehold of foreign capital on Egypt's economy. The statue was erected in 1964 to replace one of Soliman Pasha as part of the post-revolutionary rejection of foreign influences that also saw the nationalization of the famous **Groppi** patisserie, on the south side of the roundabout and built in 1925 to be an elegant Parisian-style grand café. Gilded Art Deco mosaics around the entrance hint at its former glory, but its ambience is more akin to communist Eastern Europe (see p.198).

Across the midan, Talaat Harb and Qasr el-Nil streets are divided by the wedge-shaped 1930s Art Deco **Baehler Building**, erected on the site of the *Savoy Hotel* where, in 1904, the black magician Aleister Crowley and his bride Rose Kelly performed a ritual to invoke the Ancient Egyptian gods. The adjacent **Baehler Passage** was once home to Cairo's smartest boutiques and now specializes in lingerie. It was here that the fictional aged roué Zaki Bey lived, taking an hour to walk each morning to his office in the nearby **Yacoubian Building**, immortalized in Alaa Al Aswany's bestselling novel of the same name (see p.271). Though the real Yacoubian Building at 34 Talaat Harb differs somewhat from the fictional version, it's easy to imagine events in the story unfolding here. The book's author (a dentist by profession) had his first dental surgery in the building.

Sharia Qasr el-Nil

Sharia Qasr el-Nil is equally busy with traffic (in the opposite direction), but less thronged with pedestrians than Talaat Harb. Travel agents dominate the initial stretch from Midan Tahrir to Midan Talaat Harb, also featuring the Egyptian – formerly Royal – **Automobile Club** at no.10, where King Farouk loved to gamble before moving on to the nightclubs of Pyramids Road in a sports car from his collection of two hundred automobiles (all painted red – a colour forbidden to other motorists). A 1920s' pastiche of Fatimid, Mamluke and Ottoman architecture, the club's decor is as grand as its exterior is grimy – but sadly, you can't look inside.

Beyond Midan Talaat Harb, boutiques selling miniskirts and crop-tops never worn on the streets invite a detour into the "Golden Triangle", a charming *belle époque* quarter surrounding Sharia el-Sherifeen. Past the carmine-and-gold Art Nouveau facade of the **Cosmopolitan Hotel** (see p.184), palm trees shade the way to a 1920s' neo-classical edifice housing the Egyptian **Stock Exchange**. When closed by Nasser in 1965, it was one of the top five exchanges in the world; the privatization of Egypt's economy since 1991 has given it a new lease of life and resulted in the quarter being given a face-lift to please its corporate clientele. Returning to Qasr el-Nil, you can't miss the flamboyant Moorish-style **Trieste Building**, built for an Italian insurance company by the prolific Italian-Egyptian architect Antonio Lasciac in 1910. Further up the road stand Art Deco blocks whose marbled lobbies have gone to pot ever since rents were fixed so low that landlords gave up on repairs. Such socialist diktats were never envisaged by earlier nationalists like **Mustafa Kamel** (1874–1908), the journalist, lawyer and founder of the National Party whose portly **statue** dignifies the roundabout at the end of Qasr el-Nil.

Sharia Champollion

Running parallel to Talaat Harb, **Sharia Champollion** has sunk socially since it was first named after Jean-François Champollion (1790–1832), the French scholar who deciphered the Rosetta Stone (1824) to read Ancient Egyptian hieroglyphs. The only traces of the street's original elegance are its mature casuarina trees and the onetime palace of Saïd Halim Pasha at no.11. Confiscated by the British in 1915 after he secretly committed Turkey to an alliance with Germany, it became the **Nasriya School**, an elite establishment until it was expropriated in Nasser's time, and is now a dramatic neo-Baroque ruin. You can admire it from a shady outdoor **teahouse**, as local residents and tourists staying at hostels on Sharia Bassiouni do. What makes this area intriguing is its juxtaposition of the ruined school with numerous car repair shops, cheap places to eat, like *Abu Tareek* (see p.196), and the **Townhouse Gallery** (see p.226), whose 2009 exhibition "Model Citizens" involved Dutch and Egyptian artists creating an amazingly detailed 1:35 scale model of the neighbourhood, photos of which are still displayed here. During the 2011 revolution, local engineering students built a medieval-style catapult from scrap wood, with which they hurled rocks over the rooftops of Champollion at pro-Mubarak thugs on the 6th October flyover.

Sharia Adly

If you turn off Talaat Harb near the Yacoubian Building and walk along **Sharia Adly** ("Adly Pasha"), you'll see a temple-like edifice worthy of a Cecil B. de Mille movie. This is the **Shaar HaShamayim Synagogue** (daily 10am–3pm, Fri until 6pm; bring your passport to get in; donations appreciated), the main house of prayer for Cairo's now much reduced Jewish community (see p.268). Because of the threat of attack or vandalism, the synagogue is surrounded by armed police, who don't take kindly to tourists pointing cameras at it – which is a pity, because it's one of downtown Cairo's most photogenic buildings. Though it looks Art Deco, it was actually built well before that era, in 1907 (by Eduard Matasek); the palm trees on the facade are a symbol peculiar to Egyptian Jewry. The interior is also impressive, with a lofty dome, stained-glass windows and marble fittings. Nowadays services are held only at the Jewish New Year (around September), and Yom Kippur (ten days after New Year).

Further east, the junction of Adly and Emad el-Din streets is dominated by a Gothic pile that was once the **Davis Bryan Building and Welsh Store**. Leeks, thistles, shamrocks and roses carved on shields adorning its oxblood-red facade pay tribute to the Welsh, Scottish, Irish and English roots of the store's founder, and to its regular customers between the two world wars. In those days, the in-place for afternoon tea was **Garden Groppi**, nearby on Sharia Adly, where Europeans mingled with Egyptian pashas and their mistresses; founded in 1909 by a Swiss chocolatier, this was the first branch of the *Groppi* chain (see p.65).

26th July Street and the Ezbekiya Gardens

Downtown's widest thoroughfare is **Sharia Setta w'Ashreen Yulyu** – more easily rendered as **26th July Street** – whose name commemorates the date on which King Farouk abdicated in 1952 following a bloodless coup (see p.262); Egypt was declared a republic a year later. 26th July extends westwards past Egypt's **High Court** (formerly the Mixed Courts where, until 1949, foreigners were tried under separate jurisdiction), out to Zamalek and Mohandiseen, across the river. Its downtown stretch features two of Cairo's once elegant, Jewish-owned, department stores (both still open today, but far from elegant). **Cicurel** would close its doors to the public whenever King Farouk wished to shop there, and its owners managed to transfer their wealth abroad before the confiscation of foreign property in the wake of the Suez Crisis, which afflicted its nearby rival **Chemla**.

26th July begins at the **Ezbekiya Gardens**, laid out in the 1870s by the ex-chief gardener of Paris as a twenty-acre park. Subsequent road extensions reduced them to trampled islands amid a sea of traffic, but the northern half has now been enclosed to preserve its magnificent banyan tree; the eastern side remains a pitch for hawkers of Islamic gewgaws and a secondhand book market, with Cairo's **Puppet Theatre** (see p.207) in one corner. In medieval times a lake fed by a canal existed here, beside which the Mamluke general Ezbek built a palace, followed by other amirs. During the French occupation Napoleon stayed in Ezbek's palace, and General Jean-Baptiste Kléber (left in charge when Napoleon returned to France) promoted European innovations such as windmills, printing presses and wheelbarrows. Two symbols of colonialism later overlooked Ezbekiya from a site bounded by Alfi Bey and El-Gumhorriya streets: *Shepheard's Hotel* (founded in 1841) flourished alongside the Thomas Cook Agency, which pioneered tourist "expeditions" in the 1870s. Rebuilt more grandly in 1891, *Shepheard's* famous terrace, Moorish Hall and Long Bar were destroyed by arsonists in 1952.

Midan Opera and Midan Ataba

South of Ezbekiya, two squares form a traffic hub that completes the downtown area. **Midan Opera** (pronounced "*Obera*") is named after the Opera House that was the focus of the quarter in the 1860s, symbolically facing away from Islamic Cairo towards an equestrian **statue** of Khedive Ismail's father, Ibrahim Pasha. Since the opera burned down in 1971 a multi-storey car park has occupied the site, and the Opera Cinema replaced *Madame Badia's Opera Casino* nightclub, the first building to be burned on what the British called "**Black Saturday**" (January 26, 1952), when Egyptian resentments erupted after British troops killed native police near the Canal city of Ismailiya. Encouraged by the indifference of Cairo's police, citizens took the chance to loot while militants from the Muslim Brotherhood (see p.266) sped around in jeeps torching foreign premises. One that survives is the vast, moribund **Continental-Savoy Hotel**, where tourists could once buy "anything from a boa constrictor to a fully grown leopard" in the arcade outside, and Lord Carnarvon – who financed the hunt for Tutankhamun's tomb – died in his room in 1923, supposedly a victim of the pharaoh's curse.

Behind the car park, elevated freeways render **Midan Ataba** just as the novelist Yusuf Idris described it in his short story *The Dregs of the City*: "a madhouse of pedestrians and automobiles, screeching wheels, howling klaxons, the whistles of bus conductors and roaring motors". Besides being the starting point for **walking routes into Islamic Cairo** (see p.76), philatelists will want to visit the **Post Office Museum** on the second floor of the Central Post Office (Sun–Thurs 8am–3pm; £E2; tickets sold at the commemorative stamps office, then go upstairs through the guarded entrance on the east side of the building). The exhibits include the rare

Suez Canal commemorative issue stamp and a picture of the Sphinx and Pyramids composed entirely of stamps bearing an image of the same.

Don't be alarmed to see sentries with axes outside Ataba **Fire Station**, the last recognisable landmark before you reach Islamic Cairo (see p.73). Another local landmark – visible beyond the Sharia al-Azhar flyover – is a globe upheld by four Atlas figures, with the name Tiring spelt out below. Known to Egyptians as the Al-Tofaha Building after the eponymous 1997 film starring Leila Elwi – who admires the globe from her rooftop hovel – this was once the **Tiring Building**, a luxurious department store opened in 1914, long since sub-divided into shabby offices and smaller shops. The only grand emporium from those days that still functions as such is **Sednaoui**, several blocks further north – whose huge chandeliers and spectacular glass ceiling in the atrium are worth the walk.

North to Ramses

As you head further north from 26th July and Ezbekiya towards Ramses Station, 1km away, boutiques give way to hardware stores. Initially, however, you'll find yourself in Cairo's old nightclub district, **Tawfiqiya**, centred on Midan Orabi and Sharia Alfi Bey. The 1930s and 1940s were the heyday of singers Mohammed Abdel Wahab, Abdel Halim Hafez, Farid al-Atrache and his sister Asmahan, who were the Arab equivalent of Hollywood stars and all performed here. While its glamour has long faded, traces of this heritage remain in local **cafés**: *El Shems* in the passage at 4 Sharia Tawfiqiya (see p.197) is where casting agents seek models or extras, while the *Umm Kalthoum* on Sharia Azbakiya is filled with memorabilia of the eponymous Egyptian diva (see p.198), and other singers. Sharia Tawfiqiya has a colourful all-night **fruit market** and a bustling covered passageway leading through to 26th July. Further north, Sharia Orabi is home to the well-known *El-Tabei el-Domati* restaurant (see p.197), and some sleazy **bars** with blacked-out windows.

These bars are a faint vestige of the red-light quarter that flourished here during both world wars, when Allied troops packed Cairo. It was conveniently situated near the military high road that Mohammed Ali created to link the Citadel with Cairo's new railway station. These days, the road is called **Sharia Khulud,** but was previously named Sharia Clot Bey after the French physician Antoine Clot, ennobled for curing Mohammed Ali's troops of venereal disease and introducing Western ideas of public health to Egypt. By 1914 the once-fashionable area north of Ezbekiya had degenerated into a vice-ridden district known as the Wasa'a, whose bars, brothels and hashish dens all paid protection to Ibrahim el-Gharby, a fearsome transvestite Nubian gangster. During World War II, activities centred on Wagh el-Birket, nicknamed **the Berka**: a street overlooked by balconies where prostitutes sat fanning themselves.

Nowadays the area is shabbily respectable. A stroll up from the gardens along Sharia Khulud towards Ramses will take you past the hulking nineteenth-century **Cathedral of St Mark**, now superseded as Cairo's main Coptic cathedral and seat of the Patriarchate by the cathedral in Abbassiya (see p.143). The decrepit Ottoman pile at 117 **Sharia el-Gumhorriya** (at the Ramses end of the street), was the original premises of *Al-Ahram* ("The Pyramids"), the first newspaper in the Arab world (founded by two Syrian Christians in 1875).

Ramses Station

The Ramses Station area is the northern ganglion of Cairo's transport system. Splayed flyovers and arterial roads haemorrhage traffic towards darting pedestrians, keeping **Midan Ramses** busy round the clock. The square took its name from a Colossus of Ramses II, moved here from Memphis in 1955. By 2006 it had become

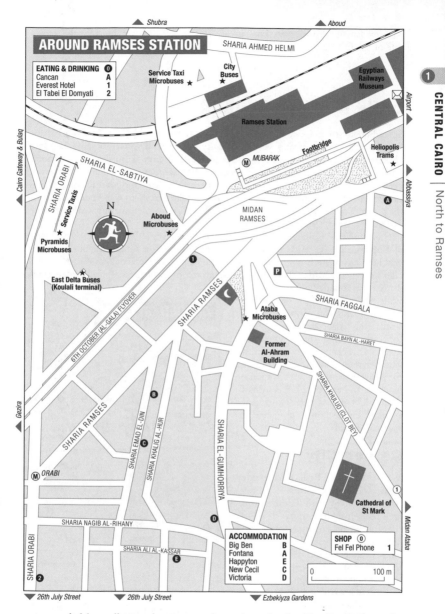

AROUND RAMSES STATION

EATING & DRINKING ⓞ	
Cancan	A
Everest Hotel	1
El Tabei El Domyati	2

SHARIA AHMED HELMI

▲ Shubra   ▲ Aboud

Service Taxi Microbuses ★

City Buses ★

Egyptian Railways Museum

Airport ▶

Ramses Station

Cairo Gateway & Bulaq ◀

SHARIA EL-SABTIYA

SHARIA ORABI

Service Taxis

MUBARAK Ⓜ

Footbridge

Heliopolis Trams ★

Abbassiya ▶

N

Pyramids Microbuses ★

Aboud Microbuses ★

MIDAN RAMSES

Ⓐ

East Delta Buses (Koulali terminal) ★

Gezira ◀

6TH OCTOBER (AL-GALA) FLYOVER

SHARIA RAMSES

❶

Ⓟ

SHARIA FAGGALA

Ataba Microbuses ★

Former Al-Ahram Building

SHARIA BAYN AL-HARET

SHARIA RAMSES

Ⓑ

SHARIA EMAD EL-DIN

Ⓒ

SHARIA KHALIG AL-HUR

SHARIA EL-GUIMHORRIYA

SHARIA KHULUD (CLOT BEY)

ORABI Ⓜ

✝

Cathedral of St Mark

❶

Midan Ataba ▶

Ⓓ

SHARIA NAGIB AL-RIHANY

SHARIA ORABI

SHARIA ALI AL-KASSAR

Ⓔ

❷

ACCOMMODATION	
Big Ben	B
Fontana	A
Happyton	E
New Cecil	C
Victoria	D

SHOP ⓞ	
Fel Fel Phone	1

0 ————— 100 m

▼ 26th July Street   ▼ 26th July Street   ▼ Ezbekiyza Gardens

so corroded by pollution that it was relocated out by the Giza Pyramids, at the junction of Pyramids Road and the Alexandria Desert Road (see p.160).

The square's main focus is **Ramses Station** itself, a quasi-Moorish shoebox-shaped building, to which a **post office** and the **Egyptian Railways Museum** are appended. At the east end of the station, the museum (daily 8am–2pm; £E10, £E20 on Fri & public holidays) houses model steam engines, stations, engineering works and even the odd airplane, plus several real steam locomotives, most notably

Khedive Ismail's private train. For a great **view** over the square, head for the terrace café of the fifteenth-floor *Everest Hotel* (see p.198), open round the clock.

Garden City and Abdin

Spreading south and east from Midan Tahrir towards Old Cairo and the Islamic districts are two disparate, yet historically interlinked, quarters. **Sharia Qasr al-Aini** divides the leafy winding lanes of **Garden City** from the grid of streets where Egypt's ministries and parliament are located, beyond which the ex-royal, now presidential Abdin Palace lends its name to the **Abdin quarter.** Some places can be reached from Midan Tahrir **by metro** (take Line 1 to the Abdeen stop for the palace, Line 2 to Sa'ad Zaghloul for Zaghloul's mausoleum), but **walking** is the easiest – or only – way to explore others.

If ten minutes' walk is your limit, head along Sharia Tahrir to the covered **Bab al-Luq market** on **Midan Falaki**. Though not for the squeamish, it's great for watching Egyptians haggling and gossiping over produce, tea and *sheeshas*. A wholesaler's shop fills **Midan Falaki** with the aroma of cardamom-spiced coffee. This district was founded outside the city walls by Arab refugees fleeing the Mongols, and for centuries afterwards was associated with vices for the working man: whenever there was a clampdown on hashish (cheaper than wine, so the drug of the poor), Bab al-Luq was always the first area to be targeted. Electronics shops, low-priced restaurants and all-night coffee houses characterize the quarter today.

Garden City

When Ibrahim Pasha's riverside palace was demolished in 1906, the British viceroy Lord Cromer had architect Joseph Lamba develop the site, laying down crescents and cul-de-sacs to create the illusion of lanes meandering through a **Garden City**. Until the Corniche road was ploughed through, embassies and villas boasted gardens running down to the Nile; nowadays, fishermen's shacks and vegetable plots line the river's edge.

Aside from the traffic, it's a pleasant walk along the Corniche towards Roda Island, past a cluster of **feluccas** available for Nile cruises (see p.209). Further inland

> ## War stories
>
> During World War II, Britain's Special Operations Executive (SOE) plotted sabotage across the Mediterranean from the **Rustum Buildings** (known to taxi drivers as the "Secret Building") on Sharia Rustum (now Sharia Mohammed el-Sayyed). Army General Headquarters (GHQ) occupied a rusticated stone pile known as **"Grey Pillars"** or "Number Ten" after its address on Sharia Tolombat (now Ittihad al-Muhamiyin al-Arab). SAS officers held wild parties in a flat crammed with captured ammunition at 13 Sharia Naguib Pasha, where the novelist Olivia Manning also lived.
>
> British sang-froid only cracked once, when the Afrika Korps seemed poised to seize Alexandria and advance on Cairo. On **"Ash Wednesday"** (July 1, 1942) GHQ and the Embassy burned their files, blanketing Garden City with smoke. Half-charred classified documents were wafted aloft to fall on the streets, where peanut vendors twisted them into cones to sell their wares in.

the heavily guarded and fortified **embassies** of the US and Britain (which enjoys grander buildings with larger grounds, a legacy of its pre-eminence in the days of Britain's veiled protectorate; see p.261) give way to streets of Art Deco apartment blocks festooned with vines.

Garden City ends at **Qasr al-Aini Hospital**, Egypt's largest medical facility, built in the 1960s on the site of a nineteenth-century medical school, which itself replaced the palace (*qasr*) of a Mamluke amir, al-Aini, which gave its name to the hospital and the neighbourhood. Antoine Clot (see p.68) was the hospital's first director, and Egypt's most famous short story writer, Yusuf Idris, practised as a doctor here before dedicating himself to writing.

Abdin

With hindsight, several rulers must have regretted the move by Khedive Ismail of the seat of state from the Citadel to what became the **Abdin quarter** – a largely working-class neighbourhood where the **Abdin Palace** made a convenient target for protestors massing on the plaza outside. The nadir of humiliation came in February 1942, when British armoured cars burst through the palace gates, and Ambassador Lampson demanded that King Farouk sack the prime minister or abdicate. Presidents Sadat and Mubarak subsequently deemed it safer to live elsewhere, designating Abdin as their "state headquarters", and staging recitations of the Koran on **Midan el-Gumhorriya** during Ramadan to stress their piety. Both were likened to pharaohs as their private luxury became an open secret – but the only glimpse of it available to ordinary mortals is the Abdin Palace Museum.

The Palace Museum

Entered from Sharia Gamae Abdine behind the palace, where tickets are sold across the street, the **Palace Museum** (daily except Fri 9am–3pm; £E15, camera £E10) kicks off with **Mubarak's Hall**, exhibiting weapons presented to him by foreign leaders, most notably a set of gold-plated automatic rifles from Saddam Hussein. Across a courtyard, beyond a shrine to local saint Sidi Badran, the **Arms Museum** has a pavilion filled with daggers (including Rommel's, and multi-bladed ones used by India's Hindu Rajputs), and a gun collection featuring such curios as an Apache-Dolene revolver which doubles as a knuckleduster and a blade, and a twenty-chamber Belgian revolver.

The section devoted to **medals** is more notable for King Farouk's *sheesha* pipes, and a vial made from a giant crab claw, which set the tone for the **Gifts Museum** of presents given to Mubarak, including a mother-of-pearl model of Jerusalem's Dome of the Rock mosque from Yasser Arafat. The **Historical Documents** room displays some letters of condolence sent to King Farouk on the death of his father King Fouad from Hitler, Emperor Hirohito and Edward VIII. The final section is devoted to **silverware**, **glassware and crockery**, including dinner services used by royalty, and a tea set belonging to King Fouad, made of solid silver instead of bone china.

The National Assembly and Sa'ad Zaghloul Mausoleum

The palace stands aloof from Egypt's parliament and bureaucracy, nearly a kilometre away on Sharia Maglis al-Shaab: an axis barricaded against car bombers, floodlit at night and guarded by machine-gunners. In the early days of the 2011 revolution, scores of protesters were killed or wounded by snipers as they attempted to march on the **National Assembly** (Maglis al-Shaab) and the **Interior Ministry** on Midan Lazoghly, which controlled the riot police and the dreaded State Security Investigations, notorious for its use of torture. **Sa'ad Zaghloul** (1859-1927), whose agitation against Britain's Protectorate earned him exile to Malta in 1919, provoking nationwide riots, compelling the British to allow his return and putting his Wafd Party in power after 1922. Zaghloul's death left the Wafd rudderless but all factions agreed on his enshrinement in a colossal pharaonic-style **mausoleum** where he was belatedly interred in 1936, seen off by fifteen thousand blue-shirted Wafdist Youth. In the intervening years it was a repository for the royal mummies that are now in the Egyptian Museum (see p.62).

Although the mausoleum has been closed for decades, it makes a dramatic landmark on the way from Sa'ad Zaghloul metro to the ethno-music **club** *MakAn* (see p.204), should you visit the latter after dark.

The serpentine **Sharia Bur Said** (Port Said Street) separating Abdin from the Saiyida Zeinab quarter of Islamic Cairo (p.107) marks the course of the medieval Khalig al-Masri canal that was filled in after the Aswan Dam reduced Cairo's dependency on Nile floodwater. Another effect of the dam's construction was to displace Egypt's Nubian population, thousands of whom ended up in Cairo as servants for the palace, embassies or rich families. To this day, many Abdin residents are of Nubian origin.

Islamic Cairo

airo's medieval old city is known as Islamic Cairo – a misleading term insofar as the city as a whole is ninety percent Muslim – but otherwise apt, for no other part of Cairo is so suffused with Islamic history and traditions. Few foreigners enter its maw without at least a little excitement and trepidation. Streets are narrow and congested; mosques, bazaars and crooked lanes abound, pungent with the aroma of *sheeshas* and frying offal, loud with *muezzins* proclaiming and beggars entreating – as integral to street life as the artisans and hawkers. The sights, sounds, smells and surprises draw you back time after time; getting lost or dispensing a little baksheesh is a small price to pay for the experience.

Here you'll find the labyrinthine bazaars of **Khan al-Khalili** and Cairo's holiest shrines – the mosques of Saiyidna Hussein and **Al-Azhar** – with a massive array of fascinating medieval monuments spread out along Sharia al-Muizz, which leads both north and south from here through the old city to its northern and southern gates. Beyond are Saladin's imposing Citadel, and the sprawling squatted cemeteries known as the Cities of the Dead.

You can have a fascinating time exploring this part of the city without knowing anything about its history or architecture, but a little understanding of the basics will undoubtedly enhance your experience – we've listed the key architectural terms in our glossary (p.282), and our Architecture colour insert goes into a little more detail. Our history section (see pp.258–260) should give you a deeper understanding of the different regimes in the Middle Ages, when what we call Islamic Cairo constituted pretty much the whole of the city.

Religious buildings in Islamic Cairo

Islamic Cairo hosts a profusion of religious buildings including **madrassas** (koranic schools), **sabil-kuttabs** (primary schools with a public fountain attached), **khanqahs** (Sufi hostels), **wikalas** (caravanserais) and, of course, **mosques**. A mosque is simply a space or building set aside for praying, but Muslims pray towards Mecca, so mosques are always aligned in that direction. The Mecca-facing **qibla wall** is marked by a niche called the **mihrab** so that people know which way to pray. In bigger mosques, a moveable wooden pulpit with stairs, called the **minbar**, is usually placed next to the *mihrab* so that the *imam* (prayer leader) can climb it to deliver his Friday sermon. This is typically amplified and broadcast into the streets around. Most mosques also have a tower, or **minaret**, from which the call to prayer is issued five times a day. All mosques have a **prayer hall** (*liwan*) in front of the *mihrab*, and most also have a **courtyard** (*sahn*), usually with an arcade around it, and often a fountain in the middle for ablutions. At midday prayers on a Friday in particular, the congregation will often spill out from the prayer hall and take up much or all of the courtyard as well.

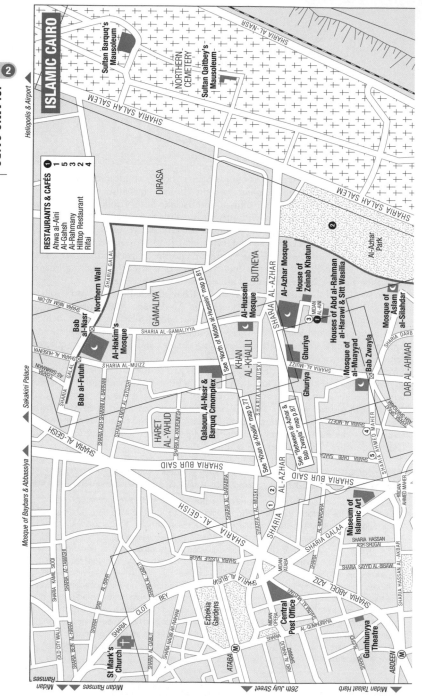

ISLAMIC CAIRO

▲ Heliopolis & Airport

RESTAURANTS & CAFÉS

Ahwa al-Aini	❶
Al-Gahsh	1
Al-Rahmany	5
Hilltop Restaurant	3
Rifai	2
	4

SHARIA SALAH SALEM

SHARIA AL-NASR

Sultan Barquq's Mausoleum

NORTHERN CEMETERY

Sultan Qaitbey's Mausoleum

SHARIA SALAH SALEM

DIRASA

SHARIA SALAH SALEM

Al-Azhar Park

❷

Al-Azhar Mosque

SHARIA AL-AZHAR

House of Zeinab Khatun

BUTNEYA

Al-Hussein Mosque

❸ MIDAN AL-AINI ❶

Houses of Abd al-Rahman al-Harrawi & Sitt Wasilia

Mosque of Aslam al-Silahdar

SHARIA DARB

DAR AL-AHMAR

Northern Wall

SHARIA GALAL

GAMALIYA

SHARIA AL-GAMALIYYA

Ghuriya

SHARIA AL-MUIZZ

Ghuriya

Mosque of al-Muayyad

Bab Zwayla

Bab al-Futuh

Al-Hakim's Mosque

SHARIA AL-HUSEINA

SHARIA GALAL

SHARIA AS-SAMMARIN

See "North of Midan al-Hussein" map p.81

KHAN AL-KHALILI

SHARIA AL-MUSKI

See "Khan al-Khalili" map p.77

SHARIA AL-MUIZZ

See "Between al-Azhar & Bab Zwayla" map p.87

Bab al-Nasr

SHARIA AMIR AL-GUISHI

Qalaoun, Al-Nasr & Barquq Cmomplex

HARET AL-YAHUD

SHARIA AS-SHARRABI

SHARIA BUR SAID

SHARIA AL-AZHAR

SHARIA AL-MUSKI

SHARIA BUR SAID

SHARIA MA-MUIZZ

Museum of Islamic Art

SHARIA AL-MOEZZ

❹

❺

SHARIA AHMED MAHER

SHARIA DARB SAADA

MIDAN AHMED MAHER

▲ Sakakini Palace

▲ Mosque of Baybars & Abbassiya

SHARIA AL-GEISH

❶ ❷

SHARIA AL-GEISH

SHARIA ABARRA

SHARIA YUSSEF NAGIB

SHARIA QALAA

SHARIA HASSAN ASH-SHUGAI

SHARIA SAYYID AL-BIBAWI

SHARIA HASSAN AL-AKBAR

SHARIA AL-BUSR

MIDAN ATABA

MIDAN ATABA

Ezbekia Gardens

MIDAN OPERA

Central Post Office

AL-GUMHURIYA

Gumhunyya Theatre

MIDAN AHMED MAHER

SHARIA ABDEL AZIZ

SHARIA AL-MINSARA

ABDEEN

St Mark's Church

OLD CITY WALL

SHARIA KAMIL SIDQI

SHARIA AL-TAWASHI

SHARIA AL-GABLIT

CLOT BEY

SHARIA BEIN AL-HARAT

SHARIA NAGIB AR-RAHMAN

SHARIA AL-KHALIG SARWAT

ATABA Ⓜ

26th July Street ▲

Midan Talaat Harb ▲

ABDEEN Ⓜ

Midan Ramses ▲▲

Midan Ramses ▲▲

Midan Ramses

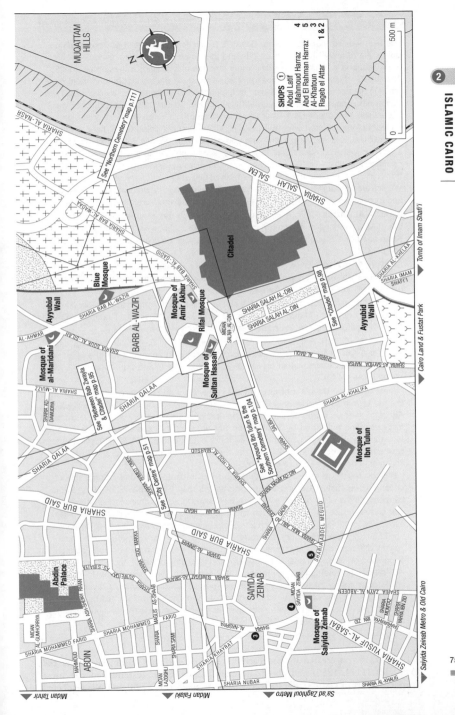

ISLAMIC CAIRO

SHOPS ①
Abdul Latif   4
Mahmoud Harraz   5
Abd El Rahman Harraz   3
Al-Khatoun   2
Rageb el Attar   1 & 2

MUQATTAM HILLS

Citadel

Blue Mosque
Ayyubid Wall
Mosque of Amir Akhur
Rifai Mosque
Mosque of Sultan Hassan
Mosque of al-Maridani
Mosque of Ibn Tulun
Abdin Palace
SAIYIDA ZEINAB
Mosque of Saiyida Zeinab
ABDIN

Tomb of Imam Shafi'i
Cairo Land & Fustat Park
Sayyida Zeinab Metro & Old Cairo
Sa'ad Zaghloul Metro
Midan Falaki
Midan Tahrir

500 m

75

Exploring Islamic Cairo: practicalities

The best way **to explore Islamic Cairo** is by **walking**. The most obvious **starting points** are Khan al-Khalili, Bab Zwayla and the Citadel; see the beginning of each of these sections for details on getting there (and the bus/minibus routes on pp.28–29). The streets of Islamic Cairo are labyrinthine and, while getting lost among them can result in the richest experiences, you may prefer to be shown round by a **guide**. The tourist office can put you in touch with authorized guides, and unofficial ones may accost you on the street. Whether you choose an official or an unofficial guide, make it clear before you start what the price is, where you are going to go, how long the tour will last, and above all insist that you do not want to visit any shops (as taking a guide in with you means the shopkeeper will be obliged to pay the guide a hefty commission, which will be added to your bill). Frankly, armed with a map and this book, you do not need a guide to visit Islamic Cairo.

There are four approaches on foot from **Midan Ataba** in downtown Cairo (see p.67, and the map on pp.50–51), using the Ataba post office and fire station for orientation:

SHARIA AL-MUSKI A narrow bazaar, identifiable by the crowds passing between the *El-Mousky* hotel and a clump of luggage stalls, this is the classic approach to **Khan al-Khalili**, though it takes slightly longer than Sharia al-Azhar. For more details, see p.78.

SHARIA AL-AZHAR Overshadowed by a flyover running to the heart of Islamic Cairo, Sharia al-Azhar buzzes with traffic and cottage industries. It's a ten-to-fifteen-minute walk along here to **Al-Azhar Mosque**.

SHARIA QALAA Across from Ataba fire station, this runs directly to the **Citadel** (2km). The stretch down to Midan Ahmed Maher – where the Museum of **Islamic Art** is located – features musical instrument shops, all-night stalls and cafés.

SHARIA AL-GEISH With a flyover running over it, "Army Street" runs out towards Abbassiya and Heliopolis. The main reason for venturing up it is to visit the Mosque of Beybars the Crossbowman on Midan Zahir (see p.143), and the Sakakini Palace beyond (see p.143).

Most of Islamic Cairo's **monuments** are self-evident and are described in detail in *Islamic Monuments in Cairo: A Practical Guide*, published by the AUC (see p.269). Although the area **maps** printed in this book should suffice, the AUC book and four fold-out maps published by SPARE (the Society for the Preservation of the Architectural Resources of Egypt) show even more detail. Shorouk, AUC, Buccellati and Lehnert & Landrock (see p.224) are the best places to look for the SPARE maps, which are not always easy to come by.

Historic buildings may charge **admission**, but mosques generally don't, though unscrupulous custodians and other opportunists may try to charge for entry. If this happens, demand an official ticket – if they have none, the charge is spurious and you should refuse to pay it, though of course custodians may expect baksheesh, especially for looking after shoes (£E1–2) or showing you round and opening things up (£E5–10). **Opening hours** are roughly 9am to 7pm daily (where they're significantly different, details are given in the text), though places may well open up later, depending on when the guardian turns up, and they may close an hour or two earlier in winter. During Ramadan, you will not be able to visit after about 4pm. Unless you are Muslim and want to pray, you will also not be welcome during **prayer times**, including the Friday noon assembly, which lasts over an hour but should be finished by 2pm. A couple of mosques (indicated in the text) are closed to non-Muslims completely.

In brief, it was created by the Fatimids in 969, and had its heyday under the Ayyubids (1171–1250) and the Mamlukes (1250–1517). It remained the most important part of Cairo under the Ottoman Empire (1517–1798), but was neglected as a "native quarter" under British colonial rule (1882–1936), and indeed until the 1980s, when its status as a tourist attraction caused the authorities to start paying it more attention. An earthquake in 1992 caused so much damage that funds were poured into restoring its monuments – an effort still underway, resulting in some places being under restoration and therefore closed to the public.

Khan al-Khalili to the Northern Gates

The bazaar quarter of **Khan al-Khalili** is the commercial and religious heart of Islamic Cairo, and the best starting point to explore it. To get here from downtown Cairo **by taxi** shouldn't cost more than £E5, although drivers often try to overcharge tourists bound for Midan al-Hussein – the square adjoining Khan al-Khalili (and the best destination to give your cab driver). A cheaper option is to catch bus #66 from the Abdel Mouneem Riyad bus station near Midan Tahrir

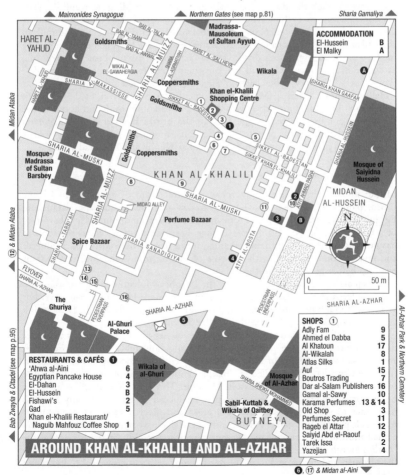

ACCOMMODATION
El-Hussein — B
El Malky — A

SHOPS
Adly Fam — 9
Ahmed el Dabba — 5
Al Khatoun — 17
Al-Wikalah — 8
Atlas Silks — 1
Auf — 15
Boutros Trading — 7
Dar al-Salam Publishers — 16
Gamal al-Sawy — 10
Karama Perfumes — 13 & 14
Old Shop — 3
Perfumes Secret — 11
Rageb el Attar — 12
Saiyid Abd el-Raouf — 6
Tarek Issa — 2
Yazejian — 4

RESTAURANTS & CAFÉS
'Ahwa al-Aini — 6
Egyptian Pancake House — 4
El-Dahan — 3
El-Hussein — B
Fishawi's — 2
Gad — 5
Khan el-Khalili Restaurant/ Naguib Mahfouz Coffee Shop — 1

AROUND KHAN AL-KHALILI AND AL-AZHAR

77

to the Al-Azhar Mosque, south of Midan al-Hussein. It's also possible to **walk** here from Midan Ataba (10–15mins); you can either follow Sharia al-Muski (as described below) or Sharia al-Azhar (beneath the flyover).

From Midan al-Hussein, the Gamaliya quarter stretches up to the Fatimid city walls, encompassing some of Cairo's most important medieval monuments, which can only be seen on foot. The area between Khan al-Khalili and the Northern Gates contains the bulk of the Fatimid city of Al-Qahira (see p.258), though most of the buildings within its limits date from slightly later than the Fatimid era. A walk through this neighbourhood is among the most rewarding in Cairo for its sheer variety of monuments and street life. For the lowdown on **shopping** in the bazaar, see p.219.

Sharia al-Muski

Though it's hard to believe today, **Sharia al-Muski** was, back in the nineteenth century, the city's first European-style shopping street, linking Islamic Cairo with Midan Ataba (see p.67). Narrow, noisy, and rubbish-strewn, it is utterly congested with shoppers and peddlers, and to negotiate it you'll have to worm your way through the throng, past windows full of wedding gear and lingerie, vendors hawking everything from salted fish to socks, and itinerant drinks vendors dispensing liquorice-water, tamarind cordial and sometimes even almond milk in their silver-spouted lemonade bottles. Water sellers have been made redundant by modern plumbing, but other drink vendors remain an essential part of street life, as do the barrow-men, who still yell out their traditional warnings – "Riglak!" (your foot!), "Dahrik!" (your back!), "Shemalak!" (your left side!).

Halfway along Sharia al-Muski you'll encounter Sharia Bur Said (see p.72), which can't be crossed directly – you'll need to head 50m south and dodge under the flyover, or use the footbridge 50m to the north. Beyond Bur Said, Sharia al-Muski is largely given over to lingerie stalls, gradually superseded by tourist souvenirs and perfume shops as it nears Khan al-Khalili and Midan al-Hussein.

Midan al-Hussein

Midan al-Hussein (Hussein Square) is a central point of reference in Islamic Cairo, flanked by the Khan al-Khalili bazaars and the Mosque of al-Hussein, Egypt's most venerated mosque. From an architectural standpoint it lacks harmony or a unifying style, but this doesn't bother Egyptians, for whom its significance has nothing to do with aesthetics. Rather, it is a place where worship, commerce and revelry come together with no sense of incongruity – and tourists get their bearings before plunging into the old city.

The square's namesake, Hussein, was the Prophet Mohammed's grandson, who was murdered at Karbala in Iraq in 680. Shi'ites revere Hussein as a martyr, but in Egypt, though its Muslim population is almost completely Sunni, Hussein is a massively popular saint, along with his sister Saiyida Zeinab (see p.107).

After the Shi'ite Fatimids conquered Egypt in 969 (see p.258), they sought to bolster their legitimacy with the population by bringing holy relics to Cairo. Foremost among these was the **head of Hussein**, transported from Palestine in 1153 to save it from the Crusaders, and installed in a marble cenotaph in the purpose-built **Mosque of Saiyidna Hussein**, or **Al-Hussein Mosque**. This tan-coloured edifice is where Egypt's president and other dignitaries pray on special occasions, but only Muslims may enter to see its magnificently cool green-and-silver interior. The three giant retractable parasols that stand outside are meant to shade worshippers during Hussein's annual **moulid** – a fortnight of religious devotion and popular revelry during the Muslim month of Rabi al-Tani (see p.216), when the Sufi brotherhoods parade with their banners and drums, and music blares all night, with vast crowds of Cairenes and *fellahin* (farmers) from the Delta. Midan al-Hussein is also a focal point during the festivals of Moulid al-Nabi, Eid al-Adha, Ramadan and Eid al-Fitr (see p.217).

Khan al-Khalili

In 1382, under the rule of the Sunni Ayyubids, the Fatimid tombs beside the Al-Hussein Mosque were demolished and the bodies unceremoniously dumped in the rubbish heaps beyond the city walls. In the tomb's place, a Master of Horse named Khalil founded a caravanserai, which became the core of a network of bazaars now known as **Khan al-Khalili**. Most of the shop fronts conceal workshops or warehouses, and the system of selling certain goods in particular areas still applies, if not as rigidly as in the past.

Goldsmiths, jewellers and souvenir-antique **shops** congregate along the lanes, which retain a few arches and walls from Mamluke times. The majority are open from 10am till 9pm or later, except on Sundays, when most shops are shut. The *khan* itself is quite compact, bounded by Hussein's mosque, Sharia al-Muizz and Sharia al-Muski, with two medieval lanes (Sikket al-Badestan and Sikket Khan al-Khalili) providing the axes for its maze-like interior – but the name is also applied to other bazaars in the vicinity.

South of Sharia Muski, along **Sharia al-Muizz**, you'll find the Souk al-Attarin or **Spice Bazaar**, selling dried crushed fruit and flowers, in addition to spices. On the corner of the same street, screened by T-shirt and *galabiyya* (long men's gown) stalls, the **Mosque-Madrassa of Sultan al-Ashraf Barsbey** (popularly known as "al-Ashrafiya") was founded by the Mamluk sultan Barsbey (ruled 1422–38), who made the spice trade a state monopoly, thus financing his 1426 capture of Cyprus. Outwardly resplendent in its red-and-white striped stonework, the interior features intricate *mashrabiya* (wooden screens), an inlaid *minbar* (pulpit), and the tombs of Barsbey's wife and son – the sultan himself is buried in the Northern Cemetery (see p.112).

Sharia Sanadiqiya (off Sharia al-Muizz) will take you into the **Perfume Bazaar**, a dark, aromatic warren sometimes called the Souk al-Sudan because much of its incense comes from Sudan. The first passage on your left off Sharia Sanadiqiya, coming from al-Muizz, leads up a flight of steps to a tiny cul-de-sac. This is Zuqaq al-Midaq, or **Midaq Alley**, immortalized by Naguib Mahfouz in his novel of the same name (see p.271), the film adaptation of which was shot here. There is no street sign apparent; it's kept in the tiny (and easy to miss) café, where they'll ask if you want to photograph it – for baksheesh, of course.

When you've tired of wandering around, duck into **Fishawi's** (see p.198), via one of the passages off Sharia al-Muski or the square. Showing its age with tobacco-stained plaster and cracked mirrors, this famous café has been open day and night every day of the year since 1773, and is an evocative place to sip mint tea, eavesdrop, and maybe smoke a *sheesha*. A more westernized, air-conditioned place to chill out is the *Naguib Mahfouz Coffee Shop* on Sikket al-Badestan; for details of both, see p.198.

Bayn al-Qasrayn

Sharia al-Muizz – named after the conquering Fatimid caliph who founded Al-Qahira – is in fact the main axis of Islamic Cairo, stretching all the way from the Northern Gates (see p.85) to Bab Zwayla (see p.91), and almost as far as the Citadel. Heading north along it from Sultan Barsbey's Mosque-Madrassa (see p.79), jewellers' shops overflowing from the **Goldsmiths Bazaar** soon give way to vendors of brass pots, basins and crescent-topped mosque finials; this stretch of Sharia al-Muizz is popularly called Al-Nahaseen, the **Coppersmiths Bazaar**.

Haret al-Yahud – the medieval Jewish quarter

From the Goldsmiths' bazaar on Sharia al-Muizz (see map, p.79), Sharia al-Makassisse leads into the **Haret al-Yahud** ("Jewish Alley"), one of the most densely populated parts of town, and Cairo's **Jewish quarter** since Al-Qahira's foundation. In the twelfth century, 97 percent of its residents were Jewish, many of whom had fled from Spain after the fundamentalist Almohad regime there offered Andalucian Jews a choice of exile, death, or conversion to Islam. Among the refugees, the rabbi, scientist and philosopher **Maimonides** (1135–1204) was appointed *nagid* (community leader) and later became Saladin's court physician. Alongside the Spanish refugees, smaller groups of Tunisian, Iraqi and Kairaite Jews each had their own synagogues – only two of which remain since Egypt's Jews left en masse in the 1950s (see p.268).

The first of these, the nineteenth-century **Maimonides Synagogue** (also called *Musa bin Maimun*, Arabic for Maimonides, or *al-mahabad*, meaning "the temple") occupies the site of a medieval original where its namesake once taught. Last used in 1960, it lay derelict until restored under a two-million-dollar project funded by the Egyptian government. A private dedication attended by Egyptian Jews, however, resulted in media reports of them "dancing and drinking alcohol", which was deemed a "provocation", and the official inauguration ceremony was cancelled. The synagogue was still closed at last check, and whether it will ever open is anybody's guess. The building is nothing special from outside but you can't miss it thanks to the police posted nearby.

The **Karaite Synagogue**, tucked up a lane branching off Haret al-Yahud (the quarter's north-south axis), stands tantalizingly close to Sharia al-Khrunfish (the quarter's northern limit), but can't be reached from there directly, and is quite difficult to find, especially as most local people are unaware of it (for its location, see the colour map at the back of the book). It belonged to the Karaites, a dissident sect of Judaism who rejected the Talmud in favour of a literal interpretation of the Torah and were known, among other things, for praying prostrated on rugs like Muslims.

In Fatimid times, this part of al-Muizz was a broad avenue culminating in a great parade ground between two vast and splendid caliphal palaces. Though the palaces themselves are long gone – bar a few carved wooden lintels in the Museum of Islamic Arts (see p.92) – they give this stretch of al-Muizz its modern name, **Bayn al-Qasrayn**, meaning "Between the Two Palaces". More recently, the street has given its name to the first novel of Naguib Mahfouz's *Cairo Trilogy*, where it is usually translated as "Palace Walk".

On the west side of the street, a minaret poking above a row of stalls betrays the otherwise unobtrusive **Madrassa-Mausoleum of Sultan Ayyub** (daily 9am–5pm; £E10), built for Egypt's last independent Ayyubid sultan, Al-Saleh Ayyub (ruled 1240–49), who introduced foreign slave-warriors, or Mamlukes, into the army. After his widow's bid for power (see p.109) the Mamlukes became kingmakers, ruling Egypt from 1250 onwards. Little remains of Ayyub's *madrassa*, which was the first to incorporate arcaded halls, or *liwans*, for teaching Sunni Islam's four schools of jurisprudence, but his mausoleum is still intact, and architecturally extremely interesting. Its dome, supported by stalactite squinches, is an early example of a design that was to become very typical of the Mamlukes' great mosque-*madrassa*-mausoleum complexes, while its minaret's *mabkhara* (incense burner) or "pepper-pot" crown is the sole example of this Ayyubid motif left in Cairo.

The Qalaoun Complex

Across the street from Ayyub's *madrassa*, the ensemble of buildings endowed by the Mamluke sultans **Qalaoun**, **Al-Nasir** and **Barquq** forms an unbroken, quite breathtaking facade. The first part that you'll see is the **Maristan, Madrassa and Mausoleum of Sultan Qalaoun**. Qalaoun, who ruled 1280–90, was a Qipchak (Tartar), purchased for the high price of a thousand dinars during Al-Saleh Ayyub's reign, hence his nickname, Al-Alfi ("the Thousand"). He rose through the ranks due to the patronage of Sultan Beybars al-Bunduqdari, whose seven-year-old son he eventually deposed in 1279. A tireless foe of the Crusaders – he died en route to boot them out of Acre, aged 79 – Qalaoun imported Circassians from

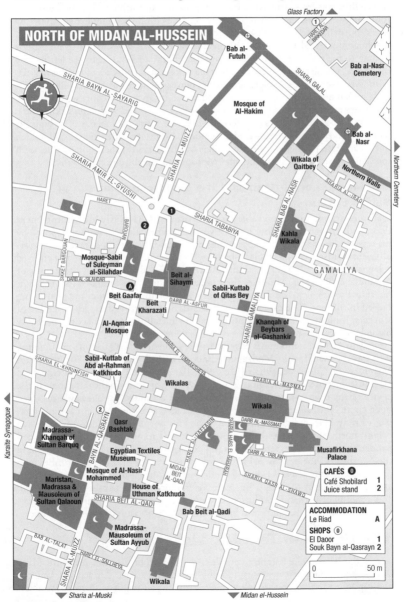

NORTH OF MIDAN AL-HUSSEIN

N

Glass Factory

Bab al-Futuh

Bab al-Nasr Cemetery

Mosque of Al-Hakim

Bab al-Nasr

SHARIA BAYN AL-SAYARIG

SHARIA GALAL

SHARIA AMIR EL-GYUISHI

SHARIA AL-MUIZZ

Wikala of Qaitbey

Northern Walls

SHARIA AL-IRAQ

Northern Cemetery

HARET

SHARIA TABABIYA

Kahla Wikala

SHARIA BAB AL-NASR

GAMALIYA

Mosque-Sabil of Suleyman al-Silahdar

Beit al-Sihaymi

SIKKET BARGOUAN

BARQUAN

DARB AL-SILAHDAR

Beit Gaafar

Beit Kharazati

DARB AL-ASFUR

Sabil-Kuttab of Qitas Bey

SHARIA GAMALIYA

Al-Aqmar Mosque

Khanqah of Beybars al-Gashankir

SHARIA EL-TUMBAKSHEYA

Sabil-Kuttab of Abd al-Rahman Katkhuda

SHARIA EL-KHRUNFISH

Wikalas

SHARIA AL-MASMAT

Wikala

DARB AL-MASSMAT

Karaite Synagogue

BAYN AL-QASRAYN

Qasr Bashtak

Madrassa-Khanqah of Sultan Barquq

Egyptian Textiles Museum

SHARIA HABS EL-RAHBA

HARET EL-RAFFISIN

DARB AL-TABLAWY

Musafirkhana Palace

Mosque of Al-Nasr Mohammed

MIDAN BEIT AL-QADI

SHARIA QASR AL-SHAWQ

CAFÉS ●
Café Shobilard   1
Juice stand   2

Maristan, Madrassa & Mausoleum of Sultan Qalaoun

House of Uthman Katkhuda

SHARIA BEIT AL-QADI

Bab Beit al-Qadi

ACCOMMODATION
Le Riad   A

SHOPS ◉
El Daoor   1
Souk Bayn al-Qasrayn 2

BAB AL-TALAT

SHARIA AL-MUIZZ

HARET EL-SALIHEYA

Madrassa-Mausoleum of Sultan Ayyub

Wikala

0   50 m

Sharia al-Muski

Midan el-Hussein

the Caucasus to offset Qipchak predominance among the Mamlukes, founding a dynasty that ruled for almost a century. Influenced by the Syrian and Crusader architecture he'd seen while fighting abroad, his complex is built on a grand scale with lavish ornamentation. By rounding up artisans and forcing passers-by to carry stones, he was able to complete it in only thirteen months (1284–85).

To endear him to the populace, it included a public hospital, or *maristan*, providing free treatment for every known illness (including cataract removals), storytellers and musicians to amuse the patients, and money to tide them over following their discharge. A modern eye clinic behind the complex continues its work, but what little of the *maristan* remains is not accessible to sightseers.

A huge door clad in bronze with geometric patterns gives access to a corridor leading to the rest of the complex (daily 9am–5pm; £E30). Off to the left lies the **madrassa**, whose sanctuary *liwan* recalls the three-aisled churches of northern Syria, with Syrian-style glass mosaics around its prayer niche – but the real highlight is Qalaoun's **mausoleum**, across the way. Preceded by an atrium court with a *mashrabiya* doorway, surmounted by a beautiful stucco arch worked with interlocking stars, floral and Koranic motifs, as intricate as lace, the tomb chamber is 30m high, its soaring dome pierced by stained-glass windows in viridian, ultramarine and golden hues. Elaborately coffered, painted ceilings overhang walls panelled in marble, with mother-of-pearl mosaics spelling out "Mohammed" in abstract calligraphy.

The Mosque of Al-Nasir and the Madrassa-Khanqah of Sultan Barquq

Qalaoun's second son, responsible for the **Mosque of Al-Nasir Mohammed** next door, had a rough succession. Only 9 years old when elected, he was deposed by his regent, then restored but kept in miserable conditions for a decade by Beybars al-Gashankir (see p.86). He finally had Beybars executed and subsequently enjoyed a lengthy reign (1293–1340, with interregnums), which marked the zenith of Mamluke civilization. Although the **mausoleum** here was intended for Al-Nasir, he actually lies next door in Qalaoun's mausoleum, his wife and son being buried in this one. The **minaret** is particularly noteworthy, a superb ensemble of stuccoed Kufic and Naskhi inscriptions, ornate medallions and stalactites, probably made by Moroccan craftsmen.

Entry to Al-Nasir's mosque is covered by the same ticket as Qalaoun's mausoleum, which is also valid for the **Madrassa-Khanqah of Sultan Barquq**. The first Burgi Mamluke, or Circassian, sultan (1382–98), Barquq seized power by intrigue and assassination. His name, meaning "plum" in Arabic, appears on the raised boss in the centre of the bronze-plated doors, behind which a vaulted passageway leads to an open court. The *madrassa*'s sanctuary *liwan* (arcaded hall), on the right as you enter, has a lovely blue and gold ceiling supported by porphyry columns of pharaonic origin; north of the prayer hall, a splendid domed **mausoleum** upheld by gilded pendentives contains the tomb of Barquq's daughter (the sultan himself is buried in the Northern Cemetery, see p.112). Upstairs are the cells of the Sufi dervishes who once inhabited the *khanqah* (a hostel for dervishes). The custodian may invite you to ascend the **minaret** to enjoy a fine view of Islamic Cairo – baksheesh is expected, and a flashlight is useful to illuminate darkened parts of the spiral staircase. Like Qalaoun's complex, Barquq's was built (1384–86) in an astonishingly short time.

The Egyptian Textiles Museum

Across the street from Barquq's complex, the **Egyptian Textiles Museum** (daily 9am–4.30pm; £E20) is a recent addition to Islamic Cairo. Attractively laid out and captioned in English throughout, it reveals all you might wish to know about the eponymous subject, from pharaonic times up until the modern era. Its collection includes one of the 145 linen loincloths found in Tutankhamun's tomb in the Valley of the Kings, mummy shrouds, Greco-Roman and Coptic tunics, cloaks and tapestries. An exporter of textiles since ancient times – linen, chiffon, mohair and fustian (the medieval equivalent of denim, named after Fustat) were all of local origin – Egypt gradually became dependent on imports from Iran, India and, eventually, Europe – a situation only remedied in the late nineteenth century. Don't miss the magnificent silver-embroidered *qiswa*, an old covering from the Ka'ba in Mecca. Egyptian pilgrims travelling to Mecca for the hajj used to replace the *qiswa* every year, until 1962, when friction between Nasser and the Saudi royal family led the Saudis to use their own *qiswa* factory instead.

The Sabil-Kuttab of Abd al-Rahman Katkhuda

At a fork in the road just north of the Qalaoun, Al-Nasir and Barquq complex and the palatial **Qasr Bashtak** (closed to the public at the time of writing), the **Sabil-Kuttab of Abd al-Rahman Katkhuda** (daily 9am–5pm; £E10) rises in tiers of airy wooden fretwork above solid masonry and grilles at street level. The *sabil* (public fountain), and *kuttab* (boys' primary school) are common charitable institutions throughout the Islamic world, but uniquely in Cairo, they were usually combined in a single building. At one time there were some three hundred such *sabil-kuttabs* in the city, of which around seventy survive (though none now supply water). This one, founded by an eighteenth-century amir who wanted to make amends for his roistering youth, betrays a strong Ottoman influence, notable in the floral carvings between the arches. As usual, the *sabil* is on the ground floor (where the Ka'ba at Mecca is depicted in Syrian tilework); exhibitions of ceramics from Fustat's Pottery Village (see p.125) are often held here. Upstairs, the *kuttab* affords a bird's eye view over Bayn al-Qasrayn.

The Al-Aqmar Mosque

Seventy metres north of the **Sabil-Kuttab of Abd al-Rahman Katkhuda** along Sharia Bayn al-Qasrayn (aka Sharia al-Muizz; bear left at the Sabil-Kuttab of Abd al-Rahman Katkhuda if heading north), the **Al-Aqmar Mosque** on the east side of the street is located at what was originally the northeast corner of one of the great Fatimid palaces (see p.80). Its most salient feature is the facade, whose ribbed shell hood, keel arches and stalactite panels were the first instance of a decorated mosque facade in Cairo. Built between 1121 and 1125 by the caliph's grand vizier, the mosque gets its name – "the moonlit" – from the glitter of its masonry under lunar light. The intricate medallion above the door bears the names of both Mohammed and his son-in-law Ali, from whom the Fatimids claimed descent and legitimacy as the Prophet's successors. In turn, an Indian Ismaili sect, the Dawood Bohara, later claimed descent from the Fatimids and dedicated itself to restoring their mosques in Cairo. They were eventually expelled from Egypt after removing several Mamluke tombs during their restoration of Al-Aqmar's interior in the 1990s. The mosque's entrance is at what was the street level when it was built. At the northern end of the facade, notice how the corner of the mosque has been cut away to allow heavily laden camels to turn more easily into the narrow lane along its north side.

Darb al-Asfur

One block north of the Al-Aqmar Mosque, the turning on the east side of al-Muizz is **Darb al-Asfur** (Yellow Street), whose pale honey-hued facades have been so thoroughly restored that it looks more like a modern reconstruction than a genuine medieval lane. The first three houses on the left are all accessible (daily 9am–5pm; £E30), via the broad wooden door of the seventeenth-century **Beit al-Sihaymi**. Its rooms surround a lovely courtyard filled with bird noises and shrubbery, overlooked by a *maq'ad* or loggia, where males enjoyed the cool northerly breezes; the ground-floor *qa'a* (reception hall), with its marble fountain, was used during winter, or for formal occasions. The *haramlik* section, reserved for women, is adorned with faïence, stained glass, painted ceilings and delicate latticework, its rooms cooled by an air-scoop (*malqaaf*) to catch night-time breezes.

From here, you pass through the nineteenth-century **Beit Kharazati** into the early eighteenth-century **Beit Gaafar**, once the residence of a coffee merchant. Both have been partially restored and offer a chance to appreciate the comfort afforded by such traditional dwellings. Visitors exit the ensemble of houses from the Beit Gaafar, on the corner of Sharia al-Muizz.

The Mosque-Sabil of Suleyman al-Silahdar

A few steps north of its junction with Darb al-Asfur, Sharia al-Muizz passes, on its western side, the **Mosque-Sabil of Suleyman al-Silahdar** (daily 9am–5pm; £E10) – recognizable by its "pencil" minaret, a typically Ottoman feature. Built in 1839, this edifice reflects the Baroque and Rococo influences that reached Cairo via Istanbul during Mohammed Ali's reign, notably in the fronds and garlands that decorate the curved exterior of its *sabil-kuttab*. Its most remarkable feature is the huge underground **cistern** discovered in 2001. An austere hall, whose only adornment is a painted ceiling frieze and ultramarine-coloured horn-shaped lamps, it is accessed through a blue door just beyond the *sabil* beneath the *kuttab*.

At the little square just north of Suleyman al-Silahdar's Mosque **Sharia Amir al-Gyushi**, leading off to the west, is a fascinating street full of **tinsmiths** manufacturing the ornate stove-pushcarts used by vendors of *fuul*, *kushari* and other street-food. If you need some rest or refreshment at this point, this is a good place to pause, with a **juice stand** on the corner of al-Muizz and Amir al-Gyushi, and the **Café Shobilard** (see p.198) just a few metres down Sharia Tababiya.

Egypt's Caligula

Al-Hakim bi-Amr Allah (Ruler by God's Command), became the sixth Fatimid caliph in 966 at the age of eleven. His 25-year reign was capricious and despotic by any standards, characterized by the persecution of Christians and Jews and a rabid misogyny. He forbade women to leave their homes and once had a group of noisy females boiled alive in a public bath. Merchants found guilty of cheating during his market inspections were summarily sodomized by his Nubian slave while the caliph stood upon their heads.

In 1020 in Fustat, Al-Hakim's followers proclaimed him a manifestation of God similar to the Christian Messiah. This blasphemous declaration provoked riots, which Al-Hakim answered by ordering Fustat's destruction, though legend also has this as being his revenge on the district where his beloved sister **Sitt al-Mulk** took her lovers; only afterwards was she examined by midwives and pronounced a virgin.

Allegedly, it was Al-Hakim's desire for an incestuous marriage with Sitt al-Mulk that impelled her in 1021 to arrange his "disappearance" during one of his nocturnal jaunts in the Muqattam Hills. Al-Hakim's follower Hamza Ibn Ali, and Ibn Ali's disciple, Mohammed al-Durzi, persuaded some foreign Muslims of Al-Hakim's divinity, giving rise to the **Druze** faith, whose tightly knit communities still exist in Syria, Lebanon and Israel, but in Coptic legend, Al-Hakim experienced a vision of Jesus, repented, and became a monk.

Al-Hakim's Mosque

The **Mosque of al-Hakim** commemorates one of Egypt's most notorious rulers (see box opposite). After his death it was shunned as a mosque, and used for profane purposes until 1980, when it was restored by the Dawood Bohara sect (see p.83), whose addition of brass lamps, glass chandeliers and a new prayer niche outraged purists – but the original wooden tie-beams and stucco frieze beneath the ceilings of its vast arcades remain. From the roof, you can admire the mosque's minarets, which resemble bastions, and gaze over Bab al-Nasr Cemetery (see below). One advantage of modernization is that the courtyard has some degree of wheelchair access (via the side door, to the left of the main one; you'll need to get someone to open it for you). Admission to the mosque (as opposed to the adjoining Northern Walls, entered from it – see below) is free.

The Northern Gates

From the rooftop of Al-Hakim's Mosque, it should be possible to climb onto, and go inside, the city's **Northern Walls**. Though they were closed at the time of research, once they have reopened to the public (possibly during 2011), you should be able to gain entry by paying a tip (£E5–10) to the caretaker of the mosque.

Erected under the Fatimid vizier Al-Gamali in 1087 to replace the original mud-brick ramparts of Al-Qahira, the walls were intended to rebuff the Seljuk Turks, but were never put to the test, although they later provided a barracks for Napoleonic, and then British, grenadiers. Two mighty gates in the walls stand either side of Al-Hakim's Mosque: **Bab al-Futuh** (the Open Gate) on the west side, and **Bab al-Nasr** (Gate of Victory) to the east. The French attempted to rename the bastions of these gates, and you can still see "Tour Julien" and "Tour Pascal" inscribed on them.

In the dark, gloomy passage that runs inside the walls between the two gates, you can see archers' slits and bombardiers' apertures, as well as shafts for pouring boiling oil onto enemies trying to enter through Bab al-Futuh, and pieces of pharaonic masonry featuring Ramses II's cartouche and a hippo that were filched from Memphis (see p.172). The ceiling of the two-hundred-metre-long tunnel is vaulted, which allowed mounted guards passage through. At its end lies a cavernous judgement room where the condemned, if found guilty, were hanged immediately, their corpses dumped through a hole in the floor, into the moat.

In times past, the annual pilgrim caravan returning from Mecca would enter Cairo via the **Bab al-Futuh** (Open Gate), drawing vast crowds to witness the arrival of the Mahmal, a decorative camel litter symbolizing the sultan's participation in the hajj. Islamic pageantry is still manifest during the **Moulid of Sidi Ali al-Bayoumi**, in early October, when the Rifai brotherhood parades behind its mounted sheikh with scarlet banners flying. The procession starts from Midan al-Hussein, progressing north along Sharia Gamiliya (where locals bombard the sheikh and his red-turbanned followers with sweets) through Bab al-Nasr, and re-entering the old city via the Bab al-Futuh.

Outside the gates, buses and microbus service taxis head westwards (to your left) along Sharia Galal to Midan Ramses.

Bab al-Nasr Cemetery

Stepping outside the Northern Gates, you can see the long-dry moat that once augmented Al-Qahira's fortifications, and gaze across Sharia Galal to the **Bab al-Nasr Cemetery**, so overbuilt with houses that you can hardly discern its tombs. Though lacking the grand mausoleums that distinguish the Northern Cemetery (see p.110), this necropolis is notable for its traditional **glass factory** (daily except Fri 9am–3pm; free) where they hand-blow Muski glass (see p.222). If you're curious to have a look (visitors are usually welcome), it's located at the far end of Haret al-Birkhader, leading off Sharia Galal; their shop at no. 14 (see p.222) can point you in the right direction.

Sharia Gamaliya

Parallel with Sharia al-Muizz, a less trodden route from Bab al-Nasr to Midan al-Hussein passes through the heart of **Gamaliya**, one of Cairo's most traditional quarters. Its name derives from the old camel road, Sharia Gamaliya, off which the quarter's alleys run. In one of them, the Arab world's greatest novelist Naguib Mahfouz (see p.271) was born, and he has always been strongly associated with this particular district. On this side, away from al-Muizz, the quarter seems poor and neglected, and the damage from the 1992 earthquake is still very apparent, with facades upheld by scaffolding and many venerable buildings still half-derelict. Yet here, just a little way off the main tourist trail, you get a much stronger feel for the day-to-day life of Islamic Cairo, and it's worth taking in at a leisurely pace, stopping off along the way for a cup of tea with the locals while checking out the street life in what is arguably Cairo's most atmospheric neighbourhood.

A short distance south of Bab al-Nast, the fifteenth-century **Wikala of Qaitbey**, one of the many caravanserais that once clustered near the city gates, is still largely derelict within following damage in the 1992 earthquake, though most of the facade remains intact.

A little further south, on the opposite side of the street (named Sharia Bab al-Nasr at this point), the **Kahla Wikala** is another old merchants' hostel, now serving as the headquarters of one of the NGOs involved in the restoration of Islamic Cairo. A block or so south of this, the modest **Sabil-Kuttab of Qitas Bey**, built in 1630, marks the eastern end of Darb al-Asfur (see p.83).

Diagonally opposite Qitas Bey's Sabil-Kuttab, the **Khanqah of Beybars al-Gashankir**, with its unmistakably bulbous dome and stumpy minaret, was founded in 1310, making it the oldest *khanqah* (Sufi hostel) in Cairo. The zig-zagging corridor through which you enter cuts off street noises from the inner courtyard, whose austerity is only enlivened by its variegated windows. The cells upstairs once housed one hundred Sufis.

The *khanqah* was commissioned in 1307 by Al-Gashankir, then a Mamluke amir (army commander), who became sultan for a year in 1309 when he usurped the throne from the previous incumbent, Al-Nasir Mohammed. After hearing a popular rhyme which mocked his name, Al-Gashankir ("the Taster", after his previous rank at court), he had three hundred people's tongues cut out for reciting it. Yet he himself came to a sticky end when Al-Nasir Mohammed retook the throne and had him garroted, closing down the *khanqah* (though it reopened fifteen years later) and having Al-Gashankir's name erased from the facade. Al-Gashankir's tomb chamber (off the entrance corridor) is nonetheless spectacular, its marbled walls inset with radiating polygons and dappled with sunbeams falling through the stained-glass windows. His cenotaph itself is shielded by an ebony *mashrabiya* screen.

Further south, two more *wikalas* precede a lane leading to the **Musafirkhana Palace** where Mohammed Ali's son and successor Khedive Ismail was born in 1830 – its blackened ruins the result of a fire in 1998. From the *wikalas* and the palace, there's a choice of routes to Khan al-Khalili Midan al-Hussein. An alley leading west passes through the **Bab Beit al-Qadi** (Gate of the Judge's House) into Midan Beit al-Qadi (where the house once stood), from which a lane joins

Bayn al-Qasrayn near Qalaoun's mausoleum (see p.81). Alternatively, the main street bends round to the left as it runs south, changing its name to Sharia Habs al-Rahdebah and then Sharia al-Hussein, before passing along the west side of Al-Hussein Mosque to emerge in Midan al-Hussein.

Al-Azhar to Bab Zwayla

Egypt's most important mosque, **Al-Azhar**, sits on the south side of Sharia al-Azhar, the main road named after it which neatly bisects the old walled Fatimid city. To avoid having to brave the traffic when you cross Sharia al-Azhar, it's best to take the pedestrian underpass from Midan al-Hussein. Alternatively, you can use the footbridge a hundred metres to the west, which connects the northern part of Islamic

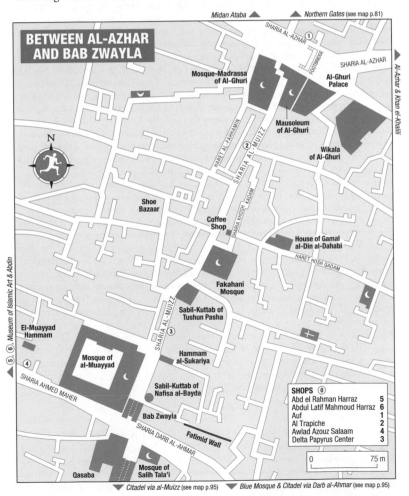

BETWEEN AL-AZHAR AND BAB ZWAYLA

Midan Ataba ▲   ▲ Northern Gates (see map p.81)

SHARIA AL-AZHAR ①

FOOTBRIDGE

SHARIA AL-AZHAR

▶ Al-Azhar & Khan el-Khalili

Mosque-Madrassa of Al-Ghuri

Al-Ghuri Palace

HARET AL-FAHHAMIN

SHARIA AL-MUIZZ

Mausoleum of Al-Ghuri

②

Wikala of Al-Ghuri

SHARIA KHOSH KADAM

Shoe Bazaar

Coffee Shop

House of Gamal al-Din al-Dahabi

HARET HOSH QADAM

Fakahani Mosque

SHARIA AL-MUIZZ

Sabil-Kuttab of Tushun Pasha

③

Hammam al-Sukariya

El-Muayyad Hammam

④

Mosque of al-Muayyad

SHARIA AHMED MAHER

Sabil-Kuttab of Nafisa al-Bayda

Bab Zwayla

SHARIA DARB AL-AHMAR

Fatimid Wall

◀ ⑤, ⑥, Museum of Islamic Art & Abdin

SHOPS ⓞ
Abd el Rahman Harraz	5
Abdul Latif Mahmoud Harraz	6
Auf	1
Al Trapiche	2
Awlad Azouz Salaam	4
Delta Papyrus Center	3

0   75 m

Mosque of Salih Tala'i

Qasaba

▼ Citadel via al-Muizz (see map p.95)   ▼ Blue Mosque & Citadel via Darb al-Ahmar (see map p.95)

Cairo's main thoroughfare, Sharia al-Muizz (covered on pp.79–85), to its southern section. Starting at the **Ghuriya** complex, al-Muizz continues south from here down to the medieval gate known as **Bab Zwayla**. It's a stretch of just 300m, but it can easily take an hour or more to walk down it if you stop to investigate the monuments on the way, most notably the Ghuriya, the **"Red Mosque" of al-Muayyad**, and the gate of Bab Zwayla iteslf. The shops in this part of al-Muizz sell mostly clothing, and each section has its own name, usually reflecting the merchandise sold there. Tucked away in the shadowy maze of side alleys to its west are small **bazaars** devoted to shoes, bedding and suchlike, while to its east, behind Al-Azhar, the shabby but lively **Butneya** quarter still retains a slightly disreputable air from the days before Mubarak (see below), when it was Cairo's main hashish market.

Al-Azhar Mosque

Across the main road from Midan al-Hussein (best reached by pedestrian underpass), Cairo's most important Islamic institution, **Al-Azhar Mosque**, has been training jurists and issuing authoritative *fatwas* since the tenth century. Though it lacks the beauty that its name implies (*al-Azhar* can be translated as "the radiant", "the blooming" or "the resplendent"), nothing can detract from its status. Founded in 970 by the Fatimid general Gawhar, it claims to be the world's oldest university (a title disputed by the Kairaouine Mosque in Fez, Morocco), and its Grand Sheikh is the ultimate theological authority for hundreds of millions of Sunni Muslims.

For over a millennium, Al-Azhar has provided students from across the Muslim world with free board and an education that remains largely as it was during the classical Islamic era. Students study every facet of the Koran and Islamic jurisprudence: logic, grammar, rhetoric, and how to calculate phases of the lunar Muslim calendar. Much of this involves listening in a circle at the feet of a sheikh, and rote memorization, but with greater knowledge, students may engage in Socratic dialogue with their teachers, or instruct their juniors.

Given all this, it's unsurprising that Al-Azhar has always been politically significant. Saladin changed it from a Shi'ite hotbed into a bastion of Sunni orthodoxy, while Napoleon's troops desecrated it to punish Cairenes for revolting against French occupation in 1798. A nationalist stronghold during colonial times, Al-Azhar was the venue for Nasser's speech of defiance during the Suez invasion of 1956.

The **mosque** itself (daily 9am–5pm, except during prayers, which last for two hours on Friday 11am–1pm) is an accretion of centuries and styles, harmonious if confusing. You enter through the fifteenth-century **Barber's Gate**, where students traditionally had their heads shaved, onto a great **courtyard** (*sahn*) that's five hundred years older, overlooked by three minarets. The *sahn* facade, with its rosettes and keel-arched panels, is mostly Fatimid, but the latticework-screened *riwaqs* (residential quarters) of the *madrassas* on your right-hand side date from the Mamluke period. While these are rarely opened for visitors, you can walk into the carpeted, alabaster-pillared prayer hall, where the *mihrab*, or Mecca-facing prayer niche, is located. The **roof** and **minarets** (closed to visitors at time of writing, but it's worth asking if you can go up) offer great views of Islamic Cairo's crumbling, dust-coloured buildings, the skyline bristling with dozens of minarets.

Butneya

The warren of lanes and tenements behind Al-Azhar, a neighbourhood known as **Butneya**, was traditionally Cairo's "Thieves' Quarter", where the main business was **hashish**, openly sold outdoors in slabs on trestle tables by local drugs barons who enjoyed high-level protection – President Sadat's brother was said to take a commission on every kilo sold. Within days of Sadat's assassination in 1981, armoured police cars entered Butneya, ending their impunity – but other rackets continued unchecked for some years. Today, Butneya has settled into being a fairly respectable quarter, and the heroin addiction now rife in Cairo's poorest neighbourhoods makes Butneya's once outrageous hashish trade seem rather quaint by comparison.

Midan al-Aini

Behind Al-Azhar Mosque, Sharia Sheikh Mohammed leads past the facade of a *sabil-kuttab* (school with drinking fountain) and *wikala* (merchants' hostel), which face the mosque's south wall, and were commissioned in 1477 by Sultan Qaitbey, who also provided a drinking trough on the next corner. The next right after the drinking trough leads into **Midan al-Aini**, a lovely little plaza with a small café (see p.198), surrounded by a trio of interesting Mamluke and Ottoman mansions, whose caretaker hangs out in the square selling tickets to visit them.

The palatial **House of Zeinab Khatun** (daily 9am–5pm; £E15), on the north side of the square, was built around 1468 and restored in 1713. You can wander around the upper and lower floors, checking out the *mashrabiya* screens and *ablaq* floors and recesses. The grand *qa'a* (reception hall) on the upper floor – very typical of Mamluke mansions of the period – boasts a beautiful red and gold painted wooden ceiling.

Opposite across the square, the 1731 **House of Abd al-Rahman al-Harawi** (daily 9am–5pm; £E15) is now a school for lute players, so a visit here is as much a musical experience as an architectural one. The entrance used today was originally the back door, and is actually a nineteenth-century addition. It leads to the *mandara*, or main downstairs hall, which is around a century older than the rest of the house, with its wooden ceiling and beautiful marble floor. The room originally centred around an octagonal fountain (you can still see where this was), flanked by two *liwans* (arcades). The built-in cupboards are worth a second glance, with their *mashrabiya* (wooden screen) doors surrounded by a little recesses, each in the shape of a doorway. Upstairs, the *qa'a*, still blue from its original paintwork, is no less impressive – note in particular the large *mashrabiya* window, which overlooks the house's original (south) entrance.

By far the most interesting house on the square, however, is the next-door **House of Sitt Wasilia** (daily 9am–5pm; £E15), named after a nineteenth-century resident (*sitt* is like "Mrs"), but actually built in 1664. Exploring it, you'll find an in-house hammam, hidden away in one of the back rooms, but the house's most impressive feature is the fresco of Istanbul in the first-floor portico overlooking the main patio, as well as one of Mecca and Medina.

The Ghuriya

The array of buildings to the west of al-Azhar, known collectively as **the Ghuriya**, were erected by the penultimate Mamluke sultan, **Qansuh al-Ghuri**. Sixty years old when he took power in 1500, Al-Ghuri loved perfume, flowers, playing polo, writing poetry and discoursing with Sufis – none of which equipped him to deal with the warlike Ottoman Turks, who signalled their intent by stripping his ambassador naked and forcing him to carry a bucket of manure on his head. In 1516 Al-Ghuri perished in battle in Syria, his intended tomb being occupied by his luckless successor Tumanbay, who was swiftly defeated by the Ottoman ruler Selim the Grim – bringing three centuries of Mamluke rule over Egypt to an inglorious end.

Al-Ghuri's legacy was a monumental ensemble instantly recognisable by its striped facades – a decorative motif termed *ablaq*, which is one of the hallmarks of latter-day Mamluke architecture. Nearest to Al-Azhar is the **Wikala of Al-Ghuri** (daily 8am–5pm; £E15), the finest example of the merchants' hostels that once characterised Cairo's bazaars. It was built in 1505, just as the Europeans' new sea route round the Cape to the East Indies was diminishing Cairo's role as a spice entrepôt. With its stables and lock-ups beneath tiers of spartan rooms, the *wikala* is uncompromisingly functional, yet the rhythm of *ablaq* arches muted by the sharp verticals of shutters, and the severe masonry lightened by *mashrabiyas* and a graceful fountain, achieves elegance. On Wednesday and Saturday evenings, it is the venue for a free, spectacular performance of Sufi **dervish dancing** (see p.206), which you shouldn't miss if you are in town. Located on a side street off Sharia al-Azhar, the *wikala* can be reached by turning left on leaving the Mosque of Al-Azhar, then following the alley round past a market.

Just to its west, the **Al-Ghuri Palace** is now used to host occasional concerts (details from the *wikala*), and stands beside **Al-Ghuri's Mausoleum** (daily 9am–5pm; £E25). This forms one half of a set-piece pair of buildings flanking Sharia al-Muizz where it meets Sharia al-Azhar, opposite a pedestrian overpass that crosses al-Azhar. Visitors can (for a little baksheesh to the caretaker) descend into a dank medieval cistern beneath the mausoleum, and climb to the mausoleum's roof to admire the view. From here, you can see the lofty wooden roof that shades the narrow **lane** between Al-Ghuri's mausoleum and mosque-*madrassa*. This formerly hosted the **Silk Bazaar**, where fine carpets were sold – the subject of a famous drawing by the Scottish artist David Roberts (of which prints and postcards are often sold in souvenir shops).

Boldly striped in buff and white across the street, the **Mosque-Madrassa of Al-Ghuri** has a lofty stalactite portal, leading to the tomb of his successor Tumanbay, who was executed by the Ottomans not far away. Its rooftop offers glimpses of the Spice Bazaar and a grand view of the neighbourhood – the door is diagonally opposite the entrance to the main part of the mosque, but you may have to ask a custodian for access.

On to Bab Zwayla

Some 200m south of the Ghuriya, the arabesque-panelled doors of the "Fruit Seller", or **Fakahani Mosque**, are all that remains of the twelfth-century original after its reconstruction in 1735. Nearby, down a side street, the **House of Gamal al-Din al-Dahabi** at 6 Haret Hosh Qadam was the home of seventeenth-century Cairo's foremost gold merchant. Though not open at the time of writing, it's worth checking whether its magnificent interior is now accessible to visitors. A spit-and-sawdust *'ahwa* opposite the western end of Haret Hosh Qadam offers a surprisingly good *'ahwa mahawega* (Turkish coffee with cardamom) for those who need a little break or a pick-me-up at this point.

South of the Fakahani Mosque, Sharia al-Muizz curves around the Rococo facade of the **Sabil-Kuttab of Tusun Pasha** (daily 10am–8pm, but often closed for no apparent reason; £E20), adorned with wrought-iron sunbursts, garlands and fronds, typical of 1820s' architecture. Unlike most of Cairo's *sabil-kuttabs* (see p.83), which have the *sabil* (public fountain) downstairs and the *kuttab* (school) upstairs, the schoolrooms here are on either side of the domed *kuttab*. Explanatory displays tell you about the building and Tusun Pasha, an upholder of tolerant Islam against the puritanical Wahhabist movement, whose ally, Ibn Saud, established today's oil-rich kingdom of Saudi Arabia.

The Mosque of al-Muayyad (Red Mosque) and around

From the Sabil-Kuttab of Tusun Pasha, the view southwards is dominated by the formidable outline of Bab Zwayla, whose twin towers are actually the minarets of the **Mosque of al-Muayyad**. Also called the "**Red Mosque**" for the colour of its exterior, it occupies the site of a prison where its founder, who was sultan from

1412 to 1421, had previously been incarcerated for plotting against Sultan Barquq. Plagued by lice and fleas, he vowed to transform it once he came to power into a "saintly place for the education of scholars". You enter via a nine-tiered stalactite portal with a red-and-turquoise geometric frame around its bronze door. From here a vestibule leads to a mausoleum, where Al-Muayyad is buried, together with his son. Beneath the roofed section of the courtyard, a carpeted sanctuary precedes the *qibla* (Mecca-facing) wall, where the prayer niche marking the direction of Mecca is located, patterned with polychrome marble and blue ceramic tiles.

Across the street from the Red Mosque, an unobtrusive door beside a jewellers' shop (no.7) fronts the eighteenth-century **Hammam al-Sukariya**, one of two former bathhouses in the vicinity of Bab Zwayla, whose boilers also once served to cook fava beans for the neighbourhood's breakfast. Like the now-derelict **Hammam al-Muayyad** behind the mosque, it once doubled as a gay brothel where, as the French novelist Gustav Flaubert described in 1839, "You reserve the bath for yourself (five francs including masseurs, pipe, coffee, sheet and towel) and you skewer your lad in one of the rooms."

This unsavoury reputation led to the baths' decline and eventual closure, but there is vague talk of restoring them in the future. Such restoration has already been carried out in the eighteenth-century **Sabil-Kuttab of Nafisa al-Bayda**, on the next corner south from the Hammam Al-Muayyad. The *sabil-kuttab* is open to the public (daily 8am–6pm; £E8; tickets sold at Bab Zwayla), though its interior is nothing special. At the end of the lane beside it stands a section of the **Fatimid city walls**.

Bab Zwayla

Islamic Cairo's walls embodied the vigour of dynasties. In 1068, Al-Qahira briefly fell to the Seljuk Turks, before being recaptured for the Fatimids by the Armenian-born general Al-Gyushi. Eleven years later, the Fatimid vizier Al-Gamali oversaw the replacement of the original mud-brick walls with stone ramparts designed by Christian architects from Anatolia and Mesopotamia. An attack from the north seemed likeliest, so the main south gate was left until 1092. Known as **Bab Zwayla** after mercenaries of the Berber al-Zwayla tribe quartered nearby, this imposing gateway lost its military function in the Mamluke city, which had outgrown the Fatimid walls and pushed up against Saladin's extensions – becoming the city's central point rather than its southern extremity – although the practice of barring the gates each night continued well into the nineteenth century. The tall minarets of Al-Muayyad's Mosque (built on top of the gate in the fifteenth century) make it a hugely impressive structure. Its full awesomeness is best seen from the south side.

For centuries Bab Zwayla was the point of departure for caravans to Mecca and the source of drum rolls greeting the arrival of Mamluke generals (titled "Amirs of One Hundred"). Besides dancers and snake charmers, punishments were another spectacle: dishonest merchants were hung from hooks; common criminals were garrotted, beheaded or impaled; losers in the Mamluke power struggles were nailed to the doors. It was here that Tumanbay, the last Mamluke sultan, was hanged by the Ottomans in 1517. Bab Zwayla's reputation was subsequently redeemed by its association with Mitwalli al-Qutb, a miracle-working local saint said to manifest himself to the faithful as a gleam of light within the gatehouse.

The **western gatetower**, its **bastion** and the **minarets** are open to the public (daily 8.30am–5pm; £15) and can be visited via a door just next to the Al-Muayyad Mosque. Finds from the site are on display, as well as offerings left by local residents for Mitwalli al-Qutb. You can climb to the top of the minarets for amazing **views** over Islamic Cairo and the Al-Muayyad and Salih Tala'i mosques directly below. Note the **barbells** high up on the outside of the western gatetower, used by medieval strongmen to show off their muscle power.

Beyond the gate

Passing through Bab Zwayla, you can continue south along Sharia al-Muizz (see pp.95–96), take a left along Sharia Darb al-Ahmar (see pp.96–98), or take a right along **Sharia Ahmed Maher** towards the **Museum of Islamic Art** (see below) and on to Abdin (see p.71). On the way, you'll pass a nineteenth-century *sabil-kuttab* and a fifteenth-century mosque. Named after a Wafdist prime minister assassinated by a nationalist lawyer in 1944, Sharia Ahmed Maher is notable for its stalls selling camel saddles and whips, *sheeshas* and braziers, and for a traditional apothecary 60m along on the right-hand side (see p.223). Minibuses #68 and #75 run to the museum, but it's usually quicker to walk (about ten minutes). The neighbourhood between Bab Zwayla and Abdin is known as **Bab al-Khalq** after a long-since-vanished medieval gate.

The Museum of Islamic Art

The medieval and modern cities merge at **Midan Bab el-Khalq**, the junction of Sharia Ahmed Maher, Sharia Bur Said and Sharia Qalaa, 600m west of Bab Zwayla. **Sharia Qalaa** ("Citadel Road") was constructed in the nineteenth century on the orders of Khedive Ismail, who demanded that a carriageway (originally called Boulevard Mohammed Ali) be ploughed through centuries-old neighbourhoods to link Midan Ataba with the Citadel. Ismail cared nothing for the "native quarters" demolished to make way for his European-style boulevard. "Do we need so many monuments?" his Minister of Public works asked rhetorically. "Isn't it enough to preserve a sample?" Alas, the new road didn't live up to Ismail's hopes of Continental sophistication, and was soon rife with cafés catering to soldiers with Gypsy dancers, whores and rotgut brandy. It was at this junction that it crossed the **canal** that snaked from the Nile northwards and along the western side of the old Fatimid city. Fetid and half-choked, the canal was eventually filled in to create Sharia Bur Said in 1899.

That same year, the foundations were laid for today's **Museum of Islamic Art** and **National Library** – the two sharing a neo-Mamluke edifice by Italian architect Alfonso Manescalo. The museum's origins go back to 1880, when Khedive Tewfik supported the creation of a Museum of Arab Art in Al-Hakim's mosque; consisting initially of 111 architectural pieces taken from decaying mosques and mansions, its collection grew rapidly under the direction of Max Hertz, a Hungarian historian, assisted by the English scholar K.A.C Cresswell.

Though **closed** for renovation at the time of writing, the museum is set to reopen in 2011. It's a good idea to visit while exploring Islamic Cairo, as the architecture there lends meaning to the exhibits in the museum, and you can compare the quality of crafts here with what's on sale in Khan al-Khalili (where traditional designs are still used but inferior materials and workmanship are common). If past opening times are anything to go by, the museum will be **open** daily, but closed during the noon prayer on Fridays.

The collection

The museum now has 102,000 artefacts, including glassware, jewellery, ceramics and architectural ornaments. Originating from Egypt and elsewhere in the Islamic world, they span all the major periods of Islamic history, from the early caliphates of the Mayyads, who ruled from Damascus (661–750 AD), and the Abbasids, who presided over the Arab empire from Baghdad (750–1258), as well as Egyptian dynasties such as the Tulunids (868–905 AD), the Fatimids (969–1171), the Ayyubids (1171–1250) and the Mamlukes (1250–1517), down to the Ottoman Empire, which supplanted the caliphates and ruled Egypt from 1517 until its khedives (viceroys) established their de facto independence in 1805.

Exhibits were previously grouped by crafts rather than chronologically, with dates given in years AH, *Anno Hegirae* (the Hegira being Mohammed's flight from Mecca in 622AD, the starting point of the Islamic era). As its **layout** may be very different when the museum reopens, we can only sketch some highlights. Because Sunni theologians extended the Koranic strictures against idolatry to any images of humans or animals, these are largely absent. Instead of paintings and sculptures, there are exquisite designs based on geometry, Islamic symbolism, plant motifs and Arabic calligraphy – a very different aesthetic.

Early Islamic (caliphate) period

Despite the taboo on images of people and animals, a **fresco** from Fustat depicting people and animals suggests that the taboo against representations of either was not yet established at this stage, while a wealth of **ceramics** (including tiles from Tunisia, Andalusia, Italy and Holland) attests to the extent of Fustat's foreign trade.

Treasures from the Umayyad caliphate include a **bronze ewer** with a spout in the form of a crowing cockerel, which probably belonged to the last Umayyad caliph, Marwan II; slain near Abu Sir, south of Cairo, his death heralded the start of Abbasid rule.

Some **friezes** from the Mosque of Ibn Tulun are all there is to show for the wealth of Al-Qitai and the Tulunids (see box, p.106), and even the **Fatimids** who founded the medieval city have left less behind than you might imagine. Some **panels** from their Western Palace on Bayn al-Qasrayn (see p.80), the bronze-inlaid **doors** of mosques of Al-Azhar (p.88) and Salih Tala'i (p.94), and two exquisitely inlaid, portable wooden **mihrabs** from the shrines of Saiyida Nafisa and Saiyida Ruqqaya (p.109), are the most notable objects.

Fatimid and Mamluke periods

The Fatimid art of combining different woods and coloured marbles in complex geometric patterns continued under the **Mamlukes** – evinced by a superb **fountain** from a fourteenth-century courtyard, and a **minbar** (pulpit) from the *madrassa-mausoleum* of a Tartar. Through till late Ottoman times, craftsmen created superb **interiors** combining woodwork, tiles and moulded stucco: a blue-tiled **Turkish fireplace**, and a section of a *kuttab* (Koranic school) from the Delta town of Rosetta incorporating a niche for the teacher to sit beneath its *muqarnas* (stalactite-honeycomb) ceiling, are choice examples.

Metalwork of all kinds reached its zenith under the Mamlukes, from such extravagant pieces of furniture as Sultan Al-Nasir's bronze, gold- and silver- encrusted dining table, down to a charming figurine on a horse in a "Look, no hands" pose. Although most of the Mamluke arsenal of richly-decorated weapons was carted off by Selim the Grim, the museum boasts the swords of the Ottoman sultans Mehmet II and Suleyman the Magnificent, the respective conquerors of Constantinople and the Balkans. The other great Mamluke art form was **glassware** – enamelled vases, jugs, and the ornate lamps hung from chains in every mosque.

The value placed on piety and scholarship made **books and manuscripts** another form of one-upmanship among sultans and amirs: a single illuminated Koran might cost more than the mosque that housed it. The museum's collection includes medical treatises by Ibn Sina (aka Avicenna) and Maimonides (see p.80), and medieval Korans collected by King Farouk. A display of gold dinars (roughly equal to a Venetian ducat), silver dirhams and bronze **coins** (accepted in

China, India and Europe) attests to the commerce and trade that underpinned the Mamlukes' wealth and ostentation.

② Bab Zwayla to the Citadel

After Saladin and his Ayyubid successors established the Citadel beyond the Fatimid city's southern gates, the empty land between them became an ever-growing residential zone. Under the Mamlukes, who succeeded the Ayyubids, this evolved into a maze of tenement blocks (*rab*) up to ten storeys high, looming above narrow lanes thronged with people. A single *rab* might house hundreds or even thousands; tightly packed and leaning together, they rendered alleys dark enough for bats to fly in daytime. The *hara*, or alley, was the basic unit of society: each locked itself away behind gates at night. As buildings fell into ruin and rubbish accumulated, alleys became cut off, hastening their decline into *kharab* or derelict quarters, whose masonry and timber were salvaged to build anew in a cycle of decay and renewal that continues to this day. You'll see evidence of this whichever of the two main routes you take **from Bab Zwayla to the Citadel**. One route goes via the **Qasaba**, Sharia al-Muizz and Sharia Qalaa; the other follows **Sharia Darb al-Ahmar**, after which this quarter of Islamic Cairo is named. It's possible to get the best of both worlds by combining the Darb al-Ahmar with a detour into the Qasaba and **Saddlemakers' Bazaar**, located on the other route, a total distance of about 1.5km. If you're starting from Bab Zwayla, it's logical to visit the Qasaba before embarking on the Darb al-Ahmar – whereas the reverse is true if you're coming from the Citadel, in which case you'll want to start with the "Blue Mosque" of Aqsunqur on Sharia Bab al-Wazir and backtrack through the text from there.

The Qasaba and around

Directly across the street from Bab Zwayla, Sharia al-Muizz continues southward, framed by two monuments. On its east side (to your left if heading south along al-Muizz), the **Mosque of Salih Tala'i** withdraws behind an elegant portico with five keel arches – a unique architectural feature. The last of Cairo's Fatimid mosques, the building shows assured use of the motifs that were first employed on the Al-Aqmar Mosque (see p.83): ribbed and cusped arches and panels, carved tie beams and rosettes. Around its base are shops (now restored, but as yet unoccupied); the rents from these contributed to the mosque's upkeep. Originally the shops were at street level, but this has risen well over a metre since the mosque was built in 1160.

Opposite, on the west side of al-Muizz, stands the **Zawiya of Farag ibn Barquq**, a *zawiya* being a residence for Sufi dervishes who belong to a brotherhood where they all follow a particular sheikh's *tariqa* (path). These Sufi brotherhoods were a conspicuous feature of Cairo until the 1940s when the British curtailed them for fear of public disorder, though they still flourish today. The Zawiya of Farag ibn Barquq is an early fifteenth-century Mamluke edifice whose lintels and *ablaq* panels have been restored to their original splendour.

Between the Mosque of Salih Tala'i and the Zawiya of Farag ibn Barquq, Sharia al-Muizz enters the evocatively-named **Qasaba**, meaning "throat" or "funnel". A lofty, shadowy roofed passageway commissioned in 1650 by Ridwan Bey, the Qasaba is the best-preserved example of a covered market left in Cairo. Colourful fabrics, appliqué and leatherwork are piled in dens, collectively known as the Khiyamiyya, or **Tentmakers' Bazaar**, after the printed fabrics used to make tents for moulids, weddings and funerals.

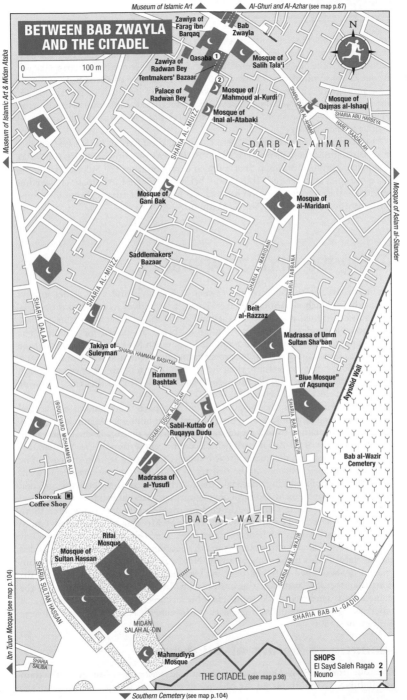

BETWEEN BAB ZWAYLA AND THE CITADEL

Museum of Islamic Art ▲   ▲ Al-Ghuri and Al-Azhar (see map p.87)

N

0   100 m

ISLAMIC CAIRO

Museum of Islamic Art & Midan Ataba ◄

Zawiya of
Farag ibn
Barqaq

Bab
Zwayla

Qasaba ①

Zawiya of
Radwan Bey   Tentmakers' Bazaar

Mosque of
Salih Tala'i

②

Palace of
Radwan Bey

Mosque of
Mahmoud al-Kurdi

Mosque of
Qajmas al-Ishaqi

SHARIA ABU HARBEYA

HARET SAKDALLAH

Mosque of
Inal al-Atabaki

SHARIA DARB AL-AHMAR

DARB AL-AHMAR

Mosque of
Gani Bak

Mosque of
al-Maridani

► Mosque of Aslam al-Silander

SHARIA AL-MUIZZ

Saddlemakers'
Bazaar

SHARIA AL-MUIZZ

SHARIA QALAA

SHARIA AL-MARIDANI

SHARIA TABBANA

Beit
al-Razzaz

Takiya of
Suleyman

SHARIA HAMMAM BASHTAK

Madrassa of Umm
Sultan Sha'ban

Ayyubid Wall

Hammm
Bashtak

(BOULEVARD MOHAMMED ALI)

SHARIA SOUK AL-SILAH

"Blue Mosque"
of Aqsunqur

SHARIA BAB AL-WAZIR

Sabil-Kuttab of
Ruqayya Dudu

Bab-al-Wazir
Cemetery

Madrassa of
al-Yusufi

Shorouk ■
Coffee Shop

BAB AL - WAZIR

Ibn Tulun Mosque (see map p.104) ◄

Rifai
Mosque

Mosque of
Sultan Hassan

SHARIA SULTAN HASSAN

SHARIA BAB AL-WAZIR

SHARIA BAB AL-GADID

SHARIA SALIBA

MIDAN
SALAH AL-DIN

Mahmudiyya
Mosque

THE CITADEL (see map p.98)

SHOPS	
El Sayd Saleh Ragab	2
Nouno	1

95

▼ Southern Cemetery (see map p.104)

South of the Qasaba

Emerging from the far end of the Qasaba, Sharia al-Muizz carries on past two mosques and the façade of Ridwan Bey's former palace. Beyond this, the monuments thin out as vegetable stalls and butchers congest the narrow street. About 150m south of the Qasaba you'll pass the **Mosque of Gani Bak**, endowed by a protégé of Sultan Barsbey, who was poisoned by rivals at the age of 25. Beyond, a few stalls selling donkey- and camel-wear constitute what remains of the Souk es-Surugiyyah, or **Saddlemakers' Bazaar**, formerly the centre of Cairo's leather industry.

Assuming you don't turn back here to pursue the Darb al-Ahmar (see below), it's a fairly mundane 350-metre walk to Al-Muizz's junction with **Sharia Qalaa** (see p.76). Turning left down Sharia Qaloa here, you'll see the Sultan Hassan and Rifai mosques at its far end, 300m away below the Citadel. Alternatively, use bus services in the opposite direction to reach the Museum of Islamic Art (p.92); some buses continue on to Midan Ataba, Abdin or Al-Azhar.

Along the Darb al-Ahmar

An alternative, more scenic route between Bab Zwayla and the Citadel follows the medieval **Darb al-Ahmar**, or Red Road, which gives its name to the neighbourhood. Originally a cemetery beyond the Fatimid city walls, this became a fashionable residential area after Sultan Al-Nasir developed the Citadel. The thoroughfare acquired its present name in 1805, when Mohammed Ali tricked the Mamlukes into staging a coup before slaughtering them; the street ran red with their blood. Stuffed with straw, their heads were sent to Constantinople as a sign of his power; six years later the surviving Mamlukes fell for another ruse, and were massacred in the Citadel (see p.100).

Since Ottoman times the neighbourhood has been poor and down-at-heel (notwithstanding local residents digging beneath their homes for Mamluke treasure), but it is now benefiting from a **regeneration** project by the Aga Khan Trust, tied in with the creation of Al-Azhar Park (p.112) and the excavation of the Ayyubid city wall which runs along the quarter's eastern edge, separating it from the park. The project has enabled residents of the quarter to study tile-making, *mashrabiya*-work and other crafts, producing materials for refurbishing historic buildings so that conservation, employment and local development go hand in hand.

If you head east along Derb al-Ahmar from Bab Zwayla, you come after 150m to a corner where the Darb turns south. Here the **Mosque of Qajmas al-Ishaqi** looms over workshops sunk beneath street level. A marble panel with swirling leaf forms in red, black and white surmounts the entrance to a vestibule with a gilded ceiling; left off this is the mosque itself. Notice the *mihrab*'s sinuous decorations (incised grooves filled with red paste or bitumen) and the fine panelling on the floor near the *qibla* wall (ask the custodian to lift the mat). Best of all are the stained-glass windows in the tomb chamber occupied by one Abu Hurayba. A raised passage connects the mosque with a *sabil-kuttab* across the street; both were built in the 1480s.

Mosque of Aslam al-Silahdar

A detour from Darb al-Ahmar at this point leads east to the **Mosque of Aslam al-Silahdar**. To find this from the Mosque of Qajmas al-Ishaqi, walk through the tunnel on its north side and on past a shrine, where the street forks (bear right); al-Silahdar's Mosque lies 250m ahead. The marble panel outside is typical of exterior decoration during the Bahri Mamluke period; inside, the layout is that of a cruciform **madrassa**. Students used to live in rooms above the north and south *liwans*, behind an ornate facade of stucco mouldings and screened windows. The mosque is named after its founder, a Qipchak Mamluke who lost his position at court after Sultan al-Nasir believed rumours spread by his enemies and imprisoned him, only to reinstate him as *silahdar* (Swordbearer) six years later.

To return to the Darb, either retrace your steps or take the street running southwest off the square, which joins the Darb further south, beyond al-Maridani's Mosque.

Mosque of al-Maridani and around

South from the Qajmas Mosque, the Darb al-Ahmar passes the **Mosque of al-Maridani**, built in 1340 and still a peaceful retreat from the streets. The mosque is usually entered via its northern portal, offset by a stalactite frieze with complex patterns of interlocking wedges and *ablaq* panels. Inside, a splendid *mashrabiya* screen separates the open courtyard from the prayer hall with its stained-glass windows and variegated columns (Mamluke, pre-Islamic and pharaonic). Architecturally, the minaret is the earliest example in Cairo of a minaret topped by a small dome on pillars. This became the hallmark of Mamluke minarets, replacing the "pepper-pot" finial typical of mosques built under the Ayyubids.

Leaving via the southern entrance, you'll need to turn left to rejoin the Darb – or **Sharia Tabbana** as it's called at this point. Roughly 200m on, past a small Turkish mosque, stands the hulking **Madrassa of Umm Sultan Sha'ban**. Umm Sha'ban was the concubine of a son of Al-Nasir, whose own son had the *madrassa* erected (1368–69) as a gesture of gratitude after he became sultan at the age of 10. Murdered in 1376, he preceded his mother to the grave and was buried here as his own *madrassa* was unfinished. A wealth of *muqarnas* and *ablaq* rim the entrance, which is flanked by a *sabil* and a drinking trough for animals.

Behind the mosque, and entered through the doorway just to the left of its entrance, the **Beit al-Razzaz** (daily except Fri, 9am–5pm) is a rambling palace, recently restored. When you go in, the caretaker will probably appear and offer to show you around the upper rooms, with their *mashrabiya* screens, painted ceilings and stained-glass windows, for which of course he will expect a tip.

The Blue Mosque

Further south along the Darb al-Ahmar, now called **Sharia Bab al-Wazir** after the Gate of the Vizier that once stood here, is the **"Blue Mosque"** or **Mosque of Aqsunqur**, which was closed (again) for restoration on our last check. When built in 1347, the mosque was plainer: the Iznik-style tiles (imported from Turkey or Syria) were added in the 1650s by Ibrahim Agha. The pretty indigo and turquoise tiles on the *qibla* wall – with cypresses, tulips and other floral motifs either side of the magnificently inlaid *mihrab* – were added at the same time. Along with similar tiles around Ibrahim Agha's tomb (probably made in Damascus), they explain the mosque's name and its popularity with tourists. The circular minaret affords a superb **view** of the Citadel – on a clear day you can even make out the Giza Pyramids.

The mosque's founder, Shams al-Din Aqsunqur, intrigued against the successors of Sultan al-Nasir, his father-in-law, pitting al-Nasir's eight sons against each other to manipulate them. One, Al-Ashraf Kuchuk, was enthroned at the age of 6, "reigned" five months, and was strangled three years later when his brother Al-Kamil Sha'ban seized the throne (Al-Ashraf Kuchuk's tomb is just inside the mosque's entrance). The following year, Al-Kamil Sha'ban's brother-in-law Muzaffar Haji overthrew him, and promptly had the scheming Aqsunqur garrotted.

Sharia Souk al-Silah

A couple of hundred metres west of the Blue Mosque, the **Hammam Bashtak** was once a bathhouse serving the Darb al-Ahmar quarter, many of whose tenements lack washing facilities; like most such old *hammams*, it's now closed. Its elaborate portal is worth a second glance, however, the ribbed keel arch bearing the napkin motif of a *jamdar* or Master of Robes. From here, **Sharia Souk al-Silah** (formerly the Weapons Bazaar, now largely a secondhand ball-bearings market) leads 300m south to the Citadel past the now derelict Ottoman **Sabil-Kuttab of Ruqayya Dudu** at no. 41, and the 1373 **Madrassa of al-Yusufi**, whose founder was a Cupbearer, as shown by the goblet motif in the inscription above the door.

The Citadel and around

Alongside Khan al-Khalili, the **Citadel** is the natural focus of a visit to Islamic Cairo; magnificent in itself, the area just below it, around Midan Salah al-Din, features two of the city's greatest monuments – the **Sultan Hassan** and **Rifai**

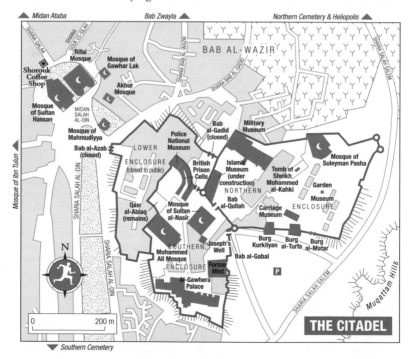

Mamluke culture

Egypt's **Mamlukes** – a caste of soldiers who were originally slaves but became so strong that they eventually took over the state – resembled Japan's Samurai in their taste for poetry, calligraphy and other refined pleasures, perhaps as an antidote to the brutal obligations of their profession. Captured, purchased or voluntarily recruited as teenagers, they had to abjure all ties to their families and homelands for sole **allegiance** to the sultan on the principle that "A Son dreams of his Father's demise; a Slave wishes only long life for his Master", and undergo exhaustive training by instructors who ruthlessly weeded-out rejects.

Mamlukes had to participate in **sports** such as polo (played on the great *midans* that were a feature of Islamic Cairo from the tenth century onwards) and *qabaq* (mounted archery), reflecting their origins among the Mongol or Turkic tribes of Central Asia and the Caucasus. Promotion to positions such as the sultan's Cupbearer (*Saqi*, responsible for his drinks and table, whose symbol was a goblet), Swordbearer (*Silahdar*, represented by a scimitar), Polo Master (*Jukandar*) and Chief Steward or Master of Robes (*Ustadar* or *Jamdar*, symbolized by a diamond-shaped napkin) were the outward manifestations of the ferocious struggle for power within the hierarchy between rival Mamluk amirs (army generals) jostling for position as would-be sultans.

Mamluke military innovations transformed warfare and were widely copied. Stirrups enabled riders to fire from the saddle using re-curved bows; the crossbow gave footmen armour-piercing firepower; mangonels and fire-missiles transformed siege warfare. (A gigantic catapult, "Mansour the Victorious", was credited with the capture of the Crusader fortress of Acre in 1291.) Much of the **pageantry** associated with medieval Europe had its origins in the Muslim world: drum-rolls, jousts and such **heraldic signs** as the *fleur-de lis*, the double-headed eagle and the lion rampant (copied from Beybars, meaning "Lord Lion" in Turkish). Even the pastime of **playing cards** came from the Mamlukes, whose insignia or titles gave rise to the suits of hearts (originally the *Saqi*'s cup), spades (originally the *Silahdar*'s sword), clubs (originally the *Jukandar*'s polo mallet) and diamonds (origi- nally the *Jamdar*'s napkin); the jack, formerly known as a knave, was originally a *Na'ib* or governor.

mosques. You need a good half a day to do justice to these, and to the Citadel itself. Depending on how much time you have, you may want to visit only the Citadel, but it is well worth stopping in **Midan Salah al-Din** to take in the arresting mix of sounds, and the views (see p.102).

Most Cairenes will assume, if you ask for the Citadel (Al-Qalaa – usually pronounced "al-'alaa"), that you want to go to Midan Salah al-Din, the large square immediately beneath it. Midan Salah al-Din can be reached from downtown by taxi (£E5–8) or by bus (see p.29 for routes); if you've got the energy, it's also an interesting walk. To actually go inside the citadel, however, you'll need to go to the **entrance** at Bab al-Gabal, which is on the Citadel's east side, on Sharia Salah Salem, nearly a kilometre by road from Midan Salah al-Din. The Bab al-Gabal entrance is served by bus #951 or minibus #105 from Abdel Mouneem Riyad terminal near Midan Tahrir, and by service-taxi microbuses from Ramses and Ataba along Sharia Salah Selim.

Heading onward from the Citadel, you could continue north from the entrance along Sharia Salah Salim to Al-Azhar Park and the Northern Cemetery (see pp.110–113), or, from Midan Salah al-Din, you could head north up Sharia al-Muizz or Sharia Darb al-Ahmar (covered in the opposite direction on pp.94–98), or west along Sharia Saliba past the Mosque of Ibn Tulun (see pp.105–107).

The Citadel

The Citadel (daily 8am–5pm; mosques closed Fri except for prayer; last entry to museums 30min before closing; £E50) presents the most dramatic feature of Cairo's skyline: a centuries-old bastion crowned by the needle-like minarets of the great Mosque of Mohammed Ali.

The whole fortified complex was begun by **Salah al-Din al-Ayyubi**, the founder of the Ayyubid dynasty – known in English as Saladin, the Crusaders' chivalrous foe. Saladin's reign (1171–93) saw much fortification of the city, though it was his nephew, Al-Kamil, who developed the Citadel as a royal residence, later to be replaced by the palaces of Sultan Al-Nasir.

The main features of the Citadel as it is today, however, are associated with **Mohammed Ali**, a worthy successor to the Mamlukes and Turks. In 1811 he feasted 470 leading Mamlukes in the Citadel palace and bade them farewell with honours, but as they rode down the narrow lane towards **Bab al-Azab**, his Albanian troops opened fire on the trapped procession. An oil painting in the Manial Palace on Roda Island (see p.130) depicts the apocryphal tale of a Mamluke who escaped by leaping the walls on his horse; in reality he survived by not attending the feast and fleeing to hide out in Upper Egypt.

On entering the Citadel, keep the wall to your right and follow it round into the southern courtyard of the **Southern Enclosure**, largely surrounded by the Al-Gawhara Palace (which is entered from the terrace to its north; see below). Also here is the former **Mint**, currently closed to the public. A passage from the courtyard's north side leads through to the Southern Enclosure's central courtyard, where you'll find the Mosque of Sultan al-Nasir (see below); to the left of this passage, stairs lead up to the back of the Citadel's most dominant structure, the great Mosque of Mohammed Ali.

Mohammed Ali's monuments

The **Mosque of Mohammed Ali**, which so ennobles Cairo's skyline, disappoints at close quarters: its domes are sheathed in tin, its alabaster surfaces grubby. Nonetheless, it exudes *folie de grandeur*, starting with the ornate clock given by France's king Louis Philippe (in exchange for the obelisk that now stands in the Place de la Concorde, Paris), which has never worked; and the Turkish Baroque ablutions fountain, resembling a giant Easter egg. Inside the mosque, whose lofty dome and semi-domes are decorated like a Fabergé egg, the use of space is classically Ottoman, reminiscent of the great mosques of Istanbul. A constellation of chandeliers and globe lamps illuminates Thuluth inscriptions, a gold-scalloped *mihrab* and two *minbars*, one faced in alabaster, the other strangely Art Nouveau. Mohammed Ali is buried beneath a white marble cenotaph, behind a bronze grille on the right of the entrance. The mosque itself was erected between 1824 and 1848, but the domes had to be demolished and rebuilt in the 1930s.

Due south of Mohammed Ali's Mosque is the entrance to what remains of his **Al-Gawhara Palace**, also known as the Bijou ("Jewelled") Palace, where he waited while the Mamlukes were butchered. Its French-style salons contain a dusty display of nineteenth-century dress, royal furniture and tableware.

Medieval remains

For an idea of the Citadel's appearance before Mohammed Ali's grandiose reconstruction programme, descend from the Mohammed Ali Mosque's front entrance into the Citadel's central courtyard. On your right, at the end of the passage from the southern courtyard, is the **Mosque of Sultan al-Nasir** (also called the Mosque of Ibn Qalaoun, after Al-Nasir's father).

The Mamlukes and the Mongols who controlled Iran enjoyed excellent relations when the mosque was constructed (1318–35), and this would appear to be reflected in the mosque's architecture: it was probably a Persian master mason from Tabriz who designed the corkscrew minarets with their bulbous finials and faïence decorations, if not the dome, which also smacks of Central Asia. Selim the Grim carted its marble panelling back to Turkey following Cairo's 1517 fall to the Ottomans, leaving the mosque's courtyard looking ruggedly austere, with rough-hewn pillars supporting *ablaq* arches linked by Fatimid-style tie-beams – although the *mihrab* itself is a feast of gold and marble. Notice the stylized crenulations around the parapet, and the blue, white and silver decorations beneath the sanctuary *liwan*.

If you leave the mosque, turn right and walk clockwise around it, past one of Mohammed Ali's cannons; you can walk up a ramp to one of the Barbicans and along the adjoining rampart. Just below it (and now filled in) is **Joseph's Well**, dug by prisoners between 1176 and 1182. Dubbed "The Well of the Snail", it spiralled down 97m to the level of the Nile, whence water percolated through fissures in the bedrock. Its steps were strewn with soil to provide a footing for the donkeys that carried up water jars.

Police National Museum

On the northwestern side of the central enclosure, a gate leads through to another courtyard, at whose northern end is the **Police National Museum**. As you pass through the gateway, the door to your right (labelled "Citadel's Prison Museum") leads to **cells** that were used until the 1980s. Famous detainees included Anwar Sadat, arrested by the British for wartime espionage (see p.137), as well as Osama Bin Laden's mentor, Ayman al-Zawahiri. Although the cells are officially closed to the public, police at the entrance may offer to let you in for a look if you show an interest.

Taken clockwise, the **exhibition** rooms of the main hall begin with Ancient Egypt (antique weapons and an exposition of the conspiracy to kill Ramses III), moving on to the Islamic period (Ottoman swords, a cartoon of prisoners from Fatimid times, and a scale model of the 1952 Battle of Ismailiya that galvanized public opinion against the British occupation). A "Political Assassination" room illustrates three famous cases – including the 1944 murder of the British minister Lord Moyne by the Zionist Stern Gang in Zamalek – but omits President Sadat's assassination in 1981. The next room contains a killer's death mask and a forger's press, leading to the "Forgery and Counterfeiting" room, whose ancient coins and seals are all clever fakes.There is a superb **view** of the entire city from the terrace outside the Police Museum, where you'll also find toilets and a **café**. At the southern end, in a pit, are the excavated remains of the **Qasr al-Ablaq**, or Striped Palace of Sultan al-Nasir. Manipulative Mamluke amirs often put underage puppet sultans on the throne so as to rule indirectly in their names, and for many of the hapless boy-sultans, the palace amounted to a luxury prison, and finally an execution cell. Nevertheless, the Citadel remained the residence of Egypt's rulers for nearly 700 years. Mohammed Ali prophesied that his descendants would rule supreme as long as they resided here, and his grandson Ismail's move to the Abdin Palace did indeed foreshadow an inexorable decline in their power (see p.261).

The Northern Enclosure

Passing through Bab al-Qullah, you'll enter the Citadel's northern enclosure, where twelve thousand Mamlukes once lived in barracks. Straight ahead, beyond a parade of tanks from four Arab–Israeli Wars, is Mohammed Ali's old Harem Palace, now a **Military Museum** full of ceremonial accoutrements, with spectacular *trompe l'oeil* murals in the main salon. By turning right at the barracks near the enclosure entrance and following the lane around, you'll emerge into a formal garden or **"Garden Museum"**, decorated with assorted columns, gateways, and the top of a minaret from the mosque of Qaitbey al-Jatkasi.

To its south, the **Carriage Museum** boasts six royal carriages and two picnic buggies (one an infant prince's); the largest state carriage was a gift to Khedive Ismail by Napoleon and his wife, Empress Eugénie. You may also come upon a **statue of Soliman Pasha**, a French soldier of fortune (1788-1862), originally named Joseph Anthelme Sève, who converted to Islam and changed his name to Soliman, becoming Soliman (or Suleyman) Pasha when he took command of Mohammed Ali's artillery in 1833. Sculpted in Zouave uniform, it once stood at the junction of Soliman Pasha (now Talaat Harb) and Qasr al-Nil streets (see p.65), in the heart of downtown Cairo.

Behind the Carriage Museum, the bastions along the Citadel's ramparts carry evocative names. Although the derivation of **Burg Kirkilyan** (Tower of the Forty Serpents) is unknown, the **Burg al-Matar** (Tower of the Flight Platform, nowadays used to mean an airport flight tower) probably housed the royal carrier pigeons. Neither is open to the public.

It's worth visiting a neglected treasure at the other end of the compound, where a cluster of verdigris domes and a pencil-sharp minaret identify the **Mosque of Suleyman Pasha** as an early sixteenth-century Ottoman creation. This is confirmed by the lavish arabesques and rosettes adorning the interior of the cupola and semi-domes. Inside, cross the courtyard to find a **mausoleum** where the tombs of amirs and their families have *tabuts* indicating their rank: turbans or hats for the men, floral-patterned *lingam*-like rods for the women. Adjacent to the courtyard is a **madrassa** where students took examinations beneath a *riwaq* upheld by painted beams.

Midan Salah al-Din

Humdrum traffic islands and monumental grandeur meet beneath the Citadel on **Midan Salah al-Din**, originally an open ground for polo matches and parades, where – even after it was built-up – Cairenes continued to stage moulids (see p.215) in honour of local saints, erecting makeshift swings and colourful tents. The tents have a long pedigree: after capturing Cairo in 1517, the Ottomans set up three marquees here, to supply their troops with beer, hashish and young boys. Today, a bevy of small mosques around the square set the scene for a confrontation of its two behemoths, the **Rifai** and **Sultan Hassan mosques**, given voice five times daily when their full-throated *muezzins* call the faithful to prayer, their cacophonous duet echoing off the surrounding tenements. This amazing aural experience is best enjoyed from one of the seats on the pavement outside the *Shorouk* **coffee shop**, on the corner of Sharia Sultan Hassan and Sharia Qalaa; check prayer times in the newspapers or by asking around.

From this vantage point you can survey both mosques, built so close as to create a knife-sharp, almost perpetually shadowed canyon between them. The dramatic angles and chiaroscuro, coupled with the great stalactite portal on this side of the Rifai, make this facade truly spectacular, although the view from the Citadel itself takes some beating. Centuries ago, all this area would have been swarming with mounted Mamlukes, escorting the sultan to polo matches or prayers. During the festivities to mark the end of Ramadan, acrobats walked a tightrope stretched between the Citadel and Sultan Hassan's mosque.

The Mosque of Sultan Hassan

Raised at the command of a son of Al-Nasir, the **Mosque of Sultan Hassan** (daily except Fri 8am–4.30pm, Fri 8–10am & 3–4.30pm; tickets from a booth between the Sultan Hassan and Rifai mosques, £E25) was unprecedentedly huge in scale when it was begun in 1356, and some design flaws soon became apparent. The plan to have a minaret at each corner was abandoned after the one directly above the entrance collapsed, killing three hundred people. Hassan himself was assassinated in 1361, two years before the mosque's completion. Its roof was used as an artillery platform during coups against sultans Barquq (1391) and Tumanbay (1517), and after another minaret toppled in 1659, the weakened dome collapsed. But the mosque is big enough to withstand a lot of battering: at 150m in length, it covers an area of 7906 square metres, with walls rising to 36m and its tallest minaret to 68m.

The mosque is best seen when the morning sun illuminates its deep **courtyard** and cavernous mausoleum, revealing subtle colours and textures disguised by shadows later in the day. Entering beneath a towering stalactite hood, you're drawn by instinct through a gloomy domed vestibule, out into the central *sahn* – a stupendous balancing of mass and void. Vaulted *liwans* soar on four sides, their height emphasized by hanging lamp chains, their maws by red-and-black rims, all set off by a bulbous-domed ablutions fountain (probably an Ottoman addition). Each *liwan* was devoted to teaching a rite of Sunni Islam, providing theological justification for the cruciform plan the Mamlukes strove to achieve regardless of the site. At Sultan Hassan, four *madrassas* have been skilfully fitted into an irregular area behind the *liwans* to maintain the internal cruciform, together with six floors of lodgings for 500 students, 120 Koran readers and 51 prayer-callers.

Soft-hued marble inlay and a band of monumental Kufic script distinguish the sanctuary *liwan* from its roughly plastered neighbours. To the right of the *mihrab* is a bronze door, exquisitely worked with radiating stars and satellites in gold and silver; on the other side is **Hassan's mausoleum**, cleverly sited to receive homage and *baraka* from prayers to Mecca while overlooking his old stamping grounds. The mausoleum is sombre beneath its restored dome, upheld by stalactite pendentives. Around the chamber runs a carved and painted Thuluth inscription, from the Throne verse of the Koran. Note also the ivory-inlaid *kursi*, or Koranic lectern.

The Rifai and Amir Akhur mosques

Adjoining Sultan Hassan, the **Rifai Mosque** (daily except Fri 8am–4.30pm, Fri 8–10am & 3–4.30pm; tickets from the same booth as the Sultan Hassan Mosque, £E25) is pseudo-Mamluke, built between 1869 and 1912 for Princess Khushyar, the mother of Khedive Ismail. With the royal entrance now closed, you enter on the side facing Sultan Hassan. Straight ahead in a sandalwood enclosure lies the **tomb of Sheikh Ali al-Rifai**, founder of the Rifai *tariqa* of Sufi dervishes, whose moulid occurs during Gumad al-Tani (see p.216). Off to your left are the *mashrabiya*-screened **tombs of King Fouad** (reigned 1917–36), his mother, the last **Shah of Iran** and **King Farouk** of Egypt (who likewise died in exile).

Finally, facing the Citadel, you can't miss the **Mosque of Amir Akhur** (on the left), with its bold red-and-white *ablaq*, breast-like dome and double minaret finial, incorporating a *sabil-kuttab* at the lower end of its sloping site.

West to Saiyida Zeinab

Two aspects of Islam are strikingly apparent in the great **Mosque of Ibn Tulun** and the quarter of the city named after Egypt's beloved saint, **Saiyida Zeinab**. The mosque evokes the simplicity of Islam's central tenet, submission to Allah,

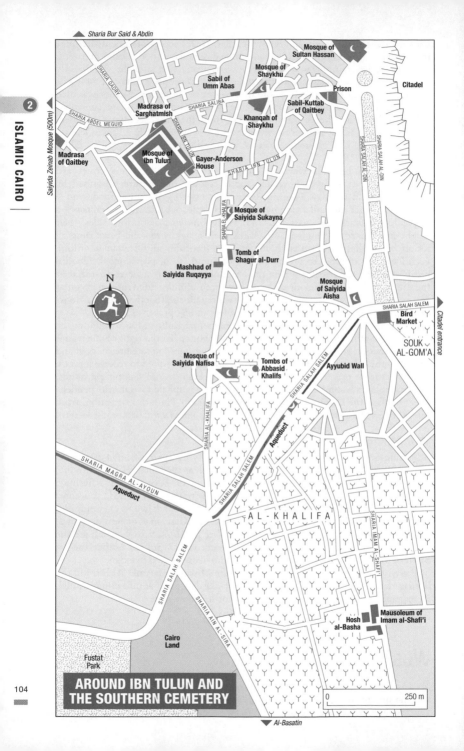

Sharia Bur Said & Abdin

Mosque of
Sultan Hassan

Mosque of
Shaykhu

Sabil of
Umm Abas

Prison

Citadel

SHARIA QADRY

SHARIA ABDEL MEGUID

Madrasa of
Sarghatmish

SHARIA SALIBA

Sabil-Kuttab
of Qaitbey

Khanqah of
Shaykhu

SHARIA SALAH AL-DIN

SHARIA SALAH AL-DIN

Madrasa
of Qaitbey

Mosque of
Ibn Tulun

Gayer-Anderson
House

SHARIA IBN TULUN

SHARIA IBN TULUN

JEBEL ENTULUN

Mosque of
Saiyida Sukayna

SHARIA EL-KHALIFA

Tomb of
Shagur al-Durr

Mashhad of
Saiyida Ruqayya

Mosque
of Saiyida
Aisha

SHARIA SALAH SALEM

N

Bird
Market

SOUK
AL-GOM'A

Citadel entrance

Mosque of
Saiyida Nafisa

Tombs of
Abbasid
Khalifs

SHARIA SALAH SALEM

Ayyubid Wall

SHARIA AL-KHALIFA

Aqueduct

SHARIA MAGRA AL-AYOUN

SHARIA SALAH SALEM

Aqueduct

AL-KHALIFA

SHARIA IMAM AL-SHAFI

SHARIA SALAH SALEM

SHARIA AIN AL-SIRA

Hosh
al-Basha

Mausoleum of
Imam al-Shafi'i

Cairo
Land

Fustat
Park

AROUND IBN TULUN AND
THE SOUTHERN CEMETERY

0   250 m

Al-Basatin

Saiyida Zeinab Mosque (500m)

whereas the surrounding neighbourhoods are urban stews seething with popular cults. **Zeinab's moulid**, which centres on the mosque, is the wildest festival in Cairo; its high-octane blend of intense devotion and sheer enjoyment is also characteristic of other **festivals** honouring Muslim "saints" whose shrines lie between Ibn Tulun and the Southern Cemetery (see pp.108–109).

The following section covers Ibn Tulun, Saiyida Zeinab and sites along Sharia Saliba – all of which could conceivably be visited in a single day. If you're not walking from Midan Salah al-Din, you can take the **metro** to Saiyida Zeinab station in the heart of the quarter, or get there by **bus** from central Cairo: #72// and #160/ **from Midan Tahrir** run through the quarter past its namesake shrine and within sight of Ibn Tulun's Mosque, towards the Citadel and on to the Mausoleum of Al-Shafi in the Southern Cemetery (see p.110). Alternatively, you can take bus #840 **from Midan Ataba**.

Sharia Saliba and around

The fifteen-minute walk from the Mosque of Sultan Hassan to Ibn Tulun takes you along **Sharia Saliba**, past a prison where inmates thrust their arms from the cell windows. Beyond stands the lofty **Sabil-Kuttab of Qaitbey**, with its bold red, white and black facade, now beautifully restored and housing an Islamic Civilization Library. Further along, beyond the **Khanqah of Shaykhu**, a Sufi hostel endowed by a kingmaking fourteenth-century amir, Sharia al-Khalifa turns off towards the Southern Cemetery (see p.108). By ignoring this and carrying on past the nineteenth-century **Sabil of Umm Abbas**, with its blue-and-red panels and gilt calligraphy, you'll see the huge walls of Ibn Tulun's Mosque on your left.

The entrance to the Mosque of Ibn Tulun (see below) is down Sharia Ibn Tulun. The portal on the main street (Sharia Salibba) belongs not to Ibn Tulun's Mosque but to the neighbouring **Madrassa of Sarghatmish**, built in 1356. Its courtyard, resplendent in white marble inlaid with red, black and green porphyry, is absolutely stunning, with a cool, light feel that makes a pleasant change from the rather heavy architecture of Cairo's classic mosques. It centres on a fountain surmounted with an *oba* (canopy), surrounded by the cell-like quarters formerly used by its students. A Mamluke commander assassinated on the orders of Sultan Hassan in 1358, Sarghatmish is interred in a chamber adjoining the courtyard.

The Mosque of Ibn Tulun

The Mosque of Ibn Tulun (daily 8am–4.30pm) is a rare survivor of the classical Islamic period of the ninth and tenth centuries, when the Abbasid caliphs ruled the Muslim world from Iraq. Their purpose-built capital, Samarra, centred upon a congregational mosque where the entire population assembled for Friday prayer, and this most likely provided the inspiration for the Ibn Tulun. You enter the mosque via a *ziyada*, or high-walled **enclosure**, that distances the mosque from its surroundings; to the left stands the Gayer-Anderson House (see p.106). It's only within the inner walls that the vastness of the mosque becomes apparent: the courtyard is 92m square, while the complex measures 140m by 122m – sufficient to accommodate the entire population of Al-Qitai, which was effectively the city of Cairo in Tulunid times (see box, p.106).

Besides its sheer size, the **mosque** impresses by its simplicity. Ibn Tulun's architects understood the power of repetition – see how the courtyard's crenulations echo the rhythm of the arcades – and also restraint: small floral capitals and stucco rosettes seem at first glance to be the only decorative motifs. Beneath the arcades you'll find a sycamore-wood **frieze** over 2km long, relating roughly one-fifth of

Ibn Tulun and Al-Qitai

It was from Iraq that the Abbasids made **Ahmed Ibn Tulun** governor of Fustat (see p.258) in 868, and smarted as he declared his independence. Ibn Tulun (the "Son of Tulun", a Turkish slave) founded the **Tulunid dynasty** that ruled Egypt until 905, and established a new city to the northeast of Fustat two years later. According to legends, Noah's Ark had come to rest on this site when the Flood receded, Moses confronted the pharaoh's magicians here, and Abraham had been ready to sacrifice his son on a nearby hillock. Unperturbed by this, nor by the existence of Christian and Jewish cemeteries on the site, Ibn Tulun ordered the construction of **Al-Qitai** ("the Wards", so called after its division into cantonments, which were said to have housed ten thousand troops in comfort). Mansions, villas and parks belied the austerity implicit in the city's name.

Ibn Tulun lived hard, and especially loved a game of polo on Al-Qitai's *midan* (now Midan Salah al-Din). When he was sick, his doctors suffered for it. Contemporary reports record that he "refused to follow their orders, flouted their prescribed diet, and when he found himself still sinking, he had their heads chopped off, or flogged them till they died". Under his successor **Khomaruya**, the *midan* was converted into a garden with a silver lake, where the insomniac sultan lolled on an airbed guarded by a blue-eyed lion. The Tulunids could afford such luxury, for their annual revenue amounted to 4,300,000 dinars.

When the Abbasids reconquered Egypt in 905, they destroyed everything here but the mosque, which became derelict. Exploited as a makeshift caravanserai and a hideout for bodysnatchers during the terrible famine of 1200, it was belatedly restored in 1296 by Sultan Laghin, who had hidden there when, as an amir, he was suspected of murdering the sultan.

the Koran in Kufic script. The severely geometric ablutions **fountain**, an inspired focal point, was added in the thirteenth century, when the *mihrab* was also jazzed up with marble and glass mosaics – the only unsuccessful note in the complex.

The **minaret** (entered from the *ziyada*) is unique for its exterior spiral staircase, which gives the structure a helical shape. Supposedly, Ibn Tulun twisted a scrap of paper into a spiral, and then justified his absent-minded deed by presenting it as the design for a minaret. But the great minaret at Samarra (itself influenced by ancient Babylonian ziggurats) seems a likelier source of inspiration. Expect to pay baksheesh to climb the minaret (£E5–10), and for looking after your shoes or providing shoe covers (£E1–2), but resist excessive demands, especially if you are told (falsely) that they are official charges.

The neighbourhood around the Ibn Tulun Mosque was one of Cairo's earliest *kharab* (derelict quarters), where the ruins of the Tulunid capital, **Al-Qitai** (see box above), merged with the vaster expanse of Fustat (see p.126), the first Muslim metropolis. Never entirely depopulated, its scavengers and squatters crept northwards over generations. They formed a settlement amid the rubbish heaps beside the Elephant Pond (drained in the late nineteenth century), which became a fashionable residential area after Sultan Al-Nasir developed the Citadel.

The Gayer-Anderson House

From the *ziyada* of Ibn Tulun's Mosque, a sign directs you to the **Gayer-Anderson House** (daily 9am–7.30pm; £E35, video camera £E20), which abuts the southeast corner of the mosque. Gayer-Anderson was a retired British major who, during the 1930s and 1940s, joined together two houses from the sixteenth and eighteenth centuries, turning the right-hand one (originally a blacksmith's) into a private *haramlik* (women's area) and the other into a semi-public *salamlik* (guests' area), before filling both with Oriental bric-a-brac (among the paintings is a self-portrait of Gayer-Anderson wearing a pharaonic headdress).

Tours of the house (the buildings are linked by a passage on the third floor) feature Persian, Chinese and Queen Anne rooms, and an amazing guest bedroom named after Damascus, from where its opulent panelling originated. It's possible to sneak through a camouflaged *dulab* (wall cupboard) into the screened gallery overlooking the *salamlik*, as women did in olden days to observe the *salamlik* without themselves being seen and thus breaking purdah. With its polychrome fountain, decorated ceiling and kilim-covered pillows, this is the finest **reception hall** left in Islamic Cairo, and served as the set for a tryst and murder in the James Bond film *The Spy Who Loved Me*.

The **well** beneath an arch in the courtyard was once reputed to contain water left behind by the Great Flood, and to serve as the entrance to the subterranean palace of the mythical King of the Jinn, who lived amid vast treasures with his seven daughters sleeping on golden beds, under a spell.

Saiyida Zeinab

The backstreets west of Ibn Tulun harbour another gem of Islamic architecture in the **Madrassa of Qaitbey**. Ignore the dust and grime and tip the curator to unlock the building, whose mosaic floors and *minbar* are superb examples of fifteenth-century craftsmanship. You can drop in en route to the **Saiyida Zeinab quarter**, where Islamic and modern Cairo merge in a confusion of tenement blocks and **markets**. Midan Lazoghli, on the edge of the Abdin quarter, hosts a daily car spares and repairs souk, while a **bird market** is held beneath an overpass in the direction of Qasr al-Aini Hospital on Mondays and Thursdays – hence its name, Souk Itnayn w Khamis. Like Saiyida Zeinab **metro** station, the market is on the quarter's periphery, where it merges with Garden City and Old Cairo.

The quarter's highlight is the annual **Moulid of Saiyida Zeinab** (see p.216) which features parades of Sufi orders by day and nocturnal festivities that attract half a million people. To see the *zikrs*, snake charmers, conjurers, nail-swallowers and dancing horses performing, you'll have to force your way through a scrum of people and tents – don't bring any valuables. The fifteen-day event takes place during Ragab, the seventh month of the Muslim calendar, currently falling in late spring.

The focal point for these celebrations is the **Mosque of Saiyida Zeinab** (closed to non-Muslims), off Sharia Bur Said. Zeinab, born in 628 AD, was the Prophet's granddaughter; she emigrated to Fustat after the Umayyads slew her brother, Hussein, and died there shortly afterwards. For Egyptian Muslims, especially women, Zeinab is a protector whose blessing (*baraka*) is sought in matters of fortune and health, while Shia Muslims revere her as Hussein's closest kinswoman.

Before heading back into town, you might want to try one of Saiyida Zeinab's many cheap but renowned **eating places** (see p.193 & p.196). To return to downtown Cairo from here, catch a bus or minibus from Sharia Khayrat opposite Zeinab's Mosque, or ask for directions to the nearest metro (ten minutes' walk). From Saiyida Zeinab station, or Sa'ad Zaghloul (which is as near), you can take the metro north to Midan Tahrir, or south to Old Cairo (Mari Girgis station). Alternatively, on foot, head up Sharia Khayrat to Midan Lazoghli, and then follow Sharia Nubar north to Midan al-Falaki, or Sharia Maglis al-Shaab west to Sharia Qasr al-Aini, where a right turn takes you to Midan Tahrir, a twenty-minute walk or so.

Cities of the Dead

It's thought that up to 500,000 Cairenes live amid the **Cities of the Dead**, two vast cemeteries that stretch away from the Citadel to merge with newer shanty-towns below the Muqattam Hills. The Southern Cemetery, sprawling to the southeast of Ibn Tulun's mosque, is only visible from the Muqattam, or at close quarters, whereas the Northern Cemetery is an unforgettably eerie sight, with dozens of mausoleums rising from a sea of dwellings along the road into town from Cairo Airport.

Although tourists generally – and understandably – feel uneasy about viewing the cemeteries' splendid **funerary architecture** with squatters living all around or in the tombs, few locals regard the Cities of the Dead as forbidding places. Egyptians have a long tradition of building "houses" near their ancestral graves and picnicking or even staying there overnight; other families have simply occupied them. By Cairene standards these are poor but decent neighbourhoods, with shops, schools and electricity, maybe even piped water and sewers. The saints buried here provide a moral touchstone and *baraka* (blessing) for their communities, who honour them with **moulids**, or festivals.

Though these are generally not dangerous quarters, it's best to exercise some caution when **visiting**. Don't flaunt money or expensive possessions, and be sure to dress modestly; women should have a male escort, and will seem more respectable if wearing a headscarf. You'll be marginally less conspicuous on Fridays, when many Cairenes visit their family plots; but remember that mosques can't be entered during midday prayers. At all events, leave the cemeteries well before dark, if only to avoid getting lost in their labyrinthine alleys – and don't stray to the east into the inchoate (and far riskier) slums built around the foothills of the Muqattam.

The Southern Cemetery

The older, larger **Southern Cemetery** – known to Cairenes as "the Great Cemetery" (Al-Qarafah al-Kubra) – is broadly synonymous with the residential quarter of **Al-Khalifa**, named after the Abbasid caliphs buried amid its mud-brick tenements. Although the Abbasid tombs aren't half as imposing as those of the Mamlukes in the Northern Cemetery, one of the approach routes passes several shrines famous for their moulids. One such festival is held at the beautiful **Mausoleum of Imam al-Shafi'i**, best reached by bus as a separate excursion. Though respectable enough by day, the whole area is noted for drug dealing and quite unsafe after dark.

Sharia al-Khalifa

The route from Sharia Saliba into the Southern Cemetery passes through one of the oldest poor neighbourhoods in Cairo, where it's thought that people started settling around their saints' graves as early as the tenth century. None of the tombs is remarkable visually, but the stories and moulids attached to them are interesting. The trail begins where **Sharia al-Khalifa** turns south off Sharia Saliba, just after the Khanqah of Shaykhu (see map, p.105). This narrow street passes a succession of tombs. The second on the left, within a yellow-and-white mosque, is that of **Saiyida Sukayna**, a great-granddaughter of the Prophet Mohammed, whose **moulid** (see p.216) is attended by several thousand people and features traditional entertainments such as stick-twisters and dancing horses.

The Tomb of Shagar al-Durr

Such saintly graves invariably acquired an oratory or mosque, unlike the **Tomb of Shagar al-Durr**, 100m further on, a derelict edifice sunk below street level. Shagar al-Durr (Tree of Pearls) was the widow of Sultan Ayyub, who ruled as sultana of Egypt for eighty days (1249–50) until the Abbasid caliph quoted the Prophet's dictum "Woe unto nations ruled by a woman". This compelled her to marry Aybak, the first Mamluke sultan, and govern "from behind the *mashrabiya*". In 1257 she ordered Aybak's murder after learning that he sought another wife, but then tried to save him; the assassins objected, "If we stop halfway through, he will kill both you and us!" Rejecting her offer to marry their new leader, the Mamlukes handed Shagar al-Durr over to Aybak's former wife, whose servants beat her to death with bath clogs and threw her body to the jackals.

Slightly further down and across the street, the oratory, or **Mashhad of Saiyida Ruqayya**, commemorates the half-sister of Saiyida Zeinab (see p.107), who came to Egypt with her; the name of their father, Ali, adorns its rare Fatimid *mihrab*, and the devotion she inspires is particularly evident during Ruqayya's moulid (see p.216).

The Saiyida Nafisa Mosque and the Abbasid Tombs

Ruqayya's devotion doesn't, however, compare with that accorded to the **Mosque of Saiyida Nafisa**, 100m to the south, by a roundabout planted with grass and flowers. This, Egypt's third-holiest shrine, is closed to non-Muslims, though visitors can still appreciate the good-natured crowd that hangs around after Friday noon prayers, or during Nafisa's **moulid** in the month of Gumad al-Tani (see p.216). Honoured during her lifetime as a descendant of the Prophet and a *hafizat al-Qur'an* (one who knows the Koran by heart), Nafisa was famed for working miracles and conferring *baraka*. Her shrine has been repeatedly enlarged since Fatimid times – the Southern Cemetery possibly began with devotees settling or being buried near her grave – and the present mosque was built in 1897.

If you walk down the alley to its left, and through the passage beyond, a green-painted gate to the right (just before the street turns) leads to a compound enclosing the **Tombs of the Abbasid Caliphs** (in principle open daily 9am–5pm; the caretaker will let you in for a small consideration if he happens to be around). Having been driven from Baghdad by the Mongols, the caliphs gratefully accepted Beybars' offer to re-establish them in Egypt, only to discover that they were mere puppets. Beybars appropriated the domed mausoleum (usually kept locked) for his own sons; the caliphs were buried outdoors in less than grandiose tombs. Notice the beautiful foliate Kufic inscription on the cenotaph of Khadiga, under the wooden shed. In 1517 the last Abbasid caliph was formally divested of his office, which the Ottomans assumed in 1538 and Ataturk abolished in the 1920s.

An alternative route back towards the Citadel passes the **Mosque of Saiyida Aisha**, whose moulid occurs during Sha'ban. To get there, retrace your steps to the junction just south of Ruqayya's shrine and take the road leading off to the right. It's roughly 500 metres' walk to Aisha's Mosque. From there, Sharia Salah Salem runs southwest alongside Saladin's medieval wall, and northeast to the Citadel entrance at Bab al-Gabal, while Sharia Salah al-Din leads north to Midan Salah al-Din. If you happen to be here on Friday, consider making a detour to the Souk al-Gom'a (see p.226), a massive **flea market** that stretches south from the Salah Salem overpass.

The Mausoleum of Imam al-Shafi'i

Two kilometres from the Citadel, at the far end of the street that bears his name, the **Mausoleum of Imam al-Shafi'i** is Egypt's largest Islamic mortuary complex in Egypt, instantly recognizable by its graceful ribbed dome, crowned by a metal boat like a weather vane. Born in Gaza in 767 AD, **Mohammed Ibn Idris al-Shafi'i** grew up in Mecca and practised law in Baghdad under Caliph Haroun al-Rashid before moving to Cairo, where he died in 820, leaving a corpus of rulings that made him the founder of the Shafi'ite school of Islamic jurisprudence, whose rulings are followed by most Egyptian Muslims.

The mausoleum was constructed in 1211 on the orders of the Ayyubid sultan Al-Kamil (Saladin's nephew), who was a great propagator of Sunni orthodoxy, like the imam himself. It was the first Sunni monument to be officially commissioned in the city following the demise of the Shi'ite Fatimids fifty years earlier. Within, Al-Shafi'i's teak cenotaph – into which the faithful slip petitions – lies beneath a magnificent dome perched on stalactite squinches and painted red and blue, with gilt designs. The walls are clad in variegated marble, dating from Qaitbey's restoration of the building in the 1480s. Al-Shafi'i's **moulid** (see p.217) attracts many sick and infirm people, seeking his *baraka*. More prosaically, the street leading northwards to the mausoleum from the Al-Basatin quarter is used for scrap, clothing and livestock **markets** every Friday morning.

By walking clockwise around the block in which the Imam's mausoleum is located, you'll find a five-domed complex directly behind it. Inside the courtyard are clumps of cenotaphs decorated with garlands and fronds, topped by a turban, fez or other headdress to indicate the deceased's rank. These constitute the **Hosh al–Basha**, where Mohammed Ali's sons, their wives, children and retainers are buried. The conspicuously plain cenotaph belongs to a princess with radical sympathies who abhorred ostentation. In a separate room, forty statues commemorate the 470 Mamlukes butchered by Mohammed Ali in the Citadel (see p.100).

You can reach the mausoleum by taxi from Midan Salah al-Din (for about £E7–10), or take bus #81 or #89 from Midan Ataba, #160 from Midan Ramses, or minibus #154 from Abdel Mouneem Riyad, which turn off Sharia Imam al-Shafi'i 100m short of the mausoleum itself.

The Northern Cemetery

The finest of Cairo's funerary monuments – erected by the Burgi Mamlukes from the fourteenth to sixteenth centuries – are spread around the **Northern Cemetery**. You can see the three main sites – Qaitbey's and Barquq's mausoleums and the Barsbey complex, plus various sites in between – over an hour or so, though it's worth stopping for tea in a café or two to get a better feel of the area. The opening hours of the monuments in the cemetery seem to change very frequently; some are open until as late as 10pm, while others close at 5pm, but it often seems to depend merely on when the caretaker happens to be around; generally you can access all of them at least between 10am and 5pm but non-Muslims will not be allowed in during prayers.

Aside from catching a taxi (ask for *al-Qarafat ash-Sharqiyyah* – the Eastern Cemetery – in Arabic), the easiest way to **get here** is to walk from Al-Azhar. This will take around fifteen minutes, following the dual carriageway Bab al-Ghuriyab past university buildings and uphill to its roundabout junction with Salah Salem. Although the tombs of Anuk and Tulbey are among the nearby mausoleums, you might prefer to head 250m north along the highway to the Dirasa bus terminal – also accessible by minibus #102 **from Midan Tahrir** or minibus #10 **from Ramses**

and Ataba – and then cut east into the cemetery. That way you start with Qaitbey's Mausoleum, whose ornate dome and minaret are clearly visible. Dirasa can also be reached by service-taxi microbus from Midan Ramses.

Sultan Qaitbey's Mausoleum

Sultan Qaitbey was the last strong Mamluke ruler and a prolific builder of monuments from Mecca to Syria; his funerary complex (depicted on £E1 notes) is among the grandest in the Northern Cemetery. His name means "the restored" or "returned", indicating that he nearly died at birth; as a scrawny lad, he fetched only fifty dinars in the slave market. The rapid turnover in rulers after 1437 accelerated his ascent, and in 1468 he was acclaimed as sultan by the bodyguard of the previous incumbent. His 28-year reign was only exceeded by Al-Nasir's, and Qaitbey remained "tall, handsome and upright as a reed" well into his eighties.

An irregularly shaped complex built in 1474, Qaitbey's **Mausoleum** (daily 10am–5pm) is dynamically unified by the bold stripes along its facade, which is best viewed from the north. The trilobed portal carries one's eye to the graceful **minaret**, soaring through fluted niches, stalactite brackets and balconies to a teardrop finial. Inside, the *madrassa liwans*, floors and walls are a feast of marble and geometric patterns, topped by elaborately carved and gilded ceilings, with a lovely octagonal roof lantern. Qaitbey's **tomb chamber** off the prayer hall is similarly decorated, its lofty dome upheld by squinches. One of Mohammed's footprints, brought over from Mecca, is also preserved in the tomb chamber. Ask to climb the minaret for a close view of the marvellous stone carving on the **dome**'s exterior: a raised star-pattern is superimposed over an incised floral one, the two designs shifting as the shadows change.

Map labels:
Abbassiya & Heliopolis
NORTHERN CEMETERY
MIDAN BARQUQ
Military Cemetery
Sultan Barquq's Mausoleum
Tomb of 'Asfur
Tombs of al-Bagasi & Amir Suleyman
Tomb of Gani Bak
Tomb of al-Saba Banaf
Sultan Barsbey's Mausoleum
Tomb of al-Rifai
DIRASA
Qaitbey's Rab
Buses
Sultan Qaitbey's Mausoleum
Footbridge
TUNNEL TO MIDAN OPERA
BAB AL-GHURIYAB
SHARIA AL-NASR
Northern Gates & Midan Ramses
Al-Azhar Mosque & Midan Ataba
Tombs of Umm Anuk & Tulbey
Al-Azhar Park
SHARIA SALAH SALEM
Muqattam Hills
Citadel (north side)
0   200 m
& Sharia Bab al-Wazir
Citadel (entrance)
& Southern Cemetery
EATING & DRINKING
Hilltop Restaurant   1

The Barsbey complex

As the street jinks northwards from Qaitbey's Mausoleum it passes (on the left) the **Rab**, or apartment building, that Qaitbey deeded to provide income for his mausoleum's upkeep and employment for poor relations. Such bequests could not be appropriated by the state, unlike merchants' and Mamlukes' personal wealth, which partly financed the **Mausoleum of Sultan al-Ashraf Barsbey** (daily 10am–10pm), 200m beyond the building. Barsbey was the sultan who acquired young Qaitbey at a knockdown rate; he himself had been purchased in Damascus for eight hundred dinars, but was "returned to the broker for a filmy defect in one of his blue eyes". Unlike other sultans, who milked the economy, Barsbey troubled to pay his Mamlukes regularly and the reign (1422–38) of this well-spoken teetotaller was characterized by "extreme security and low prices".

Based on a now-ruined *khanqah* (Sufi hostel), the complex was expanded to include a mausoleum and mosque-*madrassa* (1432) after Barsbey's funerary pile near Khan al-Khalili (see p.79) was found lacking. If there's a curator around, ask him to lift the mat hiding the marble mosaic floor inside the long mosque, which also features a superb *minbar*. At the northern end, a great dome caps Barsbey's tomb, its marble cenotaph and mother-of-pearl-inlaid *mihrab* softly lit by stained-glass windows, added at a later date. The stone carving on the dome's exterior marks a transition between the early chevron patterns seen, for example, on the domes of Sultan Barquq's Mausoleum (see below), and the fluid designs on Qaitbey's Mausoleum. Fifty metres up the street, another finely carved dome surmounts the **Tomb of Gani Bak**, a favourite of Barsbey's, whose mosque stands near the Saddlemakers Bazaar.

Sultan Barquq's Mausoleum

The third – and oldest – of the great funerary complexes can be found 50m further north, on the far side of a square, with a direct through road onto Sharia Salah Salem. Recognizable by its twin domes and minarets, the **Mausoleum of Sultan Barquq** (daily 9am–10pm) was the first royal tomb in a cemetery that was previously noted for the graves of Sufi sheikhs. Its courtyard is plain, with stunted tamarisks, but the proud chevron-patterned domes above the sanctuary *liwan* enliven the whole ensemble. Barquq and his son Farag are buried in the northern tomb chamber, his daughters Shiriz and Shakra in the southern one, with their faithful nurse in the corner. Both are soaring structures preceded by *mashrabiyas* with designs similar to the window screens in Barquq's *madrassa* on Sharia al-Muizz (see p.82). The sinuously carved *minbar* was donated by Qaitbey to what was then a Sufi *khanqah*; stairs in the northwest corner of the courtyard lead to a warren of dervish cells on the upper floors, long since deserted.

The complex was actually erected by Farag, who transferred his father's body here from the *madrassa*. Farag was crowned at the age of ten and deposed and killed in Syria after thirteen years of civil strife: all in all, it's quite amazing that the mausoleum was ever completed, but it was, in 1411.

Depending on your route out, you might pass the minor **tombs of Barsbey al-Bagasi and Amir Suleyman**, or those of **Princess Tulbey and Umm Anuk**, nearer Bab al-Ghuriyab and visible from the highway, due east of Al-Azhar Park.

Al-Azhar Park

Across Sharia Salah Salem from the cemetery's southern end is the new, much welcomed **Al-Azhar Park** (daily: summer 9am–midnight; winter 9am–11pm; usually £E5, but £E3 on Tuesdays, £E7 on public holidays; ⓦ www.alazharpark .com), whose entrance is about 200m south of Dirasa, and 500m north of the

Islamic architecture

With their geometric decoration, horseshoe arches and minarets, Islamic buildings are instantly recognizable the world over. For centuries, Cairo was the most important city in the Islamic world; unsurprisingly, the city boasts some of its greatest architectural treasures. Most typical of Cairo are the distinctive Ayyubid and Mamluke monuments with their pointed domes and striking *ablaq* (black-and-white or red-and-white stonework), and a walk through any district of Islamic Cairo will bring you upon wonderful buildings in a range of styles, from monumental ninth-century Tulunid through to flowery nineteenth-century Ottoman.

The courtyard of the mosque of Ibn Tulun ▲

Bab Zwayla ▼

Al-Aqmar Mosque ▼

The Tulunids

Cairo's earliest surviving example of a mosque is the impressively massive Mosque of **Ibn Tulun** (see p.105). This follows the eighth-century Umayyad tradition of the congregational mosque, with its great courtyard (*sahn*) flanked by arcades (*riwaq*) and a fountain for ablutions. Aside from its sheer size, the mosque's architectural impact is heightened by the rhythmic arches and parapet mouldings on the arcades that surround the courtyards. Ibn Tulun was an Abbasid viceroy who founded a breakaway dynasty in Egypt in 870 AD. His distinctive **spiral minaret** is modelled on that of the mosque at Samarra in Iraq, where the Abbasids remained in power until 1258 – and from where, in 905, they would wreak revenge on Cairo, the Tulunids' capital.

The Fatimids

In 969 Egypt was conquered by the Fatimids, Shia Muslims who founded a new capital near the ruins of Ibn Tulun's city. While the Fatimids' legendary palaces have not survived, their street plan and fortifications, including such gates as the **Bab Zwayla**, between the Northern Walls and the Citadel, still distinguish what is now called Islamic Cairo. Fatimid mosques have decorative facades with keel-shaped or scalloped arches, stucco rosettes and honeycombed *muqarnas* – motifs that became part of the lexicon of Islamic architecture. Cairo's most important Fatimid monuments are the Al-Aqmar Mosque (see p.83), Al-Hakim's Mosque (see p.84) and the Mosque of Salih Tala'i (see p.94). The most impressive examples of non-religious Fatimid architecture are the northern city gates (see p.85).

The Ayyubids

The Fatimids' Sunni successor Saladin (Salah al-Din) was responsible for Cairo's Citadel (see p.100), but his most significant innovation was the **madrassa** or Islamic seminary. *Madrassas* are usually attached to mosques, often in a cruciform pattern to provide separate lodgings for each of the four schools of Sunni law. Other contributions that Saladin's Ayyubid dynasty made to Islamic architecture were the pepperpot-style of minaret, whose only surviving example in Cairo is on the Madrassa-Mausoleum of Sultan Ayyub (see p.80), and the technique of laying alternating courses of different coloured stone to achieve a striped effect on walls and arches, known as **ablaq**.

▲ Madrassa-Khanqah of Sultan Barquq

▼ Interior of Beit al-Sihaymi

▼ Mashrabiya window, Beit al-Sihaymi

The decorative arts

The construction of public buildings stimulated decorative arts, from wood and stucco carving to glassblowing and calligraphy. The Fatimids developed bevelled carving to create monumental compositions of foliage, birds and animals, while the Ayyubids preferred to work with small polygonal panels or pieces of turned wood that were fitted together to form lattices for dividing halls or screening windows – such **mashrabiya** are a feature of traditional houses such as those in Darb al-Asfur (see p.83) and Midan al-Aini (see p.89). Though the Fatimids loved animal motifs, later mosques respected Islam's rejection of figurative art as idolatrous; instead, designs based on geometry, foliage or Arabic calligraphy and the text of the Koran adorned walls and ceilings. Vivid blue Iznik tiles were favoured in the Ottoman era (after 1517) and interiors were influenced by European Rococo under Mohammed Ali Pasha (1805–48).

Atrium court, Mausoleum of Sultan Qalaoun ▲

Sultan Qaitbey's Mausoleum ▼

Sabil-Kuttab of Abd al-Rahman Katkhuda ▼

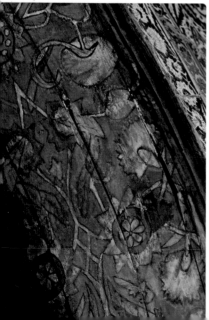

The Mamlukes

Under the Mamlukes (1250–1517), sultans such as Qalaoun and Beybars endowed Cairo with magnificent mosques and *madrassas*. A ruler or his lieutenants could show piety and court popularity by commissioning facilities such as a bathhouse (*hammam*), fountain (*sabil*) or boys' school (*kuttab*), sometimes sited above a fountain to create a dual-purpose *sabil-kuttab* such as those of **Abd al-Rahman Katkhuda** (see p.83) and **Tusun Pasha** (see p.90). Mamlukes vied to outdo their rivals with lavish materials and decorations – marble, imported tiles, cedar-wood and wrought iron. The Mamlukes also built magnificent tombs that are now known as the **Cities of the Dead**, crowned by a *qubba* (dome) such as the mausoleums of Barquq (see p.112) and Qaitbey (see p.111).

Home design

Until the seventeenth century, Islamic **domestic architecture** was far ahead of Europe's. Wealthy Cairenes had mansions with running water and Turkish baths, cooled by a rooftop ventilator and an inner courtyard, and distanced from the noisy, dusty streets by a chicaned entrance passage. Rooms had high ceilings, panelled or tiled walls, *mashrabiya* screens and cooling fountains, but were not associated with specific functions; rather, people relaxed, ate or slept in whichever room was most comfortable according to the season or time of day. The crucial distinction was between the semi-public *salamlik* and the private family quarters, or *haramlik* (which Europeans misconstrued as harems), as you'll see if you visit Mamluke- or Ottoman-period homes, such as those on Darb al-Asfur (see p.83) or around Midan al-Aini (see p.89).

Citadel's Bab Gadid. Funded by a US$45m grant from the Aga Khan Trust, the park is part of a regeneration project for the Darb al-Ahmar quarter (p.96), laid out on the old site of a stretch of waste ground, once used as a rubbish dump and the haunt of junkies. Now all that has changed: in its place is a scrupulously kept recreational area that has provided local employment and given one of Cairo's most deprived areas a new lease of life. Scattered around the park's lawns and fountains are trees, plants and shrubs from around the world, all labelled, while the western boundary includes a 1300-metre stretch of **Ayyubid city wall**, uncovered during the park's creation; its ramparts and bastions will be open to the public once work is complete. The park also contains a lakeside café and the classy **Hilltop Restaurant** (see p.193), and its highest point offers a fantastic **view** over Islamic Cairo, especially impressive at night when many monuments are illuminated.

The Muqattam Hills and Manshiyet Nasser

Beyond the Citadel and the Northern Cemetery, girdling Cairo to the east, the arid limestone **Muqattam Hills** stretch from Medinet Nasr (see p.143) in the north all the way down to Tura (see p.128) in the south. The plateau's summit is seldom visited by tourists but easily accessible by #951 bus from Abdel Mouneem Riyad, or #401 from Midan Ataba. Zigzagging up the hillside past caves and quarries, ruined shrines and guarded outposts, buses terminate at **Medinat Muqattam**, an upmarket suburb whose avenues are flanked by villas and casinos. The Corniche

The Zebaleen

Cairo's **Zebaleen** (literally, "rubbish people") are descended from poor rural migrants of the 1890s who used to dispose of household waste for landlords, and dried the organic residue to use as fuel for heating and cooking. As paraffin replaced dung in the 1930s, they teamed up with a clan of pig-breeders, whose pigs provided food for the community and a product to sell to non-Muslims; most *zebaleen* are Coptic Christians. In 1969 many were forcibly relocated from the city to shantytowns below the Muqattam Hills, where some thirty thousand live today; the total number of *zebaleen* in Cairo is thought to be seventy to eighty thousand.

Having banished donkey rubbish-carts from Cairo in 1987, the authorities had to allow them back in many neighbourhoods after garbage trucks proved unable to negotiate the congested streets, but the richer quarters were handed over to European waste-management contractors. Mechanized crushing ensures that no recycling is possible once the garbage has been compressed, so waste can only be dumped in landfill sites – whereas the *zebaleen* recycled much of it. While their filthy work remains indispensable, the *zebaleen* feel cheated of its rewards; the government's **mass-killing of pigs** on the pretext of averting a swine flu epidemic in 2008 provoked riots in the *zebaleen* colonies.

The largest of these – Manshiyet Nasser – is famous for its extraordinary cave churches and monastery of St Simeon the Tanner (see p.114). Manshiyet Nasser is also associated with Sister Emmanuelle, the "Mother Teresa of Cairo", who spent over two decades building a network of clinics, schools and gardens for children, later opening a primary school in the Muqattam and initiating development efforts, leading to several new schools, health care projects and income-generating ventures.

circling the summit has spectacular **views** of the Citadel and over most of Cairo –
an unforgettable vista at sunset.

Below the plateau's north face, off Sharia al-Nasr, lies the *zebaleen* (see box,
p.113) settlement of **Manshiyet Nasser**, known to outsiders as "Garbage City".
Donkey carts trundle through the streets, loaded with rubbish from all over Cairo,
which is sorted here into huge piles of tin cans, plastic bottles, glass, and anything
else that can be recycled.

Manshiyet Nasser would hardly be a draw for tourists were it not for the amazing
Monastery of St Simeon the Tanner (Deir Samaan Kharas; Ⓦ www.cavechurch
.com). This long-derelict seventh-century monastery was originally dedicated to
a saint by the name of Anba Hadra. In 1978, it was rededicated to St Simeon, a
one-eyed tenth-century shoemaker who is believed to have miraculously moved
the Muqattam massif after Caliph Al-Muizz demanded proof of the validity of
the gospel of Matthew 17:20 ("If ye have faith... ye shall say unto this mountain,
'Remove hence to yonder place,' and it shall remove"). The monastery has now
been reborn as seven **cave chapels**, carved with stunning coloured reliefs of
Christ, the saints, and biblical scenes, created by a Polish artist known only as
Mario, who continues to work on the site. The largest of the caves is now the
Virgin Mary and St Simeon Cathedral, a breathtaking auditorium that seats some
twenty thousand people, and hosts mass on Sunday mornings (7.30–11am).

On an eastern spur of the Muqattam stands the **Mosque of al-Guyushi**, the
Fatimid vizier Badr al-Gamali who rebuilt Cairo's Northern Walls. Ostensibly
a shrine (*mashhad*) but without anybody buried there, it may have once been a
watchtower disguised as a mosque, or a memorial to his victories over rebel tribes
in Upper Egypt. Its eleventh-century interior was restored in the 1990s by the
Dawood Bohara sect (see p.83).

A private **taxi** is the only feasible way to reach Manshiyet Nasser or Al-Guyushi's
mosque (approachable only on foot at the final stage).

Old Cairo and Roda Island

Depending on how it's defined, **Old Cairo** (Masr al-Qadima in Arabic) can mean everything south of Garden City and Saiyida Zeinab, or a relatively small area near Mari Girgis metro station, known to foreigners as "**Coptic Cairo**". Cairenes themselves distinguish between the general area of Masr al-Qadima and specific localities such as **Fumm al-Khalig** (where you can see the **Aqueduct** which brought water to the Citadel) or Qasr al-Sham'ah, the **Roman fortress of Babylon** where the Holy Family is thought to have taken refuge from King Herod. An ancient powerhouse of Egyptian Christianity, the fortress remains the heart of Cairo's Coptic community even though more Copts now live in districts such as Abbassiya and Shubra (see Chapter Five). Featuring several medieval churches, the superb **Coptic Museum** and an atmospheric synagogue, it totally eclipses the site of **Fustat** – Egypt's first Islamic metropolis, of which little remains but the much-altered **Mosque of Amr**.

From Coptic Cairo it's a short walk across a narrow channel to **Roda Island,** whose southern tip harbours a museum dedicated to the Egyptian superstar Umm Kalthoum and a medieval **Nilometer**. The sky-scraping *Grand Hyatt* hotel at the island's northern end is a conspicuous feature of the Nile waterfront, and Roda will have more to offer visitors once the magnificent Manial Palace reopens.

Coptic Cairo is readily accessible from downtown; it's only four stops (20min) by **metro** from Midan Tahrir to **Mari Girgis** station in the direction signposted "Helwan", while a **taxi** from downtown should cost about £E6. **Buses** from Tahrir (#825) and Ramses (#134 and minibus #94) to the Mosque of Amr are often packed on the outward journey but fine for getting back. The Nilometer and Umm Kalthoum Museum are within walking distance of Mari Girgis station, while the Manial Palace can be reached by bus #95 or minibus #58 from Midan Tahrir (Abdel Mouneem Riyad terminal).

Coptic Cairo

Coptic Cairo recalls the millennial interlude between pharaonic and Islamic civilization and the enduring faith of Egypt's Coptic Christians. Though not a ghetto, the quarter's huddle of dark churches suggests a mistrust of outsiders – an

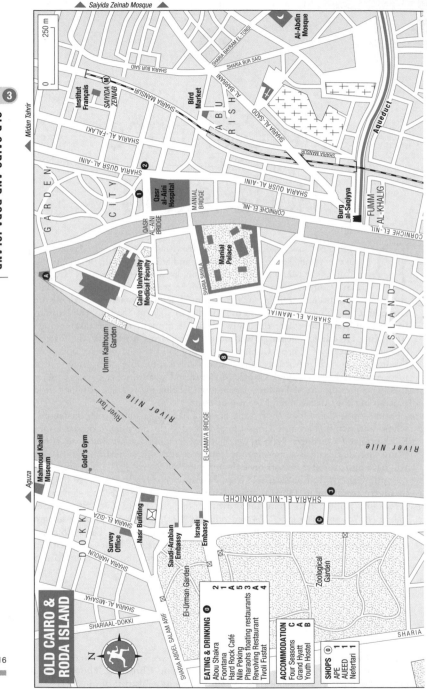

3

OLD CAIRO AND RODA ISLAND

OLD CAIRO & RODA ISLAND

N

▲ *Saiyida Zeinab Mosque* ▲

Al-Abdin Mosque

Institut Français

SAIYIDA ZEINAB Ⓜ

SHARIA MANSUR

SHARIA BUR SAID

SHARIA BAYRAM EL-TONSI

SHARIA BUR SAID

Bird Market

ABU RISHA

SHARIA AL-SAID

SHARIA AL-BARRANI

Aqueduct

SHARIA AL-FALAKI

SHARIA QASR AL-AINI

GARDEN CITY

❶

❷

Qasr al-Aini Hospital

QASR AL-AINI BRIDGE

MANIAL BRIDGE

CORNICHE EL-NIL

SHARIA QASR AL-AINI

SHARIA MANSUR

Burg al-Saqiyya Ⓜ

FUMM AL-KHALIG

CORNICHE EL-NIL

Cairo University Medical Faculty

Umm Kalthoum Garden

❹

Manial Palace

SHARIA SAYALA

SHARIA EL-MANIAL

RODA ISLAND

❽

Mahmoud Khalil Museum

Gold's Gym

River Taxi

River Nile

EL-GAMA'A BRIDGE

River Nile

DOKKI

SHARIA EL-GIZA

Nasr Building

SHARIA HAROUN

Survey Office

Saudi-Arabian Embassy

Israeli Embassy

El-Urman Garden

SHARIA EL-NIL (CORNICHE)

❸

Ⓖ

Zoological Garden

SHARIA

SHARIA AL-MISAHA

SHARIAAL-DOKKI

SHARIA ABDEL SALAM ARIF

▲ *Midan Tahrir* ▲

▲ *Aguza* ▲

▲ *Cairo University* ▲

0   250 m

EATING & DRINKING Ⓓ

Abou Shakra	2
Foontana	1
Hard Rock Café	A
Nile Peking	5
Pharaohs floating restaurants	3
Revolving Restaurant	A
Tivoli Fustat	4

ACCOMMODATION

Four Seasons	C
Grand Hyatt	A
Youth Hostel	B

SHOPS Ⓢ

APE	1
AUEED	1
Nefertari	1

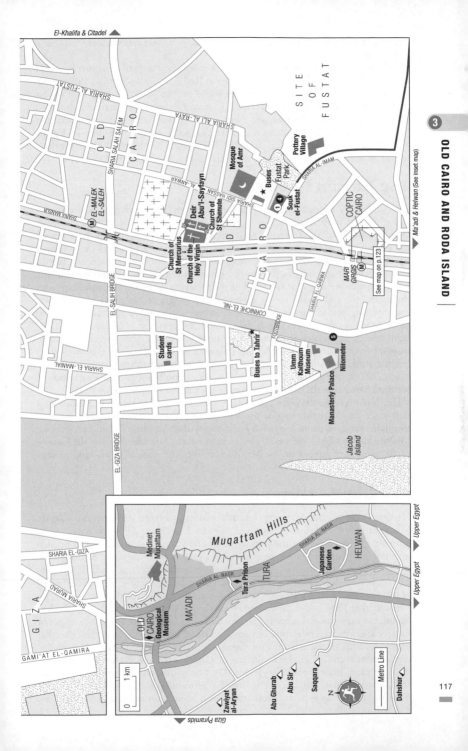

El-Khalifa & Citadel

SHARIA AL-FUSTAT

OLD CAIRO

SHARIA SALAH SALEM

SHARIA ALI AL-BAYA

SITE OF FUSTAT

Pottery Village

Mosque of Amr

Fustat Park

Buses

SHARIA SIDI HASSAN

AL-ANWAR

SHARIA AL-IMAM

Deir Abu'l-Sayfayn

Church of St Shenute

Church of St Mercurius

Church of the Holy Virgin

Souk el-Fustat

COPTIC CAIRO

MARI GIRGIS (M)

SHARIA AL-QAEWA

See map on p.123

Ma'adi & Helwan (See inset map)

SHARIA MANSUR

EL-MALEK (M) EL-SALEH

OLD CAIRO

CORNICHE EL-NIL

FOOTBRIDGE

EL-SALIH BRIDGE

Student cards

Buses to Tahrir

Umm Kalthoum Museum

Nilometer

Manasterly Palace

SHARIA EL-MANIAL

EL-GIZA BRIDGE

Jacob Island

GIZA

SHARIA EL-GIZA

SHARIA MURAD

GAMI'AT EL-QAMIRA

Giza Pyramids

OLD CAIRO

Geological Museum

Medinet Muqattam

Muqattam Hills

MA'ADI

SHARIA AL-NASR

Tura Prison

TURA

SHARIA AL-NASR

Japanese Garden

HELWAN

Upper Egypt

Zawiyat al-Aryan

Abu Ghurab

Abu Sir

Saqqara

Dahshur

N

Metro Line

0   1 km

117

attitude of mind that has its roots in the Persian conquest and centuries of Greek or Roman rule.

Perhaps as early as the sixth century BC, a town grew around a fortress intended to guard the canal linking the Nile and the Red Sea. This served as the port of ancient Heliopolis, and was named Per-hapi-On, the "River House of On" (as Heliopolis was then called). Egyptians, Jews and Babylonian Chaldeans mingled here centuries before the Romans came and Emperor Trajan raised the existing fortress in 130 AD. Some ascribe the fortress's Roman name – **Babylon-in-Egypt** – to Chaldean workmen pining after their home town beside the Euphrates; others suggest it derived from Per-hapi-On, or Bab il-On, the "Gate of Heliopolis".

The Roman fortress

Almost directly opposite Mari Girgis metro station (named after St George, who comes second to St Mark in the Coptic hierarchy of saints) you'll see the twin circular **towers** of the fortress's **western gate**. In Trajan's day, the Nile lapped the gate's base and was crossable by a 66-span pontoon bridge, via the southern tip of Roda. Today, the fortress-town's foundations are buried under ten metres of accumulated silt and rubble, so the churches within the compound and the streets outside are nearly at the level of the fortress's ramparts. Approaching from the metro, the right-hand tower is ruined, exposing a central shaft buttressed by masonry rings and radial ribs, which enabled it to withstand catapults and battering rams. Atop the other tower stands the Orthodox Church of St George (see p.122). Both towers are encased in alternating courses of dressed stone (much of it taken from pharaonic temples) and brick, a Roman technique called *opus mixtum* or "mixed work", which may have inspired the Mamluke fashion for *ablaq* masonry (see p.282). While exploring the Coptic quarter, you'll notice various sections of fortified **Roman walls**, rebuilt during the fourth and fifth centuries AD.

The fortress's **Water Gate**, beneath the Hanging Church, is accessible by a stairway behind the three stone piers supporting the back of the church. It was through this gate (then lapped by the river) that the last Byzantine viceroy, Melkite bishop Cyrus, escaped by boat under cover of darkness before the fortress of Babylon surrendered to the Muslims in 641 AD, after a seven-month siege (see p.258).

The Coptic Museum

Nestled between the Hanging Church and the fortress towers, the **Coptic Museum** (daily 9am–5pm, closing at 3pm in Ramadan; £E50; Ⓦwww.coptic museum.gov.eg) is one of the highlights of Old Cairo. Its collection can be seen in detail in a couple of hours, or covered at a pace in half that time. Although the museum is supposed to close at 5pm, officials may shoo you out (and not politely) half an hour before that, if they feel like going home early – something worth bearing in mind if you buy your ticket towards the end of the day.

Founded in 1908 under the patronage of Coptic Patriarch Cyril V and Khedive Kamil, the museum was intended to save Christian antiquities from the ravages of neglect and foreign collectors, but soon widened its mandate to embrace secular material. With artefacts from Old Cairo, Upper Egypt and the desert monasteries, the museum traces the evolution of Coptic art from Greco-Roman times into the early Islamic era (300–1000 AD). Notwithstanding debts to pharaonic and Greco-Roman culture, its spirit was refreshingly unmonumental, if not downright plebeian – its artefacts often seem homespun compared to pharaonic and Islamic craftsmanship.

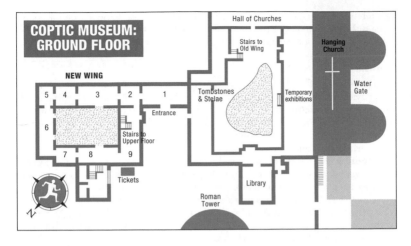

COPTIC MUSEUM:
GROUND FLOOR

Hall of Churches

Stairs to
Old Wing

Hanging
Church

Water
Gate

NEW WING

5 4 3 2 1

Tombstones
& Stelae

Temporary
exhibitions

Entrance

6

Stairs to
Upper Floor

7 8 9

Tickets

Library

Roman
Tower

Rooms 2–4

Entering the museum grounds from Sharia Mari Girgis, the **New Wing** (built in 1937) is straight ahead. Its **ground floor** is arranged in chronological order in an anticlockwise direction, starting with **Room 2**. Coptic art is renowned for its textiles, which were exported under the Roman and Byzantine empires, valued for their fine weave, intricate designs and bold colours. Proof of the weavers' skill is a double-faced **tapestry** from the fourth or fifth century, depicting a piper on one side, and people dancing and frolicking on the other. A **fresco** of saints from the Monastery of St Jeremiah shows how native monk-artists infused Byzantine murals with realism: the saints' faces in this and other frescoes are recognizably Egyptian – indeed, uncannily like people on Cairo's streets today.

Equally striking is the extent to which Christian symbolism and resurrection beliefs derived from Ancient Egypt. The **ankh** (the hieroglyph for "breath" and "life") appeared alongside the gods Anubis and Horus on second-century Coptic **gravestones** (in **Room 3**), while veneration of the Virgin Mary tapped into the cult of goddess Isis/Aphrodite that was widespread across the Roman Empire. Among the shell-shaped **cornices** from churches, one relief shows **Aphrodite** emerging from a seashell (just as she does in Botticelli's famous painting), while another image looks almost Indian. Once Christianity gained strength, other pagan gods disappeared and ankhs were transmuted into looped crosses, as you can see in **Room 4**.

Rooms 5–6

Egypt was the cradle of Christian monasticism; the "Desert Fathers" St Anthony and St Paul inspired a host of hermits, whose followers established the first monasteries at the end of the fourth century AD. **Rooms 5** and **6** display objects from the sixth-century **Monastery of St Jeremiah** at Saqqara, unearthed by the British archeologist James Quibell in 1906–10. His greatest finds were seven lovely fresco-painted **prayer niches**, some depicting Jesus holding up a copy of the Bible, others the Madonna and Child – in two of which Mary is shown breast-feeding the infant Jesus, subtly identifying her with Isis (see p.267). All were originally used to inspire the monks' devotional prayers.

Stone-carving was a craft associated with monasteries; masons combined acanthus leaves and grapevines with pharaonic palm fronds and lotus motifs, carving intricate

capitals for pillars in cloisters and churches. The oldest known example of a stone **pulpit** (*ambon*) may have been influenced by the Heb-Sed thrones of Zoser's funerary complex at Saqqara (see p.166), near the monastery.

Rooms 7–9

Another source of finds was the fourth-century **Bawit Monastery** in Middle Egypt, yielding three geometric **painted panels** (Room 7) and some wonderful frescoed **prayer niches** (Room 8). One niche from the sixth or seventh century depicts Christ enthroned on what appears to be a flaming chariot, surrounded by the creatures of the Apocalypse (eagle, ox, lion and man), and flanked by the archangels Gabriel and Michael.

In **Room 9**, a **cartoon** from the wall of a monk's cell at Bawit shows three mice (one waving a white flag, another offering a cup of wine) approaching a cat – its meaning is obscure, but it is reminiscent of the *Satirical Papyrus* in the Egyptian Museum (p.64). Directly opposite, a wooden **panel** depicts a haloed monk reaching for a pen from a case hanging on his shoulder; the peacock in the top right corner of the panel is a symbol of resurrection, held by some scholars to derive from the mythical phoenix, or firebird, of Heliopolis.

Rooms 10–14

Another early Christian resurrection symbol was the **eagle**, found on a bas-relief and a third- or fourth-century statuette from Coptic Cairo, displayed **upstairs** in **Room 10**. This harks back to Greek mythology (whose supreme deity Zeus often took an eagle's form), as do an embroidered piece of cloth and a carving depicting **centaurs** (one ridden by a faun playing pan pipes). Beyond are copies of the gospels in Coptic and Arabic, no small matter in the Middle Ages, before the advent of printing: all were written out by hand.

Minutely-detailed carving in **ivory** was as much a devotional task as copying the gospels. In **Room 11**, a **comb** depicts the raising of Lazarus, while an ivory **panel** (probably from a box) shows the resurrected Jesus appearing to the apostles Peter, James and John, and beneath, chatting to Moses and Elijah.

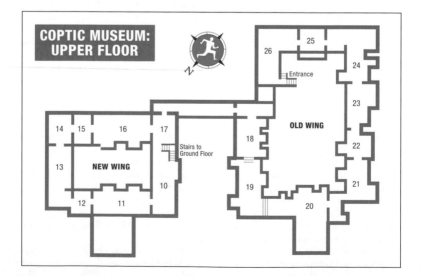

Room 12 jumps to the nineteenth century with liturgical vestments before visitors return to the fourth and fifth centuries in **Room 13**, whose **tapestries** and **embroideries** include a tiny one of Hercules feeding a lion. A strip of cloth from the same period depicts Aphrodite partying, but the goddess is notably absent from the neighbouring seventh- or eighth-century black-and-white depiction of similar scenes. In **Room 14**, the textiles get more colourful and elaborate, including a particularly good one featuring dancing animals.

Room 15

Room 15 is devoted to the **Gospels of Nag Hammadi**, whose 1200 pages shed light on the development of early Christianity and its mystic tradition. These non-canonical gospels – omitted from the Bible – were mostly translated into Coptic from Greek for local members of the heretical Gnostic church. Probably buried during the anti-Gnostic purges of the fourth and fifth centuries, they were found in a sealed jar by farmers near the Upper Egyptian town of Nag Hammadi in 1945. Sadly only two pages are on show here, along with the covers in which the gospels were found. The two pages contain the end of a book called the Apocryphon of John, and the beginning of the Gospel of Thomas, which may actually be earlier than the official, canonical gospels. Translations of these and other Nag Hammadi gospels can be found at Ⓦ www.gnosis.org/naghamm/nhl.html.

Rooms 16–19

Room 16 focuses on **books** and writing, including volumes made of paper at a time when paper was unknown in Europe, as well as a scribe's pen case similar to the one shown on the panel in Room 9, and letters and orders for grain, inscribed on potsherds or animal bone. Notice the ankh-shaped bookmark in the Book of Psalms in **Room 17**.

Passing through a corridor into the **Old Wing**, you'll find in **Room 18** wooden **panels** carved with Nile scenes including two from the fifth or sixth century that feature crocodiles, still endemic in Egypt at that time. The exquisite **painted ceiling** with stained-glass windows in **Room 19**, dating from the museum's inauguration in 1910, rather outshines the other exhibits, including some wheeled **toys** and a Fayoum **funerary portrait** (see p.63).

Rooms 20–26

Icon painting was a form of religious devotion condemned by Islam as idolatrous; churches had their icons and frescoes defaced by Muslim iconoclasts just as Christians had previously vandalized pagan tombs and temples. **Room 20** features a thirteenth-century triptych of Jesus on the cross surrounded by pictures of events preceding and following his crucifixion, and an eighteenth-century image of two saints with the heads of dogs that sits oddly on a Christian icon. An icon on a cloth was a typical souvenir sold to pilgrims in eighteenth-century Palestine, which they could roll up and take home. In **Room 22,** one of St Thomas touching Jesus's stigmata shows Christ and the disciples as they probably were – rather swarthier than as usually depicted in European churches.

Rooms 23–25 showcase **metalwork**, **glassware** and **ceramics**, all worth comparing with their contemporary equivalents in the Museum of Islamic Art (see p.92). As Muslims performed the hajj to Mecca, so Christians visited the holy city of Jerusalem, wealthy female pilgrims being transported in the kind of **Ottoman litter** exhibited in **Room 26**.

You finally descend to the **courtyard**, where you can pop into the Hall of Churches of Old Cairo, whose prime exhibit is the original fifth-century **wooden altar** from the Church of St Sergius (p.124), topped by a Fatimid-era wooden dome from the Hanging Church (see below), both of which are nearby.

The Hanging Church

Built directly above the Roman Water Gate, the **Hanging Church** (in Arabic Al-Mu'allaqah, "The Suspended"; daily 9am–4.30pm; no admission before 11am on Wed, Fri & Sun) can be reached via an ornate portal on Sharia Mari Girgis. Ascending a steep stairway, you enter a nineteenth-century vestibule displaying cassettes and videos of Coptic liturgies and papal sermons. Above this are the monks' quarters; beneath it is a secret repository for valuables, only discovered last century. Through the door and to the right, a glass panel in the floor allows you to see that the church is indeed "suspended", bridge-like, above the water gate.

The church's **nave** – whose ceiling is ribbed like an upturned boat or ark – is separated from the side aisles by sixteen pillars, formerly painted with images of saints. Behind the marble pulpit, beautifully carved **screens** hide three **haikals** (altar areas) from the congregation. Their star patterns, accentuated by inlaid bone and ivory, are similar to those found in mosques. Both pulpit and screens date from the thirteenth century, but the church was founded at least six hundred years earlier and may even have originated in the fourth century as a chapel for the soldiers of the bastion.

The thirteen pillars holding up the **pulpit** represent Jesus and the twelve disciples: as is customary in Coptic churches, one of the pillars is black, for Judas, and another, perhaps unfairly, is grey for "doubting" Thomas.

If you're curious to attend a **Coptic Mass**, the Hanging Church is the best place to do so, for its choir and atmospherics (Wed, Fri & Sun 7.30–11am).

The Monastery of St George

Heading north from the Coptic Museum along Sharia Mari Girgis, the first gateway on the right (ignore any demands for cash from "doormen") leads into the precincts of the **Monastery of St George**, now the seat of the Greek Orthodox Patriarchate of Alexandria. The monastery itself rarely admits tourists, but it's worth looking into the neighbouring **Church of St George** (daily 8am–4pm), built in 1904 after a fire destroyed the original tenth-century structure. The only round church in Egypt (so shaped because it's built atop one of the old Roman gateway towers), it has a dark interior perfumed with incense and pierced by sunbeams that filter through the stained glass. Notwithstanding the church's Greek Orthodox allegiance, its **Moulid of Mari Girgis** (on St George's Day – April 23) is one of the largest Coptic festivals in Cairo.

The Old Quarter

Fifty metres north of the Coptic Museum entrance on Sharia Mari Girgis, steps lead down to a **subterranean gateway** into the **oldest part of Old Cairo**, whose cobbled lanes flanked by high-walled houses wind between medieval churches and cemeteries. Described as a "constricted slum" by British satirist Evelyn Waugh in 1929, the quarter has been gradually sanitized and tarted up for tourists since the 1970s and now seems almost Disneyesque along the main sightseeing trail – but its back alleys are still visibly poor and neglected. The quarter and its churches and synagogue are open daily 8am–4pm, unless stated otherwise.

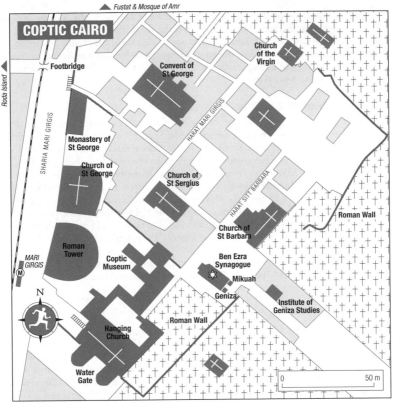

Within the map:

Fustat & Mosque of Amr

Footbridge

Roda Island

Convent of St George

Church of the Virgin

SHARIA MARI GIRGIS

HARAT MARI GIRGIS

Monastery of St George

Church of St George

Church of St Sergius

HARAT SITT BARBARA

Roman Wall

MARI GIRGIS

Roman Tower

Coptic Museum

Church of St Barbara

Ben Ezra Synagogue

Mikuah

Geniza

Institute of Geniza Studies

N

Roman Wall

Hanging Church

Water Gate

0   50 m

The Convent of St George

The most interesting of the churches is reached through the first gate on the left after you pass through the subterranean gateway. This is the Coptic **Convent of St George** (Deir Mari Girgis; daily 10am–4pm), whose main building, still a nunnery, is closed to visitors. Underneath, however – and usually open to visitors despite being under restoration – is a lofty **hall** that once belonged to a Fatimid mansion. Tall, narrow wooden doors with 66 panels depicting courtly life lead into a chapel where worshippers kiss a cedarwood casket containing relics of St George. Confusingly, this is signposted in the yard as the **Chaplet of St George**, which is in fact a separate chapel, home to the chain with which St George was restrained while being tortured by the Romans. Visitors may touch the chain for *baraka* (blessing), and the nuns may even offer to wrap it around you for a souvenir photo.

On leaving the convent, turn left and pass through the tourist bazaar to the end of the lane, where you can turn right for the churches of St Sergius and St Barbara and the Ben Ezra Synagogue, or left for the churches of St George and the Virgin.

The churches of St George and the Virgin

Fifty metres up the alley from the intersection, a doorway on the right leads to yet another **Church of St George**, founded in 681 by Athanasius the Scribe. Of the original foundation, only the Hall of Nuptials survived a conflagration in the mid-nineteenth century, after which the current structure was erected.

Beyond it, at the end of the road, stands the smaller **Church of the Virgin**, also known as Qasriyyat al-Rihan (Pot of Basil) after the favourite herb of the Orthodox Church. Because Caliph Al-Hakim's mother was of that faith, the church was given to the Greek community for the duration of his reign, but later returned to the Copts. Largely rebuilt in the eighteenth century, it's chiefly notable for several icons painted by John the Armenian in 1778.

The Church of St Sergius

Heading right from the intersection beyond St George's Convent, you reach, at the next corner, the **Church of St Sergius** (Abu Serga). The oldest extant church in Egypt, its great age is attested to by its site below modern-day street level. Probably founded in the fifth century, though most of the current building dates from the eleventh, Abu Serga retains the basilical form typical of early Coptic churches. Antique columns topped with Corinthian capitals support the women's gallery, where you can inspect the thirteenth-century *haikal* screen and bits of frescoes and mosaics in the central apse. Steps to the right of the altar descend into a **crypt** where the Holy Family are believed to have stayed, a sojourn commemorated by a Coptic **festival** (June 1). Unfortunately, the crypt itself is open only for services (Sat 6–7pm).

From St Sergius, you can wander along to the end of the lane where another thoroughfare leads to the Church of St Barbara (to the left) and Ben Ezra Synagogue (on the right).

The Church of St Barbara

The eleventh-century **Church of St Barbara** replaced an earlier Church of Saints Cyrus and John, which was razed during Al-Hakim's assault on Fustat. Unlike others in the quarter, its wooden-vaulted roof is lofty, with skylights and windows illuminating a nave flanked by Arabic arches with Fatimid tie-beams. Its *minbar*-esque pulpit and inlaid *haikal* screen would not look amiss in a mosque. The western sanctuary (remove shoes to enter) contains the cloth-wrapped relics of Saint Barbara. Tradition holds that she was the daughter of a pagan merchant who was murdered for preaching Christianity in the third century.

The Geniza

For scholars, en Ezra Synagogue is synonymous with its **Geniza**, or treasury of documents. Ever since 1041, nearly all the papers of Cairo's Jewish community were consigned to a storeroom in keeping with the tradition that any document in Hebrew, or which might bear God's name, must be preserved. A Lithuanian Talmudist was the first outsider to penetrate this cache, but failed to realise that the dusty shaft was filled with scrolls and texts, which began to leak on to the black market. In 1876, a Talmudic scholar at Cambridge University was shown a manuscript that two Scottish sisters had bought in Cairo, which he identified as a unique copy of a lost text from the Apocrypha; he immediately rushed to Egypt and acquired all that was left.

Besides religious texts there were thousands of letters, contracts and rulings, amounting to the most complete **record** of any medieval society ever discovered. It's due to these that we know so much about Fustat (see p.126) and **legends** surrounding the Ben Ezra Synagogue. According to Coptic and Jewish traditions, it was built on spot where the pharaoh's daughter found Moses in the bulrushes; Jeremiah gathered survivors here after Nebuchadnezzar destroyed Jerusalem; and a Jewish temple here provided a haven for the Holy Family, who lived among the Jews of Babylon for three months of their sojourn in Egypt.

The Ben Ezra Synagogue

Down the road, behind a wrought-iron fence, the **Ben Ezra Synagogue** is a unique relic of Cairo's ancient Jewish community. Built a thousand years after they first settled in this area, it was still revered long after most Jews had moved to Fustat or Al-Qahira. With only twelve families left here by 1864 and none a century later, the synagogue would have crumbled away were it not for one "Rabbi" Cohen, who shamelessly overcharged for souvenir postcards to fund urgent repairs until the American Jewish Congress and the Egyptian government stepped in to restore it in the 1990s.

In form, the synagogue resembles a basilical church. Some believe it incorporates a Coptic church that was sold to the Jews in 876, when the Copts were taxed to finance Ibn Tulun's Mosque. Photography isn't allowed inside, much to the chagrin of visitors dying to snap the opulent decor. The inlaid gilded marble stalactite niche dates from 1041, when the synagogue was restored by Abraham Ben Ezra, Rabbi of Jerusalem (after whom it was subsequently named). Most of its arabesque mouldings and floral swirls are the result of much later repairs, following the discovery of the Geniza (see box opposite).

The **Geniza**'s exterior can be glimpsed behind the synagogue, near a ruined **Mikvah** (ritual bath). Further on is an **Institute of Geniza Studies**, likewise off-limits to tourists.

From Fustat to the aqueduct

While the pyramids are an enduring reminder of Ancient Egypt, it's sobering to realize that the world's first Islamic metropolis (see box, p.126) has almost entirely disappeared. Under the Mamlukes Fustat's ruins became a rubbish dump, ignored until the first excavations in the 1900s. Today you can go shopping in a stylish bazaar just up the road from the Coptic quarter, or visit a pottery village amidst the flyblown vestiges of Fustat, whose sole surviving monument to its bygone glory is the nearby Mosque of Amr.

The Souk el-Fustat

The **Souk el-Fustat** (daily 10am–6pm), just up the road from the Coptic quarter, has sold handicrafts made by local communities since 2003. Its sandstone arcades are always cool due to their design, and its smart restaurant, Tivoli Fustat, makes a good lunch break before or after browsing the fifteen shops, which sell designer jewellery, textiles, ceramics and other quality handicrafts, all at fixed prices. One, APE, sells patchwork quilts, soft toys, bags and other products made from recycled garbage by the *zebaleen* (rubbish-gatherers) who have lived in this part of Cairo for centuries (see box, p.113).

The Pottery Village and the ruins of Fustat

Most of the pots, jars and plates sold in the Souk el-Fustat are made at the **Pottery Village** beyond **Fustat Park** (daily 9am–8pm; £E1), the latter a touch of greenery on the edge of Cairo's bleakest landscape. *Zebaleen* **shantytowns** (see box, p.113), potteries and smouldering rubbish tips cover a vast field of debris stretching nearly as far as the Citadel, hidden from passers-by by a high perimeter wall.

A brief history of Fustat

Fustat was founded by the victorious Arab general **Amr Ibn al-As** near the fortress of Babylon which had just fallen to his troops. According to tradition, its location was chosen by a dove, which laid an egg in Amr's tent before he was to march on Alexandria. Amr declared this as a sign from Allah, and the tent was left untouched as they went off to battle. When they returned victorious, Amr told his troops to pitch their tents around his, giving his new capital its name, **Masr al-Fustat**, "City of the Tents". From an array of tribal encampments around a mosque, it grew into a wealthy city populated by Copts, Jews, and settlers from Yemen and Arabia, communicating in Arabic and Coptic, and trading as far away as India.

The last Umayyad caliph, **Marwan II**, burned Fustat behind him as he fled to Abu Sir to die in 750 – but although the Abbasid caliphs that followed him ordered a new city to be constructed further north (Medinet al-Aksar, the "City of Cantonments"), Fustat was soon rebuilt. Awestruck tenth-century chroniclers described **high-rise buildings** housing hundreds of tenants, reaching up to seven storeys high.

Fustat kept growing even after **Ibn Tulun** founded his own capital, Al-Qitai (see p.106). In the early eleventh century, the Persian poet Nasir Khusraw saw fourteen-storey buildings with roof gardens irrigated by oxen-powered waterwheels, which drew from a piped water system that was unequalled in Europe until the eighteenth century.

This conurbation peaked demographically long after the Fatimids had created Al-Qahira (see p.258), when its population topped two hundred thousand. Even the burning of Fustat ordered by the "mad caliph" **Al-Hakim** in 1020 (see p.84) left such a vast metropolis that, in 1168, the Fatimid vizier Shawar decided to destroy it rather than let the Crusaders occupy the defenceless old city beyond Al-Qahira's walls.

Set ablaze with ten thousand torches and twenty thousand barrels of naphtha, "flames and smoke engulfed the city and rose to the sky in a terrifying scene", wrote the historian Al-Maqrizi, noting that it burned for 54 days.

It's hard to credit that such a wasteland still remains in the midst of Cairo, let alone that the great metropolis of Fustat once existed here– even if you venture in to see the paltry **ruins** (daily 9am–4pm; £E6) so far excavated. Broken columns, mud-brick foundations, bathhouse pits and water-mains are all that meet the eye. Everything of value found here is in the Museum of Islamic Art (see p.92), or foreign museums – yet more undoubtedly exists beneath the rubble of Fustat.

The Mosque of Amr

Following Sharia Mari Girgis northwards, past the Fustat turn-off and a small bus depot, you'll soon reach the **Mosque of Amr**. Its mighty enclosure walls date from 827, when it was enlarged to twice the size of the original mosque (built in 641) – the first in Egypt. A simple mud-brick, thatch-roofed enclosure without a *mihrab*, courtyard or minaret, it was large enough to contain the entire Muslim army at prayer; built on the spot where Amr pitched his tent and told his troops to settle roundabout, it has remained in use ever since.

The existing structure follows the classic congregational pattern, arched *liwans* surrounding a pebbled *sahn* centred on an ablutions well. Believers pray or snooze on fine carpets in the sanctuary *liwan*. When Amr introduced a **pulpit**, he was rebuked by Caliph Omar (a companion of the Prophet Mohammed) for raising himself above his Muslim brethren. The *mashrabiya*'d **mausoleum** of his son Abdullah marks the site of Amr's house in Fustat. A nearby column bears a gash caused by people licking it until their tongues bled to obtain miraculous cures.

The pair of **columns** on the left as you enter are said to part to allow the truly righteous to squeeze through, and another pair was supposedly whipped here all the way from Mecca by Caliph Omar.

Deir Abu'l-Sayfayn

Less than 100m past the Mosque of Amr, another Christian enclave known as **Deir Abu'l-Sayfayn** (daily 9am–5pm) is seldom visited by tourists compared to the better known Coptic quarter.

Entering the high-walled enclave by a door on Sharia Ali Salem, you'll see to your right the early seventh-century **Church of St Shenute** (Anba Shenouda), which features a lovely cedar wood and ebony altar screen. Beyond stands the **Church of St Mercurius**, which claims to be older, despite the fact that it was first mentioned in the tenth century as a sugar-cane warehouse, and totally rebuilt after the burning of Fustat (see opposite). Its claim to antecedence is based on the existence of a crypt beneath its north aisle, where St Barsum the Naked lived with a snake until his death in 317; a special Mass is held here on St Barsum's name day (September 10).

Across the way, the diminutive **Church of the Holy Virgin** (known as "Al-Damshira") was founded in the seventh century, destroyed in 785, rebuilt in 809 and restored in the eighteenth century. Outwardly modern looking, its icon-packed interior has a superb altar screen, plus a cabinet of archeological finds (unlabelled).

Adjacent to the enclave are extensive Protestant and Maronite **cemeteries**, including Commonwealth graves from World War II and a section devoted to **pets** (mostly owned by British expats, judging by the sentimental inscriptions and effigies).

The aqueduct

Travelling between Coptic and central Cairo by bus or taxi, you'll glimpse the great **aqueduct** that once carried water to the Citadel. Originally a mere conduit supported by wooden pillars, it was rebuilt in stone by Sultan Al-Nasir in 1311 and extended in 1505 by Al-Ghuri to accommodate the Nile's westward shift, to a total length of 3405m. (Al-Ghuri used it to water the ornamental gardens he had planted below the Citadel.)

River water was raised by the **Burg al-Saqiyya**, a hexagonal **water-wheel tower** (daily 9am–8pm; free) near the Corniche. On its river-facing wall, Al-Ghuri's heraldic emblem and slots for engaging the six oxen-powered water-wheels, which remained in use until 1872, can be seen. Stairs to the top allow visitors to view one of the oxen tread-wheels, and enjoy a fantastic **view** looking west over Roda

---

The Khalig al-Masri

The locality where the aqueduct meets the Nile is called **Fumm al-Khalig** (Mouth of the Canal) after a waterway that once ran inland to meet the walls of Fatimid Al-Qahira. The **Khalig al-Masri** (Egyptian Canal) was twice linked to the ancient Nile Delta–Red Sea waterway that was redug by Amr and Al-Nasir in the seventh and fourteenth centuries, but its perennial function was to supply water for the city's sanitary and industrial needs. Drinking water was drawn from the Nile and transported by an army of donkeys and *saqi* (water-carriers) to the cisterns of Cairo, since the canal became murky and dried out each year. In an annual ceremony to mark the Nile flood, the dike that separated it from the river was breached, sending fresh water coursing through the city to fill boating lakes near Bab al-Luq and Ezbekiya – a practice that continued until the taming of the Nile spelt its end, and the canal was filled in to create Bur Said and Ramses streets after 1899.

The southern suburbs

South of Old Cairo, a tendril of urban sprawl follows the east bank of the Nile out to Helwan at the end of metro Line 1. These suburbs seldom register on tourists' radar but are well-known to long-staying foreigners, harbouring a few low-key sights and two industrial complexes vital to Egypt's economy.

Cognoscenti of fossils should hunt down the **Egyptian Geological Museum** (daily except Fri 9am–1pm; free), on the Corniche el-Nil, ten to fifteen minutes' walk from Zahra metro station. Many of its exhibits are a legacy of the Tethys Sea that covered much of Egypt forty million years ago: marine invertebrates and proto-whales from the Fayoum, dinosaur bones from Baharia Oasis and the cast of a skeleton of a prehistoric pachyderm. There's also a **meteorite** that fell in the Delta in 1908, one of only 33 meteorites known to have their origin on the planet Mars.

Further out, leafy **Ma'adi** is full of villas, condos and malls where wealthy Cairenes, Gulf Arabs and Western expats rub shoulders. The suburb sits uneasily beside industrialized **Tura**, whose **quarries** have been a source of limestone for millennia, providing the casing stones for pyramids and masonry for Mamluke mansions. Tura is also notorious for its **prison**, whose high-security annexe has held such personages as the future Al-Qaida leader Ayman al-Zawahiri, and the 2005 presidential contender Ayman Nour.

Still further out, **Helwan** is synonymous with a gigantic iron- and **steelworks** that exploits power from the Aswan Dam and iron ore from the Western Desert. Five blocks east from Helwan metro (turn left as you exit) is the **Japanese Garden** (al-Hadika al-Yabaniya; daily: summer 9am–11pm; winter 9am–10pm; £E4), with Buddha statues and a pagoda.

Island or eastwards to the Muqattam Hills. Although you can **walk** beneath (not along) the aqueduct nearly as far as the Citadel, some stretches are almost as Gustav Flaubert found them in 1850: rife with streetwalkers and feral dogs.

Roda Island

The narrow channel between **Roda Island** and the mainland is bridged in such a way that the island engages more with the Garden City than with Old Cairo – a reversal of historic ties. As its much-rebuilt **Nilometer** suggests, it was the southern end of Roda that was visited by ferries between Memphis and Heliopolis, and Roman ships bound for Babylon-in-Egypt. Roda gradually reverted to agricultural use as Cairo's focus shifted northwards. Nothing remains of the pontoon bridge that linked Roda to Giza in Fatimid times, or the Ayyubid fort where the Bahri Mamlukes (see p.259) were garrisoned, whose riverside location gave rise to their name (from *bahr*, meaning "river" or "sea").

Today the island is as built-up as Zamalek but less prestigious, except for its northern tip, dominated by the **Grand Hyatt Hotel**, a five-star colossus with the finest views in Cairo (see box, p.53), reached by a private bridge. Further south, the Qasr al-Aini Bridge, just before the hospital, at the Southern end of Garden City (see p.71) offers a quieter backstreet approach to the **Manial Palace** (currently closed for restoration) than the obvious route across the Manial Bridge (which is always busy with traffic).

With the palace closed, Roda's sights are currently limited to the **Nilometer** and the **Umm Kalthoum Museum** at southern end of the island, fifteen to twenty minutes' walk from Mari Girgis station in Old Cairo. Both are in the grounds of the **Manasterly Palace,** a Rococo Turkish confection dating from 1850, later refurbished as a conference venue and now housing an International Music Center (ⓦ www.manasterly.com), which is only open to the public for **concerts** and **exhibitions**.

The Nilometer

Roda's **Nilometer** (daily 9am–4pm; £E15) is the best-preserved example of a device invented by the Ancient Egyptians (see box below), that was adopted by later civilizations and remained in use for millennia. This particular one dates from Abbasid times (861 AD), though others existed here far earlier. A stone-lined shaft descending below the level of the Nile, it was connected to the river by three tunnels (now sealed) at different heights – only the uppermost is still accessible. Around the shaft's interior are Koranic verses extolling rain as God's blessing; the central column is graduated into 16 *ells* of roughly 54cm each.

The Umm Kalthoum Museum

En route to the Nilometer, in the grounds of the Manasterly Palace, you'll pass the **Umm Kalthoum Museum** (daily 9am–4pm; £E2), commemorating Egypt's greatest singer, who actually lived in Zamalek until her death in 1975. It does a fair job of recreating the life and work of this giant of Arab music through audiovisual clips, photos, press cuttings and a film show, and the exhibits include 78rpm wax records, letters from Arab heads of state including Nasser, Sadat and King Farouk, and, most poignantly, her trademark pink scarf and dark glasses.

Umm Kalthoum was born in a Delta village some time between 1898 and 1904, when girls' births weren't registered. Her father was an imam who taught her to recite the Koran (she reportedly memorized the entire book) and, when she was twelve, disguised her as a boy and entered her in a performing troupe where, at

---

Nilometers

From ancient times until well into the twentieth century, Egyptian agriculture depended on the annual **flooding of the Nile**, which revitalized the land with fertile silt from the Ethiopian highlands and the swamps of southern Sudan. Crop yields were predicted (and taxes set) according to the river's level in August, as measured by a series of Nilometers from Aswan to Roda and the Delta. Readings were sent to Egypt's ruler and provincial governors; the basin-system of irrigation dictated that dikes must be breached at certain levels, making the Nile's rise essential to the whole nation. A reading of 16 *ells* (8.6m) foretold the valley's complete irrigation; much more or less meant severe flooding or drought. Public rejoicing followed the announcement of the Wafa el-Nil (Abundance of the Nile); any other verdict caused gloom and foreboding.

Years of drought or flood led to famine, depopulated villages and neglected irrigation works – a vicious cycle that resulted in the demise of the ancient Old and Middle Kingdoms and facilitated the Fatimid conquest of Egypt in 969 AD. In the eleventh century, a seven-year dearth saw a sack of flour rise to the exorbitant price of 1000 dinars (four and a quarter kilos of gold), reducing the rich to poverty and the poor to cannibalism. Even worse was the famine of 1200–1202 recorded by a Baghdadi doctor Abd al-Latif, whose death toll far exceeded the 110,000 registered burials as the "incalculable" dead of Fustat were simply dumped outside the city for jackals to eat. And from 950 there is the cautionary tale of an Arabic grammarian innocently humming as he walked by the Nile; taken to be a sorcerer casting a spell on the river, he was thrown in by an alarmed citizen and drowned.

sixteen, she was noticed by an established singer who taught her the Classical repertoire. Moving to Cairo in 1923 she was taught to play the lute, and mentored in Arabic literature by the poet Ahmed Rami (who wrote 137 songs for her), but never succumbed to the bohemian Tawfiqiya set (see p.68), proudly espousing her humble origins and conservative values. Known as *Kawkab al-Sharq* (the Star of the East), her funeral drew 2,500,000 mourners, so many that their combined weight almost brought down the Qasr el-Nil Bridge.

The Manial Palace

Previously Roda's chief attraction, the **Manial Palace** across from Qasr al-Aini Hospital (see p.71) is currently **closed** for restoration until sometime in 2012. Would-be visitors should enquire at the tourist office downtown or ask the policemen at the palace gates, as scheduled opening dates mean little in Egypt. Built in 1903, its fabulously eclectic decor reflects the taste of King Farouk's uncle, Prince Mohammed Ali, author of *The Breeding of Arabian Horses* and the owner of a flawless emerald that magically alleviated his ill health (so legend has it). Each of the main buildings manifests a different style – Persian, Syrian, Moorish, Ottoman and Rococo – or mixes them together with gay abandon.

In the **Reception Palace** just inside the gateway, a magnificent *salamlik* (greeting room) adorned with stained glass, polychrome tiles and ornate woodcarving prepares visitors for the opulent guest rooms upstairs. The finest is the Syrian Room, literally transplanted from Damascus. Leaving this palace and turning right, a pseudo-Moroccan tower harbours the prince's **mosque**, whose lavish decor is reminiscent of the great mosque of his namesake in the Citadel, and a grotesque **Hunting Museum** features scores of mounted ibex heads, a hermaphrodite goat, a table made from elephants' ears and a vulture's claw candlestick.

Deeper into the banyan-shaded garden, the **Prince's Residence** is richly decorated in a mixture of Turkish and Occidental styles. The drab-looking building out back contains an elongated **Throne Hall**, whose red carpet passes life-size royal portraits hung beneath a sunburst ceiling. If accessible, visitors can admire the Obsidian Salon and the private apartments of the prince's mother upstairs, enriched by a silver four-poster bed from the Abdin Palace. Lastly there's the **Private Museum**, a family hoard of manuscripts, carpets, glassware and silver plate, including some huge banqueting trays.

Gezira and
the west bank

Flowing northwards through Cairo at a leisurely three miles an hour, the Nile divides into channels around the islands of Roda (see p.128) and Gezira. Between the two, just off the southern tip of Gezira, a **fountain** in the Nile shoots an immense jet of water into the sky. **Gezira** is the larger of the two islands, and is notably less dense and more verdant than the rest of Cairo.

The southern end of Gezira is within easy walking distance of Midan Tahrir (see p.52), just over Tahrir Bridge. Museums and an opera house make this end of the island Cairo's "cultural centre", but its main tourist attraction is the **Cairo Tower**, the island's only high-rise structure and a waterfront landmark, with a panoramic view of the city. Most of the island's residents live in **Zamalek**, the prosperous neighbourhood occupying the island's northern half, which is known for its restaurants, clubs and bars.

26th July Street, elevated at this point, takes you from Zamalek across another channel of the river, to the Nile's **west bank**, which belongs to the governorate of Giza, administered separately from Cairo proper, though transport and utilities are integrated. The most vibrant district on this side of the river is **Mohandiseen**, where Arab League Street is a riot of malls and fast food, aligned directly with the Giza pyramids. The other west bank neighbourhoods are less attractive, but the Mahmoud Khalil Museum in **Dokki** and the zoo in **Giza** are among the enticements to visit.

Gezira and Zamalek

At nearly 4km long, **Gezira** (literally "island") dominates Cairo's waterfront from Garden City to Bulaq. The southern half is **Gezira** proper, and includes the **Gezira Sporting Club** (see p.210), laid out by the British Army on land given by Khedive Tewfiq (who ruled 1879–92) and occupying almost a third of the island. To its north, **Zamalek** is a genteel but nonetheless quite lively neighbourhood full of apartments, villas, offices and embassies, with a Westernized ambience and nightlife. Both Gezira and Zamalek seem so integral to Cairo that it's hard to envisage their absence, yet the island itself only coalesced out of mudbanks in the river in the early 1800s and remained unstable until the first Aswan Dam regulated the Nile's flood in the 1900s.

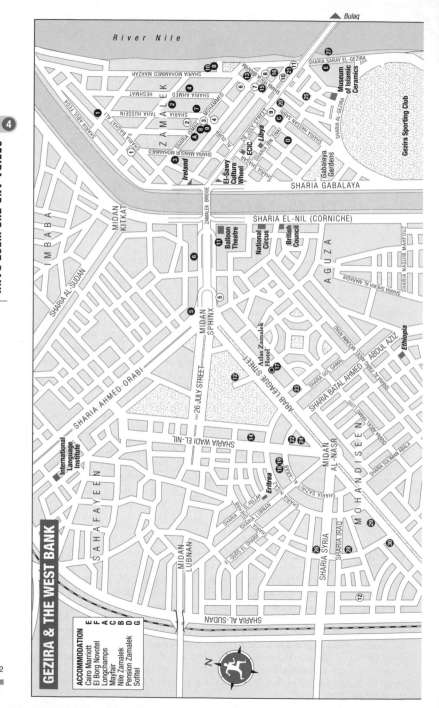

▲ Bulaq

River Nile

SHARIA SARAY EL-GEZIRA

Museum of Islamic Ceramics

Gezira Sporting Club

Gabalaya Gardens

SHARIA GABALAYA

El-Sawy Culture Wheel

Ireland

ECIC

Libya

Z A M A L E K

I M B A B A

MIDAN KITKAT

ZAMALEK BRIDGE

SHARIA EL-NIL (CORNICHE)

Balloon Theatre

National Circus

British Council

A G U Z A

MIDAN SPHINX

Atlas Zamalek Hotel

SHARIA AHMED ORABI

26 JULY STREET

ARAB LEAGUE STREET

SHARIA WADI EL-NIL

Eritrea

S A H A F A Y E E N

International Language Institute

MIDAN LUBNAN

MIDAN AL-NASR

M O H A N D I S E E N

Ethiopia

SHARIA SYRIA

SHARIA IRAQ

SHARIA AL-SUDAN

N

GEZIRA & THE WEST BANK

ACCOMMODATION
Cairo Marriott   E
El Borg Novotel   F
Longchamps   A
Mayfair   C
Nile Zamalek   B
Pension Zamalek   D
Sofitel   G

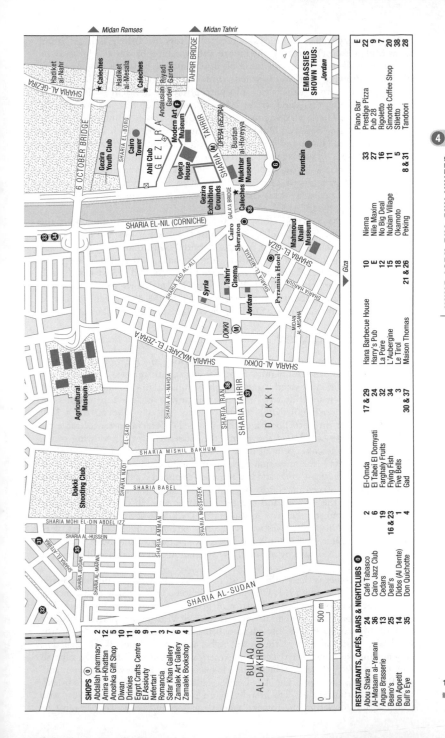

Midan Ramses ▲   Midan Tahrir ▲

★ Caleches
Hadiket
al-Nahr
SHARIA AL-GEZIRA

Hadiket
al-Mesala
★ Caleches

Andalusian Riyadi
Garden Garden

★ Caleches

TAHRIR BRIDGE

EMBASSIES
SHOWN THUS:

Jordan

6 OCTOBER BRIDGE

Gezira
Youth Club

Cairo
Tower

SHARIA EL-BORG

G E Z I R A

Modern Art
Museum

Ahli Club

Opéra
House

Gezira
Exhibition
Grounds

SHARIA TAHRIR (GEZIRA)

OPÉRA (GEZIRA)

Bustan
al-Horeyya

Mukhtar
Museum

(M)

(G)

Fountain

SHARIA EL-NIL (CORNICHE)

GALAA BRIDGE

Caleches

Mahmoud
Khalil
Museum

Cairo
Sheraton

Tahrir
Cinema

Syria

Pyramisia Hotel

SHARIA EL-GIZA

Jordan

DOKKI (M)

Giza ▼

SHARIA SAD AL-ALI

SHARIA WAZARET EL-ZERA

SHARIA AL-DOKKI

SHARIA AL-NAHDA

SHARIA IRAN

SHARIA TAHRIR

Agricultural
Museum

D O K K I

EL-SAID

SHARIA MISHIL BAKHUM

Dokki
Shooting Club

SHARIA NADI

SHARIA BABEL

SHARIA MOHI EL-DIN ABDEL IZZ

SHARIA AMMAN

SHARIA MOSSADEK

SHARIA AL-HUSSEIN

SHARIA JEDDAH

SHARIA AL-MAHWA

SHARIA AL-SUDAN

500 m

0

BULAQ
AL-DAKHROUR

SHOPS ⓘ
Abdallah pharmacy	2
Amira el-Khattan	12
Anoshka Gift Shop	5
Diwan	10
Drinkies	11
Egypt Crafts Centre	8
El Assiouty	9
Nefertari	1
Romancia	3
Safar Khan Gallery	7
Zamalek Art Gallery	6
Zamalek Bookshop	4

RESTAURANTS, CAFÉS, BARS & NIGHTCLUBS ⓞ
Abou Shakra	24	El-Omda	17 & 29	Hana Barbecue House	10	Nierna	33
Al-Mataam al-Yamani	36	El Tabei El Domyati	24	Harry's Pub	27	Nile Maxim	27
Angus Brasserie	13	Farghaly Fruits	32	La Poire	12	No Big Deal	16
Beano's	25	Flying Fish	34	L'Aubergine	15	Nubian Village	11
Bon Appetit	14	Five Bells	3	Le Tirol	18	Okamoto	5
Bull's Eye	35	Gad	30 & 37	Maison Thomas	21 & 26	Peking	8 & 31
Café Tabasco	24					Piano Bar	33
Cairo Jazz Club	36					Prestige Pizza	27
Cedars	19					Pub 28	16
Deal's	16 & 23					Rigoletto	11
Didos (Al Dente)	1					Simonds Coffee Shop	5
Don Quichotte	4					Stiletto	8 & 31
						Tandoori	

Piano Bar 33 · E 22
Prestige Pizza 27 · 9
Pub 28 16 · 7
Rigoletto 11 · 20
Simonds Coffee Shop 5 · 38
Stiletto · 28
Tandoori 8 & 31

4

Despite heavy traffic, it's enjoyable to stroll across the **Tahrir Bridge** (200m from Midan Tahrir), catching the breeze and watching barges and feluccas on the river. Walking across, you can look down and see how the Nile gives the illusion of flowing southwards when wind from the north ruffles its surface; its sluggish current is otherwise only perceptible by the drift of flotsam on the river. Once on the island, strike 200m northwards up Sharia al-Gezira and turn left down Sharia al-Borg to reach the Cairo Tower (10min), or follow the traffic heading towards Dokki along Sharia Tahrir, which brings you to the Cairo Opera House and several museums (5–10min). Alternatively, take a *calèche* (horse-drawn carriage) on a circuit of Gezira – a short trip, around the Cairo Tower area, will cost around £E40, while a half-hour circuit round the Sporting Club costs about £E60. *Calèches* can be hired by Gala'a Bridge (the bridge from Gezira to Dokki), and just off Sharia al-Gezira near the Cairo Tower (see map, pp.132–133).

Passing over the Sporting Club, the **6th October Bridge** (named after the starting date of the 1973 October War against Israel; see p.144) is a more direct link between Aguza, on the West Bank, and central Cairo than a viable approach to Gezira (though there are stairs down to both banks of the island). To get to **Zamalek** from central Cairo, save yourself a long walk and grab a **taxi** (which shouldn't cost more than £E5–8). **Buses** from Midan Tahrir to Zamalek will drop you on Sharia Gabalaya on the western side of the district, and plenty of **minibuses** run along **26th July Street** from Midan Ataba and Midan Ramses.

The Cairo Tower

Soaring 187m above Gezira, the **Cairo Tower (Borg al-Qahira** daily: summer 9am–1am; winter 8am–midnight; £E65; ⓦ www.cairotower.net) offers a stupendous view of the city's seething immensity. Entering the tower from Sharia al-Borg, visitors take a lift to a mediocre **restaurant** on the fourteenth floor (minimum charge £E100) that – when working – slowly revolves for a 360° view. Above, on the 15th floor, a similarly styled **cafeteria** serves tolerable tea (minimum charge £E30), and above that, the sixteenth floor is a viewing room, complete with telescopes. On all three levels – the restaurant, the cafeteria and the viewing room – the attraction is the **panoramic vista** of Cairo. East across the river, the *Nile Ritz–Carlton* and the antenna-festooned Radio and TV Building delineate an arc of central Cairo. Beyond lies the medieval city, bristling with minarets below the Citadel and the serene Muqattam Hills. Roda Island and deluxe hotels dominate the view south (upriver), while to the north lie Zamalek, Shubra and the Nile Delta. Westwards, the city extends to meet the desert, with the Pyramids visible on the horizon on clear days. Come a while before sunset to witness Cairo transformed by nightfall, as fifteen thousand *muezzins* call across the vast metropolis.

The Cairo Tower is the world's tallest all-concrete structure, built with Soviet help between 1956 and 1961. Combining pharaonic and socialist-realist motifs, it takes the form of a cylindrical lattice of poured concrete, flared at the top to symbolize a lotus flower. The tower was funded with money passed to Nasser by CIA bagman Kermit Roosevelt as a bribe to stay on America's side in the Cold War. Nasser spent it on the tower, to be, as historian Samir Rafaat called it, "a giant middle finger [that] even the Americans would see". Egyptian officials nicknamed it *waqf Roosevelt*, which can be taken to mean "Roosevelt's endowment" or "Roosevelt's erection". The Americans retaliated by calling it "Nasser's prick", and this was apparently taken literally by an Islamist group in the 1990s, who issued a *fatwa* declaring the tower "against religion and sharia law. It must be destroyed," they said, "as its shape and construction amid greenery could excite Egyptian women." In fact the tower is a popular locale for discreet lovers' trysts, and remains so to this day, much to the ire of the religious lobby.

The Opera House complex

Fans of postmodernist architecture should check out the 1988 **Cairo Opera House** (see p.207) near Tahrir Bridge, with its own Metro stop (signed "Opera" on the platform but marked as "Gezira" on the Metro map). Outwardly Islamic in style, it has an interior that blends pharaonic motifs with elements of the Baroque opera houses of the nineteenth century: an audacious blend of Oriental and Occidental by Japanese architect Koichiro Shikida. It was a US$30 million gift from Japan, and replaced the old building on Midan Opera, which burned down in 1971.

East of the Opera House, the **Modern Art Museum** (Tues–Sun 10am–2pm & 5–10pm; £E10; ⓦ www.modernartmuseum.gov.eg) displays paintings, sculptures and graphics created by Egyptian artists from 1908 onwards. There is always something new on show, and fans of modern art will want to make the effort to visit. The museum doesn't have any really famous works, but highlights include modern realist works by Mohamed Owais, including his 1989 "Fellah", which depicts a weeping unemployed worker, and "Factory Workers", a grim industrial piece somehow reminiscent of the Italian surrealist de Chirico. On a jollier note, Ragheb Ayad's "Cafe in Aswan" shows a traditional *'ahwa* in the 1930s, with a band playing and a rather hefty dame in the middle smoking a *sheesha*, while "Hammam" by Coptic artist Marguerite Nakhla shows the inside of a traditional Turkish bath.

Following Sharia Tahrir towards the west bank, you'll pass the old **Gezira Exhibition Grounds**, whose dilapidated pavilions formerly housed museums and a planetarium – all closed for long-term renovation. Across the road to the south, just before the Galaa Bridge, the **Mukhtar Museum** (Tues–Sun 10am–1.30pm & 5–9pm; £E5) honours the sculptor Mahmoud Mukhtar (1891–1934), who is buried in the basement. Working in limestone, bronze and marble, he created several patriotic sculptures, most famously *Nahdet Misr* ("Egypt's Renaissance"), the statue that welcomes drivers into Giza (see p.138). Mukhtar was a keen supporter of the nationalist Wafd Party, and is considered the father of modern Egyptian sculpture. His works are typified by a characteristic rounded smoothness, but they are somehow rather staid and lack any feeling of movement. The museum houses eighty-five of them, including the Henry Moore-like abstract *Khamsin* (the name refers to a hot, dusty spring wind), and *The Water Drawer*, Mukhtar's elegant homage to Egypt's hardworking village women.

Zamalek

Situated at the north end of Gezira island, Zamalek was originally a very British neighbourhood, despite its Continental-style grid of tree-lined boulevards. It still has bags of social cachet, and renting a flat here is the Cairene equivalent of moving into Manhattan. Unlike most parts of Cairo, the quarter feels very private; residents withdraw into their air-conditioned high-rises or 1930s apartment buildings and many of the streets are lifeless after dark, as the area is home to many foreign companies and **embassies**. Paradoxically, Zamalek also features some of the trendiest **bars** in Cairo (see p.202).

Children may enjoy the **aquarium grotto** in **Gabalaya Gardens** (daily 9.30am–4pm; £E1; see p.213), entered from Sharia Gabalaya. For more cultural pursuits, head for the other end of Sharia al-Gezira as it curves around the northern edge of the Sporting Club, where a graceful nineteenth-century villa houses the Museum of Islamic Ceramics (see below). The modern annexes of the adjacent **Cairo Marriott Hotel** screen what was originally a "madly sumptuous palace" built for Napoleon's wife Empress Eugénie, later sold to wealthy Copts in lieu of nineteenth-century ruler Khedive Ismail's debts, and turned into a hotel. Non-residents can wander in and recline amid khedival splendour for the price of a drink.

Although Zamalek is young by Egyptian standards, dating back only to the end of the nineteenth century, it isn't without its history. The sections of Sharia Shagar al-Durr and Sharia Mansur Mohammed due south of 26th July Street were once home to **Edwardian villas** constructed by the British in 1906–7 to house senior officials. Of the nine still standing, the grandest is at 20 Sharia Ibn Zinki (on the corner of Mansur Mohammed) with its imposing triple-arched portico. Further south, 4 Sharia Hassan Sabry occupies the site of a villa where Britain's senior minister in wartime Egypt, **Lord Moyne**, was shot in 1944, along with his driver, by members of a maverick Zionist paramilitary group known as the Stern Gang. A more recent Zamalek murder, which shocked the Middle East as much as Lord Moyne's had, was that of the popular and controversial Tunisian singer **Zikra** in 2003, at her swanky apartment on Sharia Mohammed Mazhar. She was killed by her husband, apparently in a fit of jealousy, after refusing his demand that she give up her career. Having produced two pistols and a machine gun, he pumped Zikra with 25 rounds, then shot two of their friends, and finally himself. Thousands attended the singer's funeral.

Museum of Islamic Ceramics

Housed in a white-domed villa close to the *Cairo Marriott*, the **Museum of Islamic Ceramics** (daily except Fri 10am–1.30pm & 5–9pm; £E25; ⓦ www.icm.gov.eg) is one of Cairo's most agreeable museums to visit. Commissioned by Prince Amru Ibrahim in the late nineteenth century, the structure itself is worth a look for its elaborate marble inlays and floors. The collection contains some beautiful pieces from Egypt, Persia, Syria, Turkey, Morocco, Iraq and Andalucia, ranging from the seventh century to the present. Downstairs there's an art gallery (same hours; free) exhibiting original paintings and sculptures as well as prints by modern Egyptian artists such as Asraf and Alzamzami.

Mohandiseen

West across the river from Zamalek, 26th July Street continues to Midan Sphinx and **Mohandiseen**. Laid out during the 1960s to house Egypt's new technocrats, Medinat Mohandiseen (Engineers' City), is Cairo's most thoroughly modern neighbourhood. Nowhere else in Cairo can you cruise down a boulevard glittering with boutiques and junk food outlets, squint and almost imagine that you're in LA. Even the palm trees seem to hail from Hollywood rather than the Nile.

Most of the action occurs along Mohandiseen's main axis, **Arab League Street** (Sharia Gameat al-Dowal al-Arabiya), also known as "The Mall", which is bisected by palms and shrubbery for its three-kilometre length. On a clear day (admittedly a rare occurrence in Cairo), thanks to its deliberate alignment, you can look down it and see the Giza Pyramids in the distance. During summer Cairene families picnic here – an indication of how few green spaces are available in Cairo. With lots of rich Gulf Arabs about, however, the area is not free of sleaze: outdoor tea-stands in the neighbourhood for example, where young women circulate with trays, are often a front for prostitution, allowing assignations to be made without offending public decency.

To reach Mohandiseen from central Cairo, you can catch a bus from Abdel Mouneem Riyad (#336), or from Midan Ataba (#17// or minibus #103).

Aguza and Dokki

A 100-metre-wide channel separates Zamalek and Gezira from the west bank districts of **Aguza and Dokki**, where foreigners staying in Cairo often rent flats and many Gulf Arabs settle for the summer; indeed, "Saudi flats" has become a euphemism for prostitution in this part of town. Aguza's only attraction as such – and you'd need to have a special interest to want to seek it out – is the run-down **Agricultural Museum** (Tues–Sun 9am–2pm; 25pt) in the grounds of the Ministry of Agriculture, where dusty pavilions display exhibits on ancient farming techniques and the cotton industry; the entrance is on the south side of the estate.

To the south of Aguza, **Dokki** (usually pronounced "Do'i", with a glottal stop in the middle) is most noteworthy for the **Mahmoud Khalil Museum on Sharia al-Giza** (Tues–Sun 10am–5pm; £E25; wheelchair access; Ⓦwww .mkm.gov.eg), housed in the refurbished mansion where Khalil, a prewar politician and Agriculture Minister, lived with his French-born wife. Together they built up this magnificent collection of art and sculpture, mostly French Impressionist and post-Impressionist works. Highlights include Gauguin's *Life and Death*, in which both eponymous conditions are portrayed as nude women, and Gustave Moreau's *Salome in the Garden*, a depiction of the biblical *femme fatale* in Pre-Raphaelite style. There's also one of Monet's water-lily canvases, and paintings by Renoir and Pissarro, not to mention sculptures by Rodin. Van Gogh's *Poppy Flowers* was heisted from the museum in August 2010, and was still missing at time of writing.

Dokki is served by buses #15, #19, #116, #166, #340 and #337, and minibus #183, from in front of the Arab League Building on Midan Tahrir, all running along Sharia Tahrir. Dokki metro stop is also on Sharia Tahrir, but not very convenient for the Mahmoud Khalil Museum.

Houseboat shenanigans

Aguza was once a popular mooring place for houseboats along the river, many of which were used for prostitution and illicit liaisons, and in their time generated almost as much scandal as Clot Bey (see p.68) and Butneya (see p.88) once did. During World War II, one of Aguza's houseboats was occupied by a famous belly dancer, **Hekmet Fathy**, who was used by Nazi spy Johannes Eppler to entice Allied staff officers aboard and inveigle secrets out of them. Also involved was a young Egyptian officer, **Anwar Sadat**, who attempted to convey messages to Rommel and was subsequently jailed by the British for treason. Post-revolutionary Egypt was austere by comparison, but hardly innocent. In 1988 the government tried to suppress the memoirs of **Eitimad Khorshid**, a *femme fatale* who cut a swathe through the Nasserite establishment of the 1950s, and promised to reveal all in what became an underground bestseller.

Giza

Giza proper, the area south of Dokki, is a busy, grimy but animated part of town, and a major transport hub. It's also the gateway to the Pyramids, but the only real sight in Giza itself is its zoo. The epicentre of the area is **Midan Giza** (Giza Square), a kilometre southeast of the zoo, where there are buses to the Pyramids,

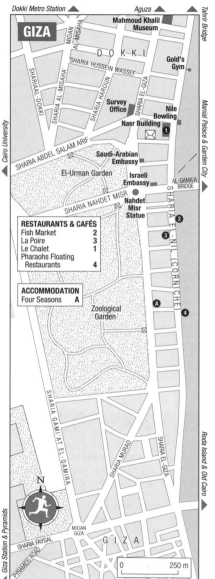

and minibuses to Tahrir, Ramses and Heliopolis, with **Giza Station** a few minutes' walk further south. From Midan Giza, Pyramids Road and Faisal Street head west towards the Giza Pyramids, which are actually 8km away and covered in chapter six (see p.153).

Coming into Giza over the El-Gama'a Bridge from Garden City and the north of Roda Island, you pass the heavily guarded entrance to the **Israeli Embassy**, to be greeted by Mahmoud Mukhtar's most famous **statue**, **Nahdet Misr** ("Egypt's Renaissance" or "Egypt Awakes"; see p.135 for more on Mukhtar). For all its pharaonic stolidity, this 1928 sculpture, of a woman lifting her veil while a sphinx stirs at her feet, was supposed to represent a cultural renewal heralded by early twentieth-century Egyptian nationalism, and was originally erected opposite the British police headquarters on Midan Ramses.

At the same road junction where the statue stands is the main entrance to **Giza Zoo** (daily 9am–5pm; £E1, camera 25pt). Originally this was part of the grounds of Khedive Ismail's palace, laid out by French landscaper Jean-Pierre Barillet-Deschamps (who was responsible for the Bois de Boulogne and the Champs de Mars in Paris, as well as Ezbekiya Gardens in Cairo; see p.67). Ismail had hoped to have the grounds converted into a botanical garden in time for the opening of the Suez Canal in 1869, but the project wasn't realized for another 22 years, by which time his son Tewfik was on the throne and the botanical garden had become a zoo.

Giza through the ages

In ancient times, Giza lay on the route between Heliopolis and Memphis (see p.257), and the skilled corps of pyramid-builders probably lived here. As Memphis declined during the Christian era, so Giza flourished, thanks to its proximity to the Fortress of Babylon across the river (now Old Cairo; see p.257). In Saladin's time (1171–93), Giza's Sunday market drew huge crowds, but from the thirteenth century, under the Mamlukes and the Ottomans, neglect of flood defences turned the area into a rural wasteland. Only when Khedive Ismail drained swamps, laid the Pyramids Road and had his palace built here in the 1860s did Giza became fashionable again. By Nasser's time, its population topped a million, and it is now more than double that, making Giza one of the busiest parts of town.

It boasts a suspension bridge by Gustave Eiffel, man-made waterfalls and grottoes, flora and fauna from Africa and Asia, and a hippo pond (£E1 to walk across on a bridge), all covering nearly eighty acres. See p.213 for details on visiting. The zoo can be reached from Abdel Mouneen Riyad by bus #8, #115, #164, #900 or #997.

Across Sharia Nahdet Misr from the zoo is the smaller **Al–Urman Garden** (daily 8.30am–4pm), a rather formal little park which was also originally part of Khedive Ismail's palace grounds, and provides a much-needed touch of green in one of the world's most densely built-up cities.

The northern suburbs

Cairo's teeming **northern suburbs** embody a cross-section of the city's social strata and a timeline from antiquity to the present. Although obvious tourist sights are few and far between, there's plenty to discover if you're curious about life in Cairo's *baladi* quarters (a term referring to the rural antecedents of their inhabitants), how Mubarak's regime was overthrown by people power, or how the Ancient Egyptians envisaged Creation.

Bulaq and **Shubra** are archetypal *baladi* quarters where residents raise poultry on the rooftops; tap overhead power-lines for free electricity and lower shopping baskets to vendors on the streets; delighting in rhyming abuse and every superstition from exorcisms to *jinn*. The two districts merge near the huge **Rod el-Farag market**, while the delectable remains of the **Shubra Palace** stand aloof from the fray, beyond the Imbrahimiya Canal.

Abbassiya is another *baladi* district whose **Coptic Cathedral** makes it a focus for Cairo's Christians (even though most live in Bulaq or Shubra). Here too are the **Mosque of Beybars the Crossbowman** – the second largest in Cairo – and the **Sakakini Palace**, worth seeing from outside even if you don't bother trying to bribe your way in.

Further out, **Medinet Nasr** hosts Cairo's international **football stadium** and the vainglorious **October War Panorama** and **Victory Memorial**, but is primarily the home turf of Egypt's bureaucratic and military elites. The finale of Egypt's 2011 revolution occurred in nearby **Heliopolis**, where Mubarak departed from an air base as crowds marched on the Presidential Palace – one of many Moorish Art Deco edifices that give this suburb its unique visual identity.

Heliopolis should not to be confused with the ancient city of the same name, whose scant remains are out in **Matariyya**, a suburb known to Cairenes for its **Virgin's Tree** (revered by Christians), which the Ancient Egyptians identified as the site of Creation.

Bulaq and Shubra

Immediately behind the 6th October flyover that crosses central Cairo (see map, pp.50–51) lies the oldest of the northern suburbs, **Bulaq**, whose name derives from the Coptic word for "marsh". During medieval times, the westward shift of the Nile turned a sandbank into an island, which merged with the east bank as the intervening channel silted up. As the Fatimid port of Al-Maks was left high and dry, Bulaq became the new anchorage in the 1350s, developing into an entrepôt after Sultan Barsbey rerouted the spice trade and encouraged manufacturing.

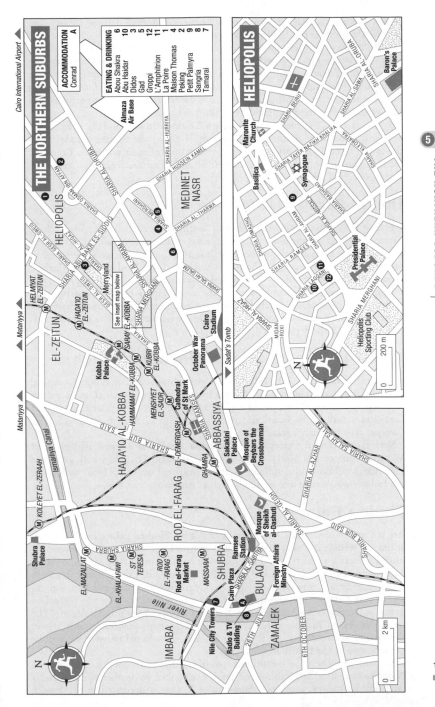

THE NORTHERN SUBURBS

▲ Cairo International Airport

ACCOMMODATION
Conrad .... A

EATING & DRINKING
Abou Shakra 6
Abu Haidar 10
Didos 3
Gad 5
Groppi 12
L'Amphitrion 1
La Poire 11
Maison Thomas 4
Peking 2
Petit Palmyra 9
Sangria 8
Tamarai 7

Almaza
Air Base

HELIOPOLIS

SHARIA OSMAN IBN AFFAN
SHARIA GESR AL-SWEIS
SHARIA ABU BAKR ES-SIDDIQ
SHARIA AL-HURRIYA
SHARIA AL-HIGAZ
SHARIA HUSSEIN KAMEL

MEDINET
NASR

SHARIA AL-THARWA

SHARIA SALAH SALEM

Merryland
See inset map below

HELMIYAT
EL-ZEITUN

▲ Matariyya

EL-ZEITUN

HADAYIQ
EL-ZEITUN

Kobba
Palace

MENSHIYET
EL-SADR

Cathedral
of St Mark

▲ Matariyya

HADA'IQ AL-KOBBA

HAMMAMAT EL-KOBBA

KUBRI
EL-KOBBA

SARAY EL-KOBBA

SHARIA BUR SAID

October War
Panorama

Cairo
Stadium

Sadat's Tomb ▼

EL-DEMERDASH

SHARIA RAMSES

ABBASSIYA

GHAMRA

Sakakini
Palace

Mosque of Beybars the
Crossbowman

KOLEYET EL-ZERA'H

Ismailiya Canal

▲ Matariyya

EL-MAZALLAT

Shubra
Palace

EL-KHALAFAWI

ST
TERESA

ROD
EL-FARAG

SHARIA SHUBRA

Rod el-Farag
Market

MASSARA

ROD EL-FARAG

SHUBRA

Ramses
Station

Mosque of
Sheikh
al-Dashuti

SHARIA AL-GALAA

Cairo Plaza

BULAQ

Foreign Affairs
Ministry

SHARIA SABTIA

IMBABA

River Nile

Nile City Towers

Radio & TV
Building

26TH JULY

ZAMALEK

6TH OCTOBER

SHARIA SALAH SALEM

SHARIA AL-AZHAR

SHARIA BUR SAID

N

0   2 km

HELIOPOLIS

Baron's
Palace

SHARIA AL-AHRAM
SHARIA AL-ORUBA

SHARIA AL-SANA

Maronite
Church

Basilica

Synagogue

SHARIA TAYER NAZIKH KHALIFA

SHARIA BEIRUT

SHARIA BAGHDAD

SHARIA AL-HIGAZ

SHARIA AL-HAMAM

SHARIA AL-MISSALA

SHARIA AL-HIGAZ

Presidential
Palace

SHARIA RAMSES

SHARIA LOQMAN

SHARIA MERGHANI

Heliopolis
Sporting Club

MIDAN
ROXI

N

0   200 m

SHARIA AL-KOBATRA

THE NORTHERN SUBURBS

5

141

When Mohammed Ali set about establishing a foundry, textiles factory and modern shipyards in the 1820s, Bulaq was the obvious site.

Today it's an uneasy juxtaposition of plutocratic and proletarian, with high-rise monoliths beside the Nile backing onto acres of *baladi* tenements. The satellite dish-festooned **Radio and Television Building** remained a bastion of state propaganda (reporting protests on Midan Tahrir as the work of foreign agents) until the final hours of Mubarak's reign; its exterior is scarred by petrol bombs thrown during the most violent days of the 2011 revolution.

By contrast, the 143-metre-high **Foreign Affairs Ministry** and the twin towers of **Cairo Plaza** were ignored as the people of Bulaq and Shubra demonstrated the solidarity typical of *baladi* quarters by marching *en masse* to Midan Tahrir, or forming vigilante groups to protect their homes when the regime unleashed its secret police and street-thugs to foment chaos.

Rod el-Farag Market

North of Bulaq, the labyrinthine **Shubra** district was originally an island (whose name, "Elephant", supposedly came from a ship that ran aground), which became attached to the mainland about the same time as Bulaq and was later given over to orchards and market gardens. The only vestige of this is **Rod el-Farag Market**, a series of warehouses used by fruit and vegetable traders from Upper Egypt. Pungently earthy, it functions around the clock but is busiest from dawn to midday, with bulk sales transacted indoors and retailing in the surrounding streets. Being far from Rod el-Farag metro station, the market is best reached by taxi (£E10–15) – ask the driver to take you to "Souk Abu el-Farag".

Nile City Towers and the Imbaba Bridge

Shubra's chief landmark is the **Nile City Towers** (Ⓦ nilecitytowers.com) complex, erected on the Corniche in 2002. Visible from as far as the Citadel, these golden skyscrapers (142m tall) are a prestige address for the super-rich, shared by a luxury hotel and a mall (daily 9am–1am) with a multiplex cinema, from which poor Cairenes are rigorously excluded.

Near the towers, the riveted steel **Imbaba Bridge** is a wonderful piece of Victorian engineering (1891) by the Englishman David Trambley, with a road on each side, a railway in the middle, and twin overhead walkways from which you can feel the whole structure tremble when a train crosses the bridge.

Shubra Palace

Ask the tourist office (see p.45) whether or not the **Shubra Palace** can be visited; at time of writing it was reserved for conferences but reportedly set to become a tourist attraction in the future. The palace was founded in 1808 by Mohammed Ali (who later died there as an insane paranoiac) and remained the summer residence of Khedive Ismail, who laid a carriage road planted with acacia and sycamore-fig trees where Cairenes promenaded and foreigners rode out to picnic in the palace grounds. Despite Ismail's hospitality, Europeans mocked the palace's decor ("The taste, alas! of an English upholsterer," sniffed *Murray's Handbook*), and a later owner – Princess Aziza – had the main building demolished rather than let it be expropriated by the British in the 1930s.

All that remains is a sumptuous **pavilion** that was once known as the Nymphaeum, after its marble-lined pool, overlooked by marble nymphs and a wrap-around gallery with four *diwans* (salons). One is decorated in the French

Empire style, another with *trompe-l'oeil* murals of mythological figures in a bucolic landscape; in a third salon, Mohammed Ali and his family cavort half-naked with Greek gods. The saucy murals are attributed to the Italian builder-decorator Pietro Avoscani, who did the interior of the original Cairo Opera House. Restored to its full glory at the beginning of the twenty-first century, the pavilion is visible behind a fence, a short walk from Koleyat el-Zeraah **metro** station, near the end of Line 2.

Abbassiya

Sprawling northeast from Ramses Station, the **Abbassiya** district is named after a palace built by Mohammed Ali's grandson, Abbas, who dreaded assassination during his brief reign (1848–54) and kept camels saddled here for rapid escape into the desert. Previously called Ridaniya, this was the site of the final battle between the Mamlukes and the Ottoman Turks before the latter took Cairo in 1517. Today it is one of Cairo's most densely populated neighbourhoods: fuel depots sitting among housing estates and flyovers running only metres past people's windows make it an object lesson in environmental dystopia.

On Sharia Sakakini, near Ghamra metro station, the Rococo **Sakakini Palace**, built in 1898 for an Italian nobleman, is supposedly being restored and due to open to the public (though they have been saying this for years). It's still worth a look for its outrageously kitsch facade, and you may be able to persuade the caretaker to let you see the marvellous interior with its huge mirrors, murals, painted ceilings and antique elevator (baksheesh expected).

At the street's far end, on Midan al-Zahir, the **Mosque of Beybars the Cross-bowman** was the first mosque to be located outside Al-Qahira's walls (in 1268). Covering ten thousand square metres – making it one of Cairo's largest religious edifices – its sturdy walls enclose a vast open courtyard surrounded by a ponderous arcade. After the mosque ceased to be a place of worship in the sixteenth century, it was used as a military storehouse by the Ottomans, a barracks by Napoleon and a slaughterhouse by the British. Restoration started in the 1990s but soon petered out; the southeast side is now again in use as a mosque, while the rest of it remains a building site.

A more conspicuous edifice is the curvaceous concrete **Cathedral of St Mark**, the seat of the Coptic Patriarchate since it was raised in the 1970s. As the position of Egypt's Coptic Christians has worsened (see p.267), the police presence outside the cathedral has grown and Coptic protests have become frequent – so don't be surprised to see Central Security troops massed outside.

Medinet Nasr

In the 1960s and 70s, the spacious suburb of **Medinet Nasr** (Victory City) was laid out on the site of the former British Rifle Ranges between Abbassiya and the Muqattam Hills. Today, football fans will need no prompting to head for **Cairo International Stadium** to experience the passion of Egyptian supporters, and anyone with an interest in military history will enjoy the pre-digital audio-visual show at the **October War Panorama**, whose specious message is rammed home by the **Victory Memorial**, where Egypt's assassinated president Anwar Sadat is buried.

Medinet Nasr is also interesting as an example of how Egypt's military dictatorship rewarded itself and its civilian minions with swanky clubs, offices and subsidized housing. That so many government departments are located here is a perpetual irritation for ordinary Cairenes, who have to trek out to obtain some rubberstamped permit or other, essential for living.

Medinet Nasr can be reached by **service taxi** from the Ahmed Helmi depot near Ramses Station (see map, p.28). Check whether your taxi's route follows Sharia al-Oruba (passing the October War Panorama en route to Heliopolis) or Sharia al-Nasr (running beside the Victory Memorial, closer to the stadium). Whichever point you arrive at, you can walk from one to the other in fifteen minutes.

The October War Panorama

It's telling that the **October War Panorama** was suggested to President Mubarak by the North Korean dictator Kim Il Sung, and inspired a similar effort in Damascus (where Syria's ruler also laid claim to victory in the same war against Israel). Both panoramas were built under North Korean supervision and resemble pavilions from a Communist theme park modified for Arab milieus; the one in Cairo has Socialist Realist reliefs of Egyptian soldiers in front of the Pyramids and statues of commandos paddling dinghies across the Suez Canal.

Shows (daily except Tues 9.30am, 11am and 12.30pm, plus in winter 5pm and 6.30pm, summer 6pm and 7.30pm; £E20, camera £E2) start with two rather silly dioramas illustrating the crossing of the canal, and culminate in an impressive three-dimensional panorama of the war in Sinai, during which the audience is rotated around 360° to take it all in. The commentary (in Arabic, with an English version via headphones) is so over-the-top in its triumphalism that you might almost think the Egyptians had actually won the October War (see below).

Cairo International Stadium and the Victory Memorial

A triumphal avenue leads southwards from Sharia al-Oruba to **Cairo International Stadium** (Al-Stad Al-Qahira Al-Dawly), Egypt's premier sporting arena. Inaugurated by President Nasser on the eighth anniversary of the 1952 revolution, it has seating for 75,000 spectators but packs in 120,000 during championship matches between Ahly and Zamalek (see p.210) or contenders in the African Cup of Nations.

Beyond the stadium rises a pyramid-shaped concrete **Victory Memorial** to the 1973 October War with Israel. By crossing the Suez Canal and breaching Israel's fortified Bar-Lev Line to recapture part of Sinai, the Egyptian Army enabled President Sadat to claim a moral victory – despite an Israeli counterattack that came within 101km of Cairo before the Superpowers imposed a ceasefire. Sadat's claim to be the "Hero of the Crossing" was rendered doubly offensive to many by his later "Peace of the Bold" (as he called it) with Israel.

In 1981, Islamic radicals infiltrated the October 6th anniversary parade at the memorial and blasted the reviewing stand with machine guns and grenades, fatally wounding Sadat. His **tomb** lies beneath the memorial, whose splayed flanks are inscribed with every male forename in Egypt, representing the soldiers whose bodies were never recovered from the battlefields of Sinai. Soldiers in hussar-style ceremonial uniforms mount a permanent **guard of honour** beside the tomb, which might otherwise be vandalized by those that detest Sadat's policies.

Heliopolis (Masr al-Gadida)

Anyone who enjoys the retro elegance of Hercule Poirot films should visit **Heliopolis**, an Art Deco suburb dating from the heyday of the British Empire, that's nowadays known in Arabic as **Masr al-Gadida** (New Cairo).

By the beginning of the last century, the doubling of Cairo's population had created a hunger for new accommodation which fired the imagination of a Belgian entrepreneur, Baron Édouard Empain (1852–1929), who was seeking new ventures after his construction of the Paris Metro. In 1905 he founded the Cairo Electric Railway and Heliopolis Oases Company, which for only £E6000 acquired 24 square kilometres of desert 15km outside Cairo. A "city of luxury and leisure", linked to downtown Cairo by tram, proved attractive to investors, as the company would collect both rents and fares from commuting residents of the new suburb, which was named after the ancient City of the Sun in nearby Matariyya (see p.147).

Laid out by British town planner Reginald Oakes in radial grid patterns, the suburb's wide avenues were lined with apartment blocks ennobled by pale yellow Moorish facades and bisected by shrubbery. It soon acquired every facility from schools and churches to a racecourse and branch of *Groppi* (see p.199). Wealthy Egyptians settled from the outset; merely prosperous ones moved in as foreigners left during the 1950s, when poorer quarters grew up around Heliopolis, ending its privileged isolation from Cairo. Today, visitors come to admire the stylish architecture along its boulevards, and many expats rent apartments or work here.

Sharia al-Ahram and around

Nouzha-line trams traverse the heart of Heliopolis. As they turn into Sharia al-Ahram across from the Sporting Club, you'll glimpse the **Presidential Palace** from which Mubarak fled Cairo on February 11, 2011, as crowds marched on the palace from Midan Tahrir. Its official name – the Unity Palace (Qasr al-Ittihadiya) – harks back to its role as the headquarters of the short-lived 1970s Federation of Arab Republics (involving Egypt, Libya and Syria). The huge building was originally a hotel, the most luxurious in Africa when it opened in 1910, with four hundred rooms, every modern amenity, and a narrow-gauge railway running the length of its basement kitchens and staff quarters. King Albert I of Belgium and the US tycoons John Pierpont Morgan and Milton Hershey (inventor of the Hershey Bar) were among its celebrity guests.

Getting to Heliopolis

Heliopolis is fifteen to thirty minutes' ride from downtown Cairo. You can get there by bus (#400, #400/ and #500) or minibus (#27) from Tahrir and Ramses but, especially during rush hour, these are slower than the suburb's original tram system, the **Heliopolis metro**, which begins at Midan Ramses. From there, its three streetcar lines follow the same track through Abbassiya, diverging shortly before Midan Roxi in Heliopolis. Each has its own colour-coded direction boards.

The most useful for sightseeing is the **Nouzha line** (signboarded in red), which follows Sharia Al-Ahram past the Basilica to Midan Triomphe, and on to Midan al-Higaz. Some local restaurants can be reached by the **Abd al-Aziz Fahmi line** (signboarded in blue) running along Sharia al-Higaz to Midan Heliopolis, or the **Merghani line** (signboarded in yellow) that follows the street of that name to Midan Triomphe. None of these trams run near the Baron's Palace, which can only be reached by bus #400.

Sharia al-Ahram is lined with elegant villas and boutiques. Here you'll find *L'Amphitrion* (as old as Heliopolis; see p.195) and *Groppi* (see p.199), where the bourgeoisie of the district's 1920s heyday would relax over cakes and coffee, as you still can today. At the far end, trams veer right to bypass the Byzantine-style Catholic **Basilica** where Baron Empain is buried. A **Maronite Church** on Sharia Beirut and a discreetly active **Synagogue** at 3 Sharia al-Missala (aka "Sharia al-Somal") can also be found in the vicinity.

Much of Heliopolis's best architecture can be seen on streets leading off Al-Ahram. **Sharia Ibrahim**, which crosses it a few blocks before the Basilica, and **Sharia Laqqani**, leading north to Midan Roxi, are lined by arcades with Andalusian-style balconies and pantiles. Sometime in May (as advertised in the foreign-language press and by street posters locally) there's a one-day **street festival** on **Sharia Baghdad** (parallel to, and two blocks south of, Al-Ahram), with a parade, live music, food and crafts.

The Baron's Palace

Floodlit at night, the **Baron's Palace** (Qasr al-Baron) makes a dramatic landmark for anyone arriving in Cairo or departing by air, visible from the airport road – **Sharia al-Oruba** – that runs past its garden. Modelled on Hindu temples from Cambodia and India, this exotic residence was commissioned by Baron Empain as Heliopolis took shape. Architect Alexandre Marcel built the whole thing from concrete (an early example of its creative use), including a revolving central tower that tracked the sun so that the interior was always in shade (since sunlight made the Baron's daughter ill).

Although you can't enter the palace – which has lain derelict for decades – its external grand staircase was the backdrop for lavish garden parties in the 1930s, when Empain's heir, Baron Jean, scandalized high society by marrying an American showgirl whom he met at a nightclub where she performed naked, painted gold. After the third generation of Empains fled Egypt in 1957, the palace was stripped bare and became infested by bats; a spooky ruin whose cellars were later used for partying by teenage heavy-metal fans. Since being bought by the state in 2005 its exterior has been spruced up and there is vague talk of turning it into a museum.

Another landmark en route to the airport is Egypt's Air Force Headquarters and **Almaza Air Base**, fronted by vintage MiG fighters of the sort that fared badly in wars with Israel; in 1967 almost the entire force was destroyed on its runways by a surprise attack. It was from Almaza that the deposed president Mubarak flew to Sharm el-Sheikh before going into exile.

From Hada'iq el-Kobba to Matariyya

Heliopolis' Presidential Palace isn't the only luxurious state residence in Cairo's northern suburbs. The Domed or **Kobba Palace** built by Khedive Ismail was until 2011 President Mubarak's main domicile when he wasn't staying at his palatial villa in Sharm el-Sheikh. Partially visible from the street near Saray el-Kobba metro, the palace lends its name to the district of **Hada'iq el-Kobba,** and its grounds (off-limits) are the sole reminder of what was once a vast swath of gardens extending to **El-Zeitun** ("The Olives").This former village (where the Ottoman sultan Selim the Grim defeated the Mamlukes before entering Cairo in 1517) is one of many that has been swallowed up by the city's relentless expansion, like **Matariyya**, now a *baladi* suburb whose ramshackle shabbiness belies its claims to fame. A pharaonic obelisk stands as a reminder of the ancient city of On (or Heliopolis) where Creation supposedly began, while the Virgin's Tree is a revered relic of the Holy Family's sojourn in Egypt. Both sites are easily reached from central Cairo by **metro** Line 1.

Ancient Heliopolis and the Obelisk of Senusret I

On existed as a solar **cult centre** as long ago as 4241 BC, when its astronomers invented the solar calendar. It evolved in tandem with Memphis, the first capital of Dynastic Egypt (located near Saqqara, southwest of Cairo). As Memphis embodied the political union of Upper and Lower Egypt (the Nile Valley and its Delta), so On incarnated its theological aspect, blending local cults into a single cosmology that proved more influential than other creation myths of the Old Kingdom. On was the site of the Benben stone, worshipped since prehistory as the primal mound where Creation began (see box, p.148). Other legends relate that the god Thoth invented writing, and that the biblical Joseph wed the high priest's daughter, on this spot. Eclipsed by Karnak (modern-day Luxor in Upper Egypt) during the New Kingdom, On was devastated by the Persians in 525 BC, but once rebuilt under the XXVIII Dynasty in the fifth century BC its intellectual renown attracted Greek luminaries such as the philosopher Plato, Eudoxus (who probably invented the sundial after studying Egyptian astronomy) and the historian Herodotus. All of them called it **Heliopolis** (City of the Sun), the Greek name that supplanted On during Egypt's Greco-Roman era. However, Heliopolis declined as Alexandria became the focus for science and religion; the first-century geographer Strabo found it nearly desolate and the Romans totally ignored it.

Today, nothing exists but the solitary **Obelisk of Senusret I** (daily 8am–5pm; £E12). This 22-metre-high pink granite monolith was one of a pair raised to celebrate Senusret's Jubilee Festival (c.1900 BC), which flanked the start of a ceremonial avenue to the Temple of Re (erected by his father, Amenemhat I). The obelisk's twin fell some time in the twelfth century AD, long after another pair from here (belonging to the XVIII Dynasty ruler Tuthmosis III) was moved by the Romans to Alexandria, whence they ended up in New York's Central Park and on London's Victoria Embankment. Known locally as "El-Misallah", Senusret's obelisk stands in a small garden amid a waste ground, 600m northwest of Matariyya metro. Leaving the exit from the northbound platform, follow the street straight ahead for 200m until it forks, then the right-hand fork to the end and turn right.

The Virgin's Tree

The ancient **Spring of the Sun** where the god Atum supposedly washed himself at the dawn of Creation (see box, p.148) now waters a venerable Christian relic, the **Virgin's Tree** (daily 9am–5pm; £E10). This gnarled sycamore fig is supposedly descended from a tree whose branches shaded the Holy Family during their Egyptian exile. Tradition has it that they rested here when travelling between Palestine and Babylon-in-Egypt (see p.268). Mary is said to have washed the clothes of baby Jesus in the stone **trough** that still lies beside the tree. Early last century, Christian souvenir-hunting was so shameless that the owner of the sycamore tied a knife to the tree and put up a notice begging people not to hack

The Creation myth of Heliopolis

The Ancient Egyptians had multiple Creation myths, which grew ever more entangled as they sought to reconcile them. In what Egyptologists term the **Heliopolitan cosmogony**, the universe was a watery, colourless ooze (Nun) from which emerged a primal

▲ Shu, Nut and Geb

mound, the **Benben** (later stylised as a pyramid). From this rose the sun in the form of **Atum**, the creator god (or a phoenix), who aroused himself "so that he could create orgasm" (as ancient texts put it), spitting forth the deities Shu (air) and Tefnut (moisture). They engendered Geb (earth) and Nut (sky), whose own union produced Isis, Osiris, Seth and Nephthys. Later texts often regarded this divine **Ennead** (Nine) as a single entity, while the universe was conventionally represented by the figures of Shu, Nut and Geb.

Meanwhile (for reasons unknown), the primal deity Atum was subsumed by **Re** (or Ra), a yet mightier aspect of the sun-god. **Re** manifested himself in multiple forms: as hawk-headed Re-herakhte (Horus of the Horizon); the beetle Khepri (the rising sun); the disc Aten (the midday sun); and as Atum (the setting sun). The Ancient Egyptians believed that Re rose each morning in the east, traversed the sky in his solar barque and sank into the western land of the dead every evening, to voyage through the netherworld during the night, emerging at sunrise. The **cult of Re** was exclusive: only the pharaoh and priesthood had access to Re's sanctuary, whose daily rituals were adopted by other divine cults and soon became inextricably entangled with Osiris-worship. Ordinary folk – whose participation was limited to public festivals – worshipped lesser, more approachable deities.

▲ Re

at it any more with axes, and to leave some of it for others. Now enclosed within a compound, it grows near the **Church of the Virgin**, a modern building on the site of far older churches. The site is 500m south of the obelisk: from the metro, follow the street ahead to a fork where you bear left down Sharia Shagaret Mariam, turning left at the end.

The Pyramids

All things dread Time, but Time dreads the Pyramids.

Anonymous proverb

For millions of people the **Pyramids** epitomize Egypt: no other monument is so instantly recognized the world over. Yet comparatively few foreigners realize that at least 118 pyramids are spread across 70km of desert, from the outskirts of Cairo to the edge of the Fayoum.

Most visitors are content to just see the **Pyramids of Giza** and part of the sprawling necropolis of **Saqqara**, both easily accessible from the city centre. Tours to Saqqara often include a flying visit to the scant remains of the ancient capital, **Memphis**. Far fewer tourists visit the **Dahshur** pyramid field to the south of Saqqara; the **Abu Sir** and **Abu Ghurab** pyramids between Saqqara and Giza (officially off-limits); or the outlying pyramids of **Maidum**, **Lahun** and **Hawara**, which entail a separate excursion (perhaps in conjunction with a visit to Dahshur).

All of the sites mentioned above are covered in further detail in this chapter, but even they do not exhaust the list: for really serious enthusiasts, there are also

Paranormal pyramidology

As befits such mysterious ancient monuments, the pyramids have generated a whole plethora of **unorthodox theories**. Generally speaking, they boil down to an assumption that primitive people living thousands of years ago couldn't possibly have put up such impressive structures unless they were part of a civilization far in advance of any we know about, or else had a little help from some passing **extra-terrestrials**.

In the first category is **Graham Hancock** (see p.270), who argues that the pyramids were part of a worldwide civilization which flourished around 12,000 BC, before the last ice age. Others believe that the pyramids are remnants of the lost civilization of **Atlantis**. This of course ignores modern archeological theories that Atlantis was on a Mediterranean island devastated by a volcanic eruption or tsunami.

The apparent alignment of the pyramids with Orion, Sirius or the Pleiades has led others to suppose that they have extra-terrestrial significance. According to one theory, the Great Pyramid points at the **Pleiades** (the Seven Sisters star cluster in Taurus) because God was actually an extra-terrestrial traveller from there. Others reckon the alien influences behind the pyramids came from **Mars**, or from **Sirius**, the Dog Star. Sirius is our near neighbour, at only nine light years away, but it's also the brightest actual star in the sky apart from the sun, and was of great importance in anicent times because the length of the solar year could be calculated from its first rising on the horizon. The three stars of Orion's belt happen to point to Sirius.

You can read up on some of the weirder theories about how and why the Pyramids were built at ⓦparanormal.about.com/cs/ancientegypt.

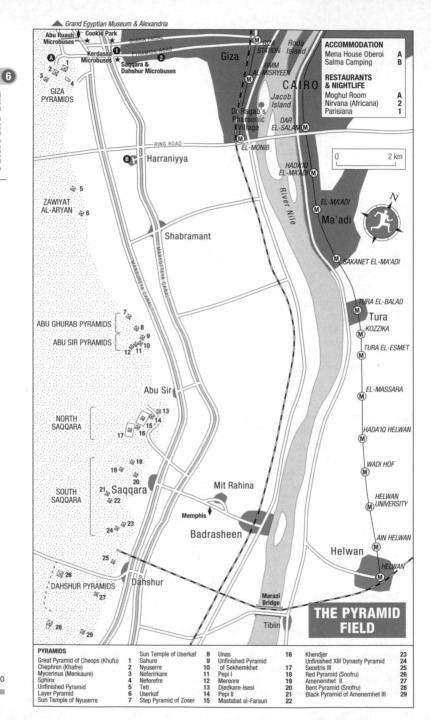

Grand Egyptian Museum & Alexandria

Abu Ruash
Microbuses

Cookie Park

Kerdassa
Microbuses

Saqqara & Dahshur Microbuses

GIZA STATION

Giza

Roda Island

OMM AL-MISRYEEN

CAIRO

Jacob Island

Dr Ragab's Pharaonic Village

DAR EL-SALAM

ACCOMMODATION
Mena House Oberoi   A
Salma Camping   B

RESTAURANTS & NIGHTLIFE
Moghul Room   A
Nirvana (Africana)   2
Parisiana   1

GIZA PYRAMIDS

RING ROAD

EL-MONIB

0   2 km

Harraniyya

HADA'IQ EL-MA'ADI

N

ZAWIYAT AL-ARYAN

EL-MA'ADI

Ma'adi

Shabramant

SAKANET EL-MA'ADI

River Nile

TURA EL-BALAD

Tura

KOZZIKA

ABU GHURAB PYRAMIDS

ABU SIR PYRAMIDS

TURA EL-ESMET

EL-MASSARA

Abu Sir

HADA'IQ HELWAN

NORTH SAQQARA

WADI HOF

HELWAN UNIVERSITY

SOUTH SAQQARA

Saqqara

Mit Rahina

Memphis

AIN HELWAN

Helwan

Badrasheen

HELWAN

Dahshur

DAHSHUR PYRAMIDS

Marazi Bridge

THE PYRAMID FIELD

Tibiin

PYRAMIDS		Sun Temple of Userkaf	8	Unas	16	Khendjer	23
Great Pyramid of Cheops (Khufu)	1	Sahure	9	Unfinished Pyramid		Unfinished XIII Dynasty Pyramid	24
Chephren (Khafre)	2	Nyuserre	10	of Sekhemkhet	17	Seostris III	25
Mycerinus (Menkaure)	3	Neferirkare	11	Pepi I	18	Red Pyramid (Snofru)	26
Sphinx	4	Neferefre	12	Merenre	19	Amenemhet II	27
Unfinished Pyramid	5	Teti	13	Djedkare-Isesi	20	Bent Pyramid (Snofru)	28
Layer Pyramid	6	Userkaf	14	Pepi II	21	Black Pyramid of Amenemhet III	29
Sun Temple of Nyuserre	7	Step Pyramid of Zoser	15	Mastabat al-Faraun	22		

remains of Pharaoh Redjedef's IV Dynasty pyramid at **Abu Ruash** and some ruinous XII Dynasty pyramids at **El-Lisht** on the edge of the Fayoum. The Abu Ruash pyramid is accessible by service taxi to the nearby village of Abu Ruash from the junction of Sharia Mansureya with Sharia Faisal, north of Pyramids Road, but the El-Lisht pyramids are accessible only by car.

If you're really determined and energetic, it's possible to visit Giza, Saqqara, Dahshur and Memphis all in one day, starting very early (say 7.30am from town). To do this, you will need to find a taxi driver who will take you, wait at each, and finally bring you back. Make sure the driver understands exactly what you want, and negotiate hard. In principle, you should be able to visit all four sites for around £E200, but £E250–300 would not be an unreasonable rate, especially if there's a group of you. Some hotels (the *Berlin*, for example) have their own drivers who are used to taking tourists on such excursions. Alternatively, you could opt for a guided tour (see p.164) that takes in both Giza and Saqqara, or Dahshur, in a day excursion.

The pyramids in history

The pyramids' sheer **antiquity** is staggering. When the Greek chronicler Herodotus visited them in 450 BC, as many centuries separated his lifetime from their creation as divide our own time from that of Herodotus, who regarded them as ancient even then. In fact, the Pyramid Age was only an episode in three millennia of pharaonic civilization, reaching its zenith within two hundred years and followed by an inexorable decline, so that later dynasties regarded the works of their ancestors with awe.

Before the pyramids, pharaohs were buried in subterranean tombs covered by large mud-brick superstructures, which were given the name **mastaba** (Arabic for "bench") by Egyptian labourers working on excavations in the nineteenth century. The **Pyramid Age** began at **Saqqara** in the twenty-seventh century BC, when the III Dynasty royal architect **Imhotep** (later revered as a minor deity) made a revolutionary change to the traditional mastaba tomb by starting with a large mastaba and placing a series of similar but increasingly smaller structures on top of it to create the first **step pyramid.** As techniques evolved, an attempt was made to convert a step pyramid at **Maidum** into a true pyramid by encasing its sides in a smooth shell, but it seems that the design was faulty, for the pyramid collapsed at some point under its own weight.

Some believe that this happened during construction of what became the **Bent Pyramid**, whose top section is at a less shallow angle than its bottom – according to the theory, the collapse of the steeper pyramid at Maidum caused the builders to alter the angle of the Bent Pyramid to prevent the same thing happening (see p.176). This then gave rise to the second, **Red Pyramid** at **Dahshur** – the first sheer-sided, true pyramid, which was followed by the **Great Pyramid** of Cheops at **Giza** – the zenith of pyramid architecture. After two more perfect pyramids at Giza, fewer resources and less care were devoted to subsequent pyramids at **Abu Sir**, South Saqqara and elsewhere, and no subsequent pyramid ever matched the standards of the Giza trio.

Although the limestone scarp at the edge of the Western Desert provided an inexhaustible source of **building material**, finer stone for casing the pyramids was quarried at Tura on the east side of the river (see p.128), or came from Aswan in Upper Egypt. Blocks were quarried using wooden wedges (which swelled when soaked, enlarging fissures) and copper chisels, then transported on rafts to the pyramid site, where the final shaping and polishing occurred. Shipments coincided with the inundation of the Nile (July–Nov), when its waters lapped the feet of the plateau and Egypt's workforce was released from agricultural tasks. Engineers have

The name and purpose of the pyramids

The derivation of the word "pyramid" is obscure. **Per-em-us**, an Ancient Egyptian term meaning "straight up", seems likelier than the Greek *pyramis* – "wheaten cake", a facetious descriptive term for these novel monuments. Then again, the word "obelisk" comes from *obeliskos*, the Ancient Greek for "skewer" or "little spit" – so perhaps it's not so unlikely.

The pyramids' **enigma** has puzzled people ever since they were built. Whereas the Ancient Greeks vaguely understood their function, the Romans were less certain, while medieval Arabs believed them to be treasure houses with magical guardians, and early European observers reckoned them the Biblical granaries of Joseph.

Most Egyptologists now agree that the pyramids' function was to preserve the pharaoh's **ka**, or double: a vital force which emanated from the sun-god to his son, the king, who distributed it amongst his subjects and the land of Egypt itself. Mummification, funerary rituals, anniversary offerings, false doors for the pharaoh's ba (soul) to escape, which are often found in pyramids, as well as the shabti figures (little model servants) which were introduced during the XI Dynasty, and are found mostly in later tombs rather than in the pyramids, were all designed to ensure that the pharaoh's ka enjoyed an afterlife similar to its earthly existence. Thus was the social order perpetuated throughout eternity and the forces of primeval chaos held at bay, a theme emphasized in tomb reliefs at Saqqara. On another level of symbolism, the pyramid form evoked the primal mound at the dawn of creation, a recurrent theme in Ancient Egyptian cosmogony, echoed in megalithic Benben (see p.162) and obelisks whose pyramidal tips were sheathed in glittering electrum.

calculated that Tura produced 330 blocks a day year-round, which were ferried across the Nile at a rate of four thousand blocks per day (averaging 6.67 blocks per minute) during the inundation.

Herodotus relates that teams of a hundred thousand slaves, relieved every three months by a fresh team, took a decade to build the causeway along which the stones for the Great Pyramid of Cheops were hauled, and a further twenty years to raise the pyramid itself. Egyptologists now believe that, far from being slaves, most of the workforce were peasants paid in food for their three-month stint (papyri enumerate the quantities of lentils, onions and leeks), while four thousand skilled craftsmen were employed full-time on its **construction**. Workmen's graffiti in the quarries at Giza boasts of the work-gangs' prowess in cutting and moving blocks, using wooden sledges and rollers lubricated with water (the wheel didn't reach Egypt until a thousand years later).

Whether or not the Ancient Egyptians deemed this work a religious obligation, these massive labour levies certainly demanded an effective bureaucracy. Pyramid-building therefore helped consolidate the state and could only be sustained while the state flourished. Thus, it waxed and waned with the zenith and decline of the **Old Kingdom** (III-VI Dynasties, c.2686–2181 BC), ceased throughout the anarchic First Intermediate Period (VIII–XI Dynasties, c.2181–2055 BC), and revived during the short-lived **Middle Kingdom** (XII-XIV Dynasties, c.2055–1650 BC), before the Second Intermediate Period (XV–XVII Dynasties, c.1650–1550 BC) brought the Pyramid Age to an end. When the Two Lands were reunited under the **New Kingdom** (XVIII–XX Dynasties, c.1550–1069 BC), its pharaohs remembered their ancestors' plundered pyramids and opted instead for hidden tombs in the Valley of the Kings, across the river from their capital Thebes (now Luxor) in Upper Egypt. A few rulers – such as Horemheb, a general under the "heretic" pharaoh Akhenaten, who later became king himself – hedged their bets by building a tomb at Saqqara, and another in the Theban Necropolis.

The Pyramids of Giza

Of the Seven Wonders of the ancient world, only the **Pyramids of Giza** have withstood the ravages of time. Resembling small triangles from afar and corrugated mountains as you approach, their gigantic mass can seem oddly two-dimensional when viewed from below. Far from being isolated in the desert as carefully angled photos suggest, they rise just beyond the outskirts of Giza City. During daytime, the tourist hordes dispel the mystique (though the site is big enough to escape them), but at sunset, dawn and late at night their brooding majesty returns.

The Pyramids' **orientation** is no accident. Their entrances are aligned with the Pole Star (or rather, its position 4500 years ago); the internal tomb chambers face west, the direction of the Land of the Dead; and the external funerary temples point eastwards towards the rising sun. Less well preserved are the causeways leading to the so-called valley temples, and various subsidiary pyramids and mastaba tombs.

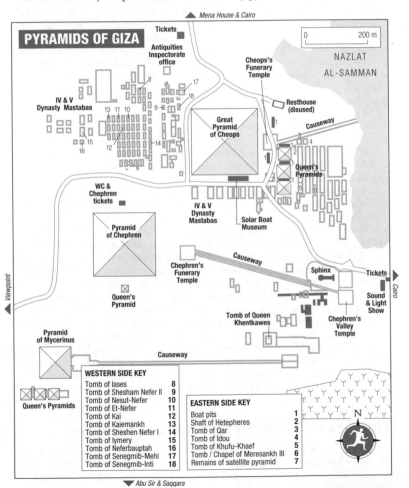

Photographing the Pyramids

The best viewpoints over the Giza Pyramids are south of Mycerinus's Pyramid. Most tourists gather along the tarmac road some 400m west of the pyramid, which is particularly popular in the late afternoon when the sun is in the right direction. In the morning, however, photos are better taken from the southeast, though it can often be hazy early on. For the best view of the Pyramids close together, the ridge to the south of Mycerinus's Pyramid is the place to head for.

Practicalities

The site is reached from Cairo by the eight-kilometre-long **Sharia al-Ahram** (Pyramids Road) built by Khedive Ismail for the inauguration of the Suez Canal. Though heavy traffic can prolong the journey, getting there is straightforward. **Taxi** drivers often quote upwards of £E30, but the proper fare is around £E20 for a one-way trip from town. A cheaper option is to take air-conditioned bus #357 (£E2), or ordinary bus #900 (50pt) from behind Ramses Station, or a microbus service taxi (£E1.25) from Ramses (by Sharia Orabi) or Abdel Mouneem Riyad (behind Midan Tahrir). Drivers heading for the Pyramids shout, "Al-Ahram, al-Ahram", but check they're going all the way. An easier one-day, minimum-effort way to visit the Giza Pyramids, while also taking in Saqqara, is to go on a guided **tour** (see p.164).

The main **entrance** to the site is just uphill from the *Mena House Oberoi*. Ignore touts and other dubious characters trying to persuade you that the ticket office is closed, or has moved to the nearby horse stables (which are worth avoiding; see p.211 for reputable stables). There's a **tourist office** (daily 8.30am–5pm; ☎02/3383-8823) across the street from *Mena House Oberoi*. There is another entrance and ticket office near the Sphinx.

Both offices sell a single ticket for **the site** (daily: summer 8am–6pm; winter 8am–4pm; Ramadan 8am–3pm; £E60), plus separate **tickets** required to enter the Great Pyramid (£E100), Chephren's Pyramid (£E30), the Pyramid of Mycerinus (£E25) and the Solar Boat Museum (£E40). Often the interiors of only two pyramids will be open, the third closed. While it was once *de rigueur* for visitors to climb the Great Pyramid, this is now forbidden. **Going inside** is quite safe, but anyone with claustrophobia or asthma should think twice, and clambering through all three shafts in the Great Pyramid will make your leg muscles ache the following day.

Plan on spending at least half a day here. The best time to come is early in the morning, ahead of the heat and crowds (tour buses start arriving around 10.30am). After nightfall there is a **Sound and Light Show**, with three one-hour performances every night accompanied by a rather crass, melodramatic commentary in different languages. For schedules, call ☎02/385-2880 or 3386-3469, or check *Egypt Today* or ⓦwww.soundandlight.com.eg. Seats cost £E75, plus £E35 for a video camera; the Arabic version costs £E11, though non-Arab nationals are not allowed to buy tickets for it. Seats are on the terrace facing the Sphinx. Bring a sweater, since nights can be cold, even in summer.

The Great Pyramid of Cheops (Khufu)

The oldest and largest of the Giza Pyramids is that of the IV Dynasty pharaoh **Khufu** – better known as **Cheops** – who probably reigned 2589 to 2566 BC. The pyramid (see colour projection) originally stood 140m high and measured 230m along its base, but the removal of its casing stones has reduced these dimensions by

Cartouches

A cartouche is an oval containing the name of a pharaoh written in hieroglyphs. Used in inscriptions, cartouches are massively important to Egyptologists for dating tombs, pyramids and other objects. It was the discovery of Cheops's cartouche in the relieving chambers (see p.156), for example, which confirmed that the Great Pyramid belonged to him. Cartouches were also inscribed on amulets and stone scarabs placed in ancient tombs. Nowadays, you can even have your own name made up into a gold cartouche by a jeweller (see p.221).

three metres. The pyramid is estimated to weigh six million tonnes and contain over 2,300,000 blocks whose average weight is 2.5 tonnes (though some weigh almost 15 tonnes). This gigantic mass actually ensures its stability, since most of the stress is transmitted inwards towards its central core, or downwards into the underlying bedrock. The pyramid was formerly thought to contain only three chambers: one in the bedrock and two in the superstructure. Experts believe that its design was changed twice, the subterranean chamber being abandoned in favour of the middle one, which was itself superseded by the uppermost chamber. By the time archeologists got here, their contents had long ago been looted, and the only object left *in situ* was Khufu's sarcophagus.

▲ Cartouche of Cheops

In 1993, a German team using a robot probe accidentally discovered a door with handles supposedly enclosing a fourth chamber, apparently never plundered by thieves, and excitement rose at the prospect that this might contain the mummy and treasures of Cheops himself. Another robot was sent down in 2002, and pushed a camera through a hole drilled in the door, to reveal another, similar door behind it. A third robot was sent down in 2007, and another in 2009, but so far the results of their explorations have not been announced, though there is said to have been "a major breakthrough".

Inside the Great Pyramid

You enter the pyramid via an opening created by the treasure-hunting Caliph Ma'mun in 820 AD, some distance below the original entrance on the north face (now blocked). After following this downwards at a crouch, you'll reach the junction of the ascending and descending corridors. The descending corridor leads to an unfinished chamber below the pyramid, and is best ignored or left until last. Instead, head up the 1.6-metre-high **ascending corridor**, which runs for 36m until it meets another junction, where the Great Gallery (see p.156) begins.

To the right of the junction is a **shaft** that ancient writers believed to be a well connected to the Nile; it's now recognized as leading into the subterranean chamber and thought to have been an escape passage for the workmen. Straight ahead is a horizontal passage 35m long and 1.75m high, leading to a semi-finished limestone chamber with a pointed roof, which Arabs dubbed the "**Queen's Chamber**", though there's no evidence that a queen was ever buried here. Two holes, in the northern and southern walls of the chamber, were made by archeologists in 1872. They were trying to find the chamber's ventilation shafts, but what a later team did find, in 1993, using a robot probe, was a new "secret chamber", at the end of a 65-metre passageway. The passageway, only twenty centimetres square, is aligned with the Dog Star, Sirius, which was believed to be an embodiment of the goddess Isis.

Great Pyramid entry practicalities

To keep down humidity inside the pyramid, the number of visitors allowed to enter is limited to 150 in the morning and 150 in the afternoon. If you want to buy tickets (£E100), you'll therefore need to act quickly. In the morning, tour groups tend to snap up all of them before anyone else can get a look in; it is generally less difficult to get the afternoon tickets, especially if you can be at the ticket office as soon as they go on sale at 1pm, but be prepared to jostle for position (or, if you go in the morning, to sprint to the ticket office as soon as the main gate opens). Having got your ticket, it's wise to let the tour groups all rush in and have their fill before you go in yourself. Note that photography is not allowed within the Great Pyramid.

Opening out from the same junction where the horizontal passage to the Queen's Chamber began, the **Great Gallery**, dark, sepulchral and almost church-like, is the best part of the pyramid's insides. Built of Muqattam limestone, cut so perfectly that a knife blade can't be inserted between its joints, the 47-metre-long shaft narrows at the top to form a corbelled roof 8.5m high. Some believe that the gallery once served as an astronomical observation chamber, before being roofed over when the pyramid was completed. The incisions in its walls probably held beams that were used to raise the sarcophagus or granite plug blocks up the steep incline (nowadays overlaid with wooden steps). Though no longer infested by giant bats, as nineteenth-century travellers reported, the Great Gallery is sufficiently hot and airless to be something of an ordeal, and you'll be glad to reach the horizontal antechamber at the top, which is slotted for the insertion of plug blocks designed to thwart entry to the putative burial chamber. At the far end of the Great Gallery, the so-called **King's Chamber** is 95m beneath the apex of the pyramid and half that distance from its outer walls. Built of red granite blocks, the rectangular chamber is large enough to accommodate a double-decker bus. Its dimensions (5.2m by 10.8m by 5.8m) have inspired many an abstruse calculation and wacky prophecy. Supposedly, the chamber generates infrasonic vibrations which, according to some New Age pundits, bathe the body in "sonic energy". Hitler ordered a replica built beneath the Nuremberg Stadium, where he communed with himself before Nazi rallies. To one side of the chamber lies a huge, lidless **sarcophagus** of Aswan granite, bearing the marks of diamond-tipped saws and drills. Being too large to fit through the passage from the Great Gallery to the King's Chamber, it must have been placed here while the pyramid was being built. On the northern and southern walls, at knee height, you'll notice two air shafts leading to the outer world, aligned with the stars of Orion's Belt and Alpha Draconis (representing Osiris and the hippo goddess Rer respectively).

Unseen above the ceiling, five stacked **relieving chambers** distribute the weight of the pyramid away from the burial chamber; each consists of 43 granite monoliths weighing 40 to 70 tonnes apiece. These chambers can only be reached by a ladder from the Great Gallery up shafts that were blasted out with dynamite by British adventurer and amateur archeologist Colonel Richard Howard Vyse in 1837. In the passage at the top, Vyse found Khufu's cartouche (see illustration, p.155) daubed on the ceiling in red paint, thus confirming the identity of the pharaoh for whom the pyramid was built. The relieving chambers are usually closed to the public.

On your way back down, consider investigating the 100-metre-long **descending corridor**, which leads to a crudely hewn **unfinished chamber** beneath the pyramid. There's nothing to see and it's usually closed to the public, but the nerve-racking descent is worthy of Indiana Jones.

Subsidiary tombs

East of the Great Pyramid, it's just possible to discern the foundations of Cheops's **funerary temple**, and a few blocks of the **causeway** that once connected it to his valley temple (now buried beneath the neighbouring Nazlat al-Samman village). Nearby stand three ruined **Queens' Pyramids**, each with a small chapel attached. The northern and southern pyramids belonged to Merites and Hensutsen, Cheops's principal wife (and sister), and the putative mother of Chephren, respectively; the middle one may have belonged to the mother of Redjedef, the third ruler of the dynasty. Between that and the Great Pyramid, the remains of a fourth satellite pyramid were discovered in 1993, its capstone the oldest yet found, its function so far unknown.

Just northeast of Queen Merites' pyramid is a **shaft** where IV Dynasty pharaoh Snofru's wife Queen Hetepheres' sarcophagus was found, having been stashed here following lootings at its original home in Dahshur. Beyond it are the **tombs** of **Qar** and his son **Idou**, which contain life-size statues of the deceased and various reliefs. To the east of Queen Hensutsen's pyramid are the tombs of Cheops's son **Khufu-Khaef** and Chephren's wife (also Hetepheres' daughter) **Meres-ankh**, the best preserved of all the tombs on the Giza plateau, complete with statues in the niches and reliefs showing scenes of daily life, with much of the paintwork intact. To get into these tombs, ask at the custodian's hut beside Hetepheres' shaft; naturally, he'll expect a tip for opening up.

To the west of the Great Pyramid lie dozens of **IV and V Dynasty mastabas**, where Egyptologists uncovered a 4600-year-old mummified princess, whose body had been hollowed out and encased in a thin layer of plaster – a hitherto unknown method of mummification. The **tombs** are less interesting than those on the eastern side, though one of the blocks of stone that were used to build **Neferbauptah's Tomb** has a dinosaur fossil preserved in it (it's the fifth block from the right in the second row up on its north side). Should you want to enter any of these tombs, ask at the Antiquities Inspectorate office to the north of the western group of tombs. Note that there are a number of deep shafts in among these tombs, with no fences around them, so watch your step when exploring the area.

The Solar Boat Museum

Perched to the south of the Great Pyramid, across the road from another cluster of mastabas, is a humidity-controlled pavilion (daily: summer 9am–6pm; winter 9am–4pm; £E40,) containing a 43-metre-long "**solar boat**". The boat's purpose is unknown but it seems to have been used in the funeral ceremony, after which it was dismantled and buried in a pit sunk into the ground next to the pyramid, one of five such pits around the pyramid. The boat was made of fragrant cedar, and when the pit's limestone roofing blocks were removed in 1954, a faint odour of cedarwood could still be smelt. A tiny camera inserted into another of the pits has revealed that it too contains the remains of a boat, but this has not been excavated.

After the solar boat was excavated, restorer Ahmed Yussef spent fourteen years reassembling 1200 pieces of wood that fitted together like a three-dimensional jigsaw puzzle, originally held together by halfa-grass ropes threaded from the inside that tightened when wet – thus ensuring a watertight fit. In Ancient Egyptian art, ropes were associated with royalty and divinity: enclosing cartouches, binding the Two Lands together, and dragging what Egyptologists term "solar boats" (or barques), carrying the pharaoh through the underworld (as shown in XVII–XIX Dynasty tombs in the Valley of the Kings) or accompanying the sun-god on his daily journey across the heavens (as in the Heliopolitan cosmology, see p.148).

The Pyramid of Chephren (Khafre)

Sited on higher ground, with an intact summit and steeper sides, the middle or **Second Pyramid** looks taller and is actually more imposing than Cheops's. Built for his son **Khafre** (known to posterity as **Chephren**), its base originally covered 214.8 square metres and its weight is estimated at 4,883,000 tonnes. As with Cheops's Pyramid, the original rock-hewn burial chamber was never finished and an upper chamber was subsequently constructed.

The Roman writer Pliny said that the pyramid had no entrance. In 1818, however, when Venetian explorer Giovanni Belzoni located and blasted open the sealed portal on its north face, he found that Arab tomb robbers had already gained access nearly a thousand years earlier. They had apparently been undeterred by legends that the pyramid was protected by an idol "with fierce and sparkling eyes", bent on slaying intruders.

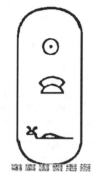

▲ Cartouche of Chephren

Inside the pyramid (£E30; no cameras allowed), you can follow one of the two entry corridors down into the bedrock, and then into a long horizontal passage leading to the **burial chamber**, where Belzoni celebrated his discovery by writing his name in black letters. Set into the chamber's granite floor is the **sarcophagus** of Khafre, who reigned c.2558–2533 BC. The square cavity near the southern wall may have marked the position of a canopic chest containing the pharaoh's viscera.

The pyramid's exterior retains a large number of **casing stones** at its summit (best viewed with binoculars, if possible). Also notice the huge **paving** blocks to the east of the pyramid, fitted precisely together in an irregular mosaic fashion. These led the nineteenth-century pyramidologist Moses Cotsworth to suggest that the entire plateau was a gigantic sundial, with the Great Pyramid casting shadows on a flat pavement (now largely destroyed), calibrated to show equinoxes and other astral events.

Chephren's Funerary Complex and the Sphinx

The funerary complex of Chephren's Pyramid is the best-preserved example of this typically Old Kingdom arrangement. When a pharaoh died, his body was ferried across the Nile to a riverside valley temple where it was embalmed by priests. Mourners then gathered there to purify themselves before escorting his mummy up the causeway to a funerary (or mortuary) temple, where further rites preceded its interment within the pyramid. Thereafter, the priests ensured his *ka*'s afterlife by making offerings of food and incense in the funerary temple on specific anniversaries.

Chephren's **funerary temple** consists of a pillared hall, central court, niched storerooms and a sanctuary, but most of the outer granite casing has been plundered over centuries and the interior is not usually accessible. Among the remaining blocks is a 13.4-metre-long monster weighing 163,000 kilos. Flanking the temple are what appear to be boat pits, although excavations have yielded nothing but pottery fragments. From here you can trace the foundations of a **causeway** that runs 400m downhill to his valley temple, near the Sphinx.

The **valley temple** lay buried under sand until its discovery by the French Egyptologist Auguste Mariette in 1852, which accounts for its reasonable state of preservation. Built of limestone and faced with polished Aswan granite, the temple faces east and used to open onto a quay. Beyond a narrow antechamber you'll find a T-shaped hall whose gigantic architraves are supported by square pillars, in front of which stood diorite statues of Chephren (one can be seen in the Egyptian Museum, which was founded by Mariette; see p.56).

The Sphinx

Everyone has seen pictures of the **Great Sphinx**, but this legendary monument is far more impressive in real life, especially from the front, where it gazes down at you from twenty metres up, with Chephren's pyramid for a backdrop. The Sphinx is carved from an outcrop of soft limestone supposedly left standing after the harder surrounding stone was quarried for the Great Pyramid, but since most of the outcrop was too friable to work on directly it was clad in harder stone before finishing. Conventional Egyptology credits Chephren with the idea of shaping it into a figure with a lion's body and a human head, which is often identified as his own (complete with royal beard), though it may represent a guardian deity. Some thousand years later, the future Tuthmosis IV is said to have dreamt that if he cleared the sand that engulfed the **Sphinx** it would make him ruler: a prophecy fulfilled, as recorded on a stele that he placed between its paws.

All these notions went unchallenged until 1991, when maverick Egyptologist **John West** – who had long claimed that Ancient Egyptian civilization was the inheritor of the ancient lost culture of Atlantis – got together a team of scientists, led by American geologist Robert Schoch, to investigate the apparent signs of water erosion on the sides of the Sphinx's enclosure. Schoch's team duly announced that the erosion could only have been caused by water, and that this meant the Sphinx was older than Egypt's last known flood era back in 10,000–15,000 BC – several millennia before the date assigned to its creation by conventional Egyptology. Despite this evidence, most Egyptologists continue to believe that the Sphinx was built to honour Chephren; apart from anything else, a New Kingdom inscription on a stele in front of it bore Chephren's name, and statues of the pharaoh have been uncovered in the neighbouring valley temple. The water erosion, they argue, can be explained by flooding from the Nile and severe storms in relatively recent times.

The name "Sphinx" was bestowed by the Ancient Greeks, after the legendary creature of Thebes (the Greek city, not the Egyptian one now known as Luxor) that put riddles to passers-by and slew those who answered wrongly. The Arabs called it Abu el-Hol (the awesome or terrible one); medieval chronicles relate how its nose and ears were mutilated by a Sufi sheikh in 1378, whereupon the Sphinx blew sand over the village at its feet and enraged residents lynched the sheikh. While there's no evidence to support the oft-repeated story that the Sphinx was used for target practice by Mamluke and Napoleonic troops, much of its beard ended up in the British Museum in London, and the British were respectful enough to sandbag the monument for protection during World War II.

Early modern repairs did more harm than good, since its porous limestone "breathes", unlike the cement that was used to fill its cracks. A more recent **restoration project** (1989–98) involved hand-cutting ten thousand limestone blocks, to refit the paws, legs and haunches of the beast, but it was decided not to replace the missing nose or beard.

Three **tunnels** exist inside the Sphinx, one behind its head, one in its tail and one in its north side. Their function is unknown, but none goes anywhere. Other tunnels have been unearthed in the vicinity of the Sphinx; again, who built them or what they were for is unknown, but one suggestion is that they were created by later Ancient Egyptians looking for buried treasure.

During Sound and Light shows, the Sphinx is given the role of narrator.

The Pyramid of Mycerinus (Menkaure)

Sited on a gradual slope into undulating desert, the smallest of the three main Giza Pyramids speaks of waning power and commitment. Though started by Chephren's successor, **Menkaure** (called **Mycerinus** by the Greeks), it was finished with unseemly haste by his son Shepseskaf, who seemingly enjoyed less power than his predecessors and depended on the priesthood. Herodotus records the legend that an oracle gave Mycerinus only six years to live, so to cheat fate he made merry round the clock, using a myriad lamps to turn night into day, thus doubling his allotted number of days. Another story (related by the Greek geographer Strabo) has it that the pyramid was actually built by Rhodophis, a Thracian courtesan who charged each client the price of a building block. As the structure is estimated to contain 200,000 blocks, she must have ended up an extremely rich woman.

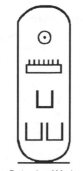
▲ Cartouche of Menkaure

Because its lower half was sheathed in Aswan granite, this is sometimes called the Red Pyramid (a name more usually applied to one of Snofru's pyramids at Dahshur). Its relative lack of casing stones is due to Saladin's son Abdel Aziz, whose courtiers persuaded him to attempt the pyramid's demolition in 1196 – a project abandoned after eight months.

The **interior** (£E25) is unlike the other pyramids, having an unfinished chamber in the superstructure and the final burial chamber underground – though no one knows why. It's also a mystery why the lower passageway (now used to enter the pyramid) and the burial chamber are lined in granite when they are hewn from the bedrock, and why the Ancient Egyptians carved a false barrel-vaulted ceiling in the burial chamber. There, nineteenth-century British amateur archeologist Richard Howard Vyse discovered a basalt sarcophagus, later lost at sea en route to Britain, plus human remains (now in the British Museum) that he assumed were Menkaure's, but which are now reckoned to be a XXVI Dynasty replacement.

The complex also features three small pyramids for the pharaoh's wives, a relatively intact funerary temple, and a causeway to the now-buried valley temple. Northwest of the latter lies the sarcophagus-shaped **Tomb of Queen Khentkawes**, an intriguing figure who appears to have bridged the transition between the IV and V dynasties. Apparently married to Shepseskaf, the last IV Dynasty ruler, it is thought that she may have wed a priest of the sun-god after Shepseskaf's demise and gone on to bear several kings who were buried at Saqqara or Abu Sir (where she also had a pyramid built).

The Grand Egyptian Museum

A swanky new **Grand Egyptian Museum** is currently under construction 2km north of the Giza Pyramids site, at the junction of the Alexandria Desert Road and the Cairo Ring Road. Scheduled to open in 2013, it is meant to alleviate the strain on Cairo's venerable Egyptian Museum (see p.53), enabling items from its basement depository to be displayed, and the downtown museum to be modernized. One exhibit, a colossal statue of Ramses II, which formerly stood outside Ramses Station, has already been moved here, and when the museum is opened, will stand at its entrance. The top floor of the museum will have commanding views over the Pyramids. This will all be part of a grandiose development, with an IMAX cinema, conference and seminar halls, and educational facilities. For news on the project's development, see Ⓦ www.gem.gov.eg.

The villages of Kerdassa and Harraniyya have no connection with the Pyramids, but tour groups often pay one or both of them a visit. **Kerdassa** (accessible by microbus from the junction of Pyramids Road with Sharia Mansureya) is where most of the scarves, *galabiyyas* and shirts sold in Cairo are made, as well as carpets, which are sold by the metre. Although no longer a place for bargains, it's still frequented by collectors of ethnic textiles, particularly Bedouin robes and veils (the best-quality ones sell for hundreds of dollars).

Guided tours often take in **Harraniyya**, the site of the famous **Wissa Wassef Art Centre** (daily 10am–5pm; ☎02/3381-5746, ⊛www.wissa-wassef-arts.com and www .wissawassef.com). Founded in 1952 by Ramses Wissa Wassef, an architect who wanted to preserve village crafts and alleviate rural unemployment, the centre teaches children to design and weave carpets, and has branched out into batik work and pottery. The pupils, supervised by his widow and the original generation of students, produce beautiful tapestries which now sell for thousands of dollars and are imitated throughout Egypt. You can see them at work (except at lunchtime and on Fridays), and admire a superb collection in the attached museum designed by Hassan Fathy, a masterpiece of mud-brick architecture. To reach the Art Centre under your own steam, take a taxi or minibus 4km south along the Saqqara road (Maryotteya Canal, west bank) from Pyramids Road, or catch bus #335 from Midan Giza (hourly), and get off at Harraniyya.

Abu Sir and Abu Ghurab

The two V Dynasty (c.2494–2345 BC) necropolises of **Abu Sir** and **Abu Ghurab** occupy an arc of desert between Giza and North Saqqara. The mortuary complexes here are smaller than the Giza Pyramids of the previous dynasty, suggesting a decline in royal power. Their ruinous state and the effort required to reach them meant that few tourists came here even before the site was closed to the public. It is not known when they will reopen – local rumour has it that this will be soon, but there's no official word to confirm this. Meanwhile, tour groups willing to pay a special fee to the Supreme Council of Antiquities have been granted **access**, and individuals may be able to persuade the custodian to let them in to look around. Visitors often feel that Abu Sir's splendid isolation compensates for its smaller-sized pyramids and inferior state of preservation.

The pyramids of Abu Sir and Abu Ghurab are a ten-minute walk (or £E2 by *tuk-tuk* – Indian-style auto-rickshaw) from Abu Sir village, which can be reached by service taxi microbus from Maryotteya Canal at Pyramids Road or by taxi from Saqqara village (£E5–8). The most adventurous option, however, is to visit them **en route between Giza and Saqqara** by horse or camel, spending three hours in the saddle (for reputable operators, see p.211). A round trip **from North Saqqara** (see p.163) is less demanding, but still requires commitment. With the Abu Sir pyramids clearly visible 6km away, you can either walk (1hr 30min–2hr) or conserve energy by renting a horse or camel from near North Saqqara's refreshments hut (£E60–100 for the round trip).

The Abu Sir pyramids

The four pyramid complexes at Abu Sir are ranged in an arc that ignores chrono-logical order. At the southern end of the site, a low mound marks the core of the unfinished **Pyramid of Neferefre**, a V Dynasty pharaoh who ruled for only three years (c.2448–2445 BC). As the pyramid's core is composed of locally quarried limestone and was never encased in finer Tura masonry, no causeway was ever built. However, the desert may yet disgorge other structures: during the 1980s, Czechoslovak archeologists uncovered another pyramid complex, thought to belong to Queen Khentkawes, the mother of Sahure.

Dominating the view north is the much larger **Pyramid of Neferirkare**, dedicated to the third ruler of the V Dynasty. Neferirkare wanted to outdo his predecessor, Sahure (see below), by building a bigger pyramid than his, and if finished, it would have been 70m high – taller than the third pyramid at Giza – but Neferirkare's premature demise forced his successor to hastily complete a modified version using perishable mud-brick.

The valley temple and grand causeway of Neferirkare's Pyramid were later usurped to serve the **Pyramid of Nyuserre**, further north. A battered mortuary temple with papyriform columns mocks the original name of this dilapidated pyramid, "The Places of Nyuserre are Enduring". The site didn't endure either: the pharaohs who followed Nyuserre preferred burial at Saqqara.

A cluster of mastabas to the northwest of Neferirkare's Pyramid includes the **Tomb of Ptahshepses**, who was Chief of Works to Sahure, the first of the V Dynasty kings to be buried at Abu Sir (see below). The tomb's most curious feature is the double room off the courtyard, which may have held solar boats. If so, the only other known example of this in a private tomb is that of Kagemni in North Saqqara.

Directly to the north of Neferirkare's pyramid, the **Pyramid of Sahure** – which the Ancient Egyptians called "The Soul of Sahure Gleams" – is badly damaged, but it's still possible to crawl through a dusty, cobwebbed passage to reach the **burial chamber**, and its associated temples have fared better than others in this group. A 235-metre-long **causeway** links the ruined **valley temple** to Sahure's **mortuary temple** on the eastern side of the pyramid. Though most of its reliefs (which were the first to show the king smiting his enemies, later a standard motif) have gone to various museums, enough remains to make this temple worth exploring. Just to the north of the causeway, a series of fascinating **reliefs** shows scenes from the building of a pyramid, with workers dragging a pyramidion (capstone) covered with white gold, while dancers celebrate the pyramid's completion. This is one of the few extant scenes depicting a pyramid's construction, but resolves none of the conundrums as to how the pyramids were built. Originally there were over eight thousand square metres of reliefs, but over the centuries, local farmers turned all but 137m into cement, whitewash or fertilizer.

The best vantage point to **photograph** the Abu Sir pyramids is halfway down the causeway between Sahure's pyramid and valley temple.

The Sun Temples of Abu Ghurab

Just northeast of the Abu Sir pyramids is the site known as **Abu Ghurab** (if you're riding between Giza and Saqqara, ask the guide to stop here). Its twin temples were designed for worship of Re, the sun-god of Heliopolis, but their proximity to a pyramid field, and reliefs on them celebrating the pharaoh's thirty-year jubilee, suggest a similar function to Zoser's *Heb-Sed* court at Saqqara (see p.166).

The **Sun Temple of Userkaf**, 400m from Sahure's Pyramid, is too ruinous to be of much interest to a non-specialist, but the more distant **Sun Temple of Nyuserre** is worth a visit. Only the base remains of the colossal megalith that stood at its western end, as tall as a pyramid, symbolizing the primordial mound, or **Benben**. The great courtyard, approached from its valley temple by a causeway, is centred on an alabaster altar where cattle were sacrificed. From the courtyard's vestibule, corridors run north to store rooms and south to the king's chapel. The "Chamber of Seasons" beyond the chapel once contained beautiful reliefs; to the south you can find the remnants of a brick model of a solar boat.

North Saqqara

During the Old Kingdom – which lasted from around 2650 BC to around 2134 BC, and was the first important phase of ancient Egypt's three thousand year history – Memphis (see p.172) was the capital, and Egypt's royalty and nobility were buried at **Saqqara**, the limestone scarp that flanks the Nile Valley to the west – the traditional direction of the Land of the Dead. During the New Kingdom (the classical period of ancient Egyptian civilization, which lasted from around 1550 BC to around 1069 BC), Saqqara was supplanted by the Theban necropolis (including

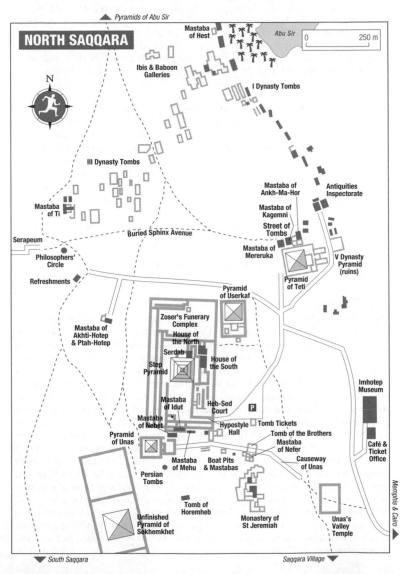

Map labels: Pyramids of Abu Sir; NORTH SAQQARA; Mastaba of Hest; Abu Sir; 0 250 m; Ibis & Baboon Galleries; I Dynasty Tombs; N; III Dynasty Tombs; Mastaba of Ankh-Ma-Hor; Antiquities Inspectorate; Mastaba of Kagemni; Mastaba of Ti; Street of Tombs; Buried Sphinx Avenue; Mastaba of Mereruka; V Dynasty Pyramid (ruins); Serapeum; Philosophers' Circle; Pyramid of Teti; Refreshments; Pyramid of Userkaf; Mastaba of Akhti-Hotep & Ptah-Hotep; Zoser's Funerary Complex; House of the North; Serdab; House of the South; Step Pyramid; Imhotep Museum; Mastaba of Idut; Heb-Sed Court; P; Mastaba of Nebet; Hypostyle Hall; Tomb Tickets; Tomb of the Brothers; Mastaba of Nefer; Pyramid of Unas; Causeway of Unas; Café & Ticket Office; Mastaba of Mehu; Boat Pits & Mastabas; Persian Tombs; Tomb of Horemheb; Monastery of St Jeremiah; Unas's Valley Temple; Unfinished Pyramid of Sekhemkhet; South Saqqara; Saqqara Village; Memphis & Cairo; 163

THE PYRAMIDS | North Saqqara

Pyramid tours

If getting down to the Giza and Saqqara pyramids on public transport sounds too strenuous and complicated, you could save time and energy by taking a **tour**, such as the ones run by Samo Tours (℡02/2299-1155 or 012/313-8446, ⊛www .samoegypttours.com), which leave around 8am in summer, 9am in winter. You'll be driven in an air-conditioned minibus to Memphis, North Saqqara, the Wissa Wassef tapestry school at Harraniyya and the Pyramids of Giza – all accompanied by an English-speaking Egyptologist – before returning to Cairo at 4–5pm. Be sure to ask to see the Mastaba of Ti (see p.170) during your trip. The price of the tour (US$23.50) doesn't include admission tickets, but *Rough Guide* readers who book direct get a £E5 discount, with a free airport transfer to your hotel on arrival also thrown in. Misr Travel and American Express also run tours to Saqqara for around £E200 per person. Another option is to rent a **private taxi** for the day (around £E200–250 for just Giza and Saqqara, £E250–300 if you add on Dahshur). Be sure to specify which sites are included and how long you expect to stay when you negotiate with the driver.

the Valley of the Kings, near Luxor in Upper Egypt), but Saqqara remained in use for burying sacred animals and birds, especially in Ptolemaic times (305 BC to 30 BC), when these cults enjoyed a revival. Over three thousand years it grew to cover 7km of desert – not including the associated necropolises of Abu Sir and Dahshur, or the Giza Pyramids. As such, it is today the largest archeological site in Egypt. Its name – usually pronounced "sa'-'ah-rah" by Cairenes, with the q's as glottal stops – probably derives from Sokar, the Memphite god of the dead, though Egyptians may tell you that it comes from *saq*, the Arabic word for a hawk or falcon, the sacred bird of Horus.

The Saqqara necropolis divides into two main sections: **North Saqqara** – the more interesting area (covered here) – and **South Saqqara** (see p.173). North Saqqara boasts a score of sights, so anyone with limited time should be selective. The **highlights** are Zoser's funerary complex, the Mastaba of Ti, and the Double Mastaba of Akhti- and Ptah-Hotep; if time allows, add the museum and some more tombs to your itinerary.

Practicalities

North Saqqara (daily: summer 8am–6pm, winter 8am–4pm, Ramadan 8am–3pm; £E60) lies 21km south of the Giza Pyramids as the camel strides, or 32km from Cairo by road. The quickest way there by **public transport** (about an hour) is to take a bus or service taxi to Pyramids Road, and get off at Maryotteya Canal (about 1km before the Giza Pyramids), where you'll find service taxi microbuses to Saqqara village (20min; £E1). An alternative route is to take bus #335 (hourly) from Midan Giza to Saqqara village, or bus #987 from Midan Ramses or Midan Tahrir to Badrasheen, and then a microbus to Saqqara village (15min; 50pt), by way of Memphis. A final option (which avoids rush-hour traffic) is to take the metro to Helwan station (30min; £E1), then a minibus or microbus to Tibiin, near the Marazi Bridge (15min; £E1); another service taxi (often a Peugeot rather than a microbus) across to Badrasheen on the west bank (15min; £E1); and finally one to Saqqara as above. Unfortunately, all these methods leave you in Saqqara village, still over a kilometre from the site entrance, though the service taxi from Maryotteya will drop you slightly nearer the site entrance if you ask. Getting back to Cairo, don't leave too late (anything after 5pm is pushing it) or you may not find transport in Saqqara village, and will have to either pay well over the odds for a taxi, or walk another 5km to El-Badrasheen (or at least to the Maryotteya Canal) to pick up a bus or microbus back to Cairo.

Site **tickets** are sold near the Imhotep Museum (see below). It's a good idea to check which tombs are open – especially those further afield – as they often close due to restoration work. Some guards encourage unauthorized snapping in the tombs in the expectation of baksheesh, but aside from this you're not obliged to give anything unless they help with lighting or provide a guided tour (if you don't want a running commentary, make this clear at the outset). Note that guards also start locking up the tombs at least half an hour before closing time. For a more exotic saunter round the site, you can **rent a camel** (around £E60/hr) from outside the refreshments hut towards the Serapeum.

Bear in mind **conditions** at Saqqara. Over winter, the site can be swept by chill winds and clouds of grit; during the hottest months walking around is exhausting. Beware of deep pits, which aren't always fenced off. Bring at least one litre of water per person, as vendors at Memphis and the refreshments hut at North Saqqara are grossly overpriced, like every restaurant along the Saqqara road; a packed lunch is also a good idea (not usually included in a tour). Alternatively, the **Palm Club** just over the Mansureya Canal from the site entrance (℡02/3819-1555 or 1999; daily 9am–8pm), has a swimming pool set amid pleasant gardens and charges £E95 for a day's access including lunch – definitely an option worth considering if you have kids in tow, or if you feel like a dip and a bite after a hard morning's trudge around the site.

The Imhotep Museum

Just beyond the ticket kiosk, to the right of the road leading onto the site, is the small but very interesting and well laid-out **Imhotep Museum** (site hours; included in ticket), containing many fine items found at the site. It is named after Imhotep, the architect who started the whole pyramid craze by designing the step pyramid for Pharaoh Zoser back in 2650 BC or thereabouts. Revered throughout pharaonic history, he was worshipped at Saqqara in later pharaonic times as a god of healing. The Ptolemies (descendants of one of Alexander the Great's generals, who ruled Egypt as pharaohs from 305 BC until 30 BC) even identified Imhotep with Asclepius, the Greek god of medicine. Imhotep's tomb is thought to lie among a cluster of **III Dynasty tombs** to the east of the Mastaba of Ti (see p.170).

To the right of the entrance hall, a door marked "Saqqara Missions" leads to a prettily **painted mummy** from the XXX Dynasty, **Imhotep's wooden coffin** (his body has yet to be found), and some copper **surgical instruments** from the tomb of a palace physician called Qar. The main hall, dominated by a reconstruction of the facade from Zoser's tomb, contains the original green **faïence panels** found at the site, a **cobra frieze** similar to the one *in situ* (see p.166), and a bronze statuette of Imhotep made nearly a millennium after his death.

Next to the museum is a "Visual Setting Hall", which features a large scale model of Zoser's funerary complex. A nine-minute **film** about Imhotep and Saqqara (narrated by Omar Sharif) is sometimes shown in this hall, and is worth seeing if you aren't pressed for time.

The Step Pyramid

The funerary complex of King Zoser (or Djoser) is the largest in Saqqara, and its **Step Pyramid** heralded the start of the Pyramid Age. When Imhotep, Zoser's chief architect, raised the pyramid in the 27th century BC, it was the largest structure ever built in stone – the "beginning of architecture", according to one historian. Imhotep's achievement was to break from the tradition of earthbound mastabas, raising level upon level of stones to create a four-step, and then a six-step pyramid, which was clad in dazzling white limestone. None of the blocks was very large, for Zoser's builders still thought in terms of mud-brick rather than megaliths, but the concept, techniques and logistics all pointed towards the true pyramid, finally attained at Giza.

Before it was stripped of its casing stones and rounded off by the elements, Zoser's **Step Pyramid** stood 62m high and measured 140m by 118m along its base. The original entrance on the northern side is permanently blocked, and access to the **interior** via a gallery on the opposite side (dug in the XXVI Dynasty) has long been suspended for vital structural repairs to its subsidence-ruptured innards.

Zoser's funerary complex

Surrounding the Step Pyramid is an extensive **funerary complex**, originally enclosed by a finely cut limestone wall, 544m long and 277m wide, now largely ruined or buried by sand. False doors occur at intervals for the convenience of the pharaoh's *ka*, but visitors can only enter at the southeastern corner, which has largely been rebuilt. Beyond a vestibule with simulated double doors (detailed down to their hinge pins and sockets) lies a narrow colonnaded corridor, whose forty "bundle" columns are ribbed in imitation of palm stems, which culminates in a broader **Hypostyle Hall** (hypostyle meaning "columned" in Greek).

The Heb-Sed court

From the Hypostyle Hall you emerge onto the **Great South Court**, where a rebuilt section of wall (marked ★ on our site plan) is topped by a **frieze of cobras**, like the one in the Imhotep Museum (see p.165). Worshipped in the Delta as a fire-spitting goddess of destruction called Wadjet or Edjo, the cobra was adopted as the emblem of royalty and always appeared on pharaonic headdresses – a figure known as the *uraeus*. Nearby, a deep shaft plummets into Zoser's **Southern Tomb**, decorated with blue faïence tiles and a relief of the king running the Heb-Sed race. During the jubilee festival marking the thirtieth year of a pharaoh's reign, he had to sprint between two altars representing Upper and Lower Egypt and re-enact his coronation, seated first on one throne, then upon another, symbolically reuniting the Two Lands.

Although the festival was held at Memphis, pairs of altars, thrones and shrines were incorporated in Zoser's funerary complex to perpetuate its efficacy on a cosmic timescale. The B-shaped structures near the centre of the Great Court are the bases of these altars; the twin thrones probably stood on the platform at the southern end of the adjacent **Heb-Sed Court**. Both shrines were essentially facades, since the actual buildings were filled with rubble. This phoney quality is apparent if you view them from the east: the curvaceous roof line and delicate false columns wouldn't look amiss on a yuppie waterfront development. A shelter near the northern end of the court covers four **stone feet** which once belonged to ancient statues.

North of the Step Pyramid

North of the Heb-Sed court, near the Step Pyramid's northeastern corner, is the partially ruined **House of the South**, whose chapel is fronted by proto-Doric columns with lotus capitals, and a spearhead motif above the lintel. Inside you'll find several examples of XVIII–XIX Dynasty tourist graffiti, expressing admiration for Zoser or the equivalent of "Ramses was here". Continuing northwards, you'll pass a relatively intact row of casing stones along the eastern side of Zoser's Pyramid. The **House of the North** has fluted columns with papyrus capitals; the lotus and the papyrus were the heraldic emblems of Upper and Lower Egypt.

On the northern side of the pyramid, a tilted masonry box or **serdab** contains a life-size statue of Zoser gazing blindly towards the North and circumpolar stars, which the ancients associated with immortality; seated thus, his *ka* was assured of eternal life. Zoser's statue is a replica, however; the original is in the Egyptian Museum (see p.55).

South of the complex

South of Zoser's funerary complex are several tombs and other ruins, dating from various dynasties. Three mastabas stand outside the southern wall of Zoser's complex; they are often closed for no apparent reason, but it's usually just a question of locating and tipping the caretaker for opening them up.

The **Mastaba of Idut** is the most worthwhile, with interesting reliefs in five of its ten rooms. Among the fishing and farming scenes, notice the crocodile eyeing a newborn hippo, and a calf being dragged across a river to induce a herd of cows to follow it and ford the river. The chapel contains a false door painted in imitation of granite, scenes of bulls and buffaloes being sacrificed, and Idut herself. Idut was the daughter of Pharaoh Unas and his queen, Nebet. Appropriately therefore, **Nebet's mastaba** stands between the mastaba of Idu and the Pyramid of Unas (see below), just to the southeast of Idu's mastaba. The reliefs in **Nebet's mastaba** are worth seeing: in one scene, Nebet smells a lotus blossom.

A kiosk by the car park for the Step Pyramid sells tickets for other mastabas next to the causeway of Unas (£E30). The ticket is supposed to cover three tombs, but their caretaker usually insists that only two are open, and is more interested in baksheesh anyway. The finest is the so-called **Tomb of the Brothers**, Niankh-khnum and Khnum-hotep, two V Dynasty officials depicted kissing each other and performing various activities together. Some historians have conjectured that they may have been a gay couple, but it's more likely they were brothers, possibly twins, and their families are also pictured in the tomb. The nearby **Tomb of Nefer** is smaller and less interesting; that of **Ruka–Ptah**, if the caretaker can be persuaded to open it up, has no lights inside, so you'd need a torch.

The Pyramid of Unas

From the tombs of Nefer and the Brothers (see above), a causeway leads west to the **Pyramid of Unas**. Though it looks like a mound of rubble from the front, Unas's pyramid retains many casing stones around the back, some carved with hieroglyphs. Thomas Cook & Sons sponsored Gaston Maspero's 1881 excavation of the interior, which (if it is open) can be entered via a low passageway on the northern side. This leads into its **burial chamber**, whose alabaster walls are covered with inscriptions listing the rituals and prayers for liberating the pharaoh's *ba* and the articles for his *ka* to use in the afterlife. These **Pyramid Texts**, forming the basis of the New Kingdom Book of the Dead, are the earliest-known example of decorative writing within a pharaonic tomb chamber, and speak of the pharaoh becoming a star and travelling to Sirius and the constellation of Orion. Painted stars adorn the ceiling, while the sarcophagus area is surrounded by striped, checked and zigzag patterns.

Unas was the last pharaoh of the V Dynasty, so his pyramid came after those of Abu Sir, which in turn show a marked decline from the great pyramids of Giza. Given the duration of pharaonic civilization, it's sobering to realize that this sad reminder of past glories was built only 350 years after the Step Pyramid began the whole pyramid-building cycle. Reliefs inside

▲ Cartouche of Unas

167

the reconstructed section of Unas's kilometre-long **causeway** depict the transport of granite from Aswan, archers, prisoners of war, and a famine caused by the Nile failing to rise. At its eastern end are the ruins of Unas's valley temple, overlooking the Museum of Imhotep (see p.165). To the south of the causeway, two gaping, brick-lined **boat pits** may have contained solar barques like the one at Giza (see p.157), but they may have been merely symbolic, as nothing was found inside the pits when they were excavated.

Other tombs and ruins

A stone hut to the south of Unas's Pyramid gives access to a spiral staircase that descends 25m underground, where three low corridors lead into the vaulted **Persian Tombs**. Chief physician Psamtik, Admiral Djenhebu and Psamtik's son Pediese were all officials of the XXVII Dynasty of Persian kings founded in 525 BC, yet the hieroglyphs in their tombs invoke the same spells as those written two thousand years earlier. The dizzying descent and claustrophobic atmosphere make this an exciting tomb to explore. It's often locked, and guards may tell you that entry is "forbidden", but a little baksheesh usually induces them to reconsider.

Further to the southeast lies the **Tomb of Horemheb**. Built when he was a general, it became redundant after Horemheb seized power from Pharaoh Ay in 1348 BC and ordered a new tomb to be dug in the Valley of the Kings, the royal necropolis of the New Kingdom. Many of the finely carved blocks from his original tomb are now in museums around the world. Another set of paving stones and truncated columns marks the nearby **Tomb of Tia**, sister of Ramses II, and the **Tomb of Maya**, Tutankhamun's treasurer, was found nearby in 1986. Unfortunately, all of these were closed to the public at last check.

Due east of Horemheb's tomb lie the sanded over mud-brick remains of the Coptic **Monastery of St Jeremiah** (Deir Apa Jeremiah), founded in the fifth or sixth century and destroyed by the Arabs in 960. Excavations by James Quibell between 1906 and 1910 uncovered numerous stone-carvings, murals and artefacts, now in the Coptic Museum in Old Cairo (see p.119), but nothing remains on site bar a few sand-blown bits of wall.

The **unfinished Pyramid of Sekhemkhet** would, if finished, have been a step pyramid and funerary complex like those of **Sekhemkhet's** predecessor, Zoser, and may also have been designed by Imhotep. Buried in sand, and forgotten for centuries, it was only rediscovered in 1950. The alabaster sarcophagus inside the pyramid (which is unsafe to enter) was apparently never used, but the body of a child was found inside an auxiliary tomb.

From Sekhemkhet's pyramid it's roughly 700m to the nearest part of South Saqqara (see p.173).

Userkaf and Teti's pyramids

Two more pyramids – belonging to **V Dynasty founder Userkaf**, and VI Dynasty founder Teti – stand to the northeast of Zoser's funerary complex. While neither amounts to very much, the mastabas near Teti's edifice contain some fantastic reliefs.

The pulverized **Pyramid of Userkaf** is just outside the northeast corner of Zoser's funerary complex. Userkaf's V Dynasty successors apparently gave up on Saqqara as a burial site, and had their own pyramids built at Abu Sir (see p.161). Teti, the first pharaoh of the VI Dynasty, had his own pyramid built at Saqqara however, to the northwest of Userkaf's, overlooking the valley from the edge of the plateau. Excavated

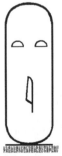

▲ Cartouche of Teti

by French Egyptologist Auguste Mariette in the 1850s, it has since been engulfed by sand but can still be entered; in its funeral chamber (accessible by a sloping shaft and low passageway), the star-patterned roof blocks have slipped inwards due to an earthquake some time in the last 4500 years.

Although most of the VI Dynasty kings who followed Teti chose to be buried at South Saqqara (see p.173), several of their courtiers were interred in a **"street of tombs"**, immediately to the north of his pyramid, which was linked to the Serapeum (see p.171) by an Avenue of Sphinxes, which is now sanded over. It was a mention of this avenue by the ancient Greek geographer Strabo that led Egyptologist Auguste Mariette to the Serapeum in the nineteenth century. To do justice to the tombs' superbly detailed reliefs takes well over an hour, but it's rare to find all of them open.

The Mastaba of Mereruka

The largest tomb in the **"street of tombs"** belongs to **Mereruka**, Teti's vizier and son-in-law, whose 32-room complex includes separate funerary suites for his wife Watet-khet-hor, priestess of Hathor, and their son Meri-Teti. Well-preserved wall paintings in the entry passage show Mereruka playing a board game and painting at an easel. Reliefs in the chamber beyond depict him hunting in the marshes with Watet-khet-hor (the frogs, birds, hippos and grasshoppers are beautifully rendered), along with the usual farming scenes. Goldsmiths, jewellers and other artisans are inspected by the couple on the walls of a room beyond the rear door, which leads into another chamber showing taxation and the punishment of defaulters. A pillared hall to the right portrays them watching sinuous dancers; a room to the left depicts offerings, sacrifices and birds being fed, with a *serdab* at the far end.

Beyond the transverse hall, with its tomb shaft, false door and reliefs of grape-treading and harvesting, lies the main offerings hall, dominated by a statue of Mereruka emerging from a false door. The opposite wall shows his funeral procession; around the corner are boats under full sail, with monkeys playing in their rigging. To the left of the statue, Mereruka is supported by his sons and litter-bearers, accompanied by dwarfs and dogs; on the other side, children frolic while dancers sway above the doorway into Meri-Teti's undecorated funerary suite.

To reach **Watet-khet-hor's suite**, return to the first room in the mastaba and take the other door. After similar scenes to those in her husband's tomb, Watet-khet-hor is carried to her false door in a lion chair.

The Mastabas of Kagemni, Ankh-ma-hor and Nilcaisesi

East of Mereruka's tomb and left around the corner, the smaller **Mastaba of Kagemni** features delicate reliefs, which are unfortunately not as well preserved as those in **Mereruka's tomb**. Catfish, perch, crocodiles and hippopotamuses appear in the entrance corridor, while the pillared hall beyond shows dancers and acrobats, the judgement of prisoners, a hippo hunt and agricultural work, all rich in naturalistic detail. Notice the boys feeding a puppy and trussed cows being milked. The door in this wall leads to another chamber where Kagemni inspects his fowl pens while servants trap marsh birds with clap-nets; on a stone pylon beyond this he relaxes on a palanquin as they tend to his pet dogs and monkeys. As usual in the offerings hall, scenes of butchery appear opposite the false door. On the roof of the mastaba (reached by stairs from the entrance corridor) are two boat pits. As vizier, Kagemni was responsible for overseeing prophets and the estate of Teti's pyramid complex.

East of Kagemni's tomb, the **Mastaba of Ankh-ma-hor** is also known as the "Doctor's Tomb" after its reliefs showing circumcision, toe surgery and suchlike, as practised during the VI Dynasty. If the tomb is open, it's definitely worth a look. The **Mastaba of Nilcaisesi**, in the "lane" behind it, contains scenes of oxen being butchered, and a deep burial shaft. Don't bother slogging out to the sand-choked **I Dynasty tombs** that straggle along the edge of the scarp beyond the **Antiquities Inspectorate**.

The Double Mastaba of Akhti-Hotep and Ptah-Hotep

This mastaba belonged to **Ptah-Hotep**, a priest of Maat during the reign of Unas's predecessor, Djedkare, and his son **Akhti-Hotep**, who served as vizier, judge and overseer of the granaries and treasury. Though it's smaller than Ti's mastaba, its reliefs are interesting for being at various stages of completion, showing how a finished product was achieved. After the preliminary drawings had been corrected in red by a master artist, the background was chiselled away to leave a silhouette, before details were marked in and cut. The agricultural scenes in the entrance corridor show this process clearly, although with the exception of Ptah-Hotep's chapel, none of these reliefs was ever painted.

Off the pillared hall of Akhti-Hotep is a T-shaped chapel whose inside wall shows workers making papyrus boats and jousting with poles. More impressive is the chapel of his father, covered with exquisitely detailed reliefs. Between the two door-shaped stelae representing the entrance to the tomb, Ptah-Hotep enjoys a banquet of offerings, garbed in the panther-skin of a high priest. Similar scenes occur on the facing wall, whose upper registers show animals being slaughtered and women bringing offerings from his estates. The left-hand wall swarms with activity, as boys wrestle and play *khaki la wizza* (a leapfrog game still popular in Nubia); wild animals mate or flee from hunting dogs, while others are caged. A faded mural above the entrance shows the priest being manicured and pedicured. The chapel originally contained two wooden statues of Ptah-Hotep, now in the Imhotep Museum (see p.165).

The Mastaba of Ti

Discovered by Auguste Mariette in 1865, the V Dynasty **Mastaba of Ti** has been a rich source of information about life in the Old Kingdom. A royal hairdresser who made an advantageous marriage, **Ti** acquired stewardship over several mortuary temples and pyramids, and his children bore the title "royal descendant".

Ti makes his first appearances on either side of the doorway, receiving offerings and asking visitors to respect his tomb **[a on the map opposite]**. The reliefs in the courtyard have been damaged by exposure, but it's possible to discern men butchering an ox **[b]**, Ti on his palanquin accompanied by dogs and dwarfs **[c]**, servants feeding cranes and geese **[d]**, and Ti examining accounts and cargo **[e]**. His unadorned tomb (reached by a shaft from the courtyard) contrasts with the richly decorated interior of the mastaba.

Near his son's false door, variously garbed figures of Ti **[f]** appear above the portal of a corridor where bearers bring food and animals for the sustenance of his *ka* **[g]**. Beyond a doorway **[h]** over which Ti enjoys the marshes with his wife, funerary statues are dragged on sledges, animals are butchered, and boats sail through the Nile Delta **[i]**. Potters, bakers, brewers and scribes occupy the rear wall of a storage room **[j]**, while dancers

▲ Cartouche of Ti

shimmy above the doorway to Ti's chapel.

In the harvesting scene, notice the man twisting a donkey's ear to make it behave **[k]**. Further along, Ti inspects shipwrights shaping tree trunks, and sawing and hammering boards **[l]**. Goldsmiths, sculptors, carpenters, tanners and market life are minutely detailed **[m]**, like the musicians who entertain Ti at his offerings table **[n]**. Peer through one of the apertures in the north wall and you'll see a cast of his statue inside its *serdab*. The original is in the Egyptian Museum.

Reliefs on the northern wall depict fishing and trapping in the Delta **[o]**; Ti sailing through the marshes while his servants spear hippopotami **[p]**; harvesting papyrus for boat-building; and ploughing and seeding fields **[q]**. The scene of hunting in the marshes is also allegorical, pitting Ti against the forces of chaos (represented by fish and birds) and evil (hippos were hated and feared). If you aren't

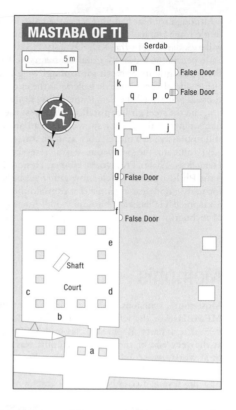

claustrophobic and like cold, dark spaces, it is possible to squeeze down the steps of a shaft into the burial chamber below.

The Serapeum

Saqqara's weirdest monument, the **Serapeum**, is a spacious but gloomy catacomb whose main attractions are the sarcophagi of mummified bulls from an ancient cult once practised here. The rock-cut galleries that make it up lie deep underground at the western end of the buried avenue of sphinxes which starts at the "street of tombs" by Teti's pyramid (see p.169). Discovered by Auguste Mariette in 1851 from clues left by the first-century Greek geographer Strabo, the **Serapeum** held the mummified corpses of the Apis bulls, which the Memphites regarded as manifestations of the god Ptah (see box, p.173) and identified with Osiris after death. The **cult of the Apis bulls** was assailed by Egypt's Persian conqueror, Cambyses, who stabbed one to disprove its divinity, while Cambyses's successor Artaxerxes I avenged his nickname "the donkey" by having a namesake beast buried here with full honours. The Ptolemies, on the other hand, a Greek dynasty who supplanted the Persians as Egypt's rulers after Alexander the Great's 332 BC conquest of the country, encouraged traditional Egyptian cults, including that of the Apis bulls, and even synthesized their own using both Greek and Egyptian elements. The name "Serapeum" thus derives from a fusion of the Egyptian Osarapis (Osiris in his Apis form) and the Greeks' Dionysus into the cult of Serapis, whose temple stood in Alexandria.

Although robbers had plundered the galleries centuries before, Mariette found a single tomb miraculously undisturbed for four thousand years. The oldest of the galleries dates from the XIX Dynasty (1320–1200 BC); the second is from the Saïte period (664–525 BC), and the main one from Ptolemaic times (305–30 BC). Enormous granite or basalt **sarcophagi** weighing up to seventy tonnes are ranged either side of the Ptolemaic gallery, at the end of which is a narrow shaft whereby robbers penetrated the Serapeum. Sadly, none of the mummified bulls remains *in situ*, and the steel girders installed to buttress the collapsing roof make it look more like a nineteenth-century subway than an ancient catacomb, but the tunnels are still impressive in a melancholy kind of way.

En route to the Serapeum, a concrete slab shelters broken statues of Plato, Heraclitus, Thales, Protagoras, Homer, Hesiod, Demetrius of Phalerum and Pindar – the **Philosophers' Circle**, now rather rubbish-strewn and neglected. The statues formerly stood near a temple that overlaid the Serapeum, proof that the Ptolemies juxtaposed Hellenistic philosophy and Ancient Egyptian religion with no sense of incongruity.

Memphis

Most tour excursions to Saqqara include a flying visit to the scant remains of **MEMPHIS** by the village of **Mit Rahina**. In its heyday – which lasted from the very first dynasty of pharaohs around 3100 BC all the way up to Roman times at the very end of the BCs – Memphis was either Egypt's most important city, or at worst, its second most important. For all that, very little remains to stir the imagination of visitors today, and the city, buried under centuries of Nilotic silt, now lies several metres below Mit Rahina's rustling palm groves and ox-ploughed

Memphis in history

The foundation of Memphis is attributed to Menes, the quasi-mythical ruler (known also as Narmer – and possibly a conflation of several rulers) who was said to have unified Upper and Lower Egypt and launched the I Dynasty around 3100 BC. At that time, Memphis stood at the apex of the Nile Delta (which has gradually moved northwards since then) and thus controlled overland and river communications. It was surrounded by levees and battlements, giving it its original name, the White Wall.

Egypt's capital throughout the Old Kingdom (III–IV Dynasty, c.2650–2134 BC), Memphis regained its role through the Middle Kingdom (XI–XIV Dynasty, c.2040–1640 BC) and was still Egypt's second most important city during the New Kingdom (the classic period of ancient Egypt, XVIII–XX Dynasty, c.1550–1040 BC), when Thebes was the capital. Memphis remained the nation's second city until well into the Ptolemaic era, but Alexandria gradually took over, while the creation of Babylon-in-Egypt (Old Cairo) by the Persians sowed the seed of the city that would supplant it (see p.257). By Roman times Memphis was in terminal decline, though it did not become deserted until early Muslim times, after four thousand years of continuous occupation.

At its peak, the population of Memphis may have exceeded one hundred thousand, making it the most populous city in the ancient world until the rise of Mesopotamian Babylon in the seventh century BC. Core-sampling has shown that, in Roman times, Memphis was the shape and size of Manhattan, stretching for over 19km along the west bank of the Nile, to the outskirts of modern-day Giza.

The cults of Ptah and Sokar

In pre-Dynastic times, **Ptah** was the Great Craftsman or Divine Artificer, who invented metallurgy and engineering. However, the people of Memphis esteemed him as the Great Creator who, with a word, brought the universe into being – and invented all the creation deities worshipped by other cities such as Heliopolis (see p.148). Like most creator gods, Ptah was subsequently linked with death cults, and is shown dressed in the shroud of a mummy. The Ancient Greeks associated him with Hephaestus, their god of fire and the arts, and the Romans with their own deity, Vulcan.

Another deity closely associated with Memphis is **Sokar**, originally the god of darkness but subsequently of death, with special responsibility for necropolises. He is often shown with a falcon's head, seated in the company of Isis and Osiris. Although his major festival occurred at Memphis towards the end of the inundation season, Sokar also rated a shrine at Abydos in Upper Egypt, where all the Egyptian death gods were represented.

▲ Ptah

fields. However, something of its glory is evident in the great, pyramid-studded necropolises ranged across the desert, which served as burial grounds for its kings and aristocrats.

The remains

Unfortunately for posterity, most of the buildings in this garden city were built of mud-brick, which eventually merged back into the Nile silt from where it came, and everyone from the Romans onwards plundered its stone temples for fine masonry. Nowadays, all that's left is a little garden (daily 8am–4pm; £E35) with leftover statues and stelae, and a souvenir kiosk. The star attraction, found in 1820, is a limestone **Colossus of Ramses II**, similar to the one that used to stand in Midan Ramses, but laid supine within a concrete shelter. A giant **alabaster sphinx** weighing eighty tonnes is also mightily impressive. Both of these figures probably stood outside the vast Temple of Ptah, the city's patron deity (see box above).

By leaving the garden and walking back along the road, you'll notice (on the right) several alabaster **embalming slabs**, where the holy Apis bulls were mummified before burial in the Serapeum at Saqqara. In a pit across the road are excavated chambers from Ptah's temple complex; climb the ridge beyond them and you can gaze across the cultivated valley floor to the Step Pyramid of Saqqara.

South Saqqara

Like their predecessors at Abu Sir, the pharaohs of the VI Dynasty (c.2345–2181 BC) established another necropolis – nowadays called **South Saqqara** – which started 700m beyond Sekhemkhet's unfinished pyramid (see p.168) and extended for over 3km. Unfortunately, the most interesting monuments are those at the southern end of the site, furthest away from North Saqqara; renting a donkey, horse or camel (£E30–50 for the round trip) will minimize slogging over soft sand. It's also possible to walk to South Saqqara from Saqqara village (see p.164): just keep heading west until you emerge from the palm trees. If you stop to ask directions, bear in mind that, whatever you say (even if you say it in Arabic – the key word is "Pepi"), the villagers will almost certainly assume you are looking for the Step Pyramid, and direct you accordingly. The site is quite large, with the northern part (around Pepi I's pyramid) pretty much due west of the village, while the southern area (around the Mastabat al-Faraun) lies to the village's southwest. There is no official entrance fee to the site, and you probably won't see another tourist. Apart from the tranquillity, what you get here – with North Saqqara's pyramids clearly visible to the north, and Dahshur's to the south – is the feeling of being in the midst of a massive pyramid field, somewhere vast and very ancient.

The northern part of the site

South Saqqara's northern section centres on a low mound of rubble identified as the **Pyramid of Pepi I**. The name "Memphis", which Classical authors bestowed upon Egypt's ancient capital and its environs, was actually derived from one of this pyramid's titles, Men-nefer-Pepi (The Beauty of Pepi Endures). To the southwest, another dusty heap is what's left of the **Pyramid of Merenre**, the tomb of Pepi's VI Dynasty successor. French Egyptologists have been excavating the Pepi's pyramid, but neither site is really worth a detour.

Directly east of Merenre's pyramid, sand drifts over the outlying temples of the **Pyramid of Djedkare-Isesi**. Known in Arabic as the "Pyramid of the Sentinel", it stands 25m high and can be entered via a tunnel on the north side. Although a shattered basalt sarcophagus and mummified remains were found here during the 1800s, it wasn't until 1946 that Abdel Hussein identified them as those of Djedkare, the penultimate king of the V Dynasty. Far from being the first ruler to be entombed in South Saqqara, he was merely emulating Shepseskaf, whose own mortuary complex (see below) is actually the oldest in this necropolis.

The southern part of the site

The mortuary complex of **Shepseskaf** is the most important monument in south Saqqara, and lies well to the south of Pepi I's, Menere's and Djedkare-Isesi's, about as far from them as they are from North Saqqara. Built of limestone blocks, the complex rather resembles a gigantic sarcophagus with a rounded lid. Locally, it's known as **Mastabat al-Faraun** – the Pharaoh's Bench. If you can find a guard, it's possible to venture through descending and horizontal corridors to reach the burial chamber and various storerooms. The monument was almost certainly commissioned by Shepseskaf, who evidently felt the need to distance himself from the pyramid of his father, Mycerinus (see p.160). However, the early twentieth-century Swiss Egyptologist Gustave Jéquier doubted that the complex was ever used for any actual burial and Shepseskaf's final resting place remains uncertain.

Just northwest of Shepseskaf's complex lie the mortuary temple and pyramid of **Pepi II**. These form the most complete VI Dynasty mortuary complex still in existence, even though they are short of casing stones and other masonry that was plundered in medieval times. The **mortuary temple**, whose vestibule and sanctuary retain fragments of their original reliefs, stands at the end of a causeway, which starts 600m to the northeast, where Pepi's valley temple once stood. Immediately to the west of the mortuary temple rises the **Pyramid of Pepi II**, whose reign supposedly lasted 94 years, after which the VI Dynasty expired. A descending passage leads to his rock-cut **burial chamber**, whose ceiling and walls are inscribed with stars and Pyramid Texts (also found within the subsidiary pyramids of Pepi's queens, Apuit and Neith, which imitate his mortuary complex on a smaller scale).

Dahshur

The Dahshur site (daily 8am–4pm, last ticket sold an hour before closing; £E30) contains some of the most impressive of all the pyramids, and some of the most significant in the history of pyramid-building.

Dahshur's pyramids are in two groups. To the east are three **Middle Kingdom complexes**, dating from the revival of pyramid-building (c.1991–1790 BC) that culminated near the Fayoum. Though the pyramids proved unrewarding to nineteenth-century excavators, their subsidiary tombs yielded some magnificent jewellery (now in the Egyptian Museum, see p.62). To the north, the pyramids of XII Dynasty pharaohs Sesostris III and Amenemhat II are little more than piles of rubble, but the southernmost of the three, the **Black Pyramid of Amenemhat III** (Joseph's pharaoh in the Old Testament, according to some; see p.180), is the oddest-looking pyramid of them all: with its limestone casing long gone, the pyramid's black mud-brick core is left as a huge, misshapen hulk rising out of the sand. The pyramid's black basalt capstone has been recovered and is in the Egyptian Museum.

More intriguing are the two **Old Kingdom pyramids** further into the desert, which have long tantalized Egyptologists with a riddle (see box, p.176). Both of them are credited to **Snofru** (c.2613–2588 BC), father of Cheops and founder of the IV Dynasty, whose monuments constitute an evolutionary link between the stepped creations of the previous dynasty at North Saqqara and the true pyramids of Giza.

The Red Pyramid

The first pyramid you come to if you follow the road from the village past the ticket office is the northern **Red Pyramid** (see colour projection), so named after the pinkish limestone from which it is built. No less impressive than any of the Giza trio (see p.153), it differs from them by standing in perfect isolation. Despite its lower angle (43.5°) and height (101m), the Red Pyramid clearly prefigures Cheops's edifice at Giza, which is also the only pyramid that exceeds it in size. It was probably Snofru's final attempt at pyramid building, but he was not laid to rest here, as no sarcophagus was ever found. Indeed, the Red and Bent pyramids are only attributed to Snofru because his cartouche (see right) appears on their respective mortuary temples.

▲ Cartouche of Snofru

Getting to Dahshur

The easiest way to reach Dahshur is by **taxi**, but there are **service taxi** microbuses to Dahshur village from Saqqara village, and occasionally direct ones from Maryotteya Canal by Pyramids Road (otherwise get one from there to Saqqara and change). Infrequent service taxis run the 2km to the site entrance from Dahshur village, but it's generally easier to walk or take a taxi. The latter is a good idea since the site is extremely spread out: it's one kilometre from the gate to the Red Pyramid, and another from there to the Bent Pyramid. A **tuk-tuk** should cost £E3 from the village to the site entrance, but actually it's a pleasant walk. Getting back to Cairo should not be left too late or you may find yourself stranded with the nearest public transport 5km away in Saqqara – transport from Dahshur tends to dry up at around 5pm. Or you can take a half-day guided **tour** from Samo Tours (see p.164), costing US$19.50 per person (minimum two people; site tickets not included).

The Red Pyramid's **interior** configuration is unusual: a typical entrance shaft on the north face leads down to just above bedrock level, where you pass through two large chambers with corbelled ceilings (slabs laid overlapping the ones below until they meet in the middle) and ascend a (modern) staircase to reach the burial chamber, situated on a higher level, perpendicular to the other two. You may well be alone to absorb the rather eerie, fetid atmosphere – in any case, photography is allowed.

The Bent Pyramid

From the Red Pyramid, a road leads south to the **Bent Pyramid** (see colour projection), which is not only the most intriguing of all the pyramids, but, because of its state of preservation, also the most breathtaking. What makes it different from all the other pyramids is its change of angle towards the top: it rises more steeply (54.3°) than the Red or Giza pyramids for three-quarters of its height, before abruptly tapering at a gentler slope (43.2°) – hence its name. The explanation for its shape, and why Snofru should have had two pyramids built barely a kilometre apart, is a longstanding conundrum of Egyptology (see box below).

Of all the pyramids, the Bent Pyramid is the only one constructed with two entrance shafts at right angles to each other – one on the north side (as usual) and the other on its western face. The former leads to two chambers carved from the bedrock, connected to a separate upper chamber within the superstructure, directly accessible by the latter shaft. All three chambers have corbelled ceilings.

The riddle of Snofru's pyramids

Snofru, the founder of the IV Dynasty, is associated with three different pyramids: the Red and Bent Pyramids at Dahshur (see p.175 & above), and the Collapsed Pyramid at Maidum (see opposite). Given that a pyramid was the pharaoh's tomb, the question arises, why would Snofru want three of them? And why is the Bent Pyramid such a funny shape, changing its angle halfway up?

Some scholars reasoned that the **Bent Pyramid**'s strange form resulted from a change of plan prompted by fears for its stability, and when these persisted, a second, safer pyramid was built to guarantee Snofru's afterlife. But for this theory to hold, it's necessary to dismiss Snofru's claim to have commissioned the pyramid at **Maidum** as a mere usurpation of an earlier structure. Two pyramids can be explained, three cannot.

Then, in 1977, Oxford professor **Kurt Mendelssohn** came up with a better answer. He suggested there was something like a pyramid production line. As one pyramid neared completion, surplus resources were deployed to start another. The reason for this was that building a single pyramid required gigantic efforts over ten to thirty years; inevitably, some pharaohs lacked the time and resources. A stockpile of half-constructed, perhaps even finished, pyramids was thus an insurance policy on the afterlife.

According to Mendelssohn, Snofru did indeed start off by commissioning the pyramid at Maidum. Unfortunately, this was built at too steep an angle and its outer layer collapsed. When this happened, the Bent Pyramid was already under construction, so its angle was hastily altered to make it more stable. The **Red Pyramid**, which followed, was then built at this new, shallower angle.

Not everyone agrees with Mendelssohn: other scholars argue that the Bent Pyramid's shape had nothing to do with the Collapsed Pyramid, but expressed a deliberate symbolic duality, echoed in its two burial chambers and the two entrance shafts at right angles to each other. At any rate, Snofru decided against using either Maidum or the Bent Pyramid, and was finally interred in the Red Pyramid.

While they are unlikely to be open to the public in the near future, you can see inside on ⓦ www.guardians.net/egypt.

Externally, the pyramid is remarkable for its largely intact **limestone casing**, whose smooth, once pristine white, surface gives a clear impression of how it once looked. All the Old Kingdom pyramids were originally clad in limestone, their surfaces as smooth as this one, but most have been stripped, their stone burned for lime. The Bent Pyramid escaped that fate because its narrower angle made it harder to remove the facing, though this has disappeared from much of the base. Where the casing blocks have fallen away at the northwest corner (now being repaired), you can see how closely they were slotted together, and also pits and grooves carved into the bedrock, presumably carved before the pyramid was begun, marking out its base on the plateau.

To its south is a subsidiary **Queen's Pyramid**, possibly belonging to Snofru's wife Hetepheres. If it did, she didn't stay there very long: after robbers had entered both of Snofru's pyramids at Dahshur, her sarcophagus was moved to Giza for safekeeping and hidden down a shaft beside the Great Pyramid of her son Cheops.

Even if one discounts the attribution of the Collapsed Pyramid of Maidum to Snofru, it is a staggering fact that, during his twenty-five-year reign, the construction of the Bent and Red pyramids involved the quarrying, transport and shaping of some nine million tonnes of stone – more than three times the quantity of the Great Pyramid of Giza. Yet Herodotus wrote that Snofru was remembered by the Egyptians as benign, and his successor Cheops as a tyrant.

Maidum, Lahun and Hawara

The pyramid field extends for 60km across the desert to the edge of the **Fayoum**, a fertile depression that has been cultivated since antiquity thanks to a network of canals fed by the River Nile. Of the four separate pyramid sites on the Fayoum's eastern periphery, by far the finest is **Maidum**, with its dramatic-looking Collapsed Pyramid that marks an evolutionary step between the Old Kingdom pyramids at Saqqara and Giza.

Lahun and **Hawara** are less spectacular relics, and represent a revival of pyramid building after many centuries. They date from the XII Dynasty (c.1991–1786 BC). The dynasty's founder, Amenemhat I, started the revival off when he had his own pyramid built at **El-Lisht**, 2km north of Maidum near his capital of Itj-tway, where his son and successor Senusret (aka Sesostris) I also had a pyramid built. The least interesting and least accessible of the four pyramid sites, El-Lisht cannot be reached by public transport, and is not open to the public.

Because of their distance from Cairo, one thing that all the pyramid sites around the Fayoum have big-time is a beautiful undisturbed charm: while Maidum might get one tourist coach every couple of days, Lahun and Hawara often see no visitors for weeks on end.

The Collapsed Pyramid of Maidum

The **Collapsed Pyramid of Maidum** (daily 8am–4pm; £E35; see colour projection) is visible from afar, looking like some craggy medieval fortress rising out of the desert in sheer-walled tiers from mounds of debris – a vision almost as dramatic as the act of getting inside used to be, when "visitors had to hang by their hands from the ledge above and drop into the entry guided by a guard". Nowadays you

Getting to Maidum, Lahun and Hawara

It's just about feasible to reach Maidum by **public transport**, by catching an early-morning train to El-Wasta in the Nile Valley (1hr 30min), and then a service taxi to the village of Maidum (15min). From the western end of the village it's a short walk across the fields and two canals into the desert; the pyramid is visible from the Nile Valley road, and during the last stage of the train journey.

However it's far easier by car, as Maidum is connected by a 6km spur to the Assyut Desert Road from Giza. As few Cairo **taxi** drivers are familiar with the Fayoum they may appreciate directions: follow the Assyut Desert Road south for 83km until you see the *Al-Assiouty Resthouse* on the far side of the highway. Make a U-turn, drive back past the resthouse and you'll find the turn-off for Maidum, whose pyramid is visible on the horizon. With excellent roads and little traffic, you can drive here from Giza in an hour or so. Expect to pay £E300–500 to persuade drivers to venture as far as Maidum (possibly including a visit to Dahshur on the way back). The additional 45km to **Lahun** (likewise accessible by a spur off the Assyut highway) or **Hawara** (somewhat nearer, using back roads) may incur an extra charge, depending on your negotiating skills.

climb a thirty-metre iron stairway on the north side, then descend 57m to the bedrock by a steep passageway (high enough to walk comfortably), to duck through a low portal into the **burial chamber**. Its lofty corbelled ceiling of limestone slabs resembles the chambers in the Bent Pyramid at Dahshur (see p.176), and its atmosphere is cool and slightly humid.

Evidently Maidum began as a step pyramid (like Zoser's at Saqqara), with four levels, which was then enlarged to an eight-step pyramid, and finally given an outer shell to make it a "true" pyramid. It seems, however, that the design was faulty, distributing stresses outwards rather than inwards, so that its own mass blew the structure apart. When exactly this happened is unknown.

No inscriptions appeared on the red granite coffin found there, but New Kingdom graffiti in the pyramid's mortuary temple led archeologists to attribute it to the IV Dynasty ruler **Snofru** or to his father **Huni** (2637–2613 BC). Partisans of Huni argue that Snofru commissioned the Red and Bent pyramids at Dahshur, and would therefore not have needed a third repository for his *ka*. Most scholars accept Kurt Mendelssohn's theory (see box, p.176) that the design of the Bent Pyramid at Dahshur was hastily altered because Maidum collapsed during construction. But critics argue that there is no evidence for the collapse having happened while the pyramid was under construction – indeed, its mortuary temple would not have been built had this happened – and the collapse might have occurred as late as medieval times.

Other sights

Around the pyramid are several unfinished mastabas, reduced to piles of mud-brick lumps. It was here that the exquisite "Maidum Geese" frieze and the famous statue of Prince Rahotep and his wife Nofret were found, which are both now in the Egyptian Museum (see p.57 & p.36). Nearest the pyramid, **Mastaba #17** is exciting to explore, but very dusty and likely to rip your clothing as you descend an extremely low and narrow 47-metre-long corridor and a makeshift wooden ladder to the burial chamber. Its sarcophagus is larger than the chamber's entrance, so presumably the mastaba was built around it.

The site ticket also covers admission to a more distant mastaba and a ruined mortuary temple – but frankly they're not worth the effort of walking that far.

The Pyramid of Lahun

Built seven or eight centuries after the pyramids at Giza, the **Pyramid of Senusret II** at **Lahun** (daily 8am–4pm; £E35) is on the southeast edge of the Fayoum depression, near the village of Al-Lahun, where visitors buy their admission ticket and pick up a police escort to walk the final kilometre to the pyramid. The pyramid looks most impressive on the approach, rearing up to mark the start of the desert as you approach through the fields. It actually looks more like a natural formation than a man-made construction.

For his pyramid, Senusret, a pharaoh of the XII Dynasty who ruled 1897–1878 BC, employed a new and different technique, devised by the royal architect Anupy. The core consists of a rock knoll on which limestone pillars were based, providing the framework for the mud-brick overlay, which was finally encased in stone. The removal of its casing left the mud-brick pyramid exposed to the elements, which eroded it into its present misshapen lump. When the British Egyptologist Flinders Petrie entered the pyramid and found Senusret's sarcophagus, it had been looted long ago; however, in 1914, the American George Brunton discovered the jewellery of Princess Sat-hathor, which is now divided between Cairo's Egyptian Museum (see p.62) and the Metropolitan Museum of Art in New York. Unfortunately, you can't go inside.

In addition to the pyramid, Senusret ordered eight rock-cut mastabas for his family to the north of his pyramid, but little remains of them. To their east is the shapeless so-called **Queen's Pyramid**, apparently lacking any tomb. In 2009 the discovery of a coffin from the II Dynasty, together with grave goods including a table, a bed and two spears, showed that Lahun was used for burials a thousand years earlier than previously reckoned.

The Pyramid of Hawara

About 12km northwest of Lahun, near the village of Hawarat al-Maqta, which is on the way from Lahun to Fayoum City (Medinet Fayoum), the 54-metre-high **Pyramid of Amenemhat III** at **Hawara** (daily 8am–4pm; £E35) gets hardly any visitors. Sadly, there isn't all that much to see, as the pyramid has degenerated into a blackened mud-brick lump since its limestone casing was removed in antiquity. It is thought that it may have stood on the shores of a lake when it was built in the nineteenth century BC. Later, it became the finishing point of a one-hundred-kilometre **desert endurance race** instituted by the XXV Dynasty pharaoh Taharqa (690–664 BC) to train his troops; the marathon was revived in 2001 and is now held annually in November (W www.egyptianmarathon.com).

Unlike most pyramids, the entrance of Amenemhat's was on the south side: one of many ruses devised to foil tomb-robbers. Alas, due to rising ground water, you can't go inside to examine such ingenious features as the stone portcullises that sealed the corridor or the roof block that was lowered into place once the sarcophagus was in the burial chamber, both operated by sand. None of these saved the body of the pharaoh from being looted and burned; his sarcophagus was later stashed alongside that of his daughter, to be found intact with her treasures in 1956. The pyramid's most interesting feature is the column of bricks visible where the corner has fallen away; the pyramid was constructed around a natural outcrop of rock, using these brick columns to hold it together.

South of the pyramid, a few column stumps and masses of limestone chippings mark the site of the fabled **Labyrinth**. According to the Greek historian Herodotus, this contained over three thousand chambers hewn from a single rock, and in Herodotus's day was one of Egypt's top tourist attractions. Most

Egyptologists believe it was Amenemhat III's mortuary temple, but David Rohl, a maverick Egyptologist who has made a name trying to tie in archeology with the Bible, has a different theory. He argues that Amenemhat was the pharaoh in the biblical story of Joseph, and that the labyrinth could be the remains of waterworks devised by Joseph to prepare Egypt for the seven years of famine that he prophesied (Genesis 41).

It was while excavating at Hawara in 1888 that Flinders Petrie unearthed 146 brilliantly naturalistic **"Fayoum Portraits"** in the Roman cemetery to the north of the pyramid. Several of these are now in the Egyptian Museum (see p.63), with one in the Coptic Museum (see p.121), and more in the British Museum in London and other museums around the world.

Listings

Listings

Accommodation

airo's **hotels** reflect the city's diversity: deluxe chains overlooking the Nile; functional high-rises; colonial piles and homely *pensions* with the same raddled facades as bug-infested flophouses. Rates are usually the same all year, though some five-stars have variable rates which change from day to day depending on current demand. Upmarket hotels are of course always cheaper if booked through an agency at home or online, and many hotels offer discounts to guests staying for a week or two. Inexpensive hotels tend to be located on the upper floors of downtown office buildings, and one or two are locked at midnight, so if you arrive later you'll have to rouse the doorman (*bowab*), who will expect a tip for his trouble.

Downtown traffic is noisy and you may wish to bring earplugs if staying in the centre. Rooms vary in many places, so try to inspect the facilities before checking in, and establish the price and any service tax or extra charges (which should be posted in reception) at the outset. Many budget hotels in particular offer a choice between cheap rooms, with shared bathroom facilities, and slightly pricier ones with en-suite bathrooms, though sometimes that is just a shower in the corner of the room.

Budget hotels generally quote **prices** in Egyptian pounds, but upmarket hotels are more likely to quote prices in US dollars or euros. The prices given here are for the cheapest double room in high season. Many hotels also offer **tours**, usually on commission, and not uncommonly at several times over their actual price (see p.22); always shop around before buying a tour, and be especially suspicious of any hotel whose staff try to push tours on guests.

Zamalek, the northern half of Gezira Island, is quieter and less congested than central Cairo, except along 26th July Street, and women will suffer less unwelcome attention there than in the downtown area or Islamic Cairo.

Central Cairo

Unless otherwise indicated, these hotels are marked on the map on pp.50–51.

Amin 38 Midan Falaki, opposite Bab al-Luq market ☎02/2393-3813. Recently redecorated small hotel whose rooms, all with fans, are located on the sixth, seventh and tenth floors. It's worth paying a bit more for a room with private bathroom and constant hot water (£E80) as the shared facilities aren't so clean. £E45.

Berlin Fourth floor, 2 Sharia el-Shawarby ☎02/2395-7502, @berlinhotelcairo @hotmail.com. Small city-centre hotel with high-ceilinged double and triple rooms, each with its own shower, a/c and comfortable mattresses, and looking nice and fresh now that most of them have been given a facelift. The owner is extremely helpful, and services include laundry, free wi-fi and use of computer, their own drivers to take you round the pyramid sites or elsewhere at decent rates, and good-value Arabic and bellydancing lessons. B&B £E137.

Big Ben 33 Sharia Emad el-Din ☏02/2590-8881 (see map, p.68). Good-value little hotel north of the main downtown area, with clean, fresh rooms, all en-suite, not frequented much by foreign tourists, and rather cheaper than its centre-of-downtown equivalents as a result. £E80.

Carlton 21 26th July St ☏02/2575-5022, ⓦwww.carltonhotelcairo.com. A pleasantly creaky old hotel, once quite swanky, built in 1935 and still retaining some wood-panelled period charm, albeit rather worn. All rooms are a/c, and the pricier deluxe rooms have satellite TV and a minibar. Rooms at the back are much quieter than those at the front. There's a restaurant on the seventh floor and a very pleasant rooftop garden with a café-bar. You usually have to take half-board, though they may do you a bed-and-breakfast rate. Half-board £E250.

Cosmopolitan 1 Sharia Ben Talaab, off Qasr el-Nil ☏02/2392-3956, Ⓕ2393-3531. This rather grand monumental *belle époque* hotel is quite stately in a modest way, with sedate, red-carpeted rooms, a European restaurant and English-style bar, but avoid the tours sold at the travel desk. All rooms have a/c and private baths. B&B US$79.

Crown 9 Sharia Emad el-Din ☏020/591-8374, Ⓔcrowncairo@yahoo.com. Quite a well-kept place north of the main downtown area, and claiming Canadian management, though that isn't in evidence. Rooms have a/c and private bathroom, and shiny tiled floors. £E100.

🏃 **Dahab** Seventh floor, 26 Sharia Bassiouni ☏02/2579-9104, ⓦwww.dahabhostel .com. A very laid-back hostel that's like a beach camp from the Red Sea backpacker resort of Dahab transported – surprisingly convincingly – to the roof of a building in downtown Cairo, with poky rooms, friendly staff and lots of interesting people staying. Plenty of vegetation and an open area to socialize in make it a pleasant hangout; facilities include a Bedouin-style café, laundry service, free wi-fi and hot water – though the last two are a bit erratic. £E45.

Fontana Off Midan Ramses ☏02/2592-2321 (see map, p.68). A bit scuffed in places, but this hotel definitely has a slightly kitsch charm about it, with pink marble in the lobby and a touch of the Louis Farouks in the rooms (that's Louis XIV as interpreted by King Farouk). There's a small rooftop swimming pool (summer only), bar, restaurant, café, and a nightclub (see p.206). Rooms have TV, fridge and a/c; some have views as far as the Citadel, and the staff are extremely friendly. B&B US$52.

Four Seasons 1089 Corniche el-Nil, Garden City ☏02/2791-7000, ⓦwww.fourseasons.com. Sleek, sophisticated and luxurious to a fault, this branch of the *Four Seasons* chain is better suited to Western tastes than its gaudier sister establishment opposite the zoo in Giza. The rooms have a classic charm with little extras like a DVD player and high-speed internet connection. Two rooms are adapted for wheelchair users. US$502.

Garden City House Third floor, 26 Sharia Kamal al-Din Salah ☏02/2794-8400, ⓦwww .gardencityhouse.com. 1930s *pension* on the edge of the Garden City, behind the *Semiramis* (see opposite). Some rooms have Nile views, some have en-suite bathrooms, and some have a/c. For some reason it's quite popular with impecunious Egyptologists, but on the downside, the location is rather noisy. B&B £E143.

Grand 17 26th July St (entrance in the alley off Sharia Talaat Harb) ☏02/575-7801 to 5, Ⓔgrandhotel@link.net. Art Deco edifice featuring original lifts and furniture, a fountain, coffee shop and old-fashioned, homely rooms with immaculately varnished wooden floors, attached to spacious and immaculate tiled bathrooms, though the plumbing can be temperamental, and the desk staff a bit surly. They generally insist that you take half-board. Half-board £E154.

Happyton 10 Sharia Ali al-Kassar ☏02/2592 8600. Functional but friendly and excellent-value two-star hotel with en-suite a/c rooms of variable sizes, all decent and well-kept, but nothing fancy. There's a café and small restaurant, but no bar, though you can buy beer in the lobby and drink it on the roof terrace. B&B £E100.

🏃 **Isis** Marouf Tower, 16th floor, 33B Sharia Ramses ☏02/2578-1895, ⓦwww .isiscairo.com. Worth staying at for the spectacular views alone, over the river on one side, and over downtown to the Citadel on the other. Staff are friendly and rooms are spacious, with large windows, wooden floors and furnishings, and there's free internet use. On the downside, the location isn't great (two blocks off Talaat Harb among car spares shops), and the lift only reaches the fourteenth floor, so you have to walk the other two. B&B £E145.

Ismailia House Eighth floor, 1 Midan Tahrir
☎ 02/2796-3122, ⓦ www.ismailiahotel.com.
Advance booking is advisable for this easy-
going, cheerful backpackers' haven. Slightly
worn around the edges, it offers a variety
of singles, doubles, triples and dorm beds,
plus 24hr hot water and plenty of communal
areas to hang out in. The Tahrir-facing rooms
are noisy at night but have great views.
Dorm beds US$6, doubles US$16; all B&B.
King Tut Hostel Eighth floor, 37 Sharia Talaat
Harb ☎ 02/2391-7897, ⓦ www.kingtuthostel
.com. Kitsch but wonderful pharaonic decor
in the entrance and public areas welcomes
you to this bright hotel (not really a hostel,
despite the name). It's often full, so worth
booking ahead (or try the very similar
Ramses II Hotel, four floors up in the same
building, run by the same firm). Don't be
pressurized into buying their tours, however.
B&B £E150.
Lotus Seventh floor, 12 Sharia Talaat Harb
(entrance in the arcade) ☎ 02/2575-0966,
ⓦ www.lotushotel.com. Its claim to have "an
authentic Art Deco ambience" is a slight
exaggeration, though one or two of the
fittings do seem to date from the 1930s,
and the rooms are suitably sombre. There's
a restaurant and a bar, and the staff are
friendly; it's worth paying the extra $3.20
for an en-suite room with a/c (hot water
6–11am and 6–11pm), but avoid buying
tours here. B&B US$23.
🏃 **Luna** Fifth floor, 27 Sharia Talaat Harb
☎ 02/396-1020, ⓦ www.hotellunacairo
.com. Better looked-after and generally
cleaner than other hotels in this price range,
with large a/c rooms, some en suite. It's
worth asking for the Egyptian breakfast (*fuul*
and *falafel*) in preference to the Continental.
Rooms at the back are quieter and slightly
pricier. B&B £E140.
New Cecil (or New Cicil) 22 Sharia Emad el-Din
☎ 02/2591-3895 (see map, p.68). Situated
to the north of the centre, near Ramses
Station, this is a reasonable budget option
if you aren't too fussy – the rooms are a bit
grimy, but quite adequate for the price, with
fans and shared bathroom facilities. £E45.
Nile Ritz-Carlton 1113 Corniche el-Nil
☎ 02/2578-0444 or 0666, ⓦ www.ritzcarlton
.com/en/Properties/Cairo. Cairo's most central
five-star, closed for refurbishment until
2012. This 1950s building (formerly the *Nile
Hilton*) is on the river right by the Egyptian
Museum; it boasts the biggest rooms in

town, and they will no doubt be top-of-the-
range when renovation is completed.
Odeon Palace 6 Sharia Abdel Hamid Said,
just off Sharia Talaat Harb ☎ 02/2577-6637,
ⓕ 2576-7971. Creaky old place with a certain
sombre, old-fashioned charm, but give
your room a once-over, and make sure
the shower and plug sockets are working,
before taking the room. The hotel's biggest
attractions are 24hr room service and a
24hr roof bar. US$60.
🏃 **Pension Roma** 169 Sharia Mohammed
Farid (entrance around the side of
Gattegno department store) ☎ 02/2391-1088,
ⓦ www.pensionroma.com.eg. The stylish
1940s ambience of this charming little
pension, immaculately maintained by
Madame Cressaty, is highly recommended
and it's wise to book in advance. The rooms
are cosy, spic and span, some with private
bathrooms, though most have shared
bathroom facilities. B&B £E104.
Select Eighth floor, 19 Sharia Adly, beside the
synagogue ☎ 02/393-3707, ⓔ hostelselect
@yahoo.com. A bright little place, homely and
very friendly, in a 1930s building with one or
two period touches. B&B £E100.
Ramses Hilton Corniche el-Nil ☎ 02/2577-7444,
ⓦ www.hilton.com. Cairo's tallest hotel,
rooms on the upper stories giving excellent
views over the city and as far as the
Pyramids, but it gets rather mixed reports,
and is largely used by tour groups, so it isn't
quite as posh as you might expect from
a Hilton, and there always seems to be a
queue at the reception desk. US$250.
Semiramis Intercontinental Corniche el-Nil
☎ 02/2795-7171, ⓦ www.intercontinental.com.
Spacious, elegant rooms, plus a gym, a
pool, the *Haroun al-Rashid* nightclub (see
p.205), and seven restaurants offering
cuisine from around the world. Rooms on
the upper floors give excellent views, and
in fact the views over Cairo from the slightly
cheaper city-side rooms are better than
from the Nile side. US$397.
Shepheard Corniche el-Nil ☎ 02/2792-1000,
ⓦ www.shepheard-hotel.com. Nile-side version
of the famous nineteenth-century establishment that stood on Midan Opera, rebuilt on
the present site in 1957, and still retaining
a certain 1950s feel. Rooms on the quieter
side facing the Muqattam Hills are cheaper
than those facing the Nile. Facilities include
two restaurants, a casino and the *Castle*
disco, but no swimming pool. US$270.

Sultan First floor, 4 Sharia Tawfiqia ☏02/2577-2258, ✉hotel.sultan@hotmail.com. Dorm beds only in this friendly ultra-cheapy located in a colourful market street near Midan Orabi, very handy for inexpensive eating and groceries, and just the right distance from the centre of downtown. Guests get free use of the kitchen and there's satellite TV in the common room. Dorm beds £E15.

Talisman in the passage by 39 Sharia Talaat Harb ☏02/2393-9431, ⓦwww.talisman-hotel.com. Well-situated boutique hotel with some five-star facilities (a/c, satellite TV, minibar, safe) but no pool or fitness centre. Excellent service and attentive staff give it a real personal touch. The whole hotel is decorated with antiques and *objets d'art*, and rooms are double-glazed to keep out the street noise. €81.50.

Tulip First floor, 3 Midan Talaat Harb ☏02/2393-9433, ⓦwww.tulip-hotel.com. Decently refurbished old place facing *Groppi's* across Midan Talaat Harb. It's extremely well-located and the rooms are bright and cheerful. Wi-fi is available for £E10 a day. B&B £E101.

Venice Hosokawaya Fourth floor, 4 Sharia Tawfiqia ☏02/273-5307, ⓦwww.venice hosokawaya.net. In the same building as the *Sultan* (see above) but pricier, this is the

Japanese backpackers' budget hotel of choice in Cairo, and ninety percent of its clientele are from Japan. It's very clean and well-run, with dorm beds and private rooms, free wi-fi, and a laundry service. Dorm beds £E35, doubles £E120, all B&B.

Victoria 66 Sharia el-Gumhorriya ☏02/2589-2290 to 94, ⓦwww.victoria.com.eg (see map, p.68).** A three-star 1930s hotel once frequented by George Bernard Shaw. Lots of wood panelling, attractive a/c rooms with shiny wooden floors and a comfortably worn, lived-in feel (some with mahogany furniture), plus a bar, restaurant and spacious lounge area, make this one of the best deals in town. Advance reservation advisable. B&B €54.

Windsor 19 Sharia Alfi Bey ☏02/2591-5810, ⓦwww.windsorcairo.com. This colonial hotel retains much character and is home to one of the nicest bars in Cairo (the *Barrel Lounge*, see p.201), but has definitely seen better days and is overpriced, not tremendously friendly, and not tremendously clean. They may also insist on your paying for a (not very nice) breakfast. All rooms have a/c and satellite TV; all but the very cheapest are en suite. Fifteen percent discount for *Rough Guide* readers, but avoid buying tours here. US$46.22.

Islamic Cairo

El-Hussein Muski, entered via a passage to Fishawi's ☏02/2591-8089 (see map, p.77). Rather grimy, and rooms overlooking the square are harangued by Cairo's loudest *muezzins*, and festivals are celebrated all night long in Midan al-Hussein, just outside. On the other hand, if you don't mind the noise, a balcony overlooking the square gives you a ringside view, and if you want to be in the thick of it, this really is right in the heart of Islamic Cairo. B&B £E165.

El Malky 4 Sharia el-Hussein ☏02/2589-0804, ⓦwww.server2002.net/malky (see map, p.77). Behind the Saiyidna Hussein Mosque, this quiet little hotel, with a mainly Muslim clientele, is good value, and well located. It's less than 100m from El-Hussein, but out of

the noise and bustle. Rooms are carpeted, with a/c and private bathrooms, and are generally comfortable though the beds are a bit on the hard side. B&B £E100.

Le Riad 114 Sharia al-Muizz ☏02/2787-6074, ⓦwww.leriad -hoteldecharme.com (see map, p.81). Immaculate boutique hotel in the heart of Gamaliya, containing seventeen individually themed suites (including a a pharaoh suite, a Mamluke suite and a King Farouk suite), all with sparkling bathrooms, free wi-fi (plus loan of a laptop if you need it) and plasma TV with DVD player. There's a library of DVDs and books, and a roof terrace with great views over Islamic Cairo. B&B £E240.

Elsewhere in the city

Cairo Marriott Sharia Saray al-Gezira, off 26th July St, Zamalek ☏02/2728-3000, ⊛www.cairo marriotthotel.com (see map, pp.132–133). A classy five-star where you can choose between garden rooms or slightly pricier tower rooms with a better view (some of the river and downtown), all built around a lavish palace constructed to house Napoleon III's wife Empress Eugénie. The hotel's extensive facilities include five restaurants, two bars, a casino, nightclub and, of course, a pool. Rooms have fast internet connections and the hotel is wi-fi-enabled throughout. US$620.

Conrad 1191 Corniche el-Nil, Bulaq ☏02/2580-8000, ⊛www.conradhotels.com (see map, p.141). Palm trees welcome you into the lobby of this modern five-star hotel run by the Hilton chain, but calmer and more sedate than the *Ramses Hilton* (see p.185). As well as some of the most comfortable rooms in Cairo, it boasts international dining, a pool and a health club. US$313.

El Borg Novotel 3 Sharia Saraya el Gezira ☏02/3735-6725, ⊛www.novotel.com (see map, pp.132–133). Just over Tahrir Bridge in Gezira, this hotel is rather ugly on the outside but cool and stylish inside, with modern cream and beige rooms, plus the usual deluxe accessories such as a/c and plasma TV. US$300.

Grand Hyatt ☏02/2365-1234, ⊛www.cairo .grand.hyatt.com (see map, pp.116–117). Superior five-star at the northern tip of Roda Island, best accessed via its own bridge from Garden City. Stylish rooms, all in a sumptuous new wing; north-facing ones offer killer views of central Cairo and the Nile. As for the facilities, there's everything you'd expect from a top hotel, including a sauna, health club, business centre and two swimming pools. There are also no less than nine restaurants, including a revolving restaurant with panoramic views (see p.194). B&B US$438.

Le Meridien Pyramids Midan al-Remaya, Alexandria Desert Rd, Giza Pyramids ☏02/3377-3388 or 7070, ⊛www.lemeridien .com/pyramids (see map, p.150). Just over 1km from the pyramids, and a 20min drive from central Cairo, the vast sandy-coloured *Le Méridien Pyramids* has spacious rooms with subdued decor and balconies, but the real draw are the stunning views of the pyramids that many of the rooms boast. Service is smart and efficient, and there's an appealingly curvy pool and a spa. You'll find several decent restaurants in-house, and breakfasts are bountiful. You can usually find good deals online. B&B US$364.

Longchamps 5th floor, 21 Sharia Ismail Mohammed, Zamalek ☏02/2735-2311, ⊛www.hotellongchamps.com (see map, pp.132–133). Spotless, quiet and well-run three-star hotel with a/c, satellite TV, internet connection and a fridge in all rooms, plus a pleasant terrace and meals available. It's advisable to book at least a couple of weeks ahead, but if it's full, the similarly priced *Horus House* downstairs isn't a bad fallback. B&B US$87.

Mena House Oberoi Near the Giza Pyramids ☏02/3377-3222, ⊛www.oberoihotels.com /oberoi_menahouse (see map, p.150). Set in lush grounds by the Giza Pyramids, and with views of them from the pricier rooms, this one-time khedival hunting lodge witnessed Roosevelt and Churchill initiate the D-Day plan, and the formal signing of the peace treaty between Israel and Egypt. Its renovated arabesque halls and nineteenth-century "palace" rooms are delightful; the modern Mena Gardens annexe isn't so grand, though the rooms are plush enough. Facilities include the *Moghul* restaurant (the best Indian restaurant in Egypt; see p.195), a pool, golf course and tennis courts. €211.

Mayfair 9 Sharia Aziz Osman, 1st floor above ground ☏02/2735-7315, ⊛www.mayfaircairo .com (see map, pp.132–133). Small hotel in

Staying near the pyramids

It is possible to stay within striking distance of **Saqqara** (see p.163): Nasser Abu Ghoneim rents rooms in Abu Sir village by arrangement (☏010 393-1853; @nasser abughoneim@yahoo.co.uk; £E500); the price includes full board, transfer to and from the airport, Ramses Station or any bus terminal, plus free transport to and from Cairo and Saqqara, Dahshur and Giza pyramids; this also offers a taste of Egyptian village life, far removed from the frenzy of Cairo.

a quiet location, with immaculate rooms, all with balconies. There's a great Art Deco entrance lobby and a breakfast terrace overlooking the street. They offer a ten percent discount for *Rough Guide* readers, but avoid buying tours here. B&B £E250.

Nile Zamalek 21 Sharia Aziz Abaza ☎02/735-1846 (see map, pp.132–133) . This riverside two-star boasts spacious rooms with bath, phone, TV and a/c, plus some with a balcony overlooking the Nile (best views from the top floors, of course). B&B £E210.

Pension Zamalek 6 Sharia Salah al-Din, Zamalek ☎02/735-9318, ⓔpensionzamalek@msn.com (see map, pp.132–133). A European-style *pension*: clean, quiet and secluded, with a pleasant family atmosphere, and one bathroom to every two rooms, but note that they don't accept unmarried couples.

Salma Camping Harraniyya, past Giza ☎02/3381-5062 or 010 487-1300, ⓔpsalma .camp@yahoo.com (see map, p.150). Cairo's only campsite is a bit run-down, but handy for the Pyramid sites at Giza and Saqqara. It's £E30 per person, including electricity and free hot showers, whether camping or caravanning, and there are huts and double rooms. Breakfast isn't included, but there is use of a kitchen. It's reached by turning off Pyramids Road towards

Saqqara at Maryotteya Canal (1km before the pyramids), and then after 4km taking a signposted turn-off at Harraniyya village; continue for 100m, and the site is about 100m away on your right. £E100.

Sofitel 3 Sharia Maglis el-Thawra, Gezira ☎02/3737-3737, ⓦwww.sofitel.com (see map, pp.132–133). The location is the main draw at this tall five-star at the southern tip of Gezira looking up the Nile, with great views from the swimming pool, and even better ones from the upper floors (billed as "deluxe", though the rooms themselves aren't any different from the standard ones). The food is overpriced, however, and not all that good. Four rooms are adapted for wheelchair users. US$370.

Youth Hostel 135 Sharia Abdel Aziz al-Saoud, by Kobri al-Gamaa, El-Manial ☎02/2364 0729, ⓔinfo@egyptyha.com (see map, pp.116–117). Apart from double rooms, there's a choice of six-bed dorms (£E15 per person) and a triple room (£E100), but bookings must be made by e-mail. Rooms are clean and en-suite but the location is inconvenient, staff are not very friendly and don't usually speak English, and doors are closed from midnight to 8am. The only advantage, aside from the ultra-cheap price, is that you can meet young Egyptians and practise your Arabic here. B&B £E90.

Long stays and flat-hunting

If you're staying in the city for longer than a week or two, renting an apartment is worth considering. Upscale areas popular with foreigners include **Ma'adi** (home to most of Egypt's American community), **Zamalek** (favoured by embassies and European expats) and **Heliopolis**. **Aguza** and **Mohandiseen** are also possible, but few flats are available downtown except in **Bulaq, Qasr al-Aini** or **Abdin**.

Places to look for apartment rentals include the small ads in *Egypt Today*, the *Egyptian Gazette* and *Community Times* and expat community newssheets such as the *Maadi Messenger* or *British Community News*. It's also worth checking the noticeboards at English-language institutes and cultural centres (see p.41), and the American University. Flats are also advertised online, at ⓦwww.e-dar.com and www .algomhoria.com. The AUC's regularly updated *Cairo: the Practical Guide* contains a lot of useful advice on apartment rental and Cairo living in general; it can be found at the AUC's bookshop (see p.224), or ordered online at ⓦwww.aucpress.com.

Foreigners working or studying in Cairo often seek flatmates or want to sublet during temporary absences. Aside from checking the newssheets and noticeboards mentioned above, another way of finding a flat is via a *simsar* (flat agent), who can be found in any neighbourhood by making enquiries at local shops and cafés. Unless you spend a long, fruitless day together, *simsars* are only paid when you settle on a place; ten percent of your first month's rent is the normal charge. Flat agencies in Ma'adi levy the same commission on both tenant and landlord. You can usually rent a flat in the centre for around £E1500–2500 per person per month, and occasionally even £E1000 or less; prices are lower in winter than in summer.

8

Eating

C airo offers a fair range of foreign cuisines, but **Egyptian food** is almost always tastier and better value for money. Some dishes may be familiar from Lebanese, Turkish, Greek or French cuisine; spicier Nubian recipes from Upper Egypt, and all kinds of Mediterranean seafood, can also be enjoyed in Cairo (and Alexandria).

Menu **prices** do not include service and taxes (which may amount to 22 percent), though these are only added to your bill in upmarket or tourist-oriented restaurants, rather than the kind of places where ordinary Cairenes eat. **Tipping** (from a couple of pounds in cheap places, to ten or fifteen percent in pricier establishments) is expected if a service charge isn't listed on your bill.

Egypt's staples are **bread** (*'aish*, which also means "life"), **fuul** and **taamiya**. Bread, eaten with all meals and snacks, comes either as pitta-type *'aish shamsi* (sun-raised bread made from white flour) or *'aish baladi* (made from coarse wholewheat flour). *Fuul* (mashed fava beans) is extremely cheap and can be served as a stew or stuffed into *'aish baladi* to make a sandwich. *Taamiya* (falafel) is usually served in pitta bread with salad, pickles and *tahina* (a sauce made from sesame paste), for which you can expect to pay the grand sum of £E1.50 or so. Lastly there's *shawarma*, consisting of marinaded lamb (or chicken) carved from a vertical kebab. A *shawarma* sandwich from a street stall can cost as little as £E2, while a plate of *shawarma* in a cheap diner will set you back around £E5.

Another cheap café perennial is *makarona* – macaroni baked into a cake with minced lamb and tomato sauce. It's rather bland but very filling. Similarly common is *kushari*, a tasty, calorific mixture of noodles, rice, macaroni, lentils and crispy onions, in a spicy tomato sauce (other sauces, made of chilli or garlic and lemon, are supplied free of charge in bulbous steel shakers). It's served in small, medium and large portions (£E3–5) in tiled stand-up or sit-down diners, also called *kushari*.

The classic Egyptian restaurant meal is a lamb **kebab** or **kofta** (spiced mince patties), accompanied or preceded by a couple of **mezze** – usually *tahina* or *babaghanoug* and a green salad. Roast chicken (*firakh*) is another standard dish, both in cafés and as takeaway food from spit-roast stands. **Pigeon** (*hamam*) is common too, often served with *freek* (spicy wheat) stuffing. In slightly fancier places, you may also encounter pigeon in a *tageen* or *ta'gell*, **stewed** with onions, tomatoes and rice in an earthenware pot.

Confusingly, pasta, rice, chips (French fries) and even crisps (potato chips) are often considered interchangeable – so you may order rice and get chips instead. Also note that the shaker with one hole is for pepper, the one with several holes for salt.

It's worth bearing in mind that you can pay a few pounds or ten times as much to eat the same simple Egyptian dishes, with little or no difference in **quality** between cheap diners and swanky restaurants. Particularly in central Cairo, you'll get far better value for money at local diners than at tourist traps like *Café Riche*. As rule

Local specialities and food terms

For ordinary food vocabulary, see pp.278–281.

Babaghanoug *Tahina* mashed with aubergine.

Fatta Mutton or chicken stew, cooked with pitta bread.

Fiteer A cross between pizza and pancake, made of flaky filo pastry stuffed with feta cheese, peppers, mince, egg, onion and olives, or with raisins, jams, curds or a dusting of icing sugar.

Fuul Fava beans, usually boiled and mashed with tomatoes, onions and spices (*fuul madammes*), often served in a bowl for breakfast, or stuffed into a pitta bread to make a sandwich.

Kibda Fried liver and green chilli sandwiches, sold from pushcarts at breakfast time in the backstreets all over Cairo.

Kofta Minced lamb, usually grilled on a spit and often served as a kebab.

Kushari Pasta and rice with lentils, fried onions and a spicy tomato sauce.

Mahshi Vegetables stuffed with rice and meat.

Mezze Mixed Middle Eastern hors d'oeuvres in the form of salads and dips.

Molukhiyya Jew's mallow stewed in stock and served with meat, making a stew with a slimy texture that some people love, and others hate.

Shawarma Marinated lamb kebab grilled on a vertical spit, carved and stuffed into pitta bread or a roll and garnished with salad and *tahina*; resembles a doner kebab, but far superior.

Shish tawoouk Chicken grilled over charcoal.

Torshi A mixture of pickled radishes, turnips, gherkins and carrots; luridly coloured, and something of an acquired taste, it's served as an accompaniment.

Taamiya (falafel) Deep-fried patty of spiced broad beans, usually served in pitta bread with salad, pickles and *tahina*.

Tahina Dip made from tahini (sesame paste).

Desserts

Baklava Layers of filo pastry and nuts, soaked in syrup.

Basbousa A confection made from semolina, nuts and syrup.

Burma Slices of syrup-drenched shredded wheat around a pistachio or hazelnut core.

Mahalabiyya Rice pudding.

Sobia A gloopy rice-based dessert, often sold as a drink in juice bars.

Umm Ali Cake soaked in cream, sugar, raisins, coconut and cinnamon – named after a Mamluke sultan's widow who had her husband's killer beaten to death, on the basis that revenge is sweet, and nothing is sweeter than this confection.

of thumb, you can enjoy a full meal in a diner for under £E10, an Egyptian-style pizza for £E20 or a mixed grill for £E35–50. At anywhere that charges more than this, you're really paying for the service and ambience rather than the quality of the food.

Our **listings** run the gamut from upmarket establishments to humble diners. The former tend to be concentrated in central Cairo, Garden City, Mohandiseen and Zamalek, whereas the latter can be found all over the city. European and Asian restaurants tend to be in (or near) chain hotels in central Cairo or Zamalek, but there is no distinct "ethnic quarter" for eating.

Alcohol is not served in restaurants or cafés, unless stated otherwise in our listings.

We have noted **Ramadan** opening hours if they differ significantly from normal hours.

Restaurants

The distinction between **restaurants** and **cafés** is blurred, if only because most Cairenes with a modest disposable income regard fast-food chains as fancy places to eat out, and only an affluent minority is aware of the finer points of service or decor that foreigners notice. Our listings are arranged according to locality; floating restaurants, diners and street food are covered separately.

Seafood and *kofta* and kebab are sold in many restaurants by weight: a quarter of a kilo is one portion, while a full kilo is usually enough for three to four people. Phone numbers are given for establishments where a **reservation** is advisable.

Central Cairo

All the restaurants below are marked on the map on pp.50–51 unless otherwise stated.

Alfi Bey 3 Sharia Alfi Bey ☎02/577-1888. A classic colonial-era restaurant, with teak panelling, chandeliers and gilt furniture, *Alfi Bey* is best for lamb dishes such as neck of mutton (£E37). Daily 1pm–1am.

Al-Haty in the passage by 8 26th July St. Go through the door marked "Salle Orientale", and up the stairs, to find this once grand restaurant. Though now rather faded and empty, the menu here includes such sophisticated dishes as turkey in walnut sauce (£E45). Daily 10am–midnight.

Aly Hassan Al-Haty 3 Sharia Halim, off 26th July St, behind the Windsor Hotel. Vintage colonial decor, with mirrors and fans, and traditional good-value fare, including *mezze*, roast lamb, *kofta* and kebab. Their tasty chargrilled half-chicken (£E18) is a meal in itself. Daily noon–1am.

Arabesque 6 Sharia Qasr el-Nil ☎02/574-8677. Its Art Deco fittings and soft lighting make this a nice place for a date, or just to relax with a drink at the bar. Serves Egyptian, French and Levantine cuisine, and is strong on soups and meat dishes; if you like Jews' mallow, try the rabbit *molukhiyya* (£E55). Daily noon–2am.

Bon Appetit Sharia Mohammed Mahmoud, opposite the AUC Library. Downtown branch of the Mohandiseen café-restaurant (see p.201) favoured by students from the AUC. There are sub-style sandwiches (£E18.25–27.25) and tasty dishes such as *shish tawouk* (£E27.50). Daily 9am–1am.

Café Riche 17 Sharia Talaat Harb. This one-time haunt of Cairo's intelligentsia now mostly draws tourists for its authentic 1908 decor and liveried Nubian waiters. Unfortunately, its dishes (£E15–85) are mediocre, and there's a £E4 cover charge per person – the bar, however, is a nice retreat (see p.201).

Centro Recreativo Italiano 26th July St, behind the Italian embassy (ring the bell to enter) ☎02/2575-9590. This is a club for the city's Italian expats, but they usually let in foreigners on payment of a £E10 guest fee (plus £E3 cover charge). As you'd expect, the pizzas (£E25–40) and pasta dishes (£E20–35) are excellent. The dining room is air-conditioned but most people prefer to dine outside on the terrace. There's wine and aperitifs such as Campari and vermouth. Reservations compulsory on Thurs. Daily 7–11pm.

Vegetarian eating

Most Egyptians eat vegetables most of the time – meat and fish are luxuries – yet the concept of **vegetarianism** is almost incomprehensible. Even if you say that you're vegetarian (in Arabic, *ana nabati* if you're male, *ana nabatiya* if you're female) people may offer you chicken or fish as a substitute. Still, vegetarians and vegans will have no trouble feeding themselves in *kushari* and *falafel* joints (*kushari* is deliberately vegan for the benefit of Coptic Christians on a meat-free fast), and *fatatris* (Egyptian-style pizzerias) offer reasonable pickings too, even for vegans (who can try ordering a veg or mushroom *fiteer* without cheese). Restaurants and hotels that cater particularly to tourists often feature a few vegetarian dishes on the menu, such as omelettes, vegetable *tageens*, pasta and salads.

El-Dahan 52 26th July St, Bulaq.
Branch of the Muski kebab house (see below), but the bill always seems to end up much cheaper here – a quarter kilo of kebab with salad and *tahina* costs around £E25. Daily 1pm–1am.

El Nile Fish 25 Sharia el-Bustan, just off Midan Falaki. Popular fish restaurant with choice of various denizens of the deep freshly caught and fried or grilled to order (£E22–60 per kilo), served with salad, *tahina* and pickles. Daily noon–1am.

Estoril 12 Sharia Talaat Harb ☎02/2574-3102. Tucked away in a passage off Talaat Harb, this cosy bistro-style restaurant serves mainly French and Lebanese dishes, and has a splendid 1930s-style bar. Dishes include Tripoli-style spicy grouper (£E43) and chicken in ginger and soy sauce (£E38). Daily noon–midnight.

Felfela 15 Sharia Hoda Shaarawi. A tourist favourite, serving Egyptian dishes in a long hall with a funky Arabesque decor, and waiters in traditional livery. Reliably good, though service can be a little snooty if you're scruffily dressed, and there's nothing you can get here that wouldn't be cheaper elsewhere. A portion of *kofta* and kebab costs £E50, stuffed pigeon £E35. Alcohol served. *Felfela's* takeaway, around the corner on Talaat Harb (daily 7am–midnight), serves *shawarmas* and *taamiya* sandwiches, though again slightly pricier than elsewhere. Daily 8am–midnight.

Gad 13 26th July St ☎02/2576-3353 or 3583. Cairo's shiniest, most popular takeaway is always crowded, with table seating upstairs. Besides high-quality *taamiya*, *fuul*, *shawarma* and burgers, *Gad* serves delicious specialities such as *kibda skanderani* (liver with chilli; £E18), baked-on-the-premises Syrian-style pitta bread (*'aish shaami*), and some of the best *fiteers* in town (£E5–23). They also deliver. Daily 24hr.

Greek Club Above *Groppi's* on Midan Talaat Harb; entrance on Sharia Bassiouni. The cuisine isn't particularly Greek, but the food isn't bad (fried squid and chips for £E26, stuffed vine leaves for £E10), and the summer terrace is pleasant. Serves alcohol, including ouzo. Daily 7pm–midnight.

Hati el-Guesh (aka Sayed) 32 Midan Falaki, on the corner of Tahrir and Falaki streets. A bright place serving Egyptian standards such as *kofta* and kebab (£E31) and stuffed pigeon (£E25.50), with the usual mezze and side dishes. Daily noon–midnight.

La Chesa 21 Sharia Adly ☎02/393-9360. Salubrious, Swiss-managed café serving good Western food, including fondues (£E145 for up to four people); hearty Swiss breakfasts (£E26), scrumptious pastries and great coffee. Daily 7am–midnight.

Le Bistro 8 Sharia Hoda Shaarawi ☎02/392-7694. A cheerful little bistro with immaculate service and decent French food including sea bass in mustard sauce (£E36), tournedos of beef in red wine sauce (£E48), crêpes (£E12) and chocolate mousse (£E12). Serves alcohol. Daily noon–midnight.

Paprika 1129 Corniche el-Nil, just south of the TV Building ☎02/2578-9447. A slightly faded fusion bistro frequented by media folk (including Omar Sharif) and footballers, *Paprika* gets especially busy at weekends. Its menu offers a mix of Hungarian and Egyptian food – mezze and tasty paprika-based dishes like the speciality, goulash (£E48) – and they serve alcohol. Daily noon–midnight.

Peking 14 Sharia Saray el-Azbakiya ☎02/591-2381, ⌨www.peking-restaurants.com. Central branch of a citywide chain of Chinese restaurants; not the best or most authentic Chinese food you'll ever taste, but a change at least, with branches in Zamalek, Mohandiseen and Heliopolis, plus a floating restaurant (see p.196). Daily noon–12.30am.

Pomo Doro 197 Sharia Tahrir, Abdin. A hole-in-the-wall place but very clean, with outdoor seating and a takeaway service. They only serve spaghetti, with a choice of chicken, bolognaise, vegetarian or (especially recommended) seafood, at £E15 a throw. Everything's cooked fresh, but it's worth the wait and you can watch them cooking it. Daily 3pm–1am.

Islamic Cairo and Saiyida Zeinab

Egyptian Pancake House Between Midan al-Hussein and Al-Azhar (see map, p.77). Made-to-order savoury or sweet *fiteers* (£E15–40) filled with meat, egg, cheese, or any combination of coconut, raisins, jam or honey. Check for extraneous items on the bill. Daily 24hr.

El-Dahan Sharia al-Muski, beneath the El-Hussein Hotel (see map, p.77). Excellent kebab house, where a quarter kilo of mixed kebab with salad and *tahina* costs £E45. There's also roast lamb and other meat dishes. Daily 11am–2am.

El-Hussein On the roof of the *El-Hussein Hotel* (see map, p.77). Only worth a visit for its fantastic view of Khan el-Khalili; the food is poor, but no one minds if you just drink juice or tea, or smoke a sheesha. Daily 7am–midnight.

Gad Sharia al-Azhar (see map, p.77). Al-Azhar branch of the popular downtown eatery (see opposite). Daily 24hr.

🏃 **Hilltop Restaurant Al-Azhar Park, Sharia Salah Salem (see map, pp.74–75).** Set in a lovely park with stunning views over Islamic Cairo, this restaurant pays homage to Egypt's Mamluke heritage, with Arab classical music playing in the background. Its classy ambience is matched by the quality of their grills and kebabs (mixed grill £E58), and on Friday and Saturday evenings, an all-you-can-eat buffet (£E120) with soups, salads, half-a dozen main dishes, and a gluttonous choice of desserts. Daily 1–11pm.

Khan el-Khalili Restaurant 5 Sikket al-Badestan (see map, p.77). Managed by the *Mena House Oberoi* (see p.187), this Mamluke-themed café-restaurant is a short stroll from Al-Hussein's Mosque. Western and Egyptian snacks (£E16–31) and meals (main dishes from £E55), such as rabbit *molukhiyya*, are served in the air-conditioned dining room Daily 10am–2am.

🏃 **Rifai 37 Midan Saiyida Zeinab, opposite Saiyida Zeinab Mosque (hidden up an alley by the Sabil Kuttab of Sultan Mustapha, signposted "Mongy Destrict"); see map, pp.74–75.** A renowned nighttime *kofta* and kebab joint – people are known to drive from Heliopolis for a takeaway because it's so good. A quarter-kilo of *kofta* and kebab with *tahina*, *babaghanoug*, salad and a glass of multi-vegetable juice with chilli comes to £E35. Daily 5pm–5am.

Zamalek

As befits an affluent, cosmopolitan neighbourhood, Zamalek boasts several upmarket restaurants devoted to foreign cuisine; lots of choice for vegetarians at *L'Aubergine*, and popular bars such as *Deals* and *Pub 28* (see p.202), both of which also do good food. All these are on the map on pp.132–133, as is the Zamalek branch of the Chinese *Peking* chain (see opposite; 23b Sharia Ismail Mohammed; ☎02/2736-3894).

Angus Brasserie 34 Sharia Yehia Ibrahim, inside the *New Star Hotel* ☎02/735-1865. Steaks, notably *asado* (Argentinian-style sirloin with chimichurri sauce; £E45.50), or fillet steak with a choice of mustard, blue-cheese or mushroom topping (£E45). Alcohol served. Daily 5pm–midnight.

🏃 **Didos (Al Dente) 26 Sharia Bahgat Ali ☎02/2735-9117, ⊛www.didospasta .com.** Besides good pasta (£E13–39), this little place also has excellent salads and specialities such as Portuguese-style fish (£24.50). Daily 24hr.

Don Quichotte 9a Sharia Ahmed Heshmat ☎02/2735-6415. Small, elegant, lounge-style restaurant serving French and Italian cuisine. Dishes include sole *meunière* (£E80) and steak in gorgonzola sauce (£E80), with desserts such as chocolate soufflé (£E39). Alcohol served. Reservations advisable. Daily 1pm–1am.

Five Bells Corner of Adil Abu Bakr and Ismail Mohammed ☎02/2735-8980. It's worth dressing up for this swish Italianate joint, complete with garden and fountain. Specialities include meat fondue, grill-it-yourself charbonnade (£E110 for two), and fish with squid and prawns (£E55). Alcohol served. Daily 12.30pm–2am.

Hana Barbecue House Sharia Mohammed Mahzar ☎02/2738-2972. Small, friendly place offering various Asian dishes. A huge portion of *sukiyaki* (do-it-yourself stir-fry seafood soup) costs £E45. Daily noon–10.30pm.

L'Aubergine 5 Sharia Sayed el-Bakri. Its adventurous menu is changed weekly and features a good variety of vegetarian dishes, such as cheese and spinach crêpes (£E23), or pan-fried halloumi (£E28). The food is usually delicious, though some of the more ambitious dishes may disappoint. There's also a bar upstairs. Daily 10am–1.30am.

Maison Thomas 157 26th July St, opposite the Marriott Hotel ☎02/735-7057. Deli-diner-takeaway place serving freshly made baguettes and pizzas as well as light meals (from £E40). They make their own mozzarella, and serve good breakfasts (7–11am; £E26). Daily 24hr.

Garden City and Roda Island

Abou Shakra 69 Sharia Qasr al-Aini, opposite the hospital ☎02/531-6111, ⊛www.aboushakra .com (see map, p.70). Lavishly decorated in marble and alabaster, this famous establishment specializes in *kofta* and kebab sold by weight (£E94/kg), to eat in or take out. Despite its pretensions, the food isn't as good as in humbler establishments such as *el-Dahan* or *Rifai* in Islamic Cairo. Daily 1pm–1am.

🏃 **Revolving Restaurant** Fortieth floor, *Grand Hyatt Hotel*, Roda Island ☎02/365-1234 (see map, pp.116–117). "Semi-formal" dress is required and children under 12 are barred at this tip-top restaurant, which enjoys a panoramic view of the entire city, and serves the finest French cuisine in Cairo. Start with the likes of duck liver in ginger and cherry sauce (£E145) or lobster bisque (£E50), follow with salmon in horseradish sauce (£E170) or duck with pink pepper sauce (£E160), and finish with lavender crême brulée (£E60). Alcohol served. Daily 7pm–1am.

🏃 **Taboula** 1 Sharia Amerika al-Latina, Garden City ☎ 02/2792-5261 (see map, p.70). One of Cairo's best Lebanese restaurants, whose opulent Arabesque decor complements its huge range of mezze (£E11–24), various preparations of *kofta*, and Lebanese *fattehs* (stews made with toasted pitta pieces; £E32–40). Daily noon–2am.

Mohandiseen, Aguza, Dokki and Giza

In addition to places listed below, there are branches of *Peking* (see p.192; 26 Sharia el-Atebba, Mohandiseen; ☎02/3749-6713), *Gad* (see p.192; 47a Arab League St in Mohandiseen and 97 Sharia Tahrir in Dokki), *Maison Thomas* (see p.193; 29 Sharia Shehab, Mohandiseen), *El Tabei El Domyati* (see p.197; 17 Arab League St, Mohandiseen) and *Abou Shakra* (see p.193; also at 17 Arab League St, Mohandiseen). The places reviewed here are shown on the map on pp.132–133, unless stated.

Al-Mataam al-Yamani 10 Sharia al-Iran, Dokki. This is where Cairo's Yemeni community comes to eat their native cuisine. It's worth popping in, especially around lunchtime, for wonderful Yemeni bread (*sahawuq*), lamb ribs (*okda*; £E25), or succulent lamb on the bone with rice (*mandi*; £E30). Daily 24hr.

Bon Appetit 21 Sharia Wadi el-Nil. A café and a restaurant, the former offering baguette sandwiches, salads and ice cream, the latter serving fish kebabs (£E35), chicken Kiev (£E39), and desserts such as chocolate mousse. Daily noon–2am.

Cedars 38 Sharia Gazirit al-Arab, just west off Sharia Wadi el-Nil ☎02/3347-2537. Lebanese café and restaurant, a good place for a *sheesha* on the terrace, a freshly-made smoothie (£E22) or a superior Middle Eastern meal featuring mixed mezze (£E60). Daily 9am–2am.

El Mashrabiah 4 Sharia Ahmed Nessim, opposite the El-Urman Garden, Giza ☎02/3748-2801. Elegant Moorish decor and excellent Middle Eastern and Egyptian food, including roast lamb (£E48) and stuffed pigeon (£E48). Daily 12.30pm–1am (Ramadan nightfall–3.30am).

El-Omda 6 Sharia al-Gaza'ir. An island of traditional Egyptian food (*kushari* £E8.50; *kofta* and kebab £E45) among a sea of fast-food joints. Takeaway available. There's a snazzier-looking branch at 17 Arab League Street, with outdoor dining and *sheeshas*, though the service isn't as good. Daily 8am–3am.

Fish Market Americana boat, 26 Sharia el-Nil, Giza ☎02/570-9693 or 4 (see map, p.138). This offshoot of a renowned restaurant in Alexandria (see p.252) isn't as superlative as the original, but is still one of Cairo's best seafood places. You choose the fish, and they cook it to your specifications. Alcohol served. Daily noon–3am.

🏃 **Flying Fish** 166 Corniche el-Nil, Aguza ☎02/3336-5111. A classy yet still affordable seafood restaurant, with specialities such as stuffed fish, squid and lobster (priced by the kilo, according to season). Daily 1pm–1am.

Le Chalet Nasr Building, Giza ☎02/3761-0165 (see map, p.138). Pleasant Swiss-run place with fine views of the Nile, serving salads and pasta, hot meat platters, veal sausage (£E40) and delectable pastries and ice creams. *Le Chateau*, upstairs (same phone number), is similar but a bit posher. Daily noon–11.30pm.

Le Tirol 38 Sharia Gazirit al-Arab, just west off Sharia Wadi el-Nil ☎02/3344-9725. Austrian-style chalet decor and tasty central European cuisine, with a lot of beef and veal dishes, such as Zurich-style veal with *rösti* potatoes (£E48). Serves alcohol. Daily noon–1am.

Niema 172 Corniche el-Nil, Aguza. Many drivers cross the river simply to enjoy *Niema*'s tasty *fuul* or *taamiya* sandwiches (£E1.25), hamburgers and *shawarma* rolls (£E4.50). Daily 24hr.

Nubian Village Midan Sphinx, Aguza. The main Nubian specialities here are spicy meat (£E32.50) and hot drinks (*karkaday*, of course – see p.197, plus hot ginger and herbal teas called *hargel* and *halfebar*). Otherwise, the menu is typically Egyptian, with a few European dishes. There's a £E20 minimum charge. Daily 11am–3am.

Okamoto 7 Sharia Orabi, off Midan Sphinx ☏02/3346-5264. You can tell from its Japanese clientele that the food and sake are good. Prawn tempura will set you back £E40, mixed sashimi £E50. Last orders 30min before closing. Daily except Tues noon–2.30pm & 6–10.30pm.

Prestige Pizza 43 Sharia Gazirit al-Arab, just east of Sharia Wadi el-Nil ☏02/3347-0383. A smart Italian and Continental-style restaurant offering pizzas (£E19–39) as well as more substantial dishes such as beef stroganoff (£E43), and even, for starters, snails (£E32). Daily 11am–3am.

🏃 **Tandoori 11 Sharia Shehab, 2 blocks west of Arab League St** ☏02/3748-6301. Cairo's second-best Indian restaurant, run by an ex-employee of the *Moghul Room* (see below), it serves a great tandoori chicken (£E35) and fish biryani (£E45), plus some Egyptian and European dishes. Daily 11am–10pm.

Pyramids area

Felfela Village Maryotteya Canal ☏02/3384-1515 or 1616 (see map, p.150). Unabashedly kitsch and touristic, this rambling outdoor complex includes a zoo and playground, but its chief attraction is a lavish show with camel rides, acrobats, puppets, bellydancers and dancing horses. The show (1–7.30pm) is presented daily in summer, only on Fri in winter. With a similar menu to *Felfela's*, downtown (see p.192), it's aimed at coach parties visiting the Pyramids, and only worth a special journey to see the show. Located beside a canal that crosses Pyramids Road, 1km north on the east bank. Daily 8am–1am.

🏃 **The Moghul Room *Mena House Oberoi* (see p.187)** ☏02/3377-3222. Cairo's top Indian restaurant. As the name suggests,

north Indian Mughal dishes are the mainstay here, notably rogan josh (£E98), but they also do veg curries and Goan fish curry (£E110); they usually go easy on the chilli, so tell them if you want it spicy. Daily sittings at 7pm and 9.30pm, reservation required.

Pyramids Restaurant 9 Sharia Abu el-Hol (see map, p.150). An honest-to-goodness kebab house that somehow manages to charge low prices (quarter-kilo *kofta* and kebab £E20, chicken £E28–30, salad and *tahina* extra), despite the plethora of tourists. Daily 24hr.

Heliopolis

In addition to the places listed here, Heliopolis has branches of *Maison Thomas* (see p.193; 114 Sharia Merghani; ☏02/2419-2914), *Gad* (see p.192; 99 Sharia Merghani), *Abou Shakra* (see p.193; 82 Sharia Merghani; ☏02/2488-8891), *Didos* (see p.193; 100 Sharia Shehab al-Din Khafaga, by Merryland; ☏02/2241-5250) and *Peking* (see p.192; 115 Sharia Osman Ibn Affan, off Midan Triomphe; ☏02/2418-5612).

Abou Haidar 13 Sharia Laqqani (between Midan Roxi and Sharia al-Ahram). Very popular spot for *shawarma* sandwiches (£E4.50–15.25), burgers, juices and snacks to eat in or take away. Daily 8am–1am.

L'Amphitryon 18 Sharia Ibrahim al-Laqqani (on the corner of Sharia al-Ahram). A restaurant with bar, takeaway and coffee terrace, founded in 1922, though its elegance of yesteryear is rather faded nowadays. Dishes include lamb ribs and chips (£E46), or *shish tawouk* with rice (£E37). Daily 8am–1.30am.

Petit Palmyra 27 Sharia al-Ahram (on the corner of Sharia Ibrahim) ☏02/2417 1720. Quite a stylish restaurant, its walls decked with old photos of Heliopolis, serving dishes such as veal roll stuffed with smoked turkey (£E50) or steak with a choice of sauces (£E60). There's live piano music in the evenings. Daily noon–1.30am.

Floating restaurants

Floating restaurants can be an agreeable way to enjoy the Nile, but cruise schedules change regularly so it's wise to book ahead. With the exception of the *Nile Peking* (serving Chinese food), all of these restaurants offer mezze, Egyptian and European dishes in the form of a set menu or an all-you-can-eat buffet (similar in quality to what you'd find at five-star hotels), plus alcohol (not included in the quoted prices).

Nile Maxim ☎02/2738-8888 (see map, pp.132–133). Docked in front of the *Marriott*, *Nile Maxim* runs dinner cruises (daily 8pm & 10.30pm), with a choice of set menus (£E260–346) and an impressive floorshow, including some of Cairo's very best bellydancers.

Nile Peking ☎02/2531-6388, ⊛www.peking -restaurants.com (see map, pp.116–117). Moored opposite the Nilometer, 200m west of Mari Girgis metro station, this is the floating branch of the *Peking* chain of Chinese restaurants (see p.192). The boat currently sails Sun 8pm & 10pm, Thurs 10pm & midnight, and Fri 4pm, 6pm, 8pm & 10pm. Each cruise lasts 2hr, with a £E110 set menu. Otherwise, the boat is moored and open daily noon–midnight with an à la carte menu.

The Nile Pharaoh & Golden Pharaoh ☎02/3570-1000, ⊛www.thepharaohs.com.eg (see map, p.138). A pair of mock-pharaonic barges complete with scarab friezes, picture windows, and golden lotus flowers or figures of Horus mounted on the stern and prow. Moored 1km south of the El-Gama'a Bridge and operated by *Oberoi Hotels*, they cruise for lunch (2.30 & 3.30pm in winter, 3pm & 4pm summer; £E170), early dinner (7pm and 7.45pm in winter, 7.45pm & 8.45pm in summer; £E200) or late dinner (10pm & 10.45pm in winter, 10.30pm & 11.30pm in summer; £E250). Cruises last 2hr and you should check in 30min before sailing. The early dinner cruise features music and a bellydancer, the late one an Arabic stand-up comedian and a shorter bellydance show, while lunch cruises have a Middle Eastern band instead.

Scarabee ☎02/2794-3444 (see map, pp.50–51). Docked on the Corniche near the *Shepheard Hotel*, *Scarabee* isn't as posh as the other floating restaurants. It has twice-nightly dinner cruises (7.30 & 10pm; £E185) with an "oriental" floor show, bellydancer and a dance band.

Diners and street food

Cairo abounds in cheap diners serving a single dish or variations thereof – generally either *kushari*, *fuul* and falafel, or *fiteers*. Their decor tends to be basic – tiled walls, sawdust-strewn floors and battered tables and chairs – but so long as there's running water hygiene is usually not a worry. (Anywhere with a washbasin for customers should be okay.)

Street food sold from pushcarts is somewhat riskier, but if you feel that your immune system is up to it these are the cheapest nutritious snacks going (£E2–4). Every part of Cairo has its own locality for pushcarts; in the downtown area, the junction of Sharia Hoda Shaarawi and Sharia Mustafa Abu Heil is great for fried liver and chilli sandwiches or *fuul* and falafel, served from 7am onwards. Midan Falaki has another cluster of pushcarts outside the Bab al-Luq market, active 24-hours.

Abou Tarek 40 Sharia Champollion, at the corner of Sharia Maarouf ⊛www.abou tarek.com (see map, pp.50–51). You can't miss this a/c diner, spread over two floors and lit up like a Christmas tree. It serves the best *kushari* in Cairo (£E3–7), with rice pudding for afters. Daily 7.30am–11.30pm.

Akher Saa 8 Sharia Alfi Bey, next to the Nile Christian Bookshop; see map, pp.50–51. A very popular 24hr *fuul* and falafel takeaway with a sit-down restaurant attached. Not bad for breakfast either – *fuul*, omelette, bread and *tahina* costs £E10.50. There's a takeaway branch at 14 Sharia Abdel Khaliq Sarwat, just off Talaat Harb (☎02/2579-8557).

Al-Kazaz 38 Sharia Abo Alaam (see map, pp.50–51). Clean, inexpensive 24hr diner, just off Midan Talaat Harb. Tasty *shawarma* (£E3/sandwich), *taamiya* (£E1/sandwich) and other fried food, served in a tiny a/c dining room upstairs, or downstairs to take away.

Baba Abdo Sharia Monshaat al-Kataba (see map, pp.50–51). Popular *kushari* joint, hidden away in the backstreets between Talaat Harb and Qasr al-Nil. Serves not only *kushari*, but also spaghetti and macaroni with meat sauce or liver on top (£E5). Daily 7am–midnight.

El-Gahsh Saiyida Zeinab, a block along Sharia Abdel Meguid from Midan Saiyida Zeinab, on the way to Ibn Tulun Mosque (see map, pp.74–75). This insalubrious little diner is generally held to do the finest *fuul* in Cairo. Come at night, when they lay out tables in the neighbouring streets. A plate of *fuul* with all the trimmings will set you back the princely sum of £E7. Daily 24hr.

El-Tabei el-Domiati **31 Sharia Orabi, north of Midan Orabi** ☎02/575-4391 **(see map, p.69).** The pick-and-mix mezze (£E2.50 each) is the best thing in this *fuul* and *taamiya* diner, which also does Egyptian puddings. They have a small takeaway branch in the food court of the mall on Sharia Talaat Harb. Daily 5am–1am.

El-Tahrir **Sharia Tahrir between Midan Tahrir and Midan Falaki (see map, pp.50–51).** A long-established rival to *Abou Tarek* (see opposite), its *kushari* (£E3–8) isn't quite as tasty nor its

premises so clean, but neither this nor its branch at 19 Sharia Abdel Khaliq Sarwat are a bad option. Daily 8am–2am.

🏃 Fatatri Pizza el-Tahrir **Sharia Tahrir, one block east of Midan Tahrir (see map, pp.50–51).** Its marbled facade belies its humble interior. Their *fiteers* (with meat and egg or crustier versions topped with hot sauce, cheese and olives) make a delicious meal, and they also serve pancake *fiteers* filled with apple jam and icing sugar. Prices range from £E5 to £E25. Daily 24hr.

Coffee houses, tearooms and buffets

Cairene males have socialized in hole-in-the-wall **coffee houses** (*'ahwas*) ever since the beverage was introduced from Yemen in the early Middle Ages. Coffee (also called *'ahwa*) is always Turkish coffee, served in tiny cups pre-sugared to customers' specifications: *saada* (unsugared), *'ariha* (slightly sweetened), *mazboota* (medium sweet) or *ziyaada* (syrupy). In some places you can get it with **cardamom** (*'ahwa mahawega*).

An *'ahwa* will also serve **tea** (*shai*); tea with milk is *shai bi-laban*, loose-leaf tea is *shai kushari*, while tea-bag tea is *shai libton*. Tea with a sprig of **mint** (*shai bi-na'ana'*) is particularly refreshing when the weather is hot. If you don't want caffeine, fear not: an *'ahwa* will also serve a host of **infusions**, including *karkaday*, a deep-red infusion of hibiscus flowers typical of southern Egypt, as well as *helba* (fenugreek), *yansoon* (aniseed) and *'irfa* (cinnamon).

On cold winter evenings you might enjoy *sahleb*, a warming, creamy drink made from milk thickened with ground orchid root, arrowroot or cornflower, with cinnamon and nuts sprinkled on top.

The other thing any *'ahwa* will serve is a **sheesha** (waterpipe); the traditional tobacco is *ma'azil* (with molasses), but sweeter tobaccos, designed to appeal to younger smokers, have largely taken over, and come in assorted fruit flavours, the most popular of which is apple (*bitufaah*).

Until recently, it was unusual for women to frequent *'ahwas*, and unheard of to see them puffing away on a *sheesha*, but times change, and younger, less inhibited women can now be seen sitting in *'ahwas* with a waterpipe to their lips. Foreign women may nonetheless feel uneasy, especially if unaccompanied by a man, so, for a more relaxed tea or coffee, check out one of the more modern espresso houses, where you'll pay Western prices and get a Western atmosphere to go with them, as well as the usual range of lattes, cappuccinos and the like.

There are thought to be over thirty thousand *'ahwas* in Cairo, of which we've listed only a very few. All-night *'ahwas* can be found around Midan Ramses and Sharia Qalaa and the Saiyida Zeinab end of Sharia Mohammed Farid and Sharia el-Nasireya. There are modern all-night coffee shops in the *Intercontinental*, *Nile Hilton* and other deluxe hotels.

Central Cairo

All the following are marked on the map on pp.50–51, unless otherwise stated. *El-Horea* (see p.201) is also one of the more interesting downtown *'ahwas*, and also serves beer.

Cilantro **31 Sharia Mohammed Mahmoud.** All sorts of coffees, frappés, cappuccinos and frappuccinos, plus quiches, toasties, sandwiches (£E10–22), salads (£E15–22), and cakes and pastries. Daily 7am–2am.

El Shems (Sun Café) **In the passage by 4 Sharia Tawfiqia, off Midan Orabi.** A grimy, city-centre 'ahwa, distinguished mainly by its incredibly kitsch decor.

Everest Hotel Midan Ramses (see map, p.69). The fifteenth-floor terrace café of an otherwise unremarkable cheap hotel. The coffee isn't the best in town, but you can enjoy a view over Midan Ramses and as far as the Citadel and the Muqattam Hills. Daily 24hr.

Garden Groppi 48 Sharia Abdel Khaliq Sarwat/12 Sharia Adly. The more spacious, "garden" branch of the *Groppi* chain (see p.66), a favourite with British officers during the war, when non-commissioned ranks were barred. You can sit in the salon with your coffee and pastry, or on the outside terrace and enjoy a *sheesha* with them. Minimum charge £E10. Daily 7am–11pm.

Groppi Midan Talaat Harb. The once-palatial flagship branch of this classic chain was, in its heyday, pretty much synonymous with Cairo's erstwhile European "café society". It's lost much of its charm since being renovated, and the coffee itself is pretty terrible, but it has a restful a/c salon, and the pastries are great. Moreover, it's a taste, albeit a very faded one, of what Cairo's elegant downtown Ismailiya Quarter was like in the days of King Fouad and King Farouk. Minimum charge £E10. Daily 7am–11pm.

Mondial Café 4 Sharia Darih Sa'd. For fans of international football, this unassuming 'ahwa is the place to come, and can generally be relied on to show all the most important English and European matches live. Daily 7am–11pm.

Simonds Coffee Shop 29 Sharia Sherif. A downtown branch of Zamalek's French-style café (see opposite) with espresso coffee and Egyptian and European-style pastries. Daily 7am–10pm.

Umm Kalthoum Café Sharia al-Azbakiya. Fronted by two giant busts of the Arab diva Umm Kalthoum (see p.129) and filled with memorabilia of the singer and other stars of her day, this is not, actually, the original *Umm Kalthoum Café* (21 Sharia Orabi), but it's the most fun. Daily 24hr.

Islamic Cairo

The below are marked on the map on p.77 unless otherwise stated.

'Ahwa al-Aini Midan al-Aini, Butneya (see map, pp.74–75). This hole-in-the-wall coffee house comes alive in the evening, when music plays and the square becomes a lovely open-air hangout. Daily 5pm–2am.

Café Shobilard 30 Sharia Tababiya, Gamaliya (see map, p.81). With its strange collection of furniture and bric-a-brac, it looks like a junk shop, but this is a cut above your average 'ahwa, and an excellent place to stop for a breather amid the chaos of Islamic Cairo. Daily 24hr.

Fishawi's Behind the *El-Hussein Hotel* in Khan el-Khalili. Cairo's oldest tea house has been managed by the same family – and remained open – since 1773. Soak up the atmosphere – cracked mirrors, battered furniture, haughty staff and wandering vendors – with a pot of mint tea and a *sheesha*. Prices are posted up in Arabic, but expect to be overcharged if you can't read it. Daily 24hr.

Naguib Mahfouz Coffee Shop 5 Sikket al-Badestan, Khan el-Khalili. Upmarket a/c tourist café in the heart of the bazaar, serving snacks, coffee, mint tea and orange juice. Part of the *Khan el-Khalili Restaurant*. Daily 10am–2am.

Zamalek

The following are marked on the map on pp.132–133.

Beano's 8 Sharia al-Marsafy. Hot and cold espresso-based coffee concoctions in a lovely a/c space, with free wi-fi. Also serves crêpes, pastries, salads and sandwiches. There's a downtown branch on Sharia Mohammed Mahmoud (see map, pp.50–51), but it isn't as good. Daily 6am–1am.

Café Tabasco 18b Sharia el-Marashly ☎02/2735-8465. A sophisticated, Western-style coffee house, where the TV (usually Eurosport) isn't obtrusive, there are magazines to read, and you can get coffee, juices, herb teas and food. A good place to hang out, with free wi-fi. Also in Dokki (7 Sharia Mossadek ☎02/3762-2060). Daily 7am–3am.

No Big Deal Sharia Sayed el-Bakri, next to Deals bar ⊛www.nobigdealcafe.com. Small, San Francisco-style coffee shop, with home-made cakes and such exotic beverages as Earl Grey tea. Pleasant, but not very Egyptian. Daily 7am–1am.

Rigoletto Yamaha Centre, 3 Sharia Taha Hussein. Espresso, cappuccino, cheesecake and by far the best ice cream in town (£E4 a scoop) – the cinnamon flavour is especially good. £E5 minimum charge to eat in. Daily 9am–midnight.

Simonds Coffee Shop 112 26th July St, near the Hassan Sabry intersection. Cairo's original French-style coffee shop, with cappuccino, hot chocolate, lemonade, fresh croissants, pastries and *ramequins* (cheese puffs). Daily 7am–10pm.

Groppi Heliopolis 21 Sharia al-Ahram. With its panelled interior and outside terrace, this is the only branch of the *Groppi* chain to retain any of its period elegance. Minimum charge £E10. Daily 7am–11pm.

⑧

Patisseries, juice bars and ice cream

Though available at more sophisticated coffee shops, pastries are cheaper at **patisseries**, where traditional Arab sticky sweets such as baklava and *burma* (see p.190) are sold by the kilo. Good downtown patisseries (see map, pp.50–51) include *El Abd* at 25 Sharia Talaat Harb and on the corner of 26 July and Sherif, and *El-Sharkia* on Sharia Alfi Bey. Even more renowned is the city-wide chain *La Poire*, of which the original and most central branch, at 1 Sharia Amerika al-Latina (not far from Midan Tahrir; see map, p.70), offers home-made baklava (£E65 per kilo) and éclairs (£E7 each); other branches can be found in Mohandiseen (see map, pp.132–133), Giza (Sharia el-Nil, 100m south of the Gama'a Bridge; see map, 138), and Heliopolis (92 Sharia al-Higaz, near Midan Heliopolis).

For a healthy pick-up before breakfast or lunch, you can't beat Cairo's **juice bars** (usually open 8am–10pm), selling freshly-squeezed sugar-cane, orange, guava or other seasonal fruits for £E2.50 to £E4 a glass. The best in Cairo is *Farghaly Fruits*, 71 Arab League Street, in Mohandiseen (see map, pp.132–133); in the downtown area, *Mohammed Ali* on Midan Falaki (see map, pp.50–51) is unrivalled for its vast selection, including a wonderful coconut milkshake. Cairenes also love **ice cream,** which comes in all kinds of flavours. The best outlet for ice cream is *Rigoletto* in Zamalek (see opposite).

Nightlife and entertainment

Drinking doesn't get a big profile in Cairo, given that ninety percent of the population are **Muslim**, but there's a good range of bars scattered around town none the less. Discos are generally upmarket, and rather tame compared to Western nightclubs, but can be fun. Egypt's big nightlife speciality of course is bellydancing, though even this is not as traditional as you might think, and it's worth eschewing cheap, low-life establishments to splash out and see a top dancer at a five-star venue with dinner.

For current information about **what's on** at cinemas, concert halls and nightclubs, get hold of Saturday's *Egyptian Mail*, the weekly English edition of *Al-Ahram* newspaper, the monthly *Egypt Today*, or the free monthly booklets *The Croc* (available at various shops and restaurants, and online at ⓦ www.icroc.com) and *Egypt* (issued by the Egyptian Tourist Authority and available at some hotels).

Bars

Beer, the consumption of which goes back to pharaonic times, is the most widely available form of **alcohol**. Native Stella beer is a light lager (four percent ABV), and retails in most places for £E8 to £E12, although discos may charge as much as £E25. Sakkara is a similarly light lager that most foreigners seem to prefer. Premium or "export" versions of Stella and Sakkara have a slightly fuller flavour. Also worth trying is lager, marketed under the Luxor name, which is ten percent alcohol by volume, and there are Egyptian versions of Heineken, Carlsberg, Löwenbrau and Meister, none worth the extra cost, and kamikaze (seven to ten percent) versions of Sakkara and Meister, which are worth avoiding. Marzen, a dark bock beer, appears briefly in the spring; Aswali is a dark beer produced in Aswan. There is also Birrel, a non-alcoholic beer.

A half-dozen or so Egyptian **wines**, produced near Alexandria, include Omar Khayyam (a very dry red), Cru des Ptolémées (a decent dry white) and Rubis d'Egypte (an acceptable rosé). Obélisque's red Cabernet Sauvignon is good; the rosé and white less so. In most restaurants these retail for about £E80 a bottle. Chateau des Rêves, a classy red with complex flavours, goes for £E72 in the shops, and is best left to breathe for a while before drinking.

Spirits are usually mixed with sodas or fruit juice. The favourite is **brandy**, known as *jaz* ("bottle"), and sold under three labels: Ahmar (the cheapest), Maa'tak (the best) and Vin (the most common). **Zibiba** is similar to Greek ouzo. Avoid vile

Egyptian-made **gin** and **whisky** whose labels imitate famous Western brands – they may contain wood alcohol and other poisons. A vodka-based alcopop called ID is available in various flavours at liquor stores and some bars and duty-free shops.

Tourists tend to drink at the bars of upmarket hotels, or at pub-style bars, often in Zamalek and Mohandiseen. However, there are a handful of downtown options, including a couple of rooftop bars, which are fun, and, for men at any rate, rough and ready downmarket bars can also be a laugh.

The more upmarket bars often have a minimum charge, often unadvertised (usually around £E10–20). The cheapest **bars** in the city are spit-and-sawdust **drinking dens,** euphemistically named *"cafeterias"*, found in nooks all over Central Cairo. Beer is usually served with free nibbles and lots of drunken bonhomie. They're certainly not recommended for women on their own, and even with a male escort you'll be the object of much attention. Some other bars are meeting places for men and prostitutes (the only Egyptian women found there). Most of the establishments we list are places where women shouldn't face too much hassle; there are however one or two exceptions to this, which we've noted. As throughout Egypt, the sale of alcohol to Muslims is banned during Ramadan and major religious festivals, though it is available to tourists in some hotels.

Central Cairo

All of the places listed below are marked on the map on pp.50–51.

Barrel Lounge On the first floor of the *Windsor Hotel*, Sharia Alfi Bey. Some of the furniture is actually made from old wine barrels, and the faded colonial decor and charming olde-worlde ambience here almost makes you feel like you've stepped back into the 1930s, when it was a popular watering hole for British officers. Women in particular will enjoy the hassle-free atmosphere, and foreigners can buy alcohol here during Ramadan. Daily 10am–midnight.

Bodega Orabi Sharia Orabi (no number apparent, but opposite no.25). Friendly, if rough and ready, bar with a quieter upstairs section overlooking the street. It's small, and can sometimes get quite crowded, but it's always friendly, and generally more easy-going than other downmarket Cairo bars. Women may wish to steer clear, but should be OK here with male company. Daily 11am–4am.

Cafeteria Stella On the corner of Sharia Talaat Harb and Sharia Hoda Shaarawi, next door to *Felfela's restaurant*. Patronized by local barflies, expats and backpackers, this seedy, cramped den is often buzzing with life, and the regulars are quite used to tourists popping in for a drink. Daily except Fri noon–midnight.

Café Riche 17 Sharia Talaat Harb. Once a hangout for artists and intellectuals, this bar-restaurant (not a café, despite the name) has been visited by practically every Arab revolutionary of the last century. Even former Iraqi president Saddam Hussein has been known to drink here, and the free officers whose coup toppled King Farouk in 1952 (see p.262) did much of their plotting here. The owner was a pilot during the wars with Israel. Although now largely for tourists, its teak bar still oozes history, but don't bother eating in the restaurant, as the food is very mediocre. Daily 10am–midnight.

El-Horea Midan Falaki. A large and atmospheric high-ceilinged old-school Cairo café that's hardly changed since the 1930s. Decorated with mirrors and old Stella advertisements, its walls a fine shade of nicotine, it plays host to an eclectic clientele, and serves beer as well as tea, coffee and *sheesha* pipes. Chess players meet here in the evening and people gather to watch them play – though drinking isn't allowed round the boards. Sun–Thurs 11am–3am, Fri noon–3am.

Gamayka Sharia el-Bank el-Ahly, off Sharia Sharif. Named after the island of Jamaica, this cosy little dive is really just an ordinary "cafeteria" bar (women won't feel comfortable here), but it's a little more refined than most, and you can have a *sheesha* with your beer. Daily 11am–4am.

Happy City Hotel 92C Sharia Mohammed Farid. Just up the street from the Abdeen metro stop, the rooftop café at this hotel has a view of the Muqattam and tasty complimentary mezze, served when you buy a drink. Open from 5pm till midnight (or later if there are enough drinkers).

Le Bistro 8 Sharia Hoda Shaarawi
☎012/849-1943. Pub run by the neighbouring restaurant of the same name (see p.192), with smoochy lighting, soft music and an intimate ambience; a place for a romantic rendezvous rather than a booze-up. Daily 7pm–1am.

Le Grillon 8 Sharia Qasr el-Nil, down a small passage between Qasr el-Nil and Sharia Bustan. A cosy, carpeted bar that's quite large, with lots of space for a quiet chat. It also serves mediocre food and has a smoking garden in case you want a *sheesha*. Daily noon–2am.

Napoleon Bar *Shepheard Hotel*. One of the most comfortable bars in town, with soft seating, a refined atmosphere, wood panelling and Napoleonic prints on the walls. As well as drinks, they serve mezze and light meals, and there's live music every night. Foreigners can buy alcohol here during Ramadan. Daily 5pm–2am.

Odeon Palace Hotel 6 Sharia Abdel Hamid Said. The 24hr rooftop bar here is a popular and very pleasant place for a bit of after-hours drinking, perhaps with a *sheesha*. Minimum charge £E10 7am–9pm, £E15 9pm–7am. Daily 24hr.

Zamalek and Mohandiseen

Unless otherwise stated, all the places listed here are marked on the map on pp.132–133.

Bull's Eye 32 Sharia Jeddah, Mohandiseen
🌐 www.bullseyepub.com. English-style pub featuring, as its name suggests, a dartboard, as well as food, occasional live bands, cocktails and karaoke nights. See the website for schedule. Daily 6pm–2am.

Deals 5 Sharia Sayed el-Bakri, Zamalek
🌐 www.dealspub.com. This small and rather narrow but homely basement bar, where the tables hug the walls, is one of Cairo's most congenial drinking spots, and one of the few with any kind of atmosphere. It's popular with expats and Egyptians alike, and women can drink here with no fear. There's cold beer (served with popcorn), and decent food, while TVs hang from the walls playing pop videos, though the piped music never matches. There are larger branches in Mohandiseen (2 Sharia Gol Gamal) and Heliopolis (40 Sharia Baghdad). Daily 4pm–2am.

Harry's Pub *Marriott Hotel*, Zamalek. British-style bar with live music from 10pm, a favourite with expats. English football is shown here regularly. Minimum charge £E125. Daily 5pm–2am.

Piano Bar *Marriott Hotel*, Zamalek. A sleek bar with lots of stately wooden decor in what was the billiard room of Empress Eugénie's palace, the *Piano Bar* is more refined than *Harry's*, and, as its name suggests, offers live piano music (from 8pm) to enhance the ambience. Much frequented by expats. Daily 6pm–2am.

Pub 28 28 Shagar al-Durr, Zamalek. A bar that's also popular as a place to eat, offering a few different beers, *sangría* by the carafe, plus English cold cuts, mezze, grills and good steaks. Daily noon–2am.

Discos and nightclubs

Egyptians make a distinction between a **disco**, where you dance to music, and a **nightclub**, where you have dinner and watch a floorshow.

Cairo has a fair number of **discos** but nowhere to rave about. The music is usually last year's hits or current Egyptian stuff, but dancefloor attitudes are good, boozy boors are at a minimum and casual dress is acceptable at all but the ritziest places. More problematic is the trend towards a **couples-only policy**. Though you might imagine this is to prevent women from being swamped, locals say that it's to stop discos from becoming gay haunts or pick-up joints for prostitutes. In practice, women can usually get into discos without escorts, but men without women will have more difficulty. Call first to avoid disappointment. Most places don't get going until midnight.

In addition to the places listed here, one or two **bars** also have dance floors, notably *Bull's Eye* (see above). *The Cancan* is a disco held Monday to Wednesday, Friday and Saturday at the *Fontana Hotel* (see p.206).

Downtown

After Eight 6 Sharia Qasr el-Nil, Downtown ☎010/339-8000, ⓦwww.after8cairo.com (see map, pp.50–51). Sweaty, smoky and atmospheric jazz club where you can sip cocktails and wiggle your bum to smoochy music under low lights. Couples over 25 only; reservation compulsory. Entry £E40 (£E100 Thurs, £E60 Fri) – this is supposed to be a minimum charge, but it's unlikely to include any drinks you buy. Sat–Wed 8pm–2am, Thur & Fri 8pm–3am.

Latex *Nile Ritz-Carlton*, 1113 Corniche el-Nil, Downtown ☎02/2578-0666 (see map, pp.50–51). The *Nile Hotel's* basement disco, rather seedy but good for a dance if you don't want to stray too far from the centre of town. Sounds are mostly house, with a smattering of hip-hop and R&B. Minimum charge £E150. Tue–Sun 10pm–4am.

Mohandiseen

Cairo Jazz Club 197 26th July St, Mohandiseen ☎02/3345-9939, ⓦwww .cairojazzclub.com (see map, pp.132–133). Food, drink, and live musicians most nights, but despite the name, jazz only once a week. Saturday is Middle Eastern music, Sunday is jazz, but many reckon the best night is Wednesday, when there's no live band, only a DJ playing an eclectic mix of dance tunes. Happy hour, with two drinks for the price of one, is 7–9pm. Couples over 25 only (at least in principle); reservation advisable. Daily 5pm–3am.

Roda Island

Hard Rock Café *Grand Hyatt Hotel*, Roda Island (see map, pp.116–117) ☎02/2532-1277, ⓦwww.hardrock.com/cairo. The Cairo branch of the international chain, popular with bright young things, and mainly notable for having a 1957 Ford (apparently once the property of President Gamal Abdel Nasser) suspended above the tables amid the usual pop paraphernalia. Daily noon–4am, with a DJ from midnight.

Giza

Nirvana (Africana) 41 Pyramids Road (see map, p.150). Officially renamed *Nirvana* but still universally known as *Africana*, this lively, downmarket club plays African and reggae music to a largely sub-Saharan crowd, though it's as much a pick-up joint as a centre for Cairo's African community. It's lively and fun, but don't order spirits here – stick to the beer. £E60 entry. Daily 11pm–3.30am.

Dokki

Stiletto Sharia Corniche el-Nil by Midan Galaa, Dokki (opposite *Cairo Sheraton* Hotel), ☎02/3331-1360 (see map, pp.132–133). Upmarket lounge bar with cocktails, music and a dancefloor, popular with Cairo's young and rich. Friday is jazz night, Sunday is salsa night. Minimum charge Sun–Thurs £E90, Fri & Sat £E110. Daily 7pm–4am.

Bulaq and Beyond

Sangria Opposite the *Conrad* Hotel, Corniche el-Nil, Bulaq ☎02/2579-6511 (see map, p.141). A bar on a boat that doubles as a nightclub after dark. It's quite laid-back, with an outside smoking area, though they sometimes refuse entry to punters they deem too casually dressed. Minimum charge £E100. Daily noon–2.30am.

Tamarai North Tower, Nile City Towers, 2005C Corniche el-Nil, Rod el-Farag ☎02/2461-9910, ⓦwww.tamarai-egypt.com (see map, p.141). Very exclusive bar-restaurant, slick in a self-consciously upmarket kind of way, and a favourite with local VIPs. It's done out with lots of wooden slats and fabric drapes, there's a dining area and a cool outside terrace, and access is strictly by reservation only. They do their own speciality Martinis, the food is good but pricey (mains around £E200), and the clientele are well-heeled. There's a dancefloor, with chilled music played during the week, and uptempo house at weekends. Minimum charge £E250. Daily noon–2am.

Gay and lesbian nightlife

In the past, venues such as *Harry's Bar* (see opposite) at the *Marriott* hotel were haunts for **gay men**, but that all changed in 2001, when police raided the *Queen Boat* floating disco, which was popular with both gay and heterosexual couples.

Though homosexuality as such is not illegal, fifty-two gay men ("the Cairo 52") were arrested, slung in a cell and charged with offences such as "debauchery" and "contempt of religion", some receiving three-year prison sentences as a result. The religious lobby were delighted, but the gay scene has since gone completely underground, and any events that begin to attract a gay crowd are quickly closed. 1980s retro nights may be worth checking out, however. There are absolutely no venues for **lesbians** in Cairo, although a very underground lesbian scene does exist.

Live music

Aside from in discos, tourist restaurants and at the Opera House, you're unlikely to hear much **live Western music**. The city has a small rock music scene, but the **SOS music festival**, which used to be held at irregular intervals, has not been held since 2009. For contemporary Arabic music, by far the liveliest time of year is after the school and university exams, from late June to November, but you'll need an Arabic-speaking friend to tell you what's happening, as none of it is advertised in the English press.

Folk, classical Arab and religious music

Folk music doesn't command a wide following today, but under Nasser (1952–1970), troupes of artists were established to preserve Egyptian folk music and dance, and some of these – most famously the Reda Troupe (see below) – still perform today, while all of the moulids listed on pp.216–218 feature religious music in the form of hypnotic Sufi chants.

Abdel Monem el Sawy Culture Wheel Under Zamalek (15th May) Bridge, 26th July St, Zamalek (see map, pp.132–133) ☎02/2736-8881, ⊛www.culturewheel.com. With a full programme of low-priced folk, jazz and classical concerts, as well as seminars, lectures and movies, the Wheel has fast become one of Cairo's most important cultural centres, and defiantly proclaimed its support for the pro-democracy movement during the 2011 uprising.

Balloon Theatre Corniche el-Nil, Aguza (see map, pp.132–133) ☎02/3347-1718. This pleasantly old-fashioned theatre by the Nile stages performances of religious and other traditional music. Most importantly, the incredible Reda Egyptian Dance Troupe (founded by Mahmoud Reda in 1959) and the slightly less well-known National Troupe perform spectacular traditional dance

compositions such as *The Gypsy Dance* or *The Mamluke*, with spectacular costumes and excellent musicians, advertised in the weekly English edition of *Al-Ahram*.

Beit al-Sihaymi Darb al-Asfur, Gamaliya (see map, p.81) ☎02/2591-3391, ⊛www.cdf-eg .org. The Al-Nil Folk Music Troupe performs here every Sunday at 8.30pm.

Genaina Theatre Al-Azhar Park (see map, pp.74–75) ☎02/2362-5057, ⊛www.mawred .org. Hosts concerts of folk, Egyptian and foreign classical music on Thursday or Friday evenings.

Gumhorriya Theatre 12 Sharia al-Gumhorriya (see map, pp.50–51) ☎02/2390-7707. As well as plays in Arabic, this downtown theatre also sometimes hosts traditional music and dance performances, usually advertised in the weekly English edition of *Al-Ahram*.

MakAn (Egyptian Centre for Culture and Art) 1 Sharia Saad Zaghloul (see map, pp.50–51) ☎02/2792-0878, ⊛www .egyptmusic.org. This basement ethnic music club hosts performances of the Zar music of the Sahara on Wednesdays at 9pm. This stirring and deliberately trance-inducing tribal music was traditionally performed by women to exorcize *jinn* (malevolent spirits) and heal disease. MakAn also hosts a weekly jam session on Tuesdays at 9pm, involving Gypsy, Nubian and Sudanese musicians. Tickets for both events cost £E20.

Bellydancing

Cairo remains the world's most important bellydancing centre, and every summer, usually in late June or early July, it hosts the world's premier bellydancing festival, the **International Oriental Dance Festival**, usually based at the *Mena House Oberoi* hotel. For the latest information on the festival, which features classes and workshops in the daytime and performances in the evenings, plus extra events such as costume shows, check Ⓦwww.raqiahassan.net. There is also a smaller and less prestigious rival festival, run by the Nile Group four times a year; for further information check Ⓦwww.nilegroup.net. If you're interested in **lessons**, Hisham Youssef at the *Berlin Hotel* (see p.183) can arrange lessons with a number of teachers (including some of Cairo's top dancers) at different levels and prices.

Upmarket venues

The best places to see the top acts are the **nightclubs** attached to some of the **five-star hotels**; reservations and smart dress are required. All provide a four-course meal to tide you through the warm-up acts; the star comes on sometime after midnight. There's usually either a minimum rate or a flat charge of around £E300–800 for the dinner and performance. The most notable are *Haroun al-Rashid* at the *Semiramis Intercontinental* (☏02/2795-7171; Tue–Thurs, Sat & Sun 11.30pm), *Empress Show Lounge* at the *Cairo Marriott* (☏02/2728-3000; Tues–Sun 10.30pm), and *Abou Nawass* at the *Mena House Oberoi* (☏02/3377-3222; Thurs & Fri 10.30pm). At the *Cairo Sheraton* (☏02/3336-9800) on Midan Galaa in Dokki, bellydancers currently appear on Wednesdays, Thursdays and Saturdays in the *Ala al-Din Bar* (7pm–midnight; set menus £E130–170), while the hotel's *Casablanca* nightclub undergoes remodelling work. **Floating restaurants** are also a good option, in particular the *Nile Maxim* (see p.196) and the *Nile Pharaoh* (see p.196). The *Nile Pharaoh's* early evening cruise in particular, at £E200, is one of the best bargains for a bellydancing performance (note that the late cruise is less worthwhile, as the main act is an Arabic stand-up comedian).

Of the **dancers** at these five-star venues, the big names include **Randa Kamel**, whose raunchy moves are very popular with foreigners, though some purists consider them vulgar; she currently performs on the *Nile Maxim* (see p.196). Other top stars are **Dina** (at the *Semiramis InterContinental Hotel*), Sorraya (*Marriott Hotel*) and Nancy (*Mena House Oberoi*). Another well-known name, **Lucy**, now more or less in retirement, puts in the odd impromptu performance at the *Parisiana* club (Pyramids Road, north side, just east of Maryotteya Canal; ☏02/3383-3911; £E300), which she runs with her husband. The *Parisiana* is quite pricey, but still employs some of the tricks used at cheaper places (see p.206), involving putting things on your table as if they

Bellydancing: a brief history

The European appetite for exotica in the late nineteenth and early twentieth centuries did much to create the bellydancing art form as it is known today: a sequinned fusion of classical *raqs sharqi* (oriental dance), stylized harem eroticism and the frank sexuality of the *ghawazee* (public dancers). During the nineteenth century, many *ghawazee* moonlighted as prostitutes, so even though most dancers today are dedicated professionals – and the top stars wealthy businesswomen – the association with prostitution has stuck, and the resulting social stigma is deterring young Egyptian women from entering the profession. As a result, most up-and-coming bellydancers today are foreigners.

were complimentary, and then charging inflated prices for them. Lucy is most likely to appear at weekends, but only if there is a big crowd.

Cheaper venues

A big step down from the upmarket bellydancing venues are the somewhat sleazy, rip-off nightclubs **along Pyramids Road**, where the entertainments are varied and sometimes good, but the food is usually poor. **Cheaper places**, with no food to speak of, lurk downtown. The majority of these are far from pleasant and, if you intend to check them out, you need to be aware of how they operate. They generally open their doors at around 10pm, though none really get going until at least midnight. Most have an entry fee or minimum charge, sometimes both, but be warned that many will also endeavour to rip you off with **hidden charges** and sharp practices. Napkins and light snacks, for example, may be placed on your table and then charged on your bill. You need to be on your toes to keep refusing these extras, as the clubs count on customers getting too drunk to notice. Venues may also add

spurious taxes, or simply refuse to give change – even for a £E100 note.

Women are unlikely to enjoy themselves at most of these places as the atmosphere is generally sleazy, drunken and lecherous. The only **exception** in the list below is the *Cancan*, where women can go, in a group or accompanied by men, and have a good time. All these venues are marked on the map on pp.50–51, except where noted.

Cancan *Fontana Hotel*, off Midan Ramses ☏02/592-2321 (see map, p.68). A lower-priced version of the nightclubs in the five-star hotels, though sufficiently upmarket to be a safe and respectable option. Thurs & Sun 8pm–2am (starts off as a disco; dancer from 11pm). Minimum charge £E38.50.

Palmyra In the passage at 16 26th July St. Dancers, singers and other acts. Used to be free from sharp practices (see above), but has now unfortunately become as bad as the rest. Daily 11pm–4am. Entry £E50 including one beer.

Scheherazade 1 Sharia Alfi Bey. The venue itself is a marvellous old vaudeville-style music hall, with a variety of acts, but the usual tricks are played, and waiters may even try to insist that snacks (lowest price £E20) are compulsory with every beer. Daily midnight–6am. Minimum charge £E45.

Whirling dervishes

The Mowlawiyya are Arab adherents of a Sufi sect known to Westerners as the **whirling dervishes**, founded in Konya, Turkey, during the mid-thirteenth century. Their Turkish name, Mevlevi, refers to their original Master, who extolled music and dancing as a way of shedding earthly ties and abandoning oneself to God's love. The Sufi ideal of attaining union with God has often been regarded by orthodox Muslims as blasphemous, and only during Mamluke and Ottoman times did whirling dervishes flourish without persecution.

In modern Egypt the sect is minuscule compared to other Sufi orders, and rarely appears at moulids, but a tourist version of the famous whirling ceremony is staged at the Wikala al-Ghuri (see map, p.77). Free ninety-minute **performances** are held at the Wikala al-Ghuri on Wednesdays and Saturdays at 8pm; arrive early to get a good seat, and at least half an hour before the performance in any case. Photos are permitted but not videos.

Each element of the **whirling ceremony** (*samaa*) has symbolic significance. The music symbolizes that of the spheres, and the turning of the dervishes that of the heavenly bodies. The gesture of extending the right arm towards heaven and the left towards the floor denotes that grace is being received from God and distributed to humanity without anything being retained by the dervishes. The camelhair hats represent tombstones; the black cloaks the tomb itself; the white skirts shrouds.

Opera and ballet

The **Cairo Opera House** on Gezira (☎02/2739-0132 or 2739-0144, ⓦwww
.cairoopera.org) is the chief centre for performing arts in the city. Its main hall
hosts performances by the **Cairo Ballet Company** (Sept–June) and prestigious
foreign acts (anything from kabuki theatre to Broadway musicals). The smaller
hall is used by the **Cairo Symphony Orchestra** (ⓦwww.cairo-symphony.com),
who have weekly concerts, usually on Saturdays, from September to mid-June.
During July and August all events move to the marble-clad open-air theatre;
a programme of youth concerts during this period includes everything from
Nubian folk-dancing to Egyptian pop. Programme listings appear in *Egypt Today*
and the *Al-Ahram* weekly, and are available in more detail from the ticket office.
All tickets (£E35–75) should be booked several days in advance (office open daily
10am–8pm). A jacket and tie are compulsory for men attending events in the main
hall. Some chamber-music concerts take place at the **Manasterly Palace** on Roda
Island (☎02/2363-1537, ⓦwww.manasterly.com).

Cinemas

Egypt has the Arab world's most prolific **film industry**, though its golden age was in
the 1940s and 1950s. After several decades of decline since then, Egyptian films have
recently seen a revival, in both comedy and drama. Most of the films shown in Cairo's
theatres are Egyptian, and will be in Arabic without subtitles, while Hollywood films
are often dubbed. Nile TV, however, shows a lot of excellent movies from the golden
age of Egyptian cinema with English (or sometimes French) subtitles.

For cinema listings, see the weekly English edition of *Al-Ahram*. The **Cairo
International Film Festival** (ⓦwww.cairofilmfest.com) is held in late autumn.
Established in 1976, it concentrates on Arabic and African cinema, or on foreign
films with an Egyptian or Arabic theme.

Cheap downtown cinemas (£E10–15) include Cosmos, 12 Emad al-Din (☎02/2577-
9537); Diana, 17 Sharia Alfi Bey (☎02/2592-4727); Metro, 35 Sharia Talaat Harb
(☎02/2393-7566); and Rivoli, 26th July St opposite the law courts (☎02/2575-
5053). Plusher venues (£E15–25), with a/c and no-smoking, no-chattering rules,
include Al-Tahrir, on Sharia Tahrir, Dokki (☎02/3335-4726), and Ramses Hilton
cinema in the mall opposite the *Ramses Hilton* hotel (☎02/2574-7435).

Theatre

Few tourists go to plays in Cairo – deterred by the language barrier – but for those
who know some Arabic, **theatre** in Cairo can be very rewarding. The rhythms and
tones of Arabic are intensely dramatic – watching a play is a bit like experiencing
an opera in a foreign language, without surtitles – and Arabic theatre's lack of a
"fourth wall" separating actors and audience creates a strong interaction between
them, which generates a real buzz.

In the same complex as the Balloon Theatre (see p.204), the **Theatre of
Tomorrow** (Masrah al-gad ☎02/3304-3187) puts on shows that mix dance, a live
traditional orchestra and famous actors from Cairo's theatre scene.

In Midan Ataba are the **Cairo Puppet Theatre** (see p.213) and the **Talia
Theatre** (☎02/2593-7948). The Talia is two theatres: a small intimate space for
unconventionally staged work, where you sit almost in the middle of the action;
and the big hall, a more conventional proscenium stage. Performances on the small

Egyptian music

Arabic pop, and especially the heart-rending love songs typical of the Arab world, are the soundtrack to a stay in Cairo, blaring out from the stereos of taxis and cafés alike, usually on cassette rather than CD. Egypt's vast young population makes it the most important market for Arab music, and Cairo today is the centre of the Arab recording industry – a dominance partly acquired thanks to the decline of its rivals in Lebanon, Libya and Kuwait, but one which is now being challenged by studios and labels in Saudi Arabia and the UAE.

For shops selling musical recordings and instruments, see p.225.

Although the call to prayer and the recitation of the Koran are not regarded in Egypt as music, they are certainly listened to for pleasure, and the *tajwid*, or musically elaborate style of Koranic recitation, reached its apogee in Egypt. Performers may be **munshids** – professionals who move from one festival to another – or simply the **muezzin** or **imam** of the local mosque. Recitals at **moulids** are often more participation than performance, with lines of Sufi devotees chanting and swaying to the accompaniment of a drum. These recitals, known as **zikrs** (originally designed to lull the congregation into a trance-like state of oneness with God) can last for days.

Classical Arabic music can be traced back to the **Bedouin** war bards of the Arabian Peninsula, whose metre matched that of a camel's stride, but also to the refined **court music** of the Caliphates and the Ottoman Empire. During the twentieth century the form was characterized by oriental scales, orchestras and male choirs, bravura rhetoric and soloists filled with yearning. Its greatest exponent was **Umm Kalthoum**, whose fifty-year career spanned the advent of gramophones, radio and long-distance broadcasting, making her the most popular singer in the Arab world. In Egypt she was a national institution, accorded a weekly concert on radio and, later, TV; her funeral in 1975 drew the largest crowd since that of President Nasser (who timed his speeches around her broadcasts).

By the mid-1980s two main styles of **popular music** had developed, though some would say that the distinction between them is pretty moot nowadays. **Shaabi** ("people") music, from Cairo's working-class quarters, blends the traditional form of the *mawal* (plaintive vocal improvisations) with a driving beat; the lyrics are often raunchy, satirical, or provocative. You will rarely hear this music on the TV or radio, as the genre has been frowned upon in official cultural circles, but it is popular at weddings and parties throughout working-class Cairo, at nightclubs along Pyramids Road – and is played on battered cassettes in taxis, buses and cafés.

The original *shaabi* singer was **Ahmed Adaweyah**, who, from 1971 on, introduced the idea of street language, to which later imitators added elements of rap and disco, in the manner of Algerian rai music. **Shababi** or "youthful" music – also known as **al-jeel** ("the generation") music – followed hot on the heels of *shaabi* in the 1980s. It took disco elements like drum tracks and synthesized backing and mixed them with Nubian and Bedouin rhythms – the latter introduced by Libyan musicians who had fled to Cairo after Gaddafi's "cultural revolution", notably **Hamid el-Shaeri**, whose 1988 back-room recording of "Lolaiki", with vocals by **Ali Hamida,** launched the genre.

Egypt's foremost pop idol, **Amr Diab**, broke into the international market with the song "Nour el Ain", released in 1996, and had another international hit in 2001 with "Aktar Wahed". Born in the Islamist stronghold of Assyut, **Ruby** has set Egyptian eyes agog with the sexuality of her videos and the assertiveness of her lyrics, which got her expelled from the musicians' union in 2007.

stage start at 8pm and cost £E10; those on the big stage start at 10pm and cost £E20. The puppet show (Fri 10.30am, Thurs & Fri 7.30pm; ☏02/2591-0954) is a good choice for kids, although the plays can be surprisingly wordy and hard to understand without some knowledge of Arabic. Tickets are £E10 and £E15, depending on how close you sit to the stage.

10

Sports and activities

Spectator sports in Cairo are dominated by football, and it's well worth going to see a big match at Cairo Stadium if you can. There are no public sports facilities in the city so to take part in any sports activity beyond kicking a ball about on the street, Cairenes are obliged to join sports clubs. Visitors wishing to work out, swim or play golf are limited to hotel gyms, pools or clubs that allow membership on a daily or monthly basis. However, you can enjoy horse- or camel-riding in the desert or a felucca cruise on the Nile without any such rigmarole – both are highly recommended.

Felucca trips

Feluccas are lateen-sailed boats that have been used on the Nile since time immemorial. The river's northward flow, coupled with a prevailing wind towards the south, made it a natural highway; the Ancient Egyptian hieroglyphs for "south" and "north" were a boat with its sail furled or unfurled.

Today, feluccas are mainly used for **pleasure cruises** on the Nile. Egyptians bring picnics and ghetto-blasters, dancing and singing as they sail past the skyscrapers on the Corniche. Visitors tend to prefer a tranquil **sunset cruise**, enjoying the sight of egrets and other water-birds, and the sound of thousands of *muezzins* uttering the call to prayer as the sun slips over the horizon of the Western Desert. Whichever sort of cruise you fancy, be sure to bring lots of mosquito repellent.

Most of the feluccas moored along the riverbank opposite the *Shepheard Hotel* and the northern tip of Roda can seat eight people; expect to pay around £E60 per hour to charter a boat. Possible destinations include Old Cairo and the Nilometer (see p.129), or the islands beyond Roda or Shubra, which abound in birdlife and are farmed using water-buffaloes (as you can see at any landfall).

Shorter felucca jaunts around Gezira or Roda can be arranged at the quay just south of Tahrir Bridge (£E2 for 30min), while larger "public" feluccas moored just south of Maspero Dock do round trips to the **Nile barrages at Qanatir** (see p.228), taking up to four hours. These cost about £E100 an hour (split between twelve passengers), and leave only when full (or if fewer people agree to pay more).

Alternatively, you can easily reach Qanatir by public **ferry** (hourly 8–10am, returning 2–4pm; 90min; £E5), or a **pleasure boat** (daily round trips departing around 9am and noon; £E10) leaving from just north of the Maspero Dock.

For an even cheaper no-frills ride on the Nile, catch a river-taxi (£E1) from Maspero Dock upriver to Giza, or downstream to Qanatir (Fri only; £E5 each way).

Football

Of the city's spectator sports, **football** (soccer) is the most exciting. During the season (Sept–May), premier league teams Ahly (Ⓦwww.ahlyegypt.com) and Zamalek (Ⓦwww.zamaleksc.org) take on rival premier league clubs like Ismailiya (Ⓦwww.ismaily.org), Mahalla and Masri at the Cairo International Stadium in Medinet Nasr (see p.144), the country's biggest football ground. Needless to say, the season's most exciting fixture is the Ahly–Zamalek derby, when tickets sell out well in advance. Should their team win, thousands of supporters drive around Cairo honking horns and waving flags attached to lances – beware of being run over or impaled.

For matches such as this, and major international fixtures (which are played at the same stadium), you'll need to enlist help from Egyptians to secure a ticket but otherwise the best way to get a ticket for a game is to simply roll up at the stadium on match day and buy one at the gate.

Fitness centres

The most convenient gyms downtown are in the five-star hotels.

Gold's Gym Aboard a boat moored at 121 Corniche el-Nil, Giza ☏02/3748-0003, Ⓦwww.goldsgymegypt.com (see map, p.138). Has weight machines, aerobics sessions, a sauna and steam jacuzzi, and charges £E110 for one-day membership, but much better rates for monthly membership or multiple visits. **Nile Ritz-Carlton Fitness Centre** Corniche el-Nil, Downtown ☏02/2578-0444 (see map, pp.50–51). Once the hotel reopens, you should be able to use its fitness room, squash and tennis courts, sauna and steam room. Daily 6.30am–10pm.

Ramses Hilton Fitness Room Corniche el-Nil, Downtown ☏02/2577-7613 (see map, pp.50–51). Well-equipped fitness centre, charging £E50 per day for non-members, but free for hotel guests. Also has a sauna. Daily 6.30am–11.30pm.

Golf

Cairo and Giza have several **golf courses**, of which the most central is the eighteen-hole course at the Gezira Sporting Club (☏02/2735-6000; £E50 plus day membership of £E100). The *Mena House Oberoi* by the Giza Pyramids (☏02/3377-3222; see p.150) also has an eighteen-hole course (£E150; free for hotel guests), and there are a couple more golf clubs around the ring road beyond Heliopolis: the eighteen-hole course at Katameya Heights (☏02/2758-0512 to 17, Ⓦwww.katameyaheights.co), and an eighteen-hole course at the *JW Marriott Hotel* (☏02/2411-5588, Ⓦgolf.jwmarriottcairo.com/golf).

You can find further information on Cairo's golf courses at Ⓦwww.touregypt.net/golfcourses.htm.

Horse and camel riding

Riding in the desert is a fantastic experience straight out of the film *Lawrence of Arabia*. Horse riders can gallop across the sands, while riding a camel is equally exciting for novices. It's strongly advisable to hire a horse or camel from one of the authorized stables near the Giza Pyramids, rather than one of the many footloose operators frequenting the site, who pull tricks such as demanding twice the agreed sum once you're miles into the desert. Authorized stables also take better care of their animals and are more safety-conscious.

Among those situated behind the Sound and Light grandstand near the Sphinx, AA (☎012/153-4142) is especially good for children, and KG Stables (☎02/3385-1065), around the corner off Sharia Abu el-Hol, is also recommended. Expect to pay £E200 to £E250 for a four-hour round trip to the next set of pyramids at Abu Sir (see p.161 for details).

Running

The **Hash House Harriers** (ⓦwww.cairohash.com) is an expat club that gets together every Friday afternoon for a two-hour run. Street running is best done on Gezira, Roda or the west bank Corniche, before 8am or after 10pm to avoid congested sidewalks, heavy traffic and air pollution.

Swimming pools

The easiest way to get a **swim** in Cairo, albeit expensive, is to use the pool at one of the five-star hotels. The largest pool is at the *Semiramis InterContinental* (£E200; see p.185); alternatives include the *Cairo Marriott* (£E240; see p.187).

For serious swimmers, the Ahli Club (☎02/2735-2202; monthly membership US$100), behind Gezira's Opera House on Sharia Om Kalthoum, offers an Olympic-size pool and women-only sessions. In Heliopolis, there's the Heliopolis Sporting Club on Sharia Merghani (☎02/2417-0061 to 0063; £E35 entry, £E35 for a swim).

Bowling

International Bowling Center behind October War Memorial, Sharia al-Oruba, Medinet Nasr ☎02/2261-2121 or 2122. Twenty-four lanes of bowling (£E5 entry plus £E7 per game), as well as table tennis, billiards, air hockey and other games, built by the Ministry of Defence, but open to all. Daily 11am–2am.

Nile Bowling 125 Corniche el-Nil, Giza ☎02/3336-1637 (see map, p.138). Eight lanes in a rather down-at-heel club, where a game will set you back £E15 per person before 5pm, or £E19 after. Daily 11am–2am.

⑪

Kids' Cairo

Children evoke a warm response in Egypt and are welcome more or less everywhere. It's not unusual to see Egyptian children out with their parents in cafés or shops past midnight. The only child-free zones tend to be bars and nightclubs.

Most **hotels** can accommodate children by adding an extra bed to a double room for a reasonable charge, and pharmacies sell formula milk, baby food and disposable nappies. Things worth considering bringing include a mosquito net for a buggy or crib, and a parasol for sun protection.

From an adult minder's standpoint, most hazards can be minimized or avoided by taking due precautions. One specific thing to beware of is the fact that elevators in some Cairo hotels have no inner doors, so you may need to keep small hands away.

Besides the places listed in this chapter, most children (and adults) should enjoy **felucca** trips (see p.209), the **Pyramids' Sound and Light show** (see p.154), and theme restaurants like *Felfela Village* on Maryotteya Canal in Giza (see p.195).

Other things in Cairo that should appeal particularly to children include **horse**, **donkey** and **camel rides**, but choose carefully – AA Stables for example (see p.211) has a good reputation for catering to children.

Parks and gardens

Cairo has few **green spaces**. Even in prosperous Mohandiseen, people use the central reservations of the main boulevards for sitting out or picnicking. Most of the city's parks are more like gardens, small with well-tended flower beds and keep-off-the-grass rules, often by the river, and they usually charge small admission fees. They tend to be empty during the day, but can get quite crowded around sunset in summer, when local families pour in to enjoy the coolness of the evening. In addition to these, there's Gabalaya Gardens in Zamalek, covered opposite.

Food and health

Children (especially young ones) are more susceptible than adults to **heatstroke** and **dehydration**, and should always wear a sunhat, and have high-factor sunscreen applied to exposed skin. The other thing that children are very susceptible to is an upset tummy. Anti-diarrhoea drugs should generally not be given to young children; read the literature provided with the medication or consult a doctor for guidance on child dosages.

If children baulk at unfamiliar **food**, outlets of all major American fast-food chains are always close at hand. Ice cream is cheap and ubiquitous, as is rice pudding and *mahalabiyya*.

Al-Azhar Park Sharia Salah Salem, opposite the Northern Cemetery (see map, pp.74–75) ⓦ www .alazharpark.com. The city's most impressive park by far, with lots of space, fly-traps to keep the flies down, the *Hilltop Restaurant* (see p.193) and a long stretch of the original Ayyubid city wall. For full details, see p.112. Daily: summer 9am–midnight; winter 9am–11pm; usually £E5, but £E3 on Tuesdays, £E7 on public holidays.

Al-Urman Garden Sharia Nahdet Misr and Sharia Abdel Salam Aref, Giza (see map, p.138). A stately remnant of Khedive Ismail's palace grounds, created in 1870 by French landscape gardener Barillet-Deschamps (see p.138). Daily 8.30am–4pm; free.

Andalusian Garden Sharia al-Gezira, entrance at the corner with Sharia Tahrir, Gezira (see map, pp.132–133). Handy for the city centre, and supposedly modelled on the Moorish gardens of Islamic Spain, this carefully laid out garden is very neat and tidy. In case it gets too crowded for your liking, there's also a more exclusive upper section. Daily: summer 9am–midnight; winter 9am–10pm; £E2 (upper section daily 9am–5pm; £E10).

Bustan al-Horeyya Sharia Maglis el-Thawra, Gezira (see map, pp.132–133). Larger than the other Gezira gardens, and decorated with statues, this one lends itself more to picnics and games. Daily: summer 9am–midnight; winter 9am–10pm; £E2.

Riyadi Garden By the river between Tahrir Bridge and Sharia al-Borg (see map, pp.132–133). Very similar to the next-door Andalusian Garden (see opposite), but narrower, with more trees, no grass, and a Cleopatra's Needle-style obelisk in the middle. It's right by the river, on three levels, stepping up from the embankment to the street. There are two more small gardens – Hadiket al-Mesala and Hadiket al-Nahr – to its north (same hours and entry fee). Daily: summer 9am–midnight; winter 9am–10pm; £E2.

Umm Kalthoum Garden Sharia Abd al-Aziz al-Saud, Roda Island (see map, pp.116–117). Smaller and less well cared-for than the Gezira gardens, but attracts fewer people, and offers a welcome, and usually quiet, spot of green by the river. Daily: summer 9am–midnight; winter 9am–10pm; £E2.

Attractions for kids

Aquarium Grotto Gabalaya Gardens, Sharia Gabalaya, Zamalek (see map, pp.132–133). Assorted live and preserved tropical fish amid a labyrinth of passageways that children will love to explore, set in a landscaped garden that was once part of Empress Eugénie's (see p.136) palace grounds. The grottos are original, dating from 1867; the fish tanks were added by British zoologist and conservationist Stanley Flower at the beginning of the twentieth century. They won't impress serious aquarium buffs, but the kids should enjoy it, and the attached gardens (same hours and ticket) are a welcome spot of green. Daily 9.30am–4pm; £E1.

Cairo Land Sharia Salah Salem, by Fustat Park (see map, p.104). Small and rather run-down amusement park, but it's relatively central. There's a mini roller coaster and a few other rides, all at low prices (£E3–5). Daily: winter 8am–11pm, summer 5pm–1am; entry £E3.

Cairo Puppet Theatre Ezbekiya Gardens, off Midan Ataba ☎02/2591-0954 (see map, pp.50–51). A traditional diversion, staging musical puppet versions of Sindbad the Sailor, Ali Baba and other favourites, all in

Arabic. There's lots of music and the shows are spectacular enough for the language not to matter too much. Fri 10.30am, Thurs & Fri 7.30pm; £E10-15.

Cairo Zoo Sharia Nahdet Misr, Giza (see map, p.138). An impressive display of flamingos greets you on entry, and the zoo (formerly part of Khedive Ismail's palace grounds; see p.138) is reasonably humane, as zoos go, with quite large enclosures for most animals, the main exception being the lion house. There's also a hippo pond, which you can walk across (£E1), and children will enjoy helping to feed the camels or the elephants. Easily reached from downtown by bus (#8, #115, #124, #900, #998, and minibus #83, from Abdel Mouneem Riyad terminal behind the Egyptian Museum). Try to avoid Fridays and public holidays, when it's packed. Daily 9am–5pm; £E1, camera 25pt.

Cookie Amusement Park Mansoreya Canal, 400m north of Pyramids Road (see map, p.150). A small selection of fairground games and rides (rides £E2–3), including dodgems, roundabouts and a big slide. Daily: summer 5pm–1am, winter 3–11pm; entry £E3.

213

KIDS' CAIRO | Attractions for kids

Dreampark **Tariq al-Fayoum al-Wahat (Fayoum–Wahat Road) on the way to 6th October City, 20km southwest of Cairo, beyond the Giza pyramids** ⓦ www.dreamparkegypt.com. A big (150-acre), modern amusement park with lots of attractions including two roller coasters (with views of the pyramids from the top), a water chute, dodgems and a little train, plus various fast-food outlets. Expect to pay around £E80 each way by taxi, or take bus #690 from Midan Ramses, or a microbus from opposite Giza metro. Daily except Fri 10am–7pm, Fri 10am–9pm, Ramadan 9pm–2am; entry £E40 including some rides (other rides £E7).

Dr Ragab's Pharaonic Village **Reached via 3 Sharia Bahr al-Azam, El Moneeb** ☏ 02/3572-2533, ⓦ www.pharaonicvillage.com. A kitsch simulation of ancient Egypt, located on Jacob Island, upriver from Roda. Visitors are taken on a three-hour tour, on which you survey the Canal of Mythology (flanked by statues of gods) and see scores of costumed Egyptians performing tasks from their floating "time machines", before being shown around a replica temple and a nobleman's villa. There's also a 3-D cinema, and a dozen mini-museums, dedicated to Hellenic, Coptic and Islamic civilization, ancient arts, mummification and (a little incongruously)

Nasser, Sadat and Napoleon. If you don't take it too seriously, it's a fun place to visit, and quite educational, demonstrating how papyrus is made and how ancient Egyptians put on their make-up. It's £E8–10 by cab from downtown), or take a bus (#987 from Ahmed Helmi behind Ramses station, or #107 from Ataba). The nearest metro station is El-Monib, 2km south (a long walk or short cab ride). Daily: summer 9am–9pm; winter 9am–6pm; £E161–204 depending on the length of the tour.

National Circus **Corniche al-Nil, Aguza** ☏ 02/3347-0612 **(see map, pp.132–133).** Old-fashioned circus, with all the traditional acrobats, clowns, magicians and trapeze artists. Performances (in Arabic, but that won't matter very much) run from 8pm to 11pm daily except Wednesday (box office open 6–9pm). Tickets £E20–50.

Sindbad Amusement Park **Sharia Josip Tito, Heliopolis, near Cairo Airport** ☏ 02/2624-4001 **or 4002 (see map, p.141).** A relatively small (one and a half acres) but modern fairground whose 21 rides (£E3–5) include bumper cars, a Ferris wheel and a small roller coaster, plus play areas for small children. Can get very crowded in summer. To get there, take the Heliopolis metro's Nozha Line from Ramses to the last stop. Daily 4–11pm; entry £E5.

Festivals

Though few foreign visitors frequent them, Cairo's **religious festivals** are quite accessible to outsiders, and a lot of fun. Many begin with a *zaffa* (parade) of Sufis carrying banners, drums and tambourines, who chant and sway themselves into a trance-like state. Meanwhile, the crowd is entertained by acrobats, stick dancers, dancing horses, fortune-tellers and other sideshows.

The only problem in attending festivals, aside from the crowds (don't bring valuables, or come alone if you're a woman), is ascertaining the **dates**. Events may relate to either the Islamic, Coptic or secular calendars, or sometimes to a particular day or week rather than a certain date, so it's best to double-check the details below locally.

Moulids

Moulids are the equivalent of medieval European saints' fairs, and are popular events that combine piety, fun and commerce. Their ostensible aim is to obtain blessing (*baraka*) from a local saint, but they are also an opportunity for people to escape the monotony of working life in several days of festivities. Upper-class Egyptians and religious conservatives, however, look down on moulids as vulgar and unorthodox, and in 2009 they used the threat of swine flu as an excuse to ban or severely curtail them. How long these restrictions will last remains to be seen.

Most moulids are local affairs, centred around the tomb (*qubba*) of a holy man or woman. **Cairo** hosts three important ones, in honour of Al-Hussein, Saiyida Zeinab and the Imam al-Shafi'i (see p.216 & p.217 for details), plus numerous smaller moulids, each neighbourhood having its own. They attract pilgrims and itinerant Sufis, and there are snake charmers, scorpion eaters, storytellers and other traditional performers, plus foodstalls, fairground competitions and rides for children. At the most important ones, people come from far and wide, camping out around the shrine of the saint whose moulid it is.

Music and singing are a feature of every moulid; at the heart of each is at least one **zikr** – a gathering of worshippers who chant and sway for hours to attain a trance-like state of oneness with God. *Zikr* participants often belong to a **Sufi brotherhood**, identified by coloured banners, sashes or turbans, and named after their founding sheikh. The current incumbent of this office may lead them in a **zaffa** (parade) through town, and in olden times would ride a horse over his followers – a custom known as "the Treading".

A moulid may be spread over a week or more as people arrive at the shrine on which it is centred, but it culminates in a *leyla kebira* (big night), when celebrations reach their climax. The *yom kebir* (main day), on which the main processions are held, is usually – but not always – the next day.

The biggest festivals – **Eid al-Fitr**, celebrating the end of Ramadan, and the sheep-slaughtering pilgrimage festival of **Eid al-Adha** (Bakr-Id, as British Muslims often call it) – are celebrated all over the Muslim world, but it's worth seeking out the neighbourhood moulids that commemorate local saints, as these are often more interesting for their popular traditions and eccentricity.

Islamic festivals

Ramadan and other Islamic holidays follow the **lunar calendar**, losing about eleven days a year against the Western (Gregorian) calendar. You can convert dates at ⓦ www.oriold.uzh.ch/static/hegira.html. A day in the Islamic calendar begins at sundown, so Islamic festivals start on the evening before the Western date.

Below is a list of festivals, with their approximate Western calendar dates – the exact dates are set on a monthly basis by the Islamic authorities on the sighting of the new moon. Those marked with a (P) are **public holidays**. For a full list of public holidays, see p.44.

In addition to the celebrations listed below, there are one or two Islamic moulids which are dated according to the solar calendar. The most important of these is the **Moulid of Sidi Ali al-Bayoumi**, held in early October (see p.85).

Moulid al-Nabi (P) Feb 4, 2012; Jan 24, 2013; Jan 13, 2014; Jan 3, 2015; Dec 23, 2015. The prophet's birthday, celebrated in the evening (of the day before) – which is known as *Leylat Mubarak* (Blessed Night) – with spectacular processions, fireworks, and performances by *munshids* (singers of poetry). Midan al-Hussein, the Rifai Mosque and Ezbekiya Gardens are the best spots to catch the celebrations.

Moulid of Al-Hussein March 21, 2012; March 6, 2013; March 5, 2014; Feb 18, 2015. This moulid, celebrating Mohammed's grandson al-Hussein and centred on his mosque (see p.78), gathers pace over a fortnight, culminating in its *leyla kebira* (see box opposite) on the last Wednesday in the Islamic month of Rabi al-Tani. Hussein's Mosque in Khan el-Khalili is surrounded by dozens of *zikrs* and amplified *munshids*, plus all the usual sideshows. The *yom kebir* (see box opposite) is the preceding Tuesday.

Moulid of Saiyida Sukayna April 4, 2012; March 20, 2013; March 12, 2014; March 4, 2015. Held at the Mosque of Saiyida Sukayna on Sharia al-Khalifa (see p.108) culminating on the second Wednesday of the Islamic month of Gumad al-Awwil. A smaller affair than that of her father, al-Hussein, and largely confined to celebrants from the local neighbourhood.

Moulid of Saiyida Ruqayya Held at the Mosque of Saiyida Ruqayya (see p.109) at much the same time as the moulid of Saiyida Ruqayya's niece Saiyida Sukayna

(see above), and just down the road from it. Saiyida Ruqayya's *leyla kebira* is held the day after Saiyida Sukayna's.

Moulid of al-Rifai May 4, 2012; April 26, 2013; April 18, 2014; April 3, 2015. Held at the Al-Rifai Mosque (see p.103) on a Thursday and Friday in the middle of the month of Gumad al-Tani, this moulid is attended by Sufis of the Rifai order from all over Egypt. Those carrying black flags belong to the mainstream Rifaiyah; subsects include the Awlad Ilwan (once famous for thrusting nails into their eyes and swallowing hot coals) and the Sa'adiya (snake charmers, who used to allow their sheikh to ride over them on horseback).

Moulid of Saiyida Nafisa Compared with the Moulid of al-Rifai, Sufi dervishes are less evident at this smaller but equally colourful event, held at the Saiyida Nafisa Mosque (see p.109) at variable dates towards the end of Gumad al-Tani, a week or two after the al-Rifai noulid.

Moulid of Saiyida Zeinab June 19, 2012; June 4, 2013; May 27, 2014; May 19, 2015. Up to three weeks of celebrations lead up to the *yom kebir (*on the last Tuesday of the month of Ragab) and the *leyla kebira* (the subsequent Wednesday evening) at the moulid for Cairo's "patron saint", held at her mosque (see p.107), which attracts up to a million people.

Moulid of Sheikh al-Dashuti June 16, 2012; June 5, 2013; May 25, 2014; May 15, 2015. A small, local moulid, held on 26 Rajab, at the Mosque of Sheikh al-Dashuti, which is on

Ramadan

Ramadan, the ninth month of the Islamic calendar, is a holy month of fasting to commemorate the revelation of the first sura of the Koran to Mohammed in that month.

Throughout the month, most Muslims (which is to say, nearly ninety percent of Cairenes) fast from dawn to sunset, abstaining during those hours from food, drink, smoking and sex. Opening times and transport schedules are affected (almost everything pauses at sunset so people can break the fast), and many cafés and restaurants close for the month.

This can pose problems for travellers, but the celebratory evenings are good times to join in the party atmosphere that takes over the streets at night. At sunset, signalled by the boom of a cannon fired from the Citadel and the lighting of lamps on the minarets, an amazing calm and sense of well-being fall on the streets, as everyone eats *fuul* and *taamiya* and gets down to a night of celebration and entertainment. Throughout the evening, cafés and squares provide venues for live music and singing, while in the poorer quarters, you will often come across *zikrs* and Koranic recitations, which draw crowds to Al-Gumhorriya and Al-Hussein squares in particular.

Non-Muslims are not expected to observe Ramadan, but should be sensitive about not breaking the fast (particularly smoking) in public, but the best way to experience Ramadan is to enter into it. You may not be able to last without an occasional glass of water, and you'll probably breakfast later than sunrise, but it is worth an attempt – and you'll win local people's respect.

Sharia Faggala near Sakakini Palace, about a kilometre northwest of Bab al-Futuh (see map, p.141).

Leylat al-Mirag Night of June 16, 2012; June 5, 2013; May 25, 2014; May 15, 2015. Celebrating a journey Mohammed made on this night from Mecca to Jerusalem on the back of a winged beast called al-Buraq, the event is commemorated with night-long prayers and *zikrs* in the mosques, and outside Abdin Palace.

Moulid of Imam al-Shafi'i June 24, 2012; June 13, 2015; June 2, 2014; May 22, 2015. One of the city's major moulids, held at the Mausoleum of Imam al-Shafi'i in the southern cemetery (see p.110). There's a long run-up over the preceding two or three weeks which gathers momentum as it approaches the *yom kebir*, held around the imam's birthday on 4 Sha'ban, and culminating on the following Wednesday.

Mid-Sha'ban Night of July 4, 2012; June 23, 2013; June 12, 2014; June 1, 2015. This is believed to be the time when Allah determines the fate of every human over the ensuing year. Some people mark it with prayers and fasting, while many visit the Mausoleum of Imam al-Shafi'i (in the aftermath of the moulid just held there, see above) in the hope of gaining *baraka* (the saint's blessing).

Ramadan The Islamic month of fasting (see box above) begins on Aug 1, 2011;

July 20, 2012; July 9, 2013; June 28, 2014; June 18, 2015.

Eid al-Fitr (P) Aug 30, 2011; Aug 19, 2012; Aug 8, 2013; July 28, 2014; July 17, 2015. A festival to mark the end of Ramadan, celebrated with a massive party in which the nighttime festivities of the holy month carry on into the next day and the day after.

Eid al-Adha (P) 10 Dhul Hajja - Nov 6, 2011; Oct 26, 2012; Oct 15, 2013; Oct 4, 2014; Sept 23, 2015. This is the biggest festival in the Muslim calendar and celebrates Abraham's willingness to sacrifice his son to God. The son in question is Ishmael rather than Isaac in the Islamic tradition, Ishmael being the putative ancestor of the Arabs. To celebrate, any family which can afford it will slaughter a sheep for the feast. Eid al-Adha is also the time when pilgrims perform their hajj to Mecca (see p.265).

Ras al-Sana al-Hegira Nov 26, 2011; Nov 15, 2012; Nov 4, 2013; Oct 25, 2014; Oct 14, 2015. The Islamic New Year, a low-key event marked with prayers rather than festivities, though the first ten days of this Islamic month (Moharram) are considered a blessed time.

Ashura Dec 5, 2011; Nov 24, 2012; Nov 13, 2013; Nov 3, 2014; Oct 23, 2015. The anniversary of the martyrdom of al-Hussein (see p.78). Until well into the last century, the eve (*Leylat Ashura*) witnessed passionate displays by Cairo's Shia minority, whose men would lash themselves with chains. Sunni Muslims observe the day itself (*Yom Ashura*) with prayers and charity; the wealthy often feed poor families, serving them personally to demonstrate humility. But aside from *zikrs* (Sufi chanting; see box, p.215) outside Hussein's Mosque, there's little to see.

Nezlet al-Hagg Weeks following Eid al-Adha. The return of the pilgrims from Mecca once occasioned great festivities at Bab al-Futuh (see p.85) when they arrived back towards the end of the Islamic month of Safar (the month after Muharram). Nowadays, pilgrims are fêted individually when they return, their homes festooned with bunting and painted with hajj scenes, but it's still customary to congregate below the Citadel a week later to render thanksgiving *zikrs* in the evening.

Coptic festivals

Cairo's Christian Copts often attend Islamic moulids – and vice versa. **Coptic moulids** share many of the functions of their Islamic counterparts and usually celebrate a saint's name-day. Major Christian festivals, as in Eastern Orthodox churches, follow the old Julian calendar, so **Christmas** is from January 6 to 7, **Epiphany** (Twelfth Night) on January 19, and the **Annunciation** on March 21. Easter and related feast days are dated according to the solar Coptic calendar, and can differ from Orthodox and Western dates by up to a month (see ⓦ www .copticchurch.net/easter.html for dates). These will be celebrated everywhere there's a large Christian community – Old Cairo (see p.115) and Manshiyet Nasser (see p.114), for example, are good places to catch them.

There are two further festivals in Old Cairo: the **Moulid of Mari Girgis** at the Church of St George (April 23, St George's Day) and the **Moulid of the Holy Family** at the Church of St Sergius (June 1). These are celebrated in much the same way as Islamic moulids (see box, p.215), but without the Sufi presence, and Muslims will join their Christian neighbours in the celebrations. In addition, all Egyptians observe the ancient pharaonic-Coptic spring festival known as **Sham al-Nessim** (literally "Sniffing the Breeze"), held the day after Coptic Easter Sunday (April 16, 2012; May 6, 2013; April 21, 2014; April 13, 2015), when families picnic in gardens and cemeteries, eating salted smoked herring, onions and coloured eggs.

Shopping

S hopping in Cairo is a time-consuming process, which suits most locals fine; Cairenes regard it as a social event involving salutations and haggling, affirmations of status and servility. **Department stores** (generally daily 10am–2pm & 6–10pm) have fixed prices, though the system for paying is rather tedious: you begin by selecting the goods you want and get a chit from the salesperson, then pay the cashier before claiming your purchases from a third counter. **Smaller shops**, usually run by the owner, stay open till 9 or 10pm and tend to specialize in certain goods – from groceries to CDs or lingerie. Although most of them have fixed prices, tourists who don't understand Arabic price tags are liable to be overcharged in certain places (especially around the Khan el-Khalili bazaar and Sharia Talaat Harb). If you know the correct price, you can avoid being overcharged by handing over the exact sum (or as near as possible). In **bazaars** and **markets**, bargaining is common, so it's worth taking a look in fixed-price stores before haggling for lower rates at bazaar stalls.

During **Ramadan** (see p.217), **shopping hours** are unpredictable, as some places close all day and operate through the night, while others open later and close earlier. As people splurge after sundown, Cairo's boutiques and bazaars are as busy then as Western stores before Christmas.

Souvenirs, antiques and collectables

Hundreds of shops sell **souvenirs**, mostly kitsch reproductions of pharaonic art – statuettes of deities, busts of Nefertiti, and sheets of **papyrus** painted (but usually

Haggling

Many Westerners are intimidated by **haggling**, but it needn't be an ordeal. Decide before you start what price you want to pay, offer something much lower, and let the shopkeeper argue you up, but not above your maximum price. If you don't reach an agreement, even after a lengthy session, nothing is lost. But if you state a price and the seller agrees, you are obliged to pay – so it is important not to start bidding for something you really don't want, nor to let a price pass your lips if you are not prepared to pay it. Haggling should be good-natured, not acrimonious, even if you know the seller is trying to overcharge you outrageously.

Don't be put off by theatrics on the part of the seller, which are all part of the game. Your own strategems can include stressing any flaws that might reduce the object's value, talking of lower quotes received elsewhere, feigning indifference, or having a friend urge you to leave. Avoid being tricked into raising your bid twice in a row, or admitting your estimation of the object's worth (just reply that you've already made an offer, and wait for their response).

printed, and pretty shoddily) with scenes from tombs; itinerant street vendors often give better deals than shops. You can sometimes see **papyrus-making** demonstrated at Dr Ragab's Pharaonic Village (p.214), one of the few places where you can be sure of buying a genuine, hand-painted article. The term "antique" (*antika*) is loosely applied to anything that appears to be old, from fakes (with spurious certificates of authenticity) to genuine pharaonic, Coptic or Islamic **antiques** (which can't be exported without a licence from the Department of Antiquities); reproductions, and antiques of foreign origin, are a safer bet.

Ahmed el Dabba Sikket al-Badestan, Khan el-Khalili (see map, p.77). Lots of belle époque, fin-de-siècle items including cigarette boxes, crockery and chandeliers, plus Egyptian and Middle Eastern inlaid chests and furniture, and Persian rugs. Daily 2–7pm.

Awlad Azouz Salaam 96 Sharia Ahmed Maher, just west of Bab Zwayla, Islamic Cairo (see map, p.87). Horse equipment including decorative saddles, reins and horsewhips. Mon–Sat 10am–9pm.

Delta Papyrus Center 3rd floor, 21 Sharia al-Guriya (part of Sharia al-Muizz), Islamic Cairo (see map, p.87). If you really want a painted papyrus, the next best thing to Dr Ragab (see p.214) is this shop set up by one of his pupils; they quite frankly tell you, "Come by yourself, not with a guide or you'll pay more". Their papyruses are good, hand-painted with pharaonic, Islamic and Orientalist motifs, most of which are copied from tombs and paintings. Mon–Sat 11am–9pm, Sun 11am–6pm.

Old Shop Sikket al-Badestan, Khan el-Khalili (see map, p.77). Large, dusty and very browsable mix of old and new knick-knacks, glassware, furniture, record players and bric-a-brac. Daily noon–10pm.

Oum el Dounia 1st floor, 3 Sharia Talaat Harb, Downtown (see map, pp.50–51). Excellent shop for books, DVDs (classic Egyptian movies with subtitles), Muski glass (see p.222), Bedouin dresses and all kinds of crafts. Daily 10am–9pm.

Salon el Ferdaos 33 Sharia Abdel Khaliq Sarwat (see map, pp.50–51). A barber with a counter at the front selling old stamps, coins and banknotes. Mon–Sat 10am–8pm.

Tarek Issa 58A Khan el-Khalili Shopping Centre, Sikket al-Badestan, Khan el-Khalili (see map, p.77). Superior bric-a-brac shop selling anything from old postcards and banknotes to vintage Bakelite telephones. Well worth a browse, though prices are high. Daily 1–9pm.

Jewellery

In Islamic Cairo, the **Goldsmiths Bazaar** (Souk es-Sagha) covers Sharia al-Muizz between the Sharia al-Muski and Sultan Qalaoun's complex, with scores more shops tucked away on Sikkets al-Badestan and Khan el-Khalili. There are also good **silversmiths** in the Wikala al-Gawarhergia. Jewellery comes in all kinds of styles, and gold and silver are sold by the gram, with a percentage added on for workmanship. The current ounce price of gold is printed in the daily *Egyptian Gazette*; one troy ounce equals about 31 grams. Barring antiques, all gold work is stamped with Arabic numerals indicating purity: usually 21 carat for Bedouin, Nubian or *fellaheen* jewellery; 18 carat for Middle Eastern and European-style charms and chains. Sterling silver (80 or 92.5 percent) is likewise stamped, while a gold camel sign in the shop window indicates that the items are gold-plated brass. Cartouche pendants (made from all of these metals) can be inscribed with your name in Ancient Egyptian hieroglyphs; as each syllable has its own symbol, longer names cost more to inscribe.

Adly Fam Muski, Khan el-Khalili (see map, p.77). Jeweller selling silver figurines, chunky bangles, silver rings and gold cartouches, but you'll need good bargaining skills. Mon–Sat noon–8pm.

Boutros Trading Sikket Khan el-Khalili ⓦ www .boutrostrading.com (see map, p.77). Old family firm selling silver jewellery and other silver-ware, mostly priced by weight, including rings, bracelets, spoons, plates, bowls

and some lovely little pillboxes inlaid with mother-of-pearl and abalone. Mon–Sat 11am–8.30pm.
Yazejian Opposite the Khan el-Khalili Restaurant on Sikket al-Badestan, Khan el-Khalili (see map, p.77). Reliable shop for gold jewellery, including gold cartouche pendants (see p.155), but expect to pay around £E600–800. Daily 1.30–8.30pm.

Clothes

As a cotton-growing country with a major textiles industry, Egypt is big on retail **clothing**. Smartly dressed Cairenes are forever window-shopping along Talaat Harb and 26th July Street (downtown), Sharia al-Ahram (Heliopolis) and Arab League Street (Mohandiseen), to name only the main clusters of **boutiques** (open till 9/10pm). The cheapest outlets for clothes are the **street vendors** along Sharia al-Muski. The heavy, woven, fringed or tassled black **shawls** worn by working-class women are sold along Muski for upwards of £E50, depending on their size and composition (nylon or silk); check for any snags or tears in the weave.

Cairo is the world centre for bellydancing costumes, and many foreign dancers come here just to buy all the gear. If you're serious, forget the rubbish sold to tourists in the bazaar and go to a specialist such as the two listed below.

Al Trapiche 36 al-Ghuriya Sharia al-Muizz, Islamic Cairo (see map, p.87). The last fez workshop in Cairo, kept alive by sales to five-star hotels and tourists. Various grades of fez are available, the cheapest going for just £E20. The fez, or *tarboush fassi*, originally from Fez in Morocco, was a mark of Ottoman allegiance, which came to represent the secular, Westernized Egyptian, as opposed to the turbaned traditionalist. Under Nasser it fell from fashion, stigmatized as a badge of the old regime. Waiters and entertainers are the main wearers nowadays, and this is where they get them. Mon–Sat 10am–9pm.
Al-Wikalah 73 Sharia Gawhar al-Qayid, just off Sharia al-Muski, Islamic Cairo (see map, p.77). Well-made and good-value bellydancing costumes: a lavishly beaded and sequinned bra and hipband, with a skirt and veil, costs £E1500–3000; the more you buy, the lower the price. There's a woman to help fit you, and anything they don't have in stock they can make within a few days. Mon–Sat 11am–9pm.
Amira el-Khattan 27 Sharia Basra, Mohandiseen ☎02/3749-0322 (see map, pp.132–133). Top-notch, bespoke bellydancing costumes. A full costume will set you back US$300–400. Visits by appointment.
Auf 116–118 Sharia al-Azhar, Islamic Cairo (on the north side by the pedestrian bridge; see map, p.77). Large store stocking a wide assortment of ready-made clothes at reasonable prices, including black dresses with Bedouin-style embroidery, plain white cotton *galabiyyas* and headscarfs, plus cloth by the metre, all at fixed prices. Daily 7am–10pm.
Atlas Silks Sikket al-Badestan, Khan el-Khalili (see map, p.77). Made-to-order garments in handwoven fabrics with intricate braidwork; slippers can be made to order too (allow several weeks; keep all receipts). Their cheapest kaftans and *galabiyyas* are dearer than most garments in other shops, but much higher quality. Mon–Sat 10am–9pm.

Carpets, textiles and furnishings

Pure wool kilims and knotted carpets are an expensive (and bulky) purchase, so serious buyers should read up on the subject before buying one. For cheaper woven **rugs** and **tapestries**, the suburban village of Kerdassa (see p.161) replicates every style imaginable.

The carpet factories around Saqqara – a stopover for many tour groups visiting that ancient site – are all imitations of the famous Wissa Wassef school (see p.161).

Beware of stitched-together seams and gaps in the weave (hold pieces up against the light) and unfast colours – if any colour wipes off on a damp cloth, the dyes will run when the rug is washed.

APE (Association for the Protection of the Environment) Souk el-Fustat, Old Cairo Ⓦ www.ape.org.eg (see map, pp.116–117). NGO working with Cairo's *zabaleen* (see p.113). The shop sells recycled rubbish, turned into bags, soft toys, patchwork quilts and other products. Profits go towards education, healthcare and improving the lives of Cairo's poorest social group. Daily 10am–5pm.

AUEED (Association of Upper Egypt for Education and Development) 26 Souk el-Fustat, Old Cairo (see map, pp.116–117). Embroidery and wood-carvings by women from Upper Egyptian villages, marketed by an NGO. Like other shops in the Souk El-Fustat, everything is sold at fixed prices. Daily 10am–5pm.

Al Khatoun 3 Sharia Mohammed Abdo, Midan al-Aini, Butneya (see map, pp.74–75). An arty boutique selling a range of furnishings and home accessories, decorated with calligraphic and cinematic motifs. Daily 11am–9pm.

Egypt Crafts Centre Apartment 8, 27 Sharia Yehia Ibrahim, Zamalek Ⓦ www.fairtradeegypt .org (see map, pp.132–133). Non-profit organization selling crafts made by people from poor communities across Egypt, with a particularly good line in clothes, textiles and

kilims. Sat–Thurs 9am–8pm, Fri 10am–6pm.

El Assiouty 118 26th July St, Zamalek (entrance in Sharia Aziz Osman; see map, pp.132–133). Upmarket carpet shop founded in 1949, whose customers include embassies and diplomats. All the carpets and kilims are Egyptian (though some incorporate Persian designs), and priced by the square metre. Mon–Sat 10am–9.30pm.

El Sayd Saleh Ragab Tentmakers' Bazaar (next to Mahmoud al-Kurdi mosque), Sharia al-Muizz, Islamic Cairo (see map, p.95). Slightly different from the other shops in the Tentmakers' Bazaar, selling bags, pouches and pocketed wall-hangings made out of *moulid* tent material. No fixed hours, but usually there at least noon–5pm daily.

Nouno Tentmakers' Bazaar (north end, west side), Sharia al-Muizz, Islamic Cairo (see map, p.95). One of a number of shops in the Tentmakers' Bazaar selling appliqué pillowcases (£E20–35), bedspreads (£E700–1500) and wall hangings (£E200–400), a traditional Cairene craft. Much cheaper is the riotously patterned printed tent fabric used for marquees at *moulids* (£E8 per metre). It's worth looking around at what the neighbours have as well, and comparing quality and prices. Daily 10am–10pm.

Glass and ceramics

Hand-blown **Muski glass** is recognizable by its air bubbles and comes in navy blue, turquoise, aquamarine, green and purple. You can watch craftsmen fashioning it into plates, glasses, vases and candle holders (often hand-painted to medieval designs). Elegant handmade **perfume bottles** are another popular souvenir. The cheaper ones (£E5–10) are made of glass and are as fragile as they look, while pyrex versions cost roughly twice as much and are a little sturdier (they should also be noticeably heavier).

El Daoor 14 Haret al-Birkedar, outside Bab al-Futuh (see map, p.81). Outlet that sells Muski glass at very low prices. The factory is just up the street; they usually allow tourists in (Sat–Thurs 9am–3pm) to watch the glass being blown. To find Haret al-Birkedar, come out of Bab al-Futuh from Sharia al-Muizz, cross the main street (Sharia Galal), and it's about 20m to your right. Daily 9am–10pm.

Perfumes Secret Khan el-Khalili, just off Sharia al-Muski in the lane opposite the *Radwan Hotel* (see map, p.77). A good, hassle-free place to buy handmade perfume bottles. Daily 10am–1pm.

Saiyid Abd el-Raouf 8 Sikket Khan el-Khalili (see map, p.77). Main outlet for hand-blown Muski glass in the Khan, selling products from factories on Haret al-Birkedar (see p.85). Daily 11am–9pm.

Spices, herbs, soaps and perfumes

Egypt produces many of the essences used by French perfumiers, sold by the ounce to be diluted 1:9 in alcohol for perfume, 1:20 for eau de toilette and 1:30 for eau de cologne. Local shops will duplicate famous perfumes for you, or you can buy fakes (sometimes unwittingly – always scrutinize labels). Salesmen boasting that their "pure" essence is undiluted by alcohol will omit to mention that oil has been used instead, which is why they rub it into your wrist to remove the sheen.

Spices such as cinnamon (*'irfa*) and sesame (*simsim*) are piled high in bazaars, but what is sold as saffron (*za'faraan*) is actually safflower, which is why it seems ridiculously cheap compared with what you'd pay for the real thing (consisting of fine red strands only, hence the ruse of dying safflower red) back home. You'll also see **dried hibiscus** (*karkaday*); the top grade should consist of whole, healthy-looking flowers.

Abd El Rahman Harraz 1 Midan Bab el-Khalq, Islamic Cairo (see map, pp.74–75). This venerable herbalist stocks everything from rice and beans to elderflower and pink peppercorns, dried lizards and flowers of sulphur. Located 100m from the Islamic Art Museum as you walk towards Bab Zwayla. Mon–Sat 9am–9pm.

Abdul Latif Mahmoud Harraz 39 Sharia Ahmed Maher (see map, pp.74–75). The most famous herbalist in Cairo, run by the same family since 1885, this is a dusty, atmospheric place with drawers and jars full of all sorts of herbs, spices, seeds and resins, from *karkaday* and ginseng to gum arabic and frankincense. It stands opposite a Mamluke fountain, 150m west of Bab Zwayla (see p.92) in the direction of the Islamic Art Museum. Mon–Sat 10am–8pm.

Karama Perfumes 114 Sharia al-Azhar (corner of Sharia al-Muizz), and also two doors north on Sharia al-Muizz, Islamic Cairo (see map, p.77).

Most of the other perfume shops in Cairo buy their essential oils here, and then adulterate them with cooking oil before selling them at inflated prices to tourists. It's worth buying your perfume here even though they, too, may try to overcharge foreigners. Essential oils such as rose or jasmine should cost around 60pt a gram. Mon–Sat 10am–10pm.

Nefertari 26A Sharia el-Gezira el-Wosta, Zamalek (see map, pp.132–133) and 27 Souk el-Fustat, Old Cairo (see map, pp.116–117) Ⓦ www.nefertaribodycare.com. Handmade soaps, organic cotton towels, loofahs, back brushes and massagers, and other bath-time luxuries, all Egyptian made and cruelty-free. Mon–Sat 10am–6pm.

Rageb el Attar 40 & 62 Sharia al-Azhar (see map, pp.74–75). Two branches selling whole and ground spices, joss sticks, and *'amar al-din* (Syrian apricot fruit leather). One is by Midan Ataba, the other by Sharia Bur Said. Mon–Sat 10am–10pm.

Books, maps and newspapers

Almost any type of **Arab literature** is available in Cairo. Aside from magazine and paperback stalls along the downtown thoroughfares, good sources include Dar al-Kitab al-Masri wal-Loubnani, on the first floor of 33 Sharia Qasr el-Nil; and Dar al-Maaref, 27 Sharia Abdel Khaliq Sarwat. Cairo also has plenty of shops selling **books in English**, many of which are published here by the American University in Cairo (AUC; see p.224).

Foreign **newspapers** can be found in bookshops at five-star hotels. The best downtown newsstand is on Sharia Mohammed Mahmoud, opposite the AUC entrance, which carries British dailies (usually one day late), the *International Herald Tribune*, *USA Today* and even sometimes the *New York Times*. It also has a big pile of **secondhand books**, but the best place to look for those is the book market in the northeast corner of Ezbekiya Gardens by Midan Ataba (see map, p.67), many of whose titles are in English. Other places selling secondhand books in English include the newsstand outside the Algerian embassy on Sharia Brazil in Zamalek.

Al-Ahram 165 Sharia Mohammed Farid, Downtown (see map, pp.50–51). An outlet for politics textbooks published by the *Al-Ahram* newspaper (see p.34) and strategic think-tank, which also sells a few maps and has a section of classic English literature downstairs. Daily except Fri 9am–5pm.

Anglo-Egyptian Bookshop 169 Sharia Mohammed Farid, Downtown (see map, pp.50–51). Another academic bookshop, specializing in Arab politics, history and culture, that also has some novels and art books, plus maps. Mon–Sat 9am–8pm.

AUC Bookshop AUC old campus, corner of Sharia Qasr al-Aini with Sharia Sheikh Rihan, Downtown; ⦿www.aucpress.com (see map, pp.50–51). The obvious place to look for AUC publications, with a huge range of stuff on all things Egyptian, plus novels, travel guides and dictionaries. Note that you need your passport to get in. There's another branch at 16 Sharia Mohammed Ibn Thakib, Zamalek (Sat–Thurs 9am–6pm, Fri 1–6pm). Sat–Thurs 9am–6pm.

Buccellati At the northwest corner of the junction of Sharia Qasr el-Nil and Sharia Mohammed Farid, Downtown (see map, pp.50–51). An art shop, but mainly of interest because it sells maps and books such as *Cairo City Key* (see p.42), which other bookshops may not stock. Mon–Sat 11am–8pm.

Dar al-Salam Publishers 120 Sharia al-Azhar, opposite the Al-Ghuri Palace (see map, p.77). Islamic publisher, frequented by lots of earnest young men in beards and crocheted skullcaps, with some books and pamphlets

in English (just next to the door). Among their publications, *Islam and Sex* (£E5) is worth perusing. Daily 9am–8pm.

Diwan 159 26th July St, on the corner of Sharia Ishaq Yaakoub, Zamalek (see map, pp.132–133). Bright, modern shop with a wide selection of books, CDs and DVDs (including a small selection of classic and modern Egyptian films on DVD with subtitles), and a coffee shop. Daily 9am–midnight.

Lehnert & Landrock 44 Sharia Sherif, Downtown (see map, pp.50–51). One of the best places to look for maps of Cairo and Egypt, in addition to postcards and greeting cards. At the back, they also have a section of prints of old photos of Cairo and Egypt. Mon–Sat 10am–7pm.

Romancia Sharia Shagar al-Durr, on the corner of Sharia Ismail Mohammed, Zamalek (see map, pp.132–133). For such a poky little shop this place packs an awful lot in – paperback novels (pulp and literary), coffee-table books on Egypt, maps, British newspapers, magazines such as *Time*, *Newsweek* and *The Economist*, and stationery as well. Sat–Thurs 8am–8pm, Fri 9.30am–8pm.

Shorouk 1 Midan Talaat Harb, Downtown (see map, pp.50–51). Centrally located and very handy for maps, Egyptian novels in translation, books on Egypt, and the latest books in English. Daily 9am–11pm.

Zamalek Bookshop Sharia Shagar al-Durr, Zamalek, opposite *Pub 28* (see map, pp.132–133). A good place to look for AUC publications, Egyptian novels in English translation, books on Egypt and Cairo in general, plus stationery and British newspapers. Mon–Sat 9am–8pm.

Liquor and smokers' supplies

Foreigners are entitled to buy a duty-free allowance of imported **alcohol** within 24 hours of arriving in Egypt; any purchases after that will cost considerably more, even at the duty-free shop at Cairo airport or the (cheaper) Egypt Free Store on Arab League Street in Mohandiseen. You'll need your passport for the transaction – don't let any Egyptians come along to "help" (see p.38). Note that liquor stores are closed during Ramadan (see p.217), though Drinkies still does home deliveries. Refilling stalls all over the city can recharge your lighter for £E1–2, or replace flints for 50pt–£E1.

Anoshka Gift Shop 162 26th July St, by Midan Sphinx, Mohandiseen (see map, pp.132–133). The closest Cairo comes to a "head shop", selling hash-pipes and suchlike. Daily 10am–7pm.

Babik In the passage by 39 Sharia Talaat Harb, Downtown (see map, pp.50–51). Wooden tobacco pipes, lighters and numerous brands of cigarette papers and other smokers' requisites. Mon–Sat 9am–9pm.

Drinkies 41 Sharia Talaat Harb, at 26th July St, Downtown (see map, pp.50–51). Retail outlet for Al Ahram, Egypt's biggest booze company, selling all their brands, including Stella, Sakkara and Heineken, as well as their wines and spirits. Other branches include 162A 26th of July St by Maison Thomas in Zamalek (see map, pp.132–133). Also does home delivery. Daily 8.30am–4am.

Nicolakis corner of Sharia Talaat Harb and Sharia Suq al-Tawfiqiya, Downtown (see map, pp.50–51). A decent selection of wines, sometimes at slightly better prices than Drinkies; also beer, zbiba (Egyptian ouzo) and dodgy lookalike spirits. Daily 7am–10.30pm.

Orphanides 4 Sharia Emad el-Din, and 9 26th July Street (opposite the High Court), Downtown (see map, pp.50–51). Booze store selling beer, wine, zbiba and Egyptian brandy, but mostly of interest for the outrageous lookalike brands of spirit it sells (Chefas Rigal, Gorodons, Finelandia Vodka of Egypt and the like), which you definitely wouldn't want to drink. Daily noon–1am.

Souk Bayn al-Qasrayn Bayn al-Qasrayn (on the east side, just south of the Sabil-Kuttab of Abd al-Rahman; see map, p.81). A covered passage full of shops selling sheesha pipes. Prices range from £E25 to £E150, depending on the size; the ones with stainless steel rather than brass fittings are better made and more durable. Neighbouring shops also sell sheeshas, but are usually slightly pricier. Mon–Sat 11am–11pm.

Musical instruments and recordings

Cairo is a good place to buy **traditional musical instruments** such as the *kanoon* (dulcimer), *oud* (lute), *nai* (flute), *rabab* (viol), *mismare baladi* (oboe), *tabla* (drum), *riq* and *duf* (both tambourines; the latter is played by Sufis). There's a whole slew of instrument shops at the top end of Sharia Qalaa (officially renamed Sharia Mohammed Ali, though everyone uses the old name), off Midan Ataba. Authorized CDs and cassettes (a format still widely used in Egypt) of **Arab music** (and pirated versions) are sold from kiosks where it's quite acceptable (indeed, advisable) to listen before buying. A good selection of Arabic music on CD is available at Diwan bookshop (see opposite).

Beit al-Oud 164 Sharia Qalaa, off Midan Ataba (see map, pp.50–51). The most renowned and well established of the several oud (lute) makers along this stretch of Sharia Qalaa. An oud here will set you back anywhere from £E150 to over ten times that much, depending on quality and decoration. Daily 11am–11pm.

Fel Fel Phone 47 Sharia Khulud (Clot Bey), Downtown (see map, p.68). This retail outlet for the Fel Fel Phone label only sells cassettes (no vinyl or CDs) and isn't set up for browsing, but there's a representative selection in the window. Mon–Sat 11am–10pm.

Gamal el-Sawy Next to Fishawi's, Khan el-Khalili (see map, p.77). Small shop selling bellydancing CDs, DVDs, tapes and videos of the great artistes. Daily 24hr.

Sono Cairo 3 Sharia al-Borsa al-Gadida (an alley between Sharia Talaat Harb and Sharia Qasr el-Nil), Downtown, and in the arcade of the Continental-Savoy Hotel on Midan Opera (see map, pp.50–51). Retail outlets for the Sono Cairo label (including quality recordings of Umm Kalthoum, Abdel Wahaab and orchestral music), plus a good selection of CDs, and DVDs and video CDs of Egyptian and foreign movies (video CDs are much cheaper than DVDs, but don't offer subtitles). Daily 10am–11pm.

Suan Music 168 Sharia Qalaa, off Midan Ataba (see map, pp.50–51). One of the better musical instrument stores, at the top end of Sharia Qalaa. This shop (whose name means "Sound of Music") sells drums, ouds and other instruments. Daily 10am–midnight.

Contemporary art

Contemporary art is not something that most people think of buying when they visit Egypt, but the country has some fine artists. In addition to the galleries listed here, ECIC (see p.41) and Abdel Monem el Sawy Culture Wheel (see p.204) both host exhibitions by up-and-coming new talents.

Espace Karim Francis 1 Sharia el-Sherifein, Downtown ⓦwww.karimfrancis.com (see map, pp.50–51). Not just painting and sculpture, but installations, video art, and anything new and fresh. Tues–Sun 5–8pm.

Mashrabia Gallery 1st floor, 8 Sharia Champollion, Downtown ⓦwww.mashrabia gallery.org (see map, pp.50–51). Well-established gallery exhibiting works by Egypt's top contemporary artists, especially those working with indigenous styles and materials; also shows work by foreign artists. Daily except Fri 11am–8pm.

Safar Khan Gallery 6 Sharia Brazil, Zamalek ⓦwww.safarkhan.com (see map, pp.132–133). Fine modern art by prominent Egyptian artists, with a permanent collection going back to the 1930s as well as regular

exhibitions. Mon–Sat 10am–2pm & 5–9pm.

Townhouse Gallery 10 Sharia Nabrawy, off Sharia Champollion, Downtown ⓦwww .thetownhousegallery.com (see map, pp.50–51). Cairo's leading gallery for contemporary art, with regular exhibitions, a stable of good artists, and a library of art books. Sat–Wed 10am–2pm & 6–9pm, Fri 6–9pm.

Zamalek Art Gallery 2nd floor, 11 Sharia Brazil, Zamalek ⓦwww.zamalekartgallery.com (see map, pp.132–133). One of the best places to see (and buy) work by contemporary Egyptian painters and sculptors. Holds monthly exhibitions, promotes up-and-coming young talent and has a permanent collection of work by pioneering Egyptian artists. Daily except Fri 10am–9pm.

Markets and bazaars

While the crafts **bazaars** of Khan el-Khalili (see p.79) are deservedly famous, Cairo has many other markets that tend to be overlooked by visitors. Central Cairo contains some colourful **food markets** open daily around the clock, located at Bab al-Luq (on the south side of Midan Falaki), Sharia Tawfiqiya (off Midan Orabi), at the eastern end of Sheikh Rihan (by Sharia Bur Said), and the northern end of Sharia Qalaa – all surrounded by 24-hour coffee houses. With the kilo price of goods displayed on stalls (in Arabic numerals), you shouldn't have to bargain unless they try to overcharge. Elsewhere haggling is *de rigueur*.

Secondhand clothing can be found in the **Imam al-Shafi'i Market**, which straggles for 1km along the road leading from Al-Basatin to the Imam's mausoleum in the area of the Southern Cemetery. On Sharia el-Geish near Midan Ataba there's a **paper market** (daily 9am–3pm), selling all types of paper, dyed leather and art materials, and for **fabrics** (from hand-loomed silk to cheap offcuts), **tools** and much else, you can't beat the **Wikalat al-Bulah** (daily 9am–2pm), on Sharia Abu'l'Ila in the Bulaq district.

Cairo's **bird markets** are more for sightseeing than shopping, with aisles of talking birds, tropical fish, cats, dogs and lizards for sale. These outdoor markets (10am–2.30pm) are named after the days on which they're held: Souk al-Ahad (Sun; Giza Station), Souk al-Gom'a (Fri; by the Salah Salem overpass, south of the Citadel, see map, p.104) and Souk Itnayn w Khamis (Mon & Thurs; in the Abu Rish area of Saiyida Zeinab, see map, pp.74–75). In fact, the Souk al-Gom'a is much more than a bird market: it's a huge **flea market** full of junk, bric-a-brac and secondhand goods, where you can find all sorts of treasures, and all sorts of rubbish.

Out of the City

Excursions from Cairo

The Pyramids aren't the only things worth seeing outside Cairo. The **camel market** at **Birqesh**, 35km northwest of the city, is one of the biggest in North Africa – an exotically visceral experience for tourists who attend it. Closer to Cairo, the **Nile Barrages** at **Qanatir** make an enjoyable excursion by river and provide a glimpse of the **Nile Delta**, Egypt's most fertile region. Home to nearly half the country's people and known since ancient times as Lower Egypt, the Delta was the cradle of several dynasties but has few ruins to show for it – unlike Upper Egypt, whose temples are unfortunately too distant for a day's excursion from Cairo.

It is, however, possible to visit **Alexandria**, a vibrant Mediterranean city whose glorious past is embodied in the underwater ruins of Cleopatra's palace and its legendary lighthouse (both viewable by divers), its spooky catacombs and stunning modern library. You can end a great day's sightseeing with a fabulous **seafood** meal and drinks in an atmospheric bar before returning to Cairo – or stay overnight to explore the city more thoroughly.

The Desert Road to Alexandria passes **Wadi Natrun**, synonymous with four **monasteries** whose timeworn chapels and purposeful monks symbolize the enduring faith of Egypt's Coptic Christians, a beleaguered minority in an overwhelmingly Muslim nation (see p.267). Besides its monasteries, Wadi Natrun is also famous for its saline lakes and birdlife, best enjoyed on an overnight stay at an ecolodge.

The Nile Barrages

Roughly 20km north of Cairo, the Nile divides into two great branches that define the Delta. Their flow was once regulated by the **Nile Barrages** at **Qanatir** (whose proper Arabic name, Qanatir al-Qahira, is truncated and pronounced by Cairenes as "Ant-*eer*"), which still stand, but no longer function. Decoratively arched and turreted, these splendid pieces of Victorian civil engineering are surrounded by shady parks and lush islets, with cool breezes offering a respite from the heat of Cairo in the summer – a popular spot for picnics.

The barrages were conceived in 1833 by Mohammed Ali's Belgian hydro-engineer, Moughel Bey – who managed to dissuade Khedive Abbas from using stones from the Giza pyramids to construct them. Consisting of a series of basins and locks on both branches of the river and two side-canals, they allowed over 754,000 acres of Delta farmland to be irrigated year-round, leading to a vast increase in cotton production. However, their faulty construction meant that

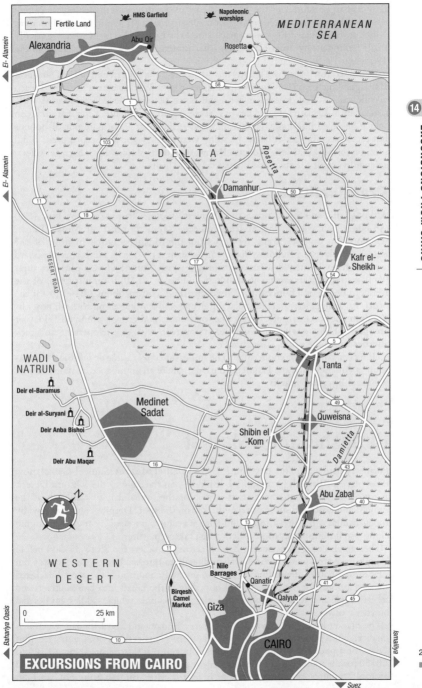

MEDITERRANEAN SEA

HMS Garfield

Napoleonic warships

Alexandria

Abu Qir

Rosetta

Fertile Land

58

1

103

D E L T A

Rosetta

Damanhur

50

11

18

Kafr el-Sheikh

54

17

DESERT ROAD

WADI NATRUN

Deir el-Baramus

12

Tanta

5

Deir al-Suryani

Deir Anba Bishoi

Medinet Sadat

49

Quweisna

Shibin el -Kom

Damietta

Deir Abu Maqar

16

43

Abu Zabal

40

13

11

WESTERN DESERT

Nile Barrages

Qanatir

1

Birqesh Camel Market

Qalyub

41

45

Giza

0   25 km

CAIRO

10

EXCURSIONS FROM CAIRO

El-Alamein

El-Alamein

Bahariya Oasis

Ismailiya

Suez

229

they had to be rebuilt in the 1880s as part of a nationwide hydrological system designed by the head of the Irrigation Department, Sir Colin Scott-Moncrieff, which revolutionized Egyptian agriculture. The Qanatir barrages were eventually made redundant by other barrages further upstream in Upper Egypt, built in the 1900s and 1970s.

Transport from Cairo (see below) terminates near the eastern end of the **Damietta Barrage**, which is 521m long with 71 sluice-gates. Walking across this you'll reach a wide spit of land, immediately to the north of which is a **Presidential Villa** (Istarahah al-Qanatir) where Egypt's **State Yacht** (originally King Farouk's, on which he sailed into exile) is often moored at the quay – both are out-of-bounds but can be seen from a distance. Heading west through the landscaped park, you'll soon reach the 438m-long **Rosetta Barrage**, with 61 sluices. Both barrages offer a splendid view of the river and the verdant Nile Delta.

Practicalities

Although it's quicker to reach the Damietta Barrage from Cairo by **bus** #210 (45-60min; £E3) from the Abdel Mouneem Riyad terminal off Midan Tahrir, it's more fun by river, using services from the **Maspero Dock** in front of the Radio & Television Building in Bulaq (see map, pp.50–51). Here you can board a public **ferry** (hourly 8–10am, returning 2–4pm; 90min; £E5), a **pleasure boat** (daily round trips departing around 9am and noon; £E10) from just north of the Maspero Dock, or a **felucca** (the slowest method, costing about £E100/hr for the boat). Passengers start dancing, playing drums and singing along to Arab pop hits the moment boats cast off. If you like loud music and crowds come on Friday or any public holiday when the barrages are overrun with day-trippers; if not, pick another time when things are quieter.

However you travel, you're sure to be importuned by *calèche* or *tuk-tuk* drivers as soon as you approach the Damietta Barrage, where an abundance of stalls offer all the usual Egyptian **snacks**.

Birqesh Camel Market

Formerly held within the city limits, Cairo's **Camel Market** (Souk el-Gamal) now takes place at **Birqesh** (pronounced "Bir'esh"), on the edge of the Western Desert. A twice-weekly event, the market is not for the squeamish, as traders beat the camels, and goats and sheep are slaughtered on the spot. Despite being hobbled by ropes, camels often break ranks and charge around, pursued by traders swinging clubs – so it's important to stay alert when taking pictures.

The camels come from Sudan, herded across the desert for 25 to 35 days before being trucked to a market near Aswan or directly to Birqesh. Here, a camel costs from £E700 to £E5000, depending on its age, sex and condition – the most knackered are sold as meat for the poor. Camel-boys chivvy the beasts into line as buyers and sellers haggle and vendors hawk camel sticks, rhino-hide whips, saddles, bridles and butcher's knives.

The market lasts from dawn till noon every Friday (and also Monday, when it is smaller), but is busiest between 6am and 8.30am. Tourists pay a £E20 entry fee, plus £E10 for a photo permit. To **get there** from Cairo by taxi costs about £E100 to £E150 for the round trip with an hour spent at the market; the journey takes around 35 to 45 minutes each way. Ask your hotel to write "Birqesh Souk el-Gamal" in

Arabic to show to drivers when opening negotiations, and try to ascertain if they actually know the route, to avoid having to stop for directions in the Delta.

By prior agreement, a taxi from Cairo could drop you at the western end of the Rosetta Barrage on the way back, allowing you to visit the Nile Barrages and return to Cairo by ferry or bus for the return journey to Cairo (see opposite).

The Monasteries of Wadi Natrun

If a visit to Old Cairo (see map, pp.116–117) has left you curious about Coptic Christianity, or if you're keen to experience a taste of the desert, **Wadi Natrun** is the place to go. This quasi-oasis, midway between Cairo and Alexandria, takes its name from deposits of natron salts, the main ingredient in ancient mummifications – but its most enduring legacy is its four Coptic **monasteries**, dating back to the infancy of Christian monasticism.

All have been ruined and rebuilt at least once since their foundation during the fourth century; most of what you see dates from the eighth century onwards. Each has a high wall surrounding its churches, a keep entered via a drawbridge, and a bakery, storerooms and wells, enabling them to withstand repeated sieges by Bedouin raiders. Nineteenth-century visitors described their monks as idle, dirty, bigoted and ignorant – the antithesis of their contemporary equivalents, who are highly educated and forward-looking.

This monastic renaissance was led by Pope Shenouda III, an ex-novice of Wadi Natrun (like previous Coptic popes). Yet despite reclaiming barren land with modern technology, the monasteries are still viewed as interlopers by some. When the monks built fences to protect their farms from criminals escaped from nearby prisons during the 2011 revolution, the army used bulldozers and live rounds against them.

Egypt's Copts revere their monasteries, coming in droves at weekends and on feast days – times to observe the passion and rituals of their faith (if you don't mind crowds). By staying overnight at an ecolodge, you can also explore the lakes beyond the monasteries – a weird terrain of salt-crusts, fossils and rare fauna, that's great for riding or biking.

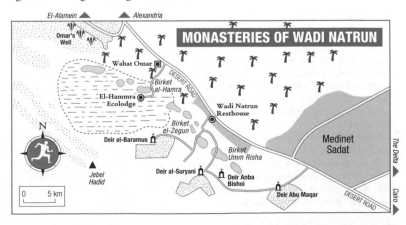

Visiting the monasteries

Wadi Natrun lies off the Desert Road to Alexandria, reached by a turning 105km from Cairo, near the **Wadi Natrun Resthouse** (known to drivers as "Rest"). The monasteries themselves are spread three to ten kilometres apart, linked by spur roads and swathes of irrigated land. Given the distances involved, they're most easily reached from Cairo by **private taxi**: a round trip should cost £E200 to £E300, depending on how many monasteries you visit.

It's cheaper but more time-consuming to catch a West Delta **bus** (hourly 6.30am–6.30pm; 90min) from Cairo Gateway (p.24), a **service taxi** from Aboud terminal (p.25; 60min) or a **microbus** (45min) from Midan el-Rameya near the *Meridien Hotel* in Giza to the Wadi Natrun Resthouse. From there you should be able to hire a local taxi to tour the monasteries for about £E25 an hour, or hope to be offered a lift by the busloads of Coptic pilgrims that come this way on Fridays, Sundays and public holidays.

Opening hours vary from monastery to monastery (see individual accounts for details), as does the extent to which each closes during the Coptic **Lents** or periods of fasting (June 27–July 10; August 7–21; November 25–January 6) – only Deir Anba Bishoi is open every day of the year. You can check if Deir al-Suryani (☎02/591-4448) or Deir el-Baramus (☎02/592-2775) are open by phoning their Cairo "residences". Deir Abu Maqar will only admit those with a letter of introduction from the Coptic Patriarchate (beside the Cathedral of St Mark, 222 Sharia Ramses, Abbassiya; ☎02/282-5374).

En route to Wadi Natrun, you'll see that palm groves, flowers and hothouse vegetables now grow beside the **Desert Road**, after decades of labour which have reclaimed over 25,000 hectares of land from the desert – a project initially financed by the sale of King Farouk's stamp collection in 1953.

At all the monasteries you're expected to dress modestly and remove your shoes at the entrance to churches (whose low doorways compel visitors to humbly stoop upon entry). You'll be assigned a guide who'll explain how Coptic churches are divided into three sections. The *haikal* (sanctuary) containing the altar lies behind the iconostasis, an inlaid screen which you can peer through with his consent. In front of this is the choir, reserved for Coptic Christians, and then the nave, where *catechumens* (would-be converts) stand nearest the choir, and sinners (known as "weepers") at the back.

Staying overnight

It's worth **staying** at Wadi Natrun purely to enjoy the beauty of its saline lakes. The ⚜ *El-Hammra Ecolodge* (☎045/355-0944, ⊕ www.elhammraeco -lodge.com) on the western side of Birket al-Hamra (see p.234) has comfortable rustic-style bungalows with up to three bedrooms, which can be rented for daytime use (£E75 for up to four people) or on a B&B, half- or full-board basis (£E125/£E150/£E175 per person). With a swimming pool, volleyball, trail-bikes, and donkeys and camels for rent you can really make the most of the great outdoors here (see p.235).

A totally different experience – open to men only, with written permission from the Patriarchate in Cairo – is to stay at Deir Anba Bishoi, Deir al-Suryani or Deir al-Baramus monasteries (the latter's lodgings are the least spartan of the three). As other guests are devout pilgrims, you're expected to make at least a token effort to attend prayers and leave a donation in return for the tea and bread that's provided (£E10 per person is appropriate).

Eating

With nowhere to eat in the vicinity of the monasteries, you can either buy **snacks** from stalls by the Resthouse or take a local taxi (£E5) 7km further along the Desert Road to the well-signposted *Wahat Omar* **restaurant**, which serves tasty Egyptian and Italian dishes and has an adjacent mini-zoo to entertain kids. With more time to spare, you can enjoy wholesome meals prepared from organic produce and freshly baked bread at the *El-Hammra Ecolodge* (see opposite).

Deir al-Suryani

The loveliest of the monasteries is **Deir al-Suryani** (Mon–Thurs 9am–6pm, Fri 3–6pm, Sat & Sun only during Lents) – a compact maze of honey-coloured buildings. Its tranquillity belies its fractious origins; the monastery was founded by monks who quit St Bishoi's (see below) in the sixth century after a dispute over the importance of the Virgin Mary. After they returned to the fold, the monastery was purchased for a group of Syrian monks, hence its name – the "Monastery of the Syrians". It was here that the English antiquarian Robert Curzon came searching for ancient manuscripts in the 1830s, and found them lying on the floor "begrimed with dirt". Nowadays, the monastery's antique volumes are lovingly maintained in a modern **library**, including a cache of manuscripts up to 1500 years old. The monastery also boasts the remains of some twelve saints and a lock of hair from Mary Magdalene.

Deir al-Suryani's principal **Church of the Virgin**, built around 980, contains a *haikal* with stucco ornamentation, and a superb, ebony **Door of Prophecies**, inlaid with ivory panels depicting the disciples and the seven epochs of the Christian era. Some lovely Byzantine-style **murals** dating back to the church's foundation have been uncovered by restorers. A dark passageway at the back of the church leads to the **cave** where St Bishoi tied his hair to a chain hanging from the ceiling to prevent himself sleeping for four days, until a vision of Christ appeared. The marble basin in the nave is used by the abbot to wash the feet of twelve monks on Maundy Thursday, emulating Christ's act during Passion Week.

Outside, the large **tamarind tree** enclosed by walls is said to have grown from the staff of St Emphram, who, as a monk, thrust it into the earth after his fellows criticized it as a worldly affectation. As Coptic pope, he established cordial relations with the Fatimid caliph in 997.

Deir Anba Bishoi

Deir Anba Bishoi (daily: summer 7am–8pm; winter 7am–6pm) is the largest of the four monasteries. Over 150 monks and novices live here, and the monastery receives a constant stream of pilgrims. The legend of **St Bishoi** suggests he was one of the earliest monks at Wadi Natrun. An angel told the saint's mother that he was chosen to do God's work even before his birth in 320; two decades later he moved here to study under St Bemoi alongside John "the Short". Since Bishoi's death in 417 his body has reportedly remained uncorrupted within its casket, which is carried in procession around the church every year on July 17. Next to him lies Paul of Tammuh, who was revered for committing suicide seven times.

St Bishoi's is the oldest of the five **churches** in the monastery, its *haikals* dating from the fourth, ninth and tenth centuries. The **keep**, built three to four hundred years later, has chapels at ground level (around the back) and on the second storey, one floor above its drawbridge. There's also a fifth-century **well** where Berber tribesmen washed their swords after massacring the 49 Martyrs of Deir Abu Maqar (see p.234).

The multi-domed building furthest from the entrance is the **residence of Pope Shenouda III**, who uses it as an occasional retreat and sometimes secludes himself here to protest at the mistreatment of Copts.

Deir Abu Maqar

Enclosed by a circular wall ten metres high, **Deir Abu Maqar** requires visitors (with the requisite letter of introduction; see p.232) to pull a bell rope to gain entrance; in times past, two giant millstones stood ready to be rolled across to buttress the door against raiders. Its founder, **St Makarius**, died in 390 "after sixty years of austerities in various deserts", the last twenty of which were spent in a hermit's cell at Wadi Natrun. A rigorous faster, his only indulgence was a raw cabbage leaf for Sunday lunch.

Over the centuries, thirty Coptic patriarchs have come from this monastery; many are buried here, together with the 49 Martyrs killed by Berbers in 444. In 1978, monks discovered what they believed to be the **head of John the Baptist**; however, this is also claimed to be held in Venice, Aleppo and Damascus. Since its nadir in 1969, when only six monks lived here, the monastery has acquired over a hundred brethren, a modern printing press and a farm employing six hundred workers. The monks have mastered pinpoint irrigation systems and bovine embryo transplant technology in an effort to meet their abbot's goal of feeding a thousand laypersons per monk, by creating orchards and dairy farms.

Deir el-Baramus

Deir el-Baramus (Fri–Sun 9am–5pm; closed during Lents) is likewise surrounded by orchards and fields. The monastery was founded by St Makarius in 340, making it the oldest of the four that remain in Wadi Natrun, and has some eighty monks and novices, one of whom will show you around.

Visitors are greeted outside by a picture of St Moses the Black, a Nubian robber who became a monk under the influence of St Isidore. The monastery's name derives from the Coptic *Pe Romios* (House of the Romans), referring to Maximus and Domidus, two sons of the Roman Emperor Valentinus who died from excessive fasting; the younger son was only 19 years old. Their bodies are reputedly buried in a crypt below the **Church of the Virgin**, whose principal altar is only used once a day, since Mary's womb begot but one child. The relics of Moses and Isidore are encased in glass; pilgrims drop petitions into the bier.

Restoration work has revealed layers of medieval **frescoes** in the nave, the western end of which incorporates a fourth-century **pillar** with Syriac inscriptions. It was behind here that St Arsanious prayed with a pebble in his mouth, grudging every word that he spoke (including a statement to that effect). The ninth-century church – whose belfries of unequal height symbolize the respective ages of Maximus and Domidus – shares a vine-laden courtyard with a **keep** and four other churches.

Birket al-Hamra

Out beyond Deir al-Baramus are **salt lakes** rimmed by crusts of **natron**, a mixture of sodium carbonate and sodium bicarbonate, which the Ancient Egyptians used for dehydrating bodies and making glass. **Birket al-Hamra** (Red Lake) is magenta-hued and highly saline, with a "miraculous" sweetwater **spring** in the middle – Copts believe that the Virgin Mary quenched her thirst here during the Holy Family's sojourn in Egypt. You can wade out to the spring (enclosed by an iron well) and taste it for yourself; the mud on the lake-bed is reputedly good for various afflictions.

The local *El-Hammra Ecolodge* (see p.232) can arrange **trail-biking** (free), camel (£E100/hr) and donkey (£E50/hr) **rides**, and **birdwatching** in the vicinity (look out for spur-winged plovers, crested larks, jacksnipes and sandpipers). The lakes harbour Egypt's last surviving wild **papyrus**, a dwarf subspecies of the plant that once flourished throughout the Nile Valley, but gradually became extinct; the last large papyrus (which could reach 6m) was found in the Delta in the mid-nineteenth century. Today it exists only on plantations, thanks to Dr Ragab (see p.214), who rediscovered the lost technique of making papyrus paper. There are also the thick fallen trunks of **petrified mangroves** from the Eocene Epoch, forty million years ago, when the environment resembled how the Florida Everglades are today.

Alexandria

Alexandria was Egypt's capital for almost a thousand years before fading into oblivion, only to be reborn in the modern age as a Europeanized metropolis. Since this was built atop the ruins of Ancient Alexandria, far more antiquities have been lost than found – but each year sees a Greek statue or Roman mosaic unearthed on construction sites or on the seabed, where the ruins of Cleopatra's palace and the city's ancient lighthouse can be seen by divers.

Another stratum of Alexandria's past is its colonial heritage: patisseries, hotels and shops whose names, sepia photographs and other bric-a-brac of a bygone Levantine world give Alexandria a strong whiff of nostalgia. Yet Alex is no less febrile than Cairo and has its own dynamic, with a youth culture that made its voice heard in the 2011 revolution. In Arabic the city is called Al-Iskandariya, after

Alexandria in literature

With relatively few monuments to show for its ancient lineage, Alexandria's past is found in its faded coffee houses, minutiae such as old nameplates, the reminiscences of aged Arabs and Greeks, and in its **literary dimension**. The English novelist **E.M. Forster** (author of *A Room with a View* and *A Passage to India*) wrote the first guidebook to Alexandria (where he had his first sexual relationship, with an Egyptian tram conductor, while serving as a nurse during World War I), but reckoned that the best thing he did was to publicize the work of the Alexandrian Greek poet **Constantine Cavafy** – odes to nostalgia, excess, loss and futility.

Cavafy was the model for Balthazar in *The Alexandria Quartet*, written by a deracinated Briton **Lawrence Durrell** (1912–1990). This verbose tetralogy of novels relating the same events from the perspective of four characters living out Ancient Greek myths in Alexandria before, during and after World War II, was widely acclaimed in the 1960s for its "relativity in space and time", but is little read today. Durrell based the character Justine on his Alexandrian Jewish lover Eve Cohen, a survivor of childhood incest. The plot twist that once shocked readers seemed far more sinister after their real-life daughter Sappho hanged herself in 1985, leaving diaries hinting at incest with Durrell, blighting his posthumous reputation.

Durrell had little time for Egyptians and his novels are not well regarded in Egypt, where people prefer the late Nobel laureate **Naguib Mahfouz**'s *Miramar* as an evocation of post-colonial Alexandria from an Egyptian standpoint.

its founder Alexander the Great (who had conquered most of the known world by the age of thirty-three).

Its magnificent modern library – a tribute to the ancient Bibliotheca Alexandrina – and the treasures of the Alexandria National Museum head the roll-call of attractions, followed closely by the Catacombs of Kom es-Shogaffa, the underwater ruins of Cleopatra's palace and the wrecks of Napoleonic warships (the last two only accessible to divers). Add to this the city's patisseries, seafood restaurants and bars, and you've got more than enough for a full day's excursion or an overnight stay. If you're hoping to dive here, make sure you book a few days beforehand (see box on p.251 for details).

Some history

When **Alexander the Great** wrested Egypt from the Persian Empire in 332 BC, he decided against Memphis, the ancient capital, in favour of building a new city linked by sea to his Macedonian homeland, choosing a site where two limestone spurs formed a natural harbour. After his belated burial in Egypt (see box, p.243), one of his Macedonian generals took power, adopting the title Ptolemy I and founding a dynasty (323–30 BC).

The **Ptolemies** made Alexandria an intellectual powerhouse. Its awesome lighthouse, the **Pharos**, was rivalled in fame only by the city's library, the **Bibliotheca Alexandrina**, and its cult of **Serapis** (a fusion of Ancient Egyptian and Greek gods). The last of the dynasty was the legendary **Cleopatra VII** (51–30 BC), who committed suicide with her lover Mark Antony to avoid the humiliation of being captured by the Roman general Octavian. Under **Roman rule** (30 BC–313 AD), Alexandria became an early beachhead of **Christianity**; after Emperor Constantine made it the state religion the city's Coptic patriarch and his monks waged war against paganism, sacking the Serapis Temple and library in 391.

Following the Arab conquest in 642, Alexandria was neglected, declining over the next millennium to a mere fishing village. Its **revival** sprang from Mohammed Ali's desire to make Egypt a commercial and maritime power; with the completion of a canal linking it to the Nile, European merchants flocked to do business here. Under the Khedives, **foreigners** enjoyed a *belle époque* that even nationalist revolts and world wars only briefly disturbed. The **revolution** that forced King Farouk to sail into exile (see p.262) didn't seriously affect them until the Suez Crisis of 1956, following which Nasser expelled all French and British citizens, and 100,000 Greeks, Jews and others emigrated. Street names and businesses were Egyptianized, and the custom of moving the seat of government to Alexandria during the hot summer months was ended.

Alexandrians whose families have lived here for generations remain proud of their multi-ethnic heritage and their openness to new ideas and influences. But their **cosmopolitanism** has been challenged by waves of settlers from the Delta, where Copts are frequently attacked by their Muslim neighbours for daring to build churches. The Muslim Brotherhood has been empowered by – and stoked – **sectarian bigotry**, making Alexandria a cockpit for competing ideologies.

In January 2011 a car bomb killed twenty-one Copts celebrating New Year Mass at the Two Saints Church in the Sidi Bishr district. Enraged Copts attacked a nearby mosque after triumphant cries of "God is great" came from the surrounding Muslim neighbourhood. Yet barely a month later Egypt was swept by a revolution where protestors asserted their unity by praying together beneath the cross and the crescent and chanting "Muslims and Christians are one hand".

However things turn out, Alexandria is sure to remain Egypt's "alternative capital", culturally, socially and politically - sometimes in sync with Cairo, sometimes making waves on its own.

Arrival

The fastest, most comfortable way of reaching Alex is **by train** from Ramses Station: Turbini and Spanish trains take two hours and thirty minutes, running non-stop or halting only at Tanta. All are air-conditioned and require seat reservations, unlike other trains, which can take over four hours. All trains terminate at **Masr Station,** from which you can walk to downtown Midan Sa'ad Zaghloul in ten to fifteen minutes, by following Sharia Nabi Daniel (see map, pp.238–239).

Arriving by other forms of public transport means ending up at the **Moharrem Bey Terminal** on Alexandria's outskirts, from which a taxi (£E15) or a minibus (£E1.25) to the Tomb of the Unknown Soldier, by the Corniche, will take fifteen to twenty minutes. The journey to Alex itself takes longer by road: three hours by Superjet bus from outside the *Ramses Hilton* in central Cairo or a less comfortable West Delta bus from Cairo Gateway in Bulaq (see map, pp.50–51), both departing hourly.

Alex can also be reached by **service taxis**, which cluster outside Ramses Station and the Aboud Terminal in Cairo, their drivers bawling "Iskandariya! Iskandariya!". West Delta buses and service taxis offer two routes, travelling by the Desert Road past the turn-off for Wadi Natrun (see p.232), or by the congested Delta Road, which is much slower, though the distance is roughly similar (about 225km).

Orientation, information and tours

Alexandria runs along the Mediterranean for 20km without ever venturing more than 8km inland – a true waterfront city. Its great Corniche sweeps around the Eastern Harbour and along the coast past a string of city beaches to **Montazah**, burning out before the final beach at **Abu Qir**. Most foreign tourists frequent the downtown quarter of **El-Manshiya**, where many of restaurants and hotels are within a few blocks either side, or inland, of **Midan Sa'ad Zaghloul**. Our map covers the downtown area, plus the peninsula leading to Fort Qaitbey in the Eastern Harbour.

The main **tourist office** (daily 8.30am–6pm; Ramadan 9am–4pm; ☏03/485-1556), off the southwest corner of Midan Sa'ad Zaghloul is quite helpful; the branch at Masr Station (daily 8.30am–6pm; ☏03/392-5985) less so. Details of **what's on** appear in two free monthly publications: *Alex Times* magazine (available at *Al-Ahram* newspaper stands and the *Fish Market* restaurant) and the booklet *Alex Agenda* (at top hotels).

If you want a personal **guide**, contact Zahraa Adel Awad (☏010 272-4324; ⓔegypt_tourguide@hotmail.com), whose encyclopedic knowledge of Alex informs her **walking tours**, which cost from $40 to $60 depending on the size of the group and the tour's duration (normally 4hr). Her Roots Tour – aimed at people with ancestral ties to the city – can be tailored to personal wishes (such as finding the house where your grandparents once lived), while other tours are devoted to Durrell, Cavafy and E.M. Forster, or Italianate and Art Deco architecture.

City transport

Downtown is compact enough to **walk** around, and strolling along the Corniche an experience not to be missed. It's worth crossing four lanes of traffic to reach the far side of Sharia 26th July, where fishermen cast their rods and couples hold hands atop the vast breakwaters. From Midan Sa'ad Zaghloul you can walk to the library (15min) or around the Eastern Harbour to Fort Qaitbey (35–50min). The Catacombs, the Royal Jewellery Museum and Montazah can only be reached by public transport or taxi.

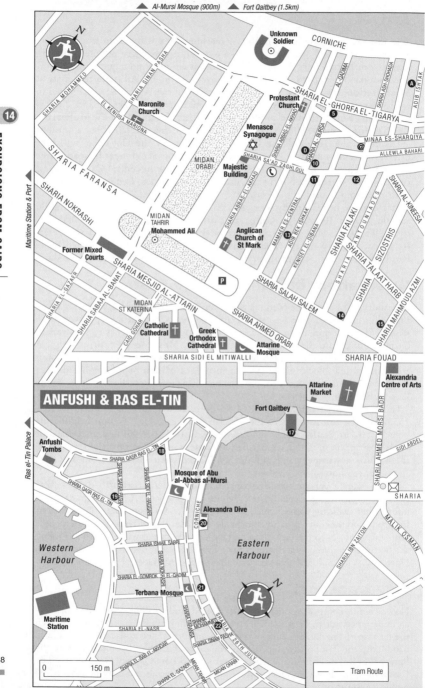

▲ Al-Mursi Mosque (900m)   ▲ Fort Qaitbey (1.5km)

CORNICHE

Unknown Soldier

SHARIA EL-GHORFA EL-TIGARYA

Protestant Church

MINAA ES-SHARQIYA

Maronite Church

ALLEWLA BAHARI

Menasce Synagogue

MIDAN ORABI

Majestic Building

Anglican Church of St Mark

MIDAN TAHRIR

Mohammed Ali

Former Mixed Courts

SHARIA MESJID AL-ATTARIN

SHARIA SALAH SALEM

SHARIA AHMED ORABI

MIDAN ST KATERINA

Catholic Cathedral

Greek Orthodox Cathedral

Attarine Mosque

SHARIA SIDI EL MITIWALLI

SHARIA FOUAD

Attarine Market

Alexandria Centre of Arts

ANFUSHI & RAS EL-TIN

Fort Qaitbey

Anfushi Tombs

SHARIA QASR RAS EL-TIN

Mosque of Abu al-Abbas al-Mursi

SHARIA QASR RAS EL-TIN

Alexandra Dive

Western Harbour

Eastern Harbour

Terbana Mosque

Maritime Station

SHARIA EL-NASR

SHARIA EL BAB EL-AKHDAR

0   150 m

— — — Tram Route

▼ Downtown Alexandria

238

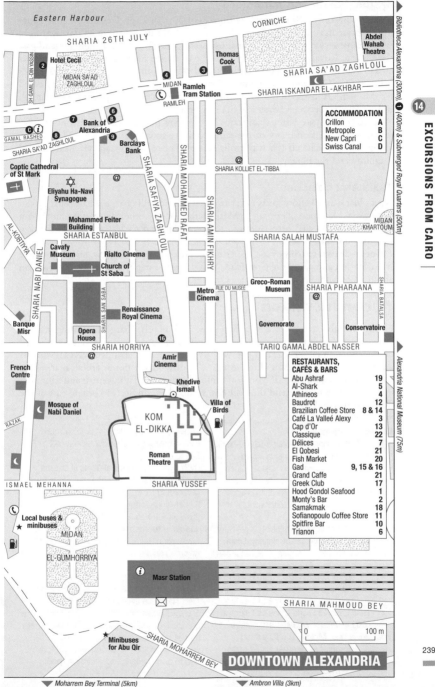

Eastern Harbour

CORNICHE

Bibliotheca Alexandrina (300m) ● (400m) & Submerged Royal Quarters (500m)

SHARIA 26TH JULY

Abdel
Wahab
Theatre

Hotel Cecil

MIDAN SA'AD
ZAGHLOUL

Thomas
Cook

SHARIA SA'AD ZAGHLOUL

MIDAN
RAMLEH

Ramleh
Tram Station

SHARIA ISKANDAR EL-AKHBAR

Bank of
Alexandria

SHARIA SA'AD ZAGHLOUL

Barclays
Bank

SHARIA KOLLIET EL-TIBBA

Coptic Cathedral
of St Mark

Eliyahu Ha-Navi
Synagogue

Mohammed Feiter
Building

SHARIA ESTANBUL

SHARIA SALAH MUSTAFA

MIDAN
KHARTOUM

Cavafy
Museum

Rialto Cinema

Church of
St Saba

Metro
Cinema

RUE DU MUSEE

Greco-Roman
Museum

SHARIA PHARAANA

Renaissance
Royal Cinema

Opera
House

SHARIA HORRIYA

Governorate

Conservatoire

TARIQ GAMAL ABDEL NASSER

Banque
Misr

Alexandria National Museum (75m)

ACCOMMODATION
Crillon	A
Metropole	B
New Capri	C
Swiss Canal	D

French
Centre

Amir
Cinema

Khedive
Ismail

Mosque of
Nabi Daniel

KOM
EL-DIKKA

Villa of
Birds

Roman
Theatre

ISMAEL MEHANNA

SHARIA YUSSEF

Local buses &
minibuses

MIDAN

EL-GUMHORRIYA

Masr Station

SHARIA MAHMOUD BEY

0   100 m

Minibuses
for Abu Qir

SHARIA MOHARREM BEY

DOWNTOWN ALEXANDRIA

239

**RESTAURANTS,
CAFÉS & BARS**
Abu Ashraf	19
Al-Shark	5
Athineos	4
Baudrot	12
Brazilian Coffee Store	8 & 14
Café La Valleé Alexy	3
Cap d'Or	13
Classique	22
Délices	7
El Qobesi	21
Fish Market	20
Gad	9, 15 & 16
Grand Caffe	21
Greek Club	17
Hood Gondol Seafood	1
Monty's Bar	2
Samakmak	18
Sofianopoulo Coffee Store	11
Spitfire Bar	10
Trianon	6

Moharrem Bey Terminal (5km)

Ambron Villa (3km)

Trams, buses and minibuses

Trams run from 5.30am to 1am, with fares of 50pt or 75pt. Destinations and route numbers are in Arabic only, so you'll need to ask for directions at **Midan Ramleh**, where most services originate. The most useful are #1 and #2 (running inland past the library, Royal Jewellery Museum and Mahmoud Said Museum), #15 (to Ras el-Tin via Anfushi, near Fort Qaitbey), and #16 (from Midan Orabi to Pompey's Pillar and the Catacombs). On trams with three carriages, the middle one is reserved for women. Over summer, a 1936-vintage wooden tram (£E1) runs from Ramleh out to Zizinia (between Glym and Stanley beach).

Buses (£E1–2) are faster than trams but grossly overcrowded; **minibuses** offer seating-only rides on many of the same routes – most usefully the #11, running along the Corniche all the way from Ras el-Tin to Montazah, via Midan Sa'ad Zaghloul and the library.

Taxis and calèches

Alex's black-and-yellow **taxis** never use meters and will charge whatever they can get away with (especially going to Masr Station or any other departure point). You should pay about £E5 for a ride across downtown, and £E30 for a trip all the way east to Montazah Beach.

Horse–drawn carriages solicit passengers with cries of *"calèche, calèche"* outside Masr Station and along the Corniche. You'll have to negotiate a price – reckon on about £E50 an hour.

Accommodation

Unsurprisingly, a sea view is a big plus, and hotels charge accordingly. One drawback of hotels near the seafront that only later becomes apparent is **tram noise** – basically, you either learn to live with it or move further inland. **Reservations** are essential in high season (June–Aug). The downtown hotels are all marked on the map on pp.238–239. If you don't mind being out of the centre and money is no object, we'd recommend the *Four Seasons* hotel at San Stefano beach, east of the downtown area.

Downtown

Crillon 5 Sharia Adib Ishtak ☎03/480-0330. This atmospheric prewar pension has a lobby full of stuffed birds, and vast Art Deco rooms with sea-view balconies on the third floor (nicer than the smaller en-suite ones upstairs). Half-board is obligatory in high season. B&B £E100.

Metropole 52 Sharia Sa'ad Zaghloul ☎03/486-1467, ⊛www.paradiseinnegypt.com. Just off Ramleh, this ornate 1900s hotel has bags of character. All rooms have a/c, while the plush suites ($165) are furnished with antiques and have jacuzzis. It's worth paying $40 extra for a sea view. B&B $119.

New Capri 23 Sharia Minaa es-Sharqiya ☎03/480-9310, ℗03/480-9703. With great views over Midan Sa'ad Zaghloul, billiards, a library, free internet and a buffet breakfast, this renovated 1930s pension is excellent value, sited on the eighth floor above the tourist office. Ask for a room with a balcony and Corniche view (£E175). B&B £E136.

Swiss Canal 14 Sharia al-Bursa al-Qadima ☎03/480-8373. Named after the Suez Canal (according its Egyptian pronunciation), this invitingly bright hotel (painted pink throughout) has an Art Deco foyer and spacious rooms that make it a fine low-budget alternative to the *Crillon* or *New Capri*. En-suite rooms from £E90.

Outside the centre

Four Seasons San Stefano, 20min by taxi from the centre ☎03/581-8000, ⊛www.fourseasons.com/alexandria. Perfect for pampering, this marbled five-star behemoth has all mod-cons and superb balcony views, in addition to a wellness spa, private beach and marina, and an infinity pool overlooking the Mediterranean. $500.

The pharaohs

The pharaohs of Ancient Egypt were absolute monarchs with the status of demi-gods. Revered as the sons of the goddess Hathor, the incarnation of Horus in life and Osiris in death, they embodied the righteous order of civilization. Their incestuous marriages and gargantuan funerary monuments were seen as a bridge between earthly life and the gods that would endure forever. The title pharaoh originally meant "great house" and referred to the king's palace, only becoming a form of address in the New Kingdom.

Pharaonic funeral motifs, Kom es-Shogaffa ▲

Cobra frieze, Saqqara ▲
Mummy of Merenre, Imhotep Museum, Saqqara ▼

Model of Pharaonic crown ▼

Ruler of the Two Lands

Much of the symbolism of kingship referred to the union of the Two Lands, the Nile Valley (Upper Egypt) and the Delta (Lower Egypt). The establishment of this union (c.3100 BC) marked the onset of the Old Kingdom, which lasted for a thousand years. Its dissolution was followed by decades of disorder until the Two Lands were reunited under the Middle Kingdom (c.2000 BC) – a cycle repeated under the New Kingdom and again during the Late Period (c.700 BC). Each Land had its own deity – the Delta had Wadjet, the cobra-goddess, and the Valley Nekhbet, the vulture-goddess. With union, their images were combined with the sun-disc of the god Re to form the winged sun-disc, a symbol which often appeared on royal jewellery and other accoutrements.

At ceremonies, the pharaoh customarily wore first the White Crown of Upper Egypt and then the Red Crown of Lower Egypt, which by the time of the New Kingdom (c.1570 BC) were often subsumed into the Combined Crown. All featured the uraeus or fire-spitting cobra, believed to be the guardian of kings. Additional symbols of authority included the crook and the flail, often shown crossed over the chest on pharaonic statues. Another ubiquitous motif was the ankh, symbolizing breath or life, which pharaohs are often depicted receiving from gods.

The archetypal symbol of kingship was the cartouche, an oval formed by a loop of rope, enclosing the hieroglyphs of the pharaoh's nomen (corresponding to a family name such as Ramses or Seti, by which they are known for posterity) and prenomen (one of four titles adopted on accession to the throne).

Life and death

The pharaoh's lifestyle was luxurious and ritualistic. His clothes, perfumes and ablutions aspired to a state of purity that enabled him to commune with the gods in the sanctuaries of cult temples, or participate in festivals celebrating the "marriage" of gods and goddesses – when the king did his bit to ensure Egypt's fertility by ejaculating into the Nile.

Polygamy and incest were an accepted part of royal life. A king married his sister and made her his Great Wife, or ranking queen, but took other wives to ensure heirs and often maintained a harem, too. Pharaohs designated their own successor from a brood of sons (Ramses II sired over one hundred), sometimes making them co-ruler to assure an uncontested succession. If not, a pharaoh's demise might precipitate a power struggle – particularly if the heir-apparent was too young to govern, in which case a regent was required.

This led occasionally to queens ruling Egypt – Khentkawes during the Old Kingdom and Hatshepsut during the New Kingdom – or resulted in regents from outside the royal line becoming pharaohs, such as vizier Ay and general Horemheb, who succeeded the boy-king Tutankhamun at the end of the XVIII Dynasty. By the Late Period, conspiracies to usurp the throne had become familiar enough to rate a section in the text on statecraft known as the *Instruction of Ankhsheshonqy*.

In death, pharaohs were mummified and buried with their treasures, to enjoy eternal life so long as their *ka* (life-force) was sustained by offerings. The pyramids of the Old and Middle Kingdoms proved vulnerable to ancient looters, so the rulers of the New Kingdom opted for hidden

▲ Statue of Ramses II, Egyptian Museum

▼ Tutankhamun's funerary mask

Bas-reliefs on mastaba tombs ▲

Snofru's Red Pyramid ▲

Akhenaten colossus, Egyptian Museum ▼

View over the Giza pyramids ▼

tombs in the Valley of the Kings – but only Tutankhamun's remained unplundered.

After the desecration of his mummy, the worst fate was the **erasure** of a pharaoh's name from his monuments, which was believed to curse the dead – a fate that befell the "heretic pharaoh" Akhenaten (see p.58) after the restoration of the old religion, and to Hatshepsut after her nephew Tuthmosis III finally gained power (see p.57).

Tellingly, both were omitted from the List of Kings in the Temple of Seti I at Abydos. Naming 34 rulers in (roughly) chronological order – from Zoser to Seti I – the list helped scholars create a chronology of Ancient Egyptian history, whose pharaonic era alone spanned thirty centuries.

Pharaonic highlights

▶▶ **Akhenaten** Four colossi suggestive of a primeval earth-goddess in the Egyptian Museum's Amarna Gallery commemorate the "heretic pharaoh" of the XVIII Dynasty. See p.59

▶▶ **Cheops** The Great Pyramid of Giza is synonymous with this IV Dynasty ruler, known to the Ancient Egyptians as Khufu. See p.154

▶▶ **Chephren** Builder of the Second Pyramid at Giza, whose valley temple yielded a superb diorite statue of Chephren (exhibited in the Egyptian Museum). See p.56

▶▶ **Snofru** No fewer than three pyramids are attributed to this IV Dynasty pharaoh – the Collapsed Pyramid at Maidum and the Bent and Red pyramids at Dahshur. See p.176

▶▶ **Tutankhamun** Tut's haunting funerary mask, gilded furniture and chariots are only some of his 1700 artefacts filling a dozen rooms in the Egyptian Museum. See p.60

▶▶ **Zoser** This III Dynasty ruler's step pyramid at Saqqara inaugurated the Pyramid Age, prefiguring the "true" pyramids of the following dynasty. See p.165

The City

The seafront library, the Alexandria National Museum and the Roman Theatre are all on the periphery of **downtown**. This has its own appeal, with atmospheric patisseries, backstreet bars and souks. With a full day to spare, you could also visit Fort Qaitbey or Pompey's Pillar and the Catacombs of Kom es-Shoqafa. By staying overnight, you could spend an extra day diving wrecks and ruins, or chilling out at Montazah. To encompass all these possibilities, our account starts with downtown and works outwards from there in several directions.

Around Midan Sa'ad Zaghloul

With its windblown palm trees and tatty lawns, **Midan Sa'ad Zaghloul** seems an ephemeral locus of history. Named after the nationalist leader (see p.72) whose **statue** gazes towards Malta – where he was exiled by the British, returning to a hero's welcome after nationwide protests – the square bears no trace of its ancient glories.

Until the 1870s, visitors could still admire **Cleopatra's Needles**, two lofty obelisks first raised at Heliopolis (see p.147) that were later taken to Alexandria to ennoble the approach to the Caesareum (see below), and finally transplanted on London's Embankment and in New York's Central Park. Their popular name is a misnomer, as they were carved fourteen centuries before Cleopatra's reign and only moved to Alexandria fifteen years after her death.

Today, the square's dominant feature is the pseudo-Moorish **Hotel Cecil**, where British Intelligence hatched the deception plan for the decisive third battle of El-Alamein (Oct–Nov 1942) from a suite on the first floor. Fought barely two hours' drive from Alex, it marked the turning point of Britain's fortunes in World War II and the end of Nazi Germany's attempts to seize Egypt.

Nearby are several **patisseries** synonymous with social life in colonial times. *Délices*, established in 1922, is a tearoom whose French name belies the fact that it was originally owned by Greeks, like the *Trianon* just behind the site of Cleopatra's Needles, and *Athineos* on nearby Midan Ramleh (see p.252–253 for reviews of these and other establishments).

Along Sharia Nabi Daniel

Starting as an inconspicuous backstreet near *Délices*, **Sharia Nabi Daniel** grows wider as it runs south along the route of the ancient **Street of the Soma**. Paved in marble and flanked by marble colonnades, this dazzled the Arabs in 641 even though its finest buildings had already fallen. Before its destruction by feuding Christians in the fourth century, the north end of the street was crowned by the **Caesareum**, a temple begun by Cleopatra for Antony, which Octavian completed and dedicated to himself; the female philosopher and mathematician Hypatia was cut to shreds here by a Christian mob in 415.

A short way down Nabi Daniel, high wrought-iron gates and police guard the **Eliyahu Ha-Navi Synagogue** (admission may be possible from 9am–2pm except on Fri & Sat; bring your passport and pretend to be Jewish if necessary), entered via an alley to the north. Built in 1885 by Baron Jacques de Menasce, its Italianate interior features stained-glass windows, giant menorahs and a collection of Torah scrolls from bygone neighbourhood synagogues that once served a Jewish community of seventy thousand, tracing its ancestry back to the city's foundation; only 26 Jews remain in the city today.

The synagogue still owns most of the premises along the eastern side of Nabi Daniel; those opposite belong to the **Coptic Cathedral of St Mark**, entered from Sharia al-Kineesa al-Kobtiyya. The cathedral is named after the Apostle martyred by pagans in 67 AD; dragged by horses through the streets of the city, his remains were held by a local church until 828, when the Venetians smuggled the body out of Muslim-ruled Alexandria in a barrel of salt pork, to rebury it at the Basilica di San Marco (see box opposite).

The Cavafy Museum

Anyone seeking a trace of bygone cosmopolitanism should wander off Nabi Daniel onto Sharia Estanbul, where the flamboyant **Mohammed Feiter Building**, emblazoned with majolica panels and monogrammed coronets, serves as a landmark for locating a narrow lane across the road, called Sharia Sharm el-Sheikh. Near the far end of this, at no. 4, a tiny sign in Greek identifies the **Cavafy Museum** (Tues–Sun 10am–3pm; £E15), which evocatively recreates the flat where the celebrated poet **Constantine Cavafy** (1863–1933) lived at the zenith of his talent above a bordello and around the corner from the Greek Orthodox Church of St Saba. "Where could I live better?" he asked. "Below, the brothel caters for the flesh. And there is the church which forgives sin. And there is the hospital where we die." Cavafy died, as he had predicted, in St Saba's hospice and was buried in the Greek Cemetery at Shatby, where his grave bears the simple epitaph, *Poet*.

The museum's custodian relates how "Cavafis" (as he's called in Arabic) had nine brothers, loved candlelight, and died of throat cancer from drinking – but draws a veil over his homosexuality ("He never married"). Visitors can see Cavafy's brass bed, icons, books and death mask, and the modest desk where he wrote *The Barbarians*, *Ithaca*, and his elegiac *The City*.

St Saba and the Opera House

Across the road stands the Greek Orthodox **Church of St Saba**, built over an ancient temple of Apollo. The seventeenth-century church contains a marble columnar tablet on which St Catherine is said to have been beheaded, a giant bronze bell, and relics of Patriarch Petros VII, killed in a helicopter crash on Mount Athos in 2004.

From here, follow Sharia San Saba southwards past Alexandria's **Opera House**, also known as the **Sayed Darwish Theatre**. A splendid Beaux Arts edifice, it fuses elements of the Odéon Théâtre in Paris and the Vienna Opera House. While in the vicinity, you could also check out the **Banque Misr** on Sharia Talaat Harb, occupying a copy of the Palazzo Farnese in Rome, built for an Italian bank by the Jewish fascist Giuseppe Loria (who also designed the *Hotel Cecil*, see p.241); its lavish Moorish-Gothic interior is worth seeing.

On to Midan el-Gumhorriya

The traffic-clogged **intersection** of Nabi Daniel, Horriya and Fouad streets is roughly located on the site of Ancient Alexandria's main crossroads. From here its east–west axis, the **Canopic Way**, extended as far as the eastern Gate of the Sun where visitors entered the city.

Many scholars believe that this crossroads was the site of the **Mouseion** (Shrine of the Muses), an institution from which our word "museum" derives. Founded by Ptolemy I (323–282 BC), it incorporated lecture halls, laboratories, observatories, and the legendary "Mother" Library (see p.247). According to ancient chronicles, the Mouseion faced the **Soma** (meaning "dead body") where Alexander the Great was buried (see box opposite) – but their descriptions leave room for doubt as to where exactly these buildings were located – and all have long since disappeared.

Further south you'll see the recessed gateway of the medieval **Mosque of Nabi Daniel** that lends its name to the street. The sanctity of the Sufi sheikh buried in

The search for Alexander's tomb

People have sought the **tomb of Alexander the Great** ever since the Dark Ages. He is known to have been interred in the **Soma**, a temple opposite the Mousieon (see opposite), at the crossroads of Ancient Alexandria, where several Ptolemies were also buried. He lay in a **gold sarcophagus** until Ptolemy IX melted it down to mint coins during a crisis, but his body remained on view long after the dynasty had fallen. The victorious Roman emperor **Octavian** paid his respects to Alexandria's founder but disdained his heirs, stating "I wished to see a king, I did not wish to see corpses." According to one chronicler, Octavian accidentally broke Alexander's nose while bending to kiss the dead conqueror.

What happened to his body later remains a mystery. Some scholars believe that the Romans reburied Alexander outside the Royal Quarter, in what is now **Shatby**, where the Christian cemeteries are today. Nineteenth-century reports that Alexander's tomb lay deep beneath a mosque on Sharia Nabi Daniel have encouraged repeated excavations, while two Greek archeologists falsely claimed to have discovered it in 1991, in Siwa Oasis, near the border with Libya.

In 2004, amateur historian Andrew Chugg advanced the novel theory that Alexander's body was actually buried in the guise of St Mark's relics after Emperor Theodosius prohibited the worship of Alexander in 391 AD, and later smuggled abroad by Venetians unaware of its true origin.

its crypt has hampered several excavations in search of the tomb of Alexander the Great which is rumoured to lie beneath it (see box above).

Sharia Nabi Daniel ends at **Midan el-Gumhorriya**, a seething mass of bus and taxi ranks outside the neo-Baroque **Masr Station**. On a corner lies one of the city's best preserved Roman ruins, Kom el-Dikka.

Kom el-Dikka

In 1959, Polish archeologists searching for Alexander's tomb beneath the Turkish fort and slums on **Kom el-Dikka** (Mound of Rubble) found a stratum of Roman ruins (daily 9am–4.30pm; Ramadan until 3pm; £E20) that they're still excavating today. During Ptolemaic times this was the Park of Pan, a hilly pleasure garden with a limestone summit carved into the shape of a pine cone. Though nothing remains of this, you can wander around a **Roman Theatre** with marble seating for seven to eight hundred, cruder galleries for the plebs, and a forecourt with two patches of mosaic flooring. Along the northern side of the theatre's portico are thirteen auditoria that might have been part of Alexandria's ancient **university**, with an annual enrolment of five thousand students.

A separate ticket, sold at the main entrance, entitles you to enter the **Villa of Birds** (£E15) – so called because of its mosaic floors, depicting nine different species of birds (and a panther). En route to the villa you'll pass a laboratory for cleaning antiques, with assorted masonry recently dredged from the seabed laid outside. You can also see archeologists at work unearthing the remains of a **Temple of Bastet**, discovered in 2010 on the northern edge of Kom el-Dikka (off-limits).

Sharia Safiya Zaghloul and the Quartier Grec

Exiting Kom el-Dikka and turning northwards round the corner of the site, you'll come to a **statue of Khedive Ismail** that once stood by the Corniche. It was removed in 1956 when he became reviled by nationalists as a dupe of colonialism, and was only granted a new home here forty years later. From the statue, cross over Sharia Horriya and head north along **Sharia Safiya Zaghloul**. In Cavafy's day this was called the Rue Missala and known for its billiard halls and rent boys; today it is named after the wife of the nationalist leader and noted for its shops and cinemas. The turning just beyond the Metro Cinema leads to the heart of what was once the **Quartier Grec**, or Greek Quarter, one of five urban zones allotted to different ethnic groups by Mohammed Ali, which became as rich and cosmopolitan as Alexandria itself.

Strolling around you'll notice the **Greco-Roman Museum**, whose Classical facade is visible at the far end of Rue du Musée. Formerly home to Egypt's best collection of Classical antiquities, the museum has been closed for years while a second floor is constructed; meanwhile its antiquities are on loan abroad and the Alexandria National Museum (see below) has been making all the running in revealing new-found Greco-Roman artefacts.

The Alexandria National Museum

A short walk east of the museum along Tariq Gamal Abdel Nasser brings you to the splendid **Alexandria National Museum** (daily 9am–4pm; £E35). Occupying an Italianate mansion once owned by a wood merchant, it displays some of the amazing archeological finds made during the past decade.

On the ground floor, pride of place is afforded to Hellenistic artefacts from **Herakleion** and **Canopus** (see p.251). A diorite sphinx, a priest of Isis carrying a Canopic jar and a statue of the goddess share the spotlight with a granite stele of Nectanebo II that once stood at the mouth of the Canopic branch of the Nile. From **Ancient Alexandria** come an effigy of Emperor Caracalla in pharaonic headgear, a **mosaic** of Medusa found beneath the Diana Cinema, a marble hand from an unknown colossus and a **head of Briniky**, the wife of Ptolemy II. The latest exhibit is a marble statue of a naked warrior, presumed to represent **Alexander the Great**, which was found beneath the Shallalat Gardens in 2009.

Upstairs, splendid mother-of-pearl-inlaid doors and *mashrabiyas* give way to **Coptic** stelae and friezes carved with lions, sheep or grapevines, followed by icons, priestly garments and accoutrements. The **Islamic** artefacts include sashes and capes of Persian or Turkish origin, gold coins minted under the Fatimid and Byzantine empires, and Mamluke and Ottoman weaponry. A final room upstairs entitled "Alexandria in the Twenty-First Century" juxtaposes photos of colonial street scenes and a satellite view of the city with tableware, jewellery and medals from King Farouk's collection. Look out for the life-size silver fish with a flexible body.

Around Midan Orabi and Midan Tahrir

The old heart of "European" Alexandria lies less than 500m west of Midan Sa'ad Zaghloul, a short walk along **Sharia Sa'ad Zaghloul**, which starts as a busy shopping street aglow with neon, and ends as a shadowy alley. Along the way you can see traces of the past in Art Deco frontages and faded plaques bearing Greek, French or Armenian names, and stop at atmospheric coffee houses or bars for refreshment (see pp.252–253). At the far end you'll find the **Majestic Building** where the novelist E.M. Forster stayed when it was a hotel, across the road from the derelict **Menasce Synagogue**, a relic of the area's social complexion a century ago, like the German, Gothic-style **Protestant Church** on Sharia el-Akkad el-Boustra.

Emerging onto **Midan Orabi**, you'll see a Neoclassical **Monument of the Unknown Soldier** facing the seafront, where a naval guard of honour is changed every hour on the hour. No trace remains of the French Gardens where expatriates once strolled among the acacia trees and shrubs, just off "Frank Square", as Europeans dubbed the elongated plaza at right angles to Midan Orabi, which once served as their social hub.

This square was later renamed in honour of **Mohammed Ali**, whose equestrian **statue** (by Jacques Mart; 1868) prances outside the former **Mixed Courts**, where foreigners were once tried under their own jurisprudence rather than Egyptian law. After the Orabi Revolt of 1882 (see p.281), rebels were shot and buried here by British forces. Not surprisingly, its name was changed to **Midan Tahrir** (Liberation Square) after the 1952 revolution, and it was here, in 1956, that Nasser delivered a three-hour speech climaxing in the announcement that Egypt had taken possession of the Suez Canal.

A parking lot marks the site of the Stock Exchange that once stood on the corner of Rue Chérif Pacha, the Bond Street of Alexandria (as the British conceived it) and Cavafy's birthplace. Now **Sharia Salah Salem**, the street is less chic than in colonial times, but still the place to find **antiques** and **jewellery**. Further along on the left, the building at 2 Sharia Mahmoud Azmi is where the **Al-Fayeds** (of Harrods fame) founded their first trading company (its sign remains) and went on to become international business moguls – a far cry from their impoverished childhood in Anfushi.

The parallel **Sharia Mesjid al-Attarin** is named after the fourteenth-century **Attarine Mosque** that stands on the site of the fourth-century Church of St Athanasius, from which Napoleon's forces removed a seven-ton sarcophagus, thought to be Alexander's but later attributed to Nectanebo I. The neighbouring **Greek Orthodox** and **Catholic cathedrals** are the heart of their respective communities, while the lane running between Sidi el Mitiwalli and Ahmed Morsi Badr streets harbours the **Attarine antique market**, an intriguing place to browse.

Anfushi

Although the **Eastern Harbour** is no longer the busy port of ancient times, its graceful curve is definitely appealing. As it sweeps around towards Qaitbey's fort, bureaucratic monoliths from the last decades of the twentieth century give way to stately palms and weathered colonial mansions, likened by TV presenter Michael Palin to "Cannes with acne". Walking at least some of the way along the Corniche is highly recommended, but you may wish to use minibuses or trams to reach the fort.

In ancient times, a seven-league dike – the **Heptastadion** – connected Alexandria to a towering lighthouse on an island. Allowed to silt up after the Arab conquest, the causeway gradually turned into a peninsula that the newcomers built over, creating the **Anfushi** quarter (or El-Anfushi). Its Ottoman mosques, *mashrabiya*'d houses and bustling streetlife make Anfushi a great place for exploration. Tram #15 runs one block inland from the Corniche, passing all the major landmarks in the Anfushi and Ras el-Tin quarters.

The seventeenth-century **Terbana Mosque** incorporates a public drinking fountain and numerous antique columns; a huge pair with Corinthian capitals supports the minaret. Further north, the **Mosque of Abu al-Abbas al-Mursi** honours the patron saint of local fishermen and sailors, a thirteenth-century Andalusian sheikh. The existing structure was built in 1938 by an Italian architect, but its keel-arched panels, elaborately carved domes and cornices look as old as the sixteenth-century original.

Fort Qaitbey

One tram stop after Al-Mursi's mosque, a short walk past the fishing port and **shipbuilding** yard full of brightly painted wooden boats, will bring you to the promontory bearing Sultan Qaitbey's fort and the **Alexandria Yacht Club**, which holds an annual regatta in October.

Fort Qaitbey (daily 9am–2pm; £E25) is an Alexandrian landmark, a doughty citadel buffeted by wind-borne spray, its flag forever rippling. Built during the

The Pharos

Alexandria's lighthouse, the Pharos, was one of the Seven Wonders of the ancient world. Transcending its practical role as a navigational beacon and early-warning system, it became synonymous with the city itself: a combination of aesthetic beauty and technological audacity, exceeding 125m (perhaps even 150m) in height, including the statue of Zeus at its summit.

Possibly conceived by **Alexander** himself, the Pharos took twelve years to build under the direction of an Asiatic Greek, Sostratus, and was completed in 283 BC. Its square base contained three hundred rooms, which, according to legend, once housed the seventy rabbis who translated the Hebrew scriptures into Greek, and perhaps also machinery for hauling fuel upto the lantern in the cylindrical third storey, whose light is thought to have been visible 56km away. Some chroniclers also mention a "mirror" that enabled the lighthouse keepers to observe ships far out at sea.

Around 700 AD the lantern collapsed, or was demolished by a treasure-hunting caliph; the base survived unscathed and **Ibn Tulun** restored the second level, until an earthquake in 1303 reduced the whole structure to rubble, which is now strewn over the seabed beyond Qaitbey's fort.

Divers have located over 2500 stone objects **underwater** at depths of 6–8m, including the head of a colossus of Ptolemy as pharaoh and the base of an obelisk inscribed to Seti I, which have been brought to the surface. In addition, there are several **monoliths**, weighing 50–70 tonnes apiece and embedded in the rock by the impact of their fall, which can only have belonged to the lighthouse. Five hundred metres offshore, **wrecks** of Greek and Roman trading vessels laden with **amphorae** of wine and fish sauce have been found, and over fifty **anchors** of all eras – more pieces in the mosaic picture of Ancient Alexandria that's emerging from surveys of the Eastern Harbour (see opposite). See p.251 for details of **diving** in the harbour.

1480s and later beefed up by Mohammed Ali, it commands great views of the city and the spume-flecked Mediterranean. Within the restored keep there's a mosque whose minaret was blown away by the British in 1882.

The fort is thought to incorporate masonry from the legendary Pharos (see box above). Several red-granite pillars from antiquity are embedded in the northwest section of its curtain wall, while huge monoliths on the seabed attest to the collapse of some vast structure.

Ras el-Tin

Tram #15 runs on from Anfushi to the **Ras el-Tin** (Cape of Figs) quarter, where you can alight at Sharia Ras el-Tin to find the rock-cut **Anfushi Tombs** (daily 9am–4.30pm; £E20), uncovered in 1901. Sited in pairs around a staircase, the four tombs are painted to simulate costly alabaster or marble and belonged to third-century BC Greek Alexandrians who adopted Ancient Egyptian funerary practices. The right-hand set has pictures of Egyptian gods, warships and feluccas; a Greek workman has also immortalized his mate's virtues in graffiti.

It's possible that the necropolis extends beneath the gardens of **Ras el-Tin Palace**, overlooking the Western Harbour. The palace was built for Mohammed Ali, its audience hall sited so that he could watch his new fleet at anchor while reclining on his divan. Rebuilt and turned into the summer seat of government under Fouad I, it witnessed King Farouk's abdication on July 26, 1952, and is now off-limits as a Presidential residence.

On the way back you could enjoy lunch at one of the many **fish restaurants** on Sharia Safar Pasha (between Ras el-Tin and Anfushi) or along the Corniche (see p.252).

The submerged Royal Quarters

The opposite arm of the Eastern Harbour is formed by a narrow promontory called **Silsileh** (the Chain), which is occupied by the navy and out of bounds. Its interest lies in the **underwater** discoveries made since 1996 by explorer Franck Goddio and his team, whose survey of the sea bed five metres down has revealed extensive submerged **ruins**, including granite columns, votive statues, sphinxes, pavements, ceramics and a pier from the **ancient Royal Quarters** of Alexandria. Samples of their salvage can be seen on Goddio's website, Ⓦ www.underwaterdiscovery.org.

Goddio was quick to claim that they had found the site of **Cleopatra's Palace** on the island of Antirrhodos (where she met her death), which had been plunged into the sea by an earthquake and a tsunami in 365 AD – an assertion disparaged by professional archeologists until Goddio found inscriptions verifying his claim. Egypt's Supreme Council of Antiquities is keen on creating the world's first underwater museum – with Plexiglas tunnels that would allow visitors to stroll below the surface – a feasibility study is now underway.

It's possible to investigate the ruins by **diving**; visibility is at its best (7–20m) from April to June and October to December. As well as seven or eight **sphinxes** (one 5m long), a giant **obelisk** and numerous columns, divers can see the wreck of a British **Beaufort bomber** that narrowly missed crashing into the *Hotel Cecil* in 1942; the pilot's flight mask is fused into the rock. See the box on p.251 for more on diving.

The Bibliotheca Alexandrina

On the mainland beyond Silsileh, another wonder of antiquity has been resurrected in a new form. The **Bibliotheca Alexandrina** (Fri 3–7pm, Sat–Thurs 11am–7pm; Ⓦ www.bibalex.org) resembles a giant discus embedded in the ground at an angle, representing a second sun rising beside the Mediterranean. Pictograms, hieroglyphs and letters from every alphabet are carved on its exterior, evoking the diversity of knowledge embodied in the ancient library and the aspirations of the new one. Built over seventeen years at a cost of $355 million, the library was controversial even before its inauguration in 2002 (when an exhibition of books from every

Ancient Alexandria's library

Founded shortly after the city itself, on the advice of Ptolemy I's counsellor Demetrius of Phalerum, Alexandria's library stood beside the Mouseion in the heart of the city (see p.242). Dedicated to "the writings of all nations", it welcomed scholars and philosophers and supported research and debates. By law, all ships docking at Alexandria were obliged to allow any scrolls on board to be copied, if they were of interest. By the mid-first century BC it held 532,800 manuscripts (all catalogued by the Head Librarian, Callimachus), and later spawned a subsidiary attached to the **Temple of Serapis** (see p.248); the two were known as the **"Mother"** and **"Daughter" libraries**, and together contained perhaps 700,000 scrolls (equivalent to about 100,000 printed books today).

As many as forty thousand (or even 400,000) were burned during Julius Caesar's assault on the city in 48 BC, when he supported Cleopatra against her brother Ptolemy XIII; as compensation, Mark Antony gave her the entire contents of the Pergamum Library (200,000 scrolls). But it was Christian mobs that destroyed this vast storehouse of "pagan" knowledge, torching the Mother Library in 293 and the Daughter Library in 391, though medieval Europe later mythologized its destruction as proof of Arab barbarism. An apocryphal tale had the Muslim leader Amr pronouncing: "If these writings of the Greeks agree with the Koran they are useless, and need not be preserved; if they disagree, they are pernicious, and ought to be destroyed."

nation featured the anti-Semitic forgery, the *Protocols of the Elders of Zion,* as Israel's entry), but no one doubts its impact on the city's cultural scene or its must-see status with tourists. Its stunning architecture (by a Norwegian-Austrian team) is matched by the diversity of **events** at the **Cultural Centre** in the block opposite the entrance to the library – see the website for what's on. The library's *Hilton* **café** is a popular meeting spot. All public areas are wheelchair accessible.

Visiting the library

On the inland side facing Sharia Bur Said, a **colossus of Ptolemy II**, dredged from the Eastern Harbour, watches over a cloakroom where all bags must be checked in, and kiosks selling **tickets** for the library (£E10; no children under 6) or a combo ticket (£E45; no student discount) that also covers the two museums inside it, individual tickets for which (£E20 each) are sold within the library. **Photography** is permitted in the lobby and reading area but not in the exhibitions or museums. You can join a free **tour** in English (every 45min) just inside the entrance, or wander at will through the vast **reading area** – a stunning cascade of levels upheld by stainless-steel pillars suggestive of the columns in pharaonic temples.

Maps, engravings and photos in the **Impressions of Alexandria** exhibit show how the city has evolved since antiquity and its ruination by the British in 1882. A fine **Antiquities Museum** in the basement displays a giant head of Serapis, a black basalt Isis salvaged from Herakleion, and two mosaic floors unearthed during the building of the library, one depicting a dog beside a brass cup, the other a gladiator locked in combat. Ancient scrolls and tomes can be seen in the **Manuscripts Museum** on the entrance level. Lastly there's the **Planetarium**, a Death Star-like spheroid on the plaza facing the sea, screening IMAX science movies for children (£E25–35).

Pompey's Pillar and the Temple of Serapis

The poor **Karmous quarter** in the southwest of the city contains two of Alex's best-known ancient monuments. Towering 25m above a limestone ridge, the red-granite column known as **Pompey's Pillar** (daily 9am–4.30pm, Ramadan 9am–3pm; £E35) was actually raised to honour the Roman emperor Diocletian, who threatened to massacre Alexandria's populace "until their blood reached his horse's knees", but desisted when his mount slipped and bloodied itself prematurely. It may have come from the **Temple of Serapis** that once stood nearby, housing Cleopatra's "Daughter Library" of 42,800 texts (see p.247), which outlived the Mother Library by almost a century, only to be destroyed by Christian mobs in 391 AD. All that remains of the temple are three subterranean galleries where the sacred Apis bulls were interred (see p.171), a Nilometer and some underground cisterns – making the site pretty disappointing considering what used to exist here. Pompey's Pillar can be reached by taxi (£E30) or tram #16 from Midan Orabi. The pillar becomes visible as the tram passes the Muslim cemetery bordered by Sharia Amoud el-Sawary.

The Catacombs of Kom es-Shoqafa

Happily, the same isn't true of the **Catacombs of Kom es-Shoqafa** (daily 9am–4.30pm, Ramadan until 3pm; £E35), whose prosaic Arabic name, "Mound of Shards", hardly does justice to their wonderful amalgam of spookiness and kitsch. To get here, turn right around the corner after leaving Pompey's Pillar and follow the road straight on for five minutes; the entrance to the catacombs is on the left, 150m beyond a square. Cameras must be left at the site entrance, as photography is not allowed inside.

Aficionados of **Lawrence Durrell** may wish to track down his last Alexandrian residence, in the suburb of Moharrem Bey, to the east of the Karmous quarter. Once home to Alexandria's mercantile elite, Moharrem Bey's mansions have become slums since the 1950s, but you can still see the **Ambron Villa** where Durrell and his muse Eve Cohen rented the top floor in 1943–44; *Prospero's Cell* and *The Dark Labyrinth* were written in the corner tower. Though it's now a listed building, the villa has been allowed to decay and developers have built flats in the garden where the painter Gilda Ambron shared a studio with their neighbour, Clea Badaro, who inspired the character Cleo in *The Alexandria Quartet*. As the villa can't be entered, only hardcore fans will find it worth the expense of a taxi (£E15–20 one-way). Get someone to write the address (19 Sharia al-Ma'amoun) in Arabic to show to the driver.

The catacombs were discovered in 1900 when a donkey disappeared through the ground. Hewn 35m into solid rock, the triple-level complex is reached via a spiral stairway, past the shaft down which bodies were lowered. From the vestibule with its scalloped niches, you can squeeze through a fissure into a lofty **hall** riddled with *loculi*, or family burial niches. Scholars named it the Hall of Caracalla after the Roman emperor who massacred Alexandrian youths at a festival in 215 AD. Relatives toasted the dead from stone couches in the **Triclinium**, where the first archeologists to enter the chamber found wine jars and tableware. In the **Central Tomb** – whose vestibule is guarded by reliefs of bearded serpents with Medusa-headed shields – you'll find muscle-bound statues of the Egyptian gods Sobek and Anubis wearing Roman armour, dating from the second century AD when, as E. M. Forster put it, "the old faiths began to merge and melt". Water has flooded the **Goddess Nemesis Hall** (still accessible) and submerged the lowest level, hastening the catacombs' decay.

Corniche beaches

Since most foreigners visit Cairo in the winter, day-trippers are likelier to find Alexandria's **beaches** swept by storms battering the Corniche rather than the tawny sands that lure millions of Egyptians between early June and late September. Except for the paying Venezia Beach at Montazah (see p.250), *baladi* modesty prevails – with women sunbathing or wading into the sea fully clothed (it's no surprise that foreigners prefer beach holidays at European-style resorts on the Red Sea).

You may still be drawn by fishermen casting their nets or boys braving the swell in rubber tyres along a string of beaches that are hard to tell apart despite their resonance for locals. **Shatby** harbours the neo-Baroque **St Mark's College** (whose dome is visible from afar) and a grandly named **Necropolis** (daily 9am–4.30pm; Ramadan 9am–3pm; £E15) from the third century BC, exposing some rock-cut ossuaries and sarcophagi.

Other beaches are notable for their historic associations: **Camp Cesar** (where Julius Caesar camped during the battle that left Cleopatra at his mercy), **Ibrahimiya** (the birthplace of Hitler's deputy Führer, Rudolf Hess), and **Roushdi** (where Octavian founded a settlement called Nikopolis to escape the decadence of Alexandria).

Roushdi retains a vestige of its origins in the form of the **Mustafa Kamel Necropolis** (daily 9am–4.30pm; £E15), whose four tombs date from the second century BC. Two are upheld by Doric columns and one contains a mural of a horseman. To get there, catch tram #2 from Ramleh to Roushdi tram station and walk towards the Corniche along Sharia al-Mo'asker al-Romani.

Travelling further east along the Corniche you'll cross the spectacular **Stanley Bridge**, whose ornate suspension towers mimic the Turko-Florentine architecture at Montazah (see below). From the bridge (carrying only eastbound traffic) you can see Stanley Bay's tiers of concrete sun terraces and bathing cabins, built by the British in the 1920s.

The Royal Jewellery Museum

Three blocks in from Glym Beach, Alexandria's **Royal Jewellery Museum** (daily 9am–2pm & 5–7pm; £E35) at 27 Sharia Ahmed Yehia, is a short walk from the El-Fenoun el-Gamila or Qasr el-Safa stops on the #2 tram line. The museum is housed in a mansion built for Mohammed Ali's granddaughter Princess Fatima el-Zaharaa and her husband, which is as splendidly vulgar as the treasures on display. Among the highlights are Mohammed Ali's diamond-inlaid snuffbox, King Farouk's gold chess set, a platinum crown with 2159 diamonds, and his diamond-studded gardening tools. The gallery downstairs is lined with stained-glass cameos of courtly love in eighteenth-century France, while images of Provençal farmers, milkmaids and food decorate the service corridors. Upstairs are the rather wild his 'n' hers bathrooms – hers with tiled murals of nymphs bathing in a waterfall, his with scenes of Côte d'Azur fishermen.

The Mahmoud Said Museum

Another treat in this part of town is the **Mahmoud Said Museum** (Tues–Sun 10am–6pm; £E10), on Sharia Mahmoud Said Pasha: take tram #1 or #2 to Gianaclis (the stop after the Jewellery Museum), cross the tracks, head up the steps to the raised road and turn right. A judge who painted as a hobby, Mahmoud Said (1897–1964) disliked official commissions such as the wall-sized *Inaugural Ceremony of the Suez Canal* that greets visitors to the museum, preferring to paint pensive, sensual women or landscapes of Alexandria and Lebanon.

Upstairs, six rooms are devoted to the brothers Seif (1906–79) and Adham (1908–59) Wanly, who founded the first Egyptian artists' studio in Alexandria in 1942. Seif was an Expressionist who depicted such bourgeois delights as casinos, nightclubs and horse-racing, while Adham was into Cubism, abstraction and Socialist Realism, producing such polemical works as *Hunger* and *Palestine*.

Montazah

Sixteen kilometres from the centre the Corniche reaches **Montazah**, a former royal retreat turned privatized recreation ground (daily 24hr; £E6). Avenues of stately palms and exotic shrubs converge on the flamboyant Turko-Florentine **Haramlik Palace** (closed to the public). Commissioned by King Fouad, it served as a Red Cross hospital during World War I (when E.M. Forster was a nurse here) and is now a presidential residence. The nearby Alpine-style **El-Salamlik Palace**, built for the homesick Austrian mistress of Khedive Abbas, has become a hotel.

The park culminates in a headland whose promontory ends in a romantic "Turkish" **Belvedere** and a **lighthouse** (you can walk out to gaze over the sea), enclosing a private bay. **Venezia Beach** (£E50 admission with a beach chair and umbrella) is where rich Alexandrians come to sunbathe (dress standards for women are relaxed), and go **windsurfing** and **snorkelling** in the summer. Equipment can be rented from the local Montazah Diving Centre (see box opposite).

Canopus, Abu Qir and Herakleion

There's no point in venturing beyond Montazah unless you're keen to eat seafood on the beach at Abu Qir (see p.252), or dive submerged ruins and shipwrecks off the coast.

Diving at Alexandria

Few other cities boast such a wealth of historic underwater sites, with blocks from the Pharos littering the sea bed near Qaitbey's fort, and Roman trading vessels lying 500m offshore. Some eleven thousand artefacts and pieces of masonry remain from what was once the Royal Quarter in the Eastern Harbour, while Napoleonic wrecks and an ancient port lie beneath Abu Qir Bay.

Visibility in the Eastern Harbour declines as the water gets warmer, whereas other, less sheltered sites are best dived in the summer, when the sea is calm. **Alexandra Dive** (℡03/483-2045 or 014 261-1115, ⒲www.alexandra-dive.com), beside the *Tikka Grill* on the Corniche, can usually forecast conditions for the next 24 hours, and offers diving at two sites for €85 per person (including lunch and the Underwater Archeology Department fee; equipment costs €15 extra). As the Pharos and Cleopatra's palace are only 5–8m underwater, even uncertified divers may be accepted if they can pass a try out – whereas the wrecks and ruins at Canopus and Abu Qir demand more than open-water experience, and the bureaucracy involved requires two to four days' notice.

The **Montazah Diving Centre** (℡012 281-4769 or 010 496-3888) at Venezia Beach is a smaller outfit whose prices are competitive with Alexandra Dive's, but it shuts up shop over winter.

A row of naval bases occupies the site of **Canopus** – a once-great city that flourished where a now-extinct branch of the Nile reached the sea by the "Canopic Mouth". Myth has it that Canopus was founded by a Greek navigator returning from the Trojan Wars, whom locals later worshipped in the form of a jar with a human head – hence the term Canopic jars, bestowed on similar receptacles used to preserve mummies' viscera.

In 2004 marine archeologists found life-size statues of Ptolemaic rulers and thousands of bronze pots and incense burners on the seabed off Canopus, together with the wreck of **HMS Garfield**, sunk by a German U-boat in 1917. The wreck can be dived in conjunction with two underwater sites off the coast of **Abu Qir** (pronounced Abu Ear), where, in 1798, England's Admiral Nelson destroyed the French fleet in the so-called Battle of the Nile.

During 1998 and 1999, divers found the **wrecks** of the French flagship *L'Orient* and its sister-ships *Sérieuse* and *Artémise,* 8km out in Abu Qir Bay. Two years afterwards, they discovered the ruins of **Herakleion**, a fabled port which fell into the sea 1300 years ago. Buried by sediment 23–30m underwater, its identity was confirmed by a stele inscribed with the city's name and part of a temple seen by Herodotus in the fifth century BC.

Diving at any of these sites is a fantastic experience that must be arranged before you come to Alexandria (see box above).

Eating and drinking

Alexandria can't match Cairo for culinary variety, but it beats the capital when it comes to **seafood restaurants**, where fish and crustaceans are laid out for diners to select their own, priced per kilo (grey mullet from £E50; clams from £E55; sea bass from £E75; crab from £E60; jumbo shrimp from £E170). **Coffee houses**, too, are an Alex speciality, and there are a couple of good **bars**.

Cafés and restaurants

We've only given phone numbers where it's wise to reserve a table. Alcohol isn't served and credit cards aren't accepted, unless stated otherwise.

Downtown

Al-Shark Sharia al-Bursa al-Qadima. Serves kebab by the kilo and traditional Egyptian dishes such as *fatta* with mutton, rice with gizzards, and baked macaroni (£E10–30), to eat indoors or take away. Daily 11am–11pm.

Café La Vallé Alexy Midan Ramleh. One of the new breed of cafes catering to young Alexandrians, with a relaxed vibe and a menu featuring fresh juices (£E12), club sandwiches (£E19), grilled calamari (£E32) and shrimp curry (£E61). Daily 9am–2am.

Gad Sharia Horriya; Sharia Mahmoud Azmi; Sharia Sa'ad Zaghloul. Three branches of the popular Egyptian chain (see p.192), selling takeaway kebab, kofta, *shawarma*, *fuul* and prawn sandwiches, all freshly prepared and under £E10 – ideal for a quick snack. Daily 24hr.

Anfushi and Ras el-Tin

Abu Ashraf 28 Sharia Safar Pasha. Accessible by tram #15, Sharia Safar Pasha is full of fish and kebab restaurants, tempting passers-by with their outdoor grills. *Abu Ashraf* is devoted to seafood, which is always excellent; try the sea bass stuffed with garlic and herbs or the creamy shrimp *kishk* (casserole). Dishes £E40–70. Daily 24hr.

Fish Market Sharia 26th July T03/480-5119. Sited above the *Tikka Grill*, this posh restaurant has a/c and a wonderful view of the harbour. Their mandatory mezze platter (£E10 per person) is a meal in itself – beware of eating your fill before the seafood arrives. Wine and beer are available, though not listed on the menu. Accepts MasterCard, Visa and Diners Club. Daily 12.30am–2pm.

Grand Caffee Sharia 26th July. Under the same management as the *Fish Market* but less formal, with pizzas (£E16–23), Caesar salad (£E30), milkshakes (£E15) or ice cream (£E14–15) to be enjoyed outdoors or indoors. Daily 9am–2am.

Greek Club Sharia Qasr Qaitbey. A great place to tuck into grilled squid or fish, *mezze* or moussaka (all £E20–35), with spacious rooms and a large terrace that catches the afternoon breeze from the harbour. There's a £E6 admission charge. Daily noon–11pm.

Samakmak 42 Sharia Qasr Ras el-Tin T03/481-1560. Owned by retired belly-dancer Zizi Salem, this upmarket fish place is renowned for its crab *tageen*, crayfish, and spaghetti with clams – dishes cost between £E40 and £E100. In the summer you can eat outdoors in a large tent. Daily noon–midnight.

Further out

Hood Gondol Seafood Corner of Sharia Omar Lofty and Sharia Mohammed Motwe. Located near the Bibliotheca Alexandrina (ask any local for directions), this popular diner does a massive plate of mixed seafood for a paltry £E35. Little English is spoken and there's no menu; just point to the seafood display and find yourself a seat. Daily noon–11pm.

Zephyrion Abu Qir beach. Fronted by a cactus garden, *Zephyrion* (Greek for "sea breeze") is the most identifiable of Abu Qir's seafood spots (some of which are simply tables on the beach) and serves alcohol. A meal will set you back around £E70. Daily noon–midnight.

Coffee houses and patisseries

Before the 1952 revolution, Alexandria's **coffee houses** and **patisseries** were the hub of bourgeois society. Artists, writers and socialites mingled and pursued affairs in such salons as *Athineos*, *Trianon* and *Pastroudis*. Since then some have closed and others depend on tourists or a loyal, dwindling clientele of elderly Egyptian gentlemen. While *Athineos* only deserves a peek for its flyblown Classical friezes and mirrors, you can spend an enjoyable hour in other places.

Downtown

Baudrot 23 Sharia Sa'ad Zaghloul. With its dark-panelled salon and vine-trellised inner courtyard, this is a traditional haunt of courting couples, serving cakes, coffee and sandwiches. Daily 8am–midnight.

Brazilian Coffee Store Corner of Nabi Daniel and Sa'ad Zaghloul, near the tourist office. An antique coffee mill and a glass map of Brazil from 1929 embellish this cosy breakfast spot with seating upstairs There's another branch decorated like a 1950s American diner, on the corner of Sharia Salah Salem and Sharia Sizostris. Both daily 6.30am–midnight.

Délices Between Midan and Sharia Sa'ad Zaghloul. A spacious, elegant air-conditioned tearoom serving a decent Continental breakfast, delicious cakes and savouries, plus soft drinks and beer (which must be drunk indoors), with tables outside when the weather is fine. Daily 7am–11pm.
Sofianopoulo Coffee Store 18 Sharia Sa'ad Zaghloul. A vintage stand-up coffee shop furnished with silver grinders and allegorical statues, with a small sit-down annexe next door. Great cappuccino and croissants. Daily 9am–11pm.

Trianon Corner of Midan Sa'ad Zaghloul and Ramleh. A vintage café featured in the classic British war film *Ice Cold in Alex*, which still does a good Continental breakfast. Daily 7am–midnight.

Further out

Classique 60 Sharia 26th July. This air-conditioned patisserie has a sumptuous array of European gateaux and Middle Eastern pastries, and is non-smoking throughout. Daily 10am–11pm.
El Qobesi Sharia 26th July. Serves wonderful mango juice in chilled glasses. Though there's no sign in English, you can't miss the hundreds of mangos stacked outside, nor the fairy-lit palm trees after dark. Daily 24hr.

Drinking

Although Alex is the centre of Egypt's wine and spirits industry and the city was once famously boozy, its few remaining bars keep a low profile.

Cap d'Or (aka Sheikh Ali) 4 Sharia Adib Bek Ishtak, off Sharia Sa'ad Zaghloul. A real slice of old Alex, furnished with Art Nouveau mouldings and engraved mirrors, where bohemians and expats rub shoulders over grilled sardines and bottles of whisky and tequila. It has a friendly atmosphere, and is popular with the gay community after midnight, when there may be live *oud* (lute) music. A seafood and salad meal with a beer costs about £E65. Daily 10am–3am.

Monty's Bar *Hotel Cecil*, Midan Sa'ad Zaghloul. General Montgomery (Monty) is said to have plotted the Battle of El-Alamein here despite being a teetotaller. Little of its 1940s character has survived a *Sofitel* makeover. Daily noon–1am.
Spitfire Bar 7 Sharia al-Bursa al-Qadima. Small hangout covered in stickers from oil companies, warships and overland travel groups (reflecting its clientele of engineers, sailors and tourists), with 70s rock music and TV sports. Mon–Sat noon–1am.

Entertainment

Thursday and Friday are the big nights out in Alex, but there's usually something happening throughout the week. The *Hotel Cecil*'s nightclub (daily except Fri & Wed midnight–4am) has two or three bellydancers to set pulses racing (minimum charge £E75 per person), and you can enjoy other performing arts at various spots in the city centre.

Music, theatre and opera

After decades in the doldrums, Alexandria's cultural scene has seen a renaissance. The library is naturally at the forefront, but money has also been spent on the city's historic opera house and other venues. The tourist office has details of their monthly programmes.

The Cultural Centre at the **Bibliotheca Alexandrina** (see p.248) stages **classical music** (Arabic as well as European), modern **dance** and **drama** (tickets £E10–20), and art house movies (free). Larger orchestral works and **ballet** are performed at the **Opera House** off Sharia Horriya (see p.242; ☏03/486-5106). A few blocks west of the opera, the **Alexandria Centre of Arts** (℡03/495-6633) hosts concerts by musicians from Egypt and abroad. The most "alternative" venue is **Garage** in Sidi Gaber (℡03/544-3246, ✉tfetouh@yatfund.org), putting on performances by local and foreign youth theatre groups, in the former garage of the Jesuit Centre at 298 Sharia Bur Said.

Other events include the two-week **Alexandria Biennial**, an exhibition of art from Mediterranean countries staged in October in odd-numbered years, and two annual sporting festivals: an **International Yachting Regatta** off the Eastern Harbour and an **International Marathon** along the Corniche from Ras el-Tin to Montazah, both staged in October.

Film

Film-going is popular in Alex throughout the year, with extra screenings at all **cinemas** during Ramadan. Downtown, the three-screen Royal Renaissance (℡03/485-5725) by the Opera House and the six-screen Amir (℡03/391-7972) on the corner of Sharia Horriya and Safiya Zaghloul screen English-language films you might have seen last year. A trendier venue is the eight-screen Renaissance San Stefano (℡ 03/490-0056), in a ritzy mall behind the *Four Seasons* hotel (see p.240).

Festivals

During Ramadan (see p.217), Alex revels in five **moulids** over five consecutive weeks, starting with *zikrs* outside the Mosque of Al-Mursi. The day after its "big night", the action shifts to Sidi Gaber's mosque, then Sidi Bishr's; these are followed by the moulids of Sidi Kamal and Sidi Mohammed al-Rahhal. And should you happen to be here over **New Year**, beware the blizzard of crockery that Alexandrians throw out of their windows at midnight.

Each September, Alexandria's **International Film Festival** gives Egyptians a rare opportunity to see foreign movies in an uncensored state: the Convention Hall en route to the library is the main venue, but every cinema in town screens a selection.

Listings

Banks Barclays, corner of Sharia Sa'ad Zaghloul and Sharia Safiya Zaghloul, and the Bank of Alexandria, 59 Sharia Sa'ad Zaghloul have ATMs. There are better rates of exchange at the Forex bureaux on Midan Ramleh and Sharia Salah Salem.

Bookshops The best for non-fiction and novels in English are Dar el-Mustaqbal, 32 Sharia Safiya Zaghloul (Mon–Thurs & Sat 9am–4pm, Sun 9am–1pm) and in the Alexandria National Museum (see p.244). Foreign newspapers are sold outside Ramleh telephone exchange and the *Metropole Hotel*.

Hospitals The German (Al-Almani) Hospital is well equipped, with English-speaking doctors; taxi drivers all know it.

Internet 10 Sharia ash-Shohada (daily 9.30am–2am), 18 Sharia Kolliet el-Tibba (Sat–Thurs 8am–1am & Fri 3pm–1am), or Sharia Dr Hassan Fadaly, off Safiya Zaghloul (Mon–Sat 11am–11pm), downtown.

Pharmacies Khalil, on Sharia el-Ghorfa el-Tigarya, off Midan Sa'ad Zaghloul (Mon–Sat 9am–10pm, Sun 10am–10pm; ℡03/480-6710), plus others on Midan Ramleh, Safiya Zaghloul and Nabi Daniel streets.

Tourist police Above the tourist office (℡03/485-0507; 24hr) and at the entrance to Montazah gardens (℡03/547-5025; 24hr).

Contexts

Contexts

History

Cairo is an agglomeration of half a dozen cities, whose varied names, ages and locations make for an unusually complex **urban history**. One constant is that new cities were usually constructed to the north of the old, for quite simple reasons: an east–west spread was constrained by the Muqattam Hills and the Nile (which ran further east than nowadays), while the prevailing northerly wind blew the smoke and smell of earlier settlements away from newer areas. Thus the original settlement in what is now Coptic Cairo (see map, pp.116–117) was replaced by the first Islamic city at Fustat (see p.125), which gave way to the Tulunids' city of Al-Qitai (around Ibn Tulun's Mosque; see p.258), and then the Fatimids' city of Al-Qahira, which forms the heart of what is now Islamic Cairo (see p.73). It was only after that that later dynasties started filling in the gaps between these older settlements, following which Khedive Ismail had what is now the downtown area (see p.64) constructed to their west.

Ancient times

The earliest major settlement in the region was at **Memphis**, near Saqqara (see p.172), built around 3100 BC by the semi-mythical ruler Menes or Narmer. Menes founded the I Dynasty of pharaohs when he united the "Two Lands" of Upper and Lower Egypt (the Nile Valley and its Delta) – siting his capital where they met at the apex of the Nile Delta (at the time further south than it is now). Memphis remained Egypt's capital throughout the Old Kingdom (c.2686–2181 BC) of the **pharaonic era**, during which vast necropolises developed along the desert's edge, as the pharaohs erected ever greater monuments, from the first **Step Pyramid** at **Saqqara** (see p.165) to the unsurpassable **Pyramids of Giza** (see p.153).

Meanwhile, across the Nile flourished a sister-city of priests and solar cults known to posterity as ancient **Heliopolis** (see p.147). Originally a village called **On**, whose venerable sun temple made it an important cult centre, it was probably eschewed by Menes as a capital because it was difficult to defend. (Millennia later, the main axis of Islamic Cairo still follows the ancient road between On and Memphis.)

Both Memphis and On were still in existence when Egypt succumbed to the **Persian invasion** of 525 BC. The conqueror Cambyses demonstrated his contempt for the Ancient Egyptian cult of the Apis bulls at Saqqara by stabbing one of the sacred creatures. (Believers must have seen the hand of divine vengeance in the disappearance of his "Lost Army" in the Western Desert a year later.) Yet the new city that the Persians founded – subsequently known as **Babylon-in-Egypt** – superseded Memphis and Heliopolis to become the root of the city we know today – and is thereby called **Old Cairo** (see map, pp.116–117).

In 332 BC, Egypt was conquered by Alexander the Great, who founded the Mediterranean city of **Alexandria** (see p.236). His Macedonian heirs, the **Ptolemies**, made it their capital and ruled Egypt as pharaohs, building temples the length of the Nile Valley and fostering the unifying cult of Serapis. The last of the dynasty was Cleopatra, whose manoeuvres to preserve Egypt's independence against the Roman Empire proved futile. For Egyptians, the **Roman** conquest of Egypt (30 BC) merely signified the exchange of one bunch of foreign rulers by another. Their resentment was reflected in the spread of **Christianity** – a faith that brought persecution at the hands of the pagan Romans. Even after the empire had adopted Christianity as its state religion and split into its Western and Eastern halves, Egypt's Coptic Christians were oppressed by **Byzantium** for their adoption of the Monophysite heresy (see p.267).

The caliphal era

Due to Byzantine persecution, Babylon-in-Egypt's citizens all but welcomed the Arab army of **Islam** that besieged it in 640 AD, after the Arabs promised to respect Christians and Jews as "people of the book". Only Alexandria's garrison resisted until the following year, when all of Egypt fell under the sway of the Islamic army. For strategic and spiritual reasons the Arab general Amr chose to found a new settlement just to the north of Babylon-in-Egypt, which became known as **Masr al-Fustat** (City of the Tent) after its tribal encampments surrounding Amr's tent.

Although Fustat evolved into a sophisticated mud-brick metropolis (see p.126), it remained a mere provincial capital in the vast Islamic empire. This was ruled from 661 until 750 by the **Umayyad** caliphs, whose capital was Damascus. The Umayyad dynasty met its eventual end at Fustat in 750, when its final ruler, Marwan II, made his last stand there. Marwan's troops burned the city down behind them as they fled the victorious **Abbasids**, who became the next dynasty of caliphs, ruling from Baghdad until 1258.

The Abbasids ordered the city to be rebuilt further north, at what was called **Medinet al-Askar** (City of Cantonments). Fustat was nonetheless rebuilt, and became famous in Europe for its hard-wearing cloth called fustian, a mix of linen and cotton woven together – the denim of its day. In the Islamic world it was already renowned as a great city in the caliphate – yet its allegiance could not be taken for granted.

In 870, the Abbasid viceroy in Egypt, **Ibn Tulun**, revolted against his masters. Like his predecessors, he founded a new city, reaching from Medinet al-Askar towards a spur of the Muqattam Hills. Inspired by the imperial capital of Samarra, it consisted of a gigantic congregational mosque, palace and hippodrome, surrounded by military quarters, after which the city was named **Al-Qitai** (The Wards).

The Tulunid dynasty proved short-lived, however, for in 905 the Abbasids reinvaded Egypt, razed Al-Qitai and ploughed it under, sparing only the great Mosque of Ibn Tulun, which stands to this day.

The city regained a shadow of its former importance under the **Ikhshidid** dynasty (935–969), who seceded from the later Abbasid caliphs. By this time distinctions between the earlier cities had blurred, as people lived wherever was feasible amid the decaying urban entity known as **Masr** (meaning both "Egypt" and "city"). The drought of 967 caused hunger, inflation and civil unrest, weakening an already shaky regime. Events in Egypt did not go unnoticed in Tunisia, where the Shi'ite **Fatimids** took power with the aim of eventually seizing the caliphate from the Abbasids. Recognizing Egypt as an ill-defended yet significant power base, they invaded it with an army of one hundred thousand in 969 and set up their own caliphate in Cairo to rival that of Baghdad.

The founding of Al-Qahira

The Fatimids distanced themselves from Masr by building an entirely new walled city – **Al-Qahira** (The Triumphant) – further north in what is now the heart of

Islamic Cairo, where certain key features remain. It was at the Al-Azhar Mosque (see p.88) that Al-Muizz, Egypt's first Fatimid ruler, delivered a sermon before withdrawing into the seclusion of his vast palaces (which survive only in the name of Bayn al-Qasrayn; see p.80). The Mosque of Al-Hakim (see p.85) commemorated the Fatimid caliph who ordered Masr's destruction after residents objected to proclamations of his divinity.

Also surviving are the great Northern Walls and Bab Zwayla gate, erected by the Armenian-born commander Al-Guyushi, after reconquering Al-Qahira for the Fatimids following its 1068 fall to the Seljuk Turks (the city's walls previously ran where Al-Hakim's mosque now stands and just north of Al-Muayyad's mosque). Meanwhile, as the Fatimid city grew, Fustat began to disintegrate as people scavenged building material from its abandoned dwellings, a process that spread to the rest of what had been the city of Masr, creating great areas of *kharab*, or **derelict quarters**.

The Ayyubids and the Mamlukes

The Fatimids ruled until 1171, when they were overthrown in the name of faith by one of Islam's great heroes, the Kurdish general Salah al-Din al-Ayyubi, known in English as **Saladin**. It was only at this point that the disparate areas of Masr and Al-Qahira assumed a kind of unity after Saladin commissioned a new **Citadel** on a rocky spur between them, and had the city walls expanded to link up with the aqueduct between the Nile and the Citadel, surrounding the whole conurbation.

Having overthrown the Shi'ite Fatimids, Saladin commissioned *madrassas* to propagate Sunni orthodoxy, but he ruled as a secular sultan rather than a calpih. His successors, the **Ayyubids**, erected pepper-pot-shaped minarets (only one remains, on Sultan Ayyub's Madrassa and Mausoleum; see p.80) and the magnificent tombs of the Abbasid Khalifs and Imam al-Shafi'i (which still exist; see p.109 & p.110) in the Southern Cemetery, but they made the mistake of depending on foreign troops and bodyguards, in particular the slave troops known as Mamlukes (from the Arabic for "owned").

Faced with invasion by an army of Crusaders, the last effective Ayyubid sultan, Al-Salih, purchased a large contingent of Mamlukes and successfully led them against the invaders, but died in battle. His son and heir angered Al-Salih's Mamlukes by favouring a rival faction, so they killed him and placed Al-Salih's wife, **Shagar al-Durr**, on the throne. As the Abbasid caliph refused to recognize a female ruler, however, she married her Mamluke lover, **Aybak**, made him sultan and ruled from behind the throne, but when she tried to do away with him, he had her slain first (see p.109) and took over, ushering in nearly three centuries of Mamluke rule.

The Mamluke era is divided into periods that are named after the factions from which the sultans intrigued their way to power: the Qipchak or Tartar **Bahri Mamlukes** (1250–1382), originally stationed by the river (*bahr* in Arabic); and their Circassian successors, the **Burgi Mamlukes** (1382–1517), quartered in a tower (*burg*) of the Citadel.

The **Mamlukes** originally hailed from Central Asia, but were later drawn from all over the Near East and the Balkans. Their price in the slave markets reflected the "value" of ethnic stock – 130–140 ducats for a Tartar, 110–120 for a Circassian, 50–80 for a Slav or Albanian – plus individual traits: sturdy, handsome youths were favoured. Often born of concubines and raised in barracks, Mamlukes advanced through the ranks under amirs (generals) who sodomized and lavished gifts upon their favourites. With the support of the right amirs, the most ruthless Mamluke could aspire to being sultan. Frequent changes of ruler were actually preferred, since contenders had to spread around bribes, not least to arrange assassinations.

Paradoxically, the Mamlukes were also renowned as aesthetes, commissioning mosques, mansions and *sabil-kuttabs* (Koranic schools and public fountains). They built throughout the city, and although urban life was interrupted by their bloody conflicts, the city nevertheless maintained public hospitals, libraries and schools, endowed by wealthy Mamlukes and merchants. Mamluke sultans like **Beybars the Crossbowman** (1260–77), **Qalaoun** (1279–90), **Barquq** (1382–89 and 1390–99) and **Qaitbey** (1468–96) commissioned mosques, mausoleums and caravanserais which still ennoble what is now known as "Islamic Cairo". The caravanserais overflowed with exotica from Africa and the spices of the East, and with Baghdad laid waste by the Mongols, Cairo had no peer in the Islamic world, its wonders inspiring many of the tales in the *Thousand and One Nights*.

Ottoman and colonial Cairo

In 1517 the **Ottoman Turks** invaded, reducing Egypt from an independent state to a vassal province in their empire, and the Mamlukes from masters to mere overseers. The last Mamluke sultan, Tumanbey, was summarily hanged at Bab Zwayla before the Ottoman Sultan Selim the Grim returned to Istanbul laden with loot. Selim left Egypt to be governed by a series of **Pashas** trained by the Ottomans, who continued to rely on the Mamlukes; in 1521, the Pasha's troops mutinied after the arrest of their favourite opium dealer, and he had to use Mamluke irregulars to restore order.

By the seventeenth century, Mamluke beys (senior officials) held every important post in Egypt, and the Ottoman governors had only a facade of authority. Between 1688 and 1755, no fewer than thirty-five Pashas were deposed by the Mamluke beys, whose in-fighting and banditry reduced Cairo to a ramshackle city living on bygone glories, introspective and archaic, its population dwindling as civil disorder increased. Eighteenth-century visitors like R. R. Madden were struck by "the squalid wretchedness of the Arabs, and the external splendour of the Turks", not to mention the lack of "one tolerable street" in a city of some 350,000 inhabitants.

In 1798, a French army under **Napoleon** landed at Alexandria, where he issued a proclamation "in the name of Allah" that he had come to liberate Egypt from this "riff-raff of slaves". Advancing rapidly, the French army clashed with the Mamlukes at the village of Imbaba and put them to flight after three-quarters of an hour, leaving the battlefield strewn with a thousand Mamlukes – the French lost only twenty-nine men. On July 24 they entered Cairo, beginning a three-year **occupation** that exposed Cairenes to such novelties as printing presses and social gatherings for both sexes.

Mohammed Ali and the Khedives

After the British forced the French out in 1801, Egypt was nominally restored to Ottoman control. Among the Turkish officers left in charge was **Mohammed Ali** of the Albanian Corps, who intrigued his way to becoming Pasha (1805) and then literally decapitated the Mamluke leadership in two infamous massacres (see p.96 & p.100). He set about modernizing Egypt with European expertise, building hospitals, railways, canals, factories and technical schools – in Bulaq, not far from his Shubra Palace (see p.142), and in Alexandria, which he revived from its 1300-year slumber (see p.236).

After he died insane in 1849, his heirs inherited the title. **Abbas Pasha** (1848–54) closed the factories and secular schools, retarding Egypt's industrialization by a century. **Said Pasha** (1854–63) granted a concession to a French engineer, Ferdinand de Lesseps, to build the **Suez Canal** – a project completed in 1869, by which time Khedive (or Viceroy) **Ismail** was in power. Ismail transformed Cairo, draining swampy tracts and founding the modern, quasi-European **Ismailiya** quarter, which nowadays constitutes downtown Cairo (see p.64). The festivities accompanying the Canal's inauguration were extraordinarily lavish, with banquets, free lodgings and transport for hundreds of guests.

Ismail's profligacy led him into **debt** with British and French banks, and the European powers demanded control of Egypt's finances. The Ottoman sultan – in debt to the same bankers – was happy to depose him in 1879 and put his malleable son **Tewfiq** on the throne. In 1882, army colonel **Ahmed Orabi** attempted a coup against the puppet regime, which gave the British an excuse to send troops in. The **British** wanted Egypt because the Suez Canal was a vital link to India, their empire's cash cow. Their occupation was supposed to be temporary but soon became a **"Veiled Protectorate"** where the British Consul-General was the power behind the throne.

Europeans flooded in: by 1910 foreigners accounted for an eighth of the city's population. Ismailiya became a truly European quarter, and Europeans also started building in Zamalek. Islamic Cairo was left a crumbling "native quarter", as new Egyptian working-class neighbourhoods grew up in areas such as Bulaq and Abbassiya. Though they ignored the needs of the poor, the British did build up Cairo's **infrastructure**. The city got a tram system, and in 1891 the Imbaba Bridge was built, allowing trains to cross the Nile. By 1920, the city's area was six times greater than that of medieval Cairo – not least due to such new **suburbs** as Heliopolis, Ma'adi and Helwan.

The struggle for independence

A **nationalist movement** founded by the lawyer **Mustafa Kamel** saw its chance in 1916, when Britain declared Egypt a protectorate and tightened its grip after Turkey (Egypt's nominal overlord) allied itself with Germany in World War I. In 1918, its leader, **Sa'ad Zaghloul**, presented Britain's High Commissioner with a demand for autonomy, which was rejected. The request to send a delegation (*wafd*) to London led to Zaghloul's arrest and deportation to Malta – rescinded after nationwide **riots**. In 1922 Britain abolished the protectorate and recognized Egypt as an independent state, but kept control of the judiciary, communications, defence and the Canal, while Khedive Fouad assumed the title of king.

The next twenty years saw a struggle for power between the king, the British and the nationalist Wafd Party. Fouad's son, **King Farouk**, succeeded him in 1935 and signed a twenty-year **Anglo-Egyptian treaty**, which ended British occupation but allowed their forces to remain in the Canal Zone. In 1937, Egypt joined the League of Nations, but the outbreak of war thwarted further moves towards independence, as Britain tightened its grip on this strategic territory.

World War II saw Rommel's Afrika Korps get within 115km of Alexandria in July 1942, precipitating panic among Cairo's British on "Ash Wednesday" (see p.71), when Egyptian nationalists prepared to welcome their Nazi "liberators" and future president Sadat tried to aid their advance (see p.137). However, the British foiled Rommel's spies in Cairo before routing the Germans at El-Alamein, 240km northwest of the capital, in October 1942.

Having kept dissent muted throughout the war on the tacit understanding that full independence would be granted afterwards, the Wafd Party resumed its agitation in 1946 supported by the radical **Muslim Brotherhood**. After British troops shot dead thirty demonstrators the following year outside the Qasr el-Nil barracks (where Midan Tahrir now is), Britain agreed to restrict its forces to the Canal Zone. In January 1952, following terrorist attacks, the British demanded the surrender of the Egyptian police barracks outside the Canal city of Ismailiya, and when this was refused stormed it, killing fifty policemen.

The next day, "**Black Saturday**", demonstrators set ablaze any Cairo institution seen as foreign, from the Opera House and *Shepheard's Hotel* to banks and liquor stores. On July 26, 1952, the pudgy bon viveur King Farouk was overthrown in a bloodless **revolution** and the so-called Free Officers took power, from whom **Gamal Abdel Nasser** later emerged as public leader. The constitution was revoked, the monarchy abolished, and Egypt declared a **republic** (July 26, 1953).

Egypt under Nasser and Sadat

The **Free Officers** were committed to Egyptian independence but differed over how to attain it. Their figurehead, General Naguib, was soon displaced by Nasser, who believed that only the construction of a **High Dam** at Aswan in Upper Egypt could avert future famine and supply the hydroelectric power for full-scale industrialization, without which Egypt was condemned to backwardness and dependency. The US flirted with Nasser – offering him a bribe that he contemptuously blew on building the **Cairo Tower** (see p.134) – but turned against him after he sought Soviet weapons to re-equip the Egyptian Army against the recently declared state of Israel.

In July 1956, Nasser nationalized the Suez Canal to fund the building of the High Dam, precipitating an unholy alliance between Britain, France and Israel. The latter's attack on Sinai was the agreed pretext for Anglo-French intervention to "safeguard" the canal by invading Port Said and Suez, but staunch Egyptian resistance and the refusal of the US to back the conspiracy resulted in a humiliating defeat for the colonial powers. Nasser emerged from the **Suez crisis** a hero throughout the Arab world.

The discovery of an Israeli sabotage network in Alexandria gave the authorities the pretext to crack down on **foreigners**, including native Jews who had never taken citizenship. Muslim Brotherhood attacks on Harat al-Yahud (see p.80), the **expropriation** of local businesses such as Cicurel, Tiring and Sednaoui (see p.67 & p.68), and all sorts of restrictions, compelled Cairo's expatriates and Jews to emigrate in droves. Feudal estates were divided among the peasantry and much of the economy was nationalized, as Nasser's regime emulated the Soviet Union (whose "fraternal gift" of the Mugamma building on Midan Tahrir remains as a monument to that era).

Expropriations and rent control changed Cairo's social complexion, as army officers and their servants moved into the ex-European downtown, and society became less bourgeois if not egalitarian (officers and engineers soon became a privileged caste, for whom the new west-bank district of **Mohandiseen** was founded in the 1960s). Pre-revolutionary café society survived only insofar as it paid tribute to Arab socialism – a restriction that the legendary diva **Umm Kalthoum** (see p.129) managed to transcend.

When Israel threatened to invade Syria in 1967, Nasser sent Egyptian forces into Sinai and cut shipping to the Israeli port of Eilat. The ensuing **Six Day War**

(June 5–10) was a shattering defeat for the Arabs, and Nasser in particular. Egypt's air force was destroyed in a surprise attack on Almaza Air Base on the edge of Cairo; Sinai was captured and the Canal Cities had to be evacuated during the subsequent two-year War of Attrition, leaving Egypt struggling to host millions of refugees from the Canal Cities. It was a trauma (called *an-Naksah*, "The Setback") from which Arab Socialism never recovered.

Following Nasser's death from a heart attack in 1970, his successor **Anwar Sadat** instituted a "corrective revolution", ending the one-party system and easing state control of the economy. Cairo's centre became more commercial again, and in working-class districts the hashish trade flourished, as Sadat declined to suppress a traditional vice that he himself enjoyed. Economically however, life for the poor became increasingly hard. In 1977, **bread riots** ensued after the government-fixed price of bread doubled; in Cairo, Islamic militants seized the chance to attack nightclubs on Pyramids Road. Lauded in the West for his unprecedented 1979 peace treaty with Israel, Sadat was increasingly hated in Egypt, seen as a "Pharaoh" who had forgotten his people. In 1981, he was fatally wounded by Islamist assassins at a military parade in Medinet Nasr (see p.144).

To the present day

After vice-president **Hosni Mubarak** took power in 1981, he focused on fixing Cairo's crumbling infrastructure, which had been neglected for decades and was far outstripped by the city's population, which rose from 1.3 million in 1937 to 8.2 million in 1977. In 1987 the **metro** opened, temporarily easing Cairo's traffic gridlock. New satellite cities such as 6th October and Sadat City were built in the desert in an effort to reduce overcrowding, even as the city continued to expand north and south, absorbing the once separate suburbs of Ma'adi and Helwan. By 1990, Cairo's **population** stood at fourteen million, making it the most populous city in Africa and second in the world only to Mexico City. With the completion of a ring road linking Cairo and Giza with 6th October, Sadat City and Qalubiyya, planners anticipated a **five-city megalopolis** with a total population of twenty-five million.

Under the **emergency laws** passed after Sadat's murder – still in force today – demonstrations and strikes were crushed by riot police; torture by the security forces was rife; and elections were shamelessly rigged. Having been "re-elected" President four times already, Mubarak was obliged to open the presidential election to other candidates when he ran for a fifth term in 2005. His opponent Ayman Nour was jailed on charges of forging signatures as MP of a new liberal party, Al-Ghad (Tomorrow), while meetings of the reformist alliance Kifaya (Enough) were broken up by government thugs.

As the octogenarian Mubarak schemed to ensure that his son Gamal would inherit the presidency, Egyptians seethed. They saw government ministers enriched by the privatization of public assets and generals enjoying sumptuous country clubs and villas, while ordinary people faced soaring food prices, unemployment, and a future without hope. With almost one third of the population aged under twenty-five, a generational tidal wave was set to emerge from the depths of despair.

The 2011 revolution

The overthrow of the Tunisian dictator Ben Ali early in 2011 inspired Arabs across North Africa and the Gulf to revolt. In Egypt, activists called for a **"Day of Rage"** on January 25, using Facebook, Twitter and SMS to mobilize protestors on Midan Tahrir. People assembled in the backstreets out of sight of the police, appearing en masse from every direction, overwhelming police cordons downtown.

As happened in Tunisia, protestors chanting *Slimiyya* ("Peacefully!) were teargassed and beaten. On the second night, crowds trying to march on the National Assembly and Interior Ministry were fired on by snipers. But each day saw people returning to Tahrir to defy the regime, with hundreds of thousands pouring onto the square after Friday prayers. Mosques became first-aid posts and wellwishers sent water, food and blankets. (State TV claimed that foreign agents were supplying Kentucky Fried Chicken or drugs to the protestors.)

As the battered riot police withdrew from central Cairo, its suburbs were hit by a wave of **looting** blamed on convicts escaped (or released) from prisons in the Delta, or on plainclothes police. This was seen as a ploy to scare protestors into returning home, but only encouraged **vigilante groups** in every neighbourhood and an even greater contempt for the regime.

When **army** tanks appeared on Tahrir many feared a Tiananmen Square-like bloodbath, but others hailed the soldiers as a shield against the *baltagiyya* (thugs). This state-hired rabble of ex-convicts and drug addicts had staged attacks on Tahrir from the 6th October flyover and even charged into the square on horses and camels. When the army announced that the protest was "legitimate", even larger crowds came onto the streets across the country.

With Egypt at a standstill and the economy losing $30 million a day, the stalemate couldn't continue for long. As protestors began a "million man march" from Tahrir to the Presidential Palace in Heliopolis, Mubarak was secretly boarding a jet at Almaza Air Base, bound for his villa in Sinai. His **resignation** on February 11 was announced by his spymaster (and vice-president) Omar Suleiman and the High Command, who pledged to oversee the transition to democracy.

Egyptians are immensely proud of themselves for overthrowing their dictator, and determined that **future elections** should be free. Several ministers have had to resign and investigations have begun into the fortunes made by Mubarak and his cronies. People are free to strike for better wages, demand decent public services, and state their opinions without fear of arrest. With so much hope in the air Cairo has never been so exciting – but only time will tell if those hopes are fulfilled.

Religion

Egyptian law requires all citizens to have a religion, stated on their ID cards; the only recognized faiths are Islam, Christianity and Judaism. Baha'is were recently grudgingly allowed to leave this category on their ID cards blank, but the whole issue of registering other faiths – or allowing conversion from Islam to other religions – remains hugely controversial. Up to three hundred Egyptians are currently imprisoned for "apostasy" (forsaking Islam), which Muslim fundamentalists wish to make a capital offence in accordance with Sharia law.

Around nine-tenths of Cairo's population is Muslim, with the rest being Coptic Christians, belonging to other Christian denominations, or the miniscule Jewish community. Most Egyptians can identify each other's religion by their forenames, never mind such visible signs as the cross that Copts tattoo on their wrists, or the callus on the forehead of devout Muslims (known as "the raisin").

Islam

Islam was born on the Arabian Peninsula, beyond the periphery of Greco-Roman civilization. Its founder, Mohammed, was a merchant from the city of Mecca, in what is now Saudi Arabia. At the age of forty (c.609 AD), he began to have visions of the Archangel Gabriel commanding him to recite divine revelations. As "God's Messenger", he proclaimed the oneness of **Allah** (God), the evil of idolatry in a city worshipping several deities (of whom Allah was one) and the need for submission (*islam*) to Allah's will. Forced to flee Mecca with his followers in 622 (the *hijira* that marks the beginning of the Muslim calendar), he spent eight years uniting the Bedouin tribes of Medina to finally conquer Mecca, dying two years later.

Mohammed's recitations – for he was illiterate – were later transcribed into Islam's holy book, the **Koran** (or "recitation"), which asserted that Allah was the same God worshipped by Jews and Christians, but that the message of Abraham (Ibrahim), Moses (Musa) and Jesus (Issa) had been distorted and was only truly expressed by Mohammed, the "Seal of the Prophets".

The Five Pillars of Islam

Islam shares a number of beliefs with Judaism and Christianity, accepting the Torah, Psalms and Gospel as divine in origin, but regarding them as corrupted texts that are superseded by the Koran. There are five fundamental duties, known as the **five pillars of Islam**, which a Muslim must perform: the **declaration of faith** (*shahada*) that there is no God but Allah, and Mohammed is His prophet; **prayer** (*salah*), recited five times daily at set times facing Mecca; the observance of **Ramadan**, the holy month when no food or drink must be taken from sunrise to sunset; the **giving of alms** (*zakat*); and the **pilgrimage** (hajj) to Mecca, which should be undertaken at least once in a lifetime. Islamic fundamentalists stress, too, the duty to wage **jihad** (holy war) to expand the faith or to defend it when under threat, as the Sixth Pillar of Islam. Friday is not a Sabbath for Muslims as Saturday is for Jews or Sunday for Christians, but a day when Muslims should all pray communally if they can. As in Judaism, meat must be slaughtered by cutting the throat and draining the blood to be **halal** (permitted). Pork is forbidden (**haram**), as are alcohol, gambling, and lending money for interest.

After his death in 632, the Prophet's successors – the four Rightly Guided Caliphs – spread Islam far beyond Arabia in a great **jihad** (holy war); within a century of the Prophet's death they had forged an Islamic Empire extending from the Atlantic Ocean to Central Asia. It was under the third caliph, Uthman, that the revelations which had been preserved by Mohammed's followers were collected and codified.

Division and the spread of Islam

Not long after Mohammed's death, the spiritual leadership of Islam became a source of contention. The first three caliphs were all related to Mohammed by marriage, but the fourth, Ali, was not only the Prophet's son-in-law but also his cousin. A substantial minority – the **Shi'ites** – supported Ali (Shi'at Ali) and broke away from the mainstream **Sunni** Muslims. Shi'ites believe that the Islamic community should be ruled only by a direct descendant of Mohammed (and therefore of Ali), called the **Imam**, a divinely appointed ruler who possesses superhuman qualities. The Sunnis, on the other hand, supported the Umayyads, descended from Mohammed's uncle Umayya, and later the Abbasids who deposed them in 749, as **caliphs**, responsible for the administration of justice through the **shari'a** (Islamic law) and for the defence of the realm of Islam. One of the offshoots of Shi'ite Islam is the **Isma'ilis**, who broke away from the Shi'ite mainstream over the question of succession on the death of the sixth Imam; the Fatimids, who ruled Egypt in the eleventh century, were Isma'ilis. Non-Isma'ili ("Twelver") Shi'ites recognize twelve Imams, the last of whom, Mohammed al-Muntazar, disappeared around 873, and is considered still to be living – the Hidden Imam, who will one day reappear as the **Mahdi**, the final prophet whose coming will herald the day of judgment and the end of the world.

Almost all Egyptian Muslims are Sunni, and Cairo's Al-Azhar Mosque is the leading theological authority of Sunni Islam. Egypt is also the birthplace of the **Muslim Brotherhood** (founded in 1928), the world's earliest and most influential Islamist movement (with branches across the Arab world, in Europe and the US). Banned under Nasser and Mubarak, the Brotherhood nonetheless had a mass organization, welfare centres and savings clubs to spread its appeal throughout society. Though it kept a relatively low profile during the protests on Midan Tahrir, it held a million-strong demonstration here after Mubarak's fall.

The Brotherhood has stressed its commitment to democratic reform but critics fear this really means "one man, one vote, once", and that its ultimate aim is a Sharia-law state – a prospect that fills Egypt's Copts in particular with dread.

Christianity

Around one in ten Cairenes is Christian, and the vast majority of these are Copts, affiliated to a church that is native to Egypt and predates Islam by centuries. Egypt's **Coptic church** belongs (along with the Armenian Orthodox and Ethiopian churches) to the Monophysite branch of Christianity, which diverged from Eastern and Roman Catholic orthodoxy very early on; the Copts even have their own pope, chosen from the monks of Wadi Natrun (see p.231). The Coptic Bible (first translated from Greek c.300 AD) predates the Latin version by a century. While Coptic services are conducted in Arabic, portions of the liturgy are sung in the old Coptic language descended from Ancient Egyptian, audibly prefiguring the Gregorian chants of Eastern Orthodoxy.

While the Copts share a common national culture with their Muslim compatriots, they remain acutely conscious of their separate identity. Mixed marriages are extremely rare and cause problems on both sides, though, under law, it is only forbidden for Muslim women to marry outside their faith.

The origins of Coptic Christianity

Tradition has it that **St Mark** the evangelist (author of the Gospel of Mark) made his first Egyptian convert – a Jewish shoemaker from Alexandria – in 45 AD. From Jews and Greeks the religion spread to the Egyptians of the Delta, which teemed with Christian communities by the third century, and thence southwards up the Nile.

Christianity appealed to Egyptians on many levels. Its message of resurrection offered ordinary folk the eternal life that was previously available only to those who could afford elaborate funerary rituals, and much of the new religion's symbolism fitted old myths and images: God created man from clay, as did Khnum on his potter's wheel, and weighed the penitent's heart, like Anubis; Confession echoed the Declaration of Innocence; the conflict of two brothers and the struggle against Satan echoed the myth of Osiris, Seth and Horus. Scholars have even traced the **cult of the Virgin** back to that of the Great Mother, Isis, who suckled Horus, and the resemblance between early **Coptic crosses** and pharaonic *ankhs* has also led some to argue that Christianity's principal symbol owes far more to Egypt than Golgotha.

Emperor Constantine's 313 AD legalization of Christianity eased matters until 451, when the Copts rejected the decision of the Council of Chalcedon that Christ's human and divine natures were unmixed, insisting that his divinity was paramount. For this **Monophysite heresy** (monophysite meaning "single nature") they were expelled from the fold, and persecuted by the Byzantines. Most Egyptians remained Christian long after the Arab conquest (640–41) and were treated well by the early Islamic dynasties. Mass **conversions to Islam** followed harsher taxation, abortive revolts, punitive massacres and indignities engendered by the Crusades, until the Muslims attained a nationwide majority (probably during the thirteenth century, earlier in Cairo). Thereafter Copts still participated in Egyptian life at every level, but the community retreated inwards and its monasteries and clergy stagnated until the nineteenth century.

The Copts today

In recent decades the **Coptic monasteries** have been revitalized by a new generation of well-educated monks, and community work and church attendances are flourishing. Coptic solidarity reflects alarm at rising Islamic fundamentalism, and the state's policy of trying to placate Islamists by discriminating against non-Muslims. With religion registered on ID cards, it is dangerous for a Muslim to convert to Christianity, while in the countryside, there have been many cases of Christian children being abducted and "converted" to Islam. To build or even repair a church requires permission from the President, which, even when given, often results in attacks by local Muslims.

Egypt's liberal intelligentsia have spoken out against sectarianism but they are swimming against the tide. All over rural and small-town Egypt, Copts and Muslims are drawing apart, and once-mixed communities are becoming polarized. These tensions are far less pronounced in Cairo, but even here, though Copts and Muslims work together, share festive celebrations, and regularly brush shoulders, intermarriage is extremely rare. Meanwhile, the Coptic diaspora, especially in the US (see ⓦwww.copts.com), rallies international support to counterbalance the Islamist influence in Egypt and protest against the bombing of a church in Alexandria or other outrages.

While the 2011 revolution witnessed unity between Copts and Muslims, future harmony is by no means assured. The Muslim Brotherhood has already laid down a challenge to the principles of secular democracy by asserting that no Christian shall be eligible for the presidency.

Judaism

Cairo's **Jewish community** is nowadays much reduced, with only around a hundred Jews *(yahud)*, living mainly in the downtown area. Twelve synagogues still exist, most in a state of disrepair. Only the Shaar HaShamayim (p.66) and Ben Ezra (p.125) are still used for services – the former for the solemn "High Holidays" of Rosh HaShanah (Jewish New Year) and Yom Kippur (Day of Atonement), the latter for happier occasions such as Hannukah, the winter festival of lights.

Egypt's Jewish community is undoubtedly ancient. Some evidence exists for the Prophet Jeremiah's foundation of a new community at Babylon-in-Egypt after the destruction of Jerusalem (585 BC), but there is no firm historical ground until the second century BC, when it is known that the Ptolemies encouraged an influx of Jews into Alexandria. The third book of Maccabees describes the Alexandrian community's struggle against anti-Semitism in Ptolemaic times.

In contrast to Alexandria's fusion of Greek and Jewish culture, the Jews of Babylon-in-Egypt were more like native Egyptians. Mutual sympathies were strengthened by the **Jewish revolt** against Roman rule (115–17 AD) and the Christian belief in the **Egyptian exile of the Holy Family**. Indeed, Babylon's Jewish community would have been a natural haven for Mary, Joseph and the baby Jesus when Herod's wrath made Palestine too dangerous.

As "people of the book", Egypt's Jews were treated about as well (or badly) as the Copts **during the medieval period** (see p.267), acting as small traders, gold- and silversmiths, moneychangers or moneylenders. In Mohammed Ali's day, the Orientalist E.W. Lane estimated that they numbered about five thousand. Until the late nineteenth century, Cairo's Jews were concentrated in the Harat al-Yahud quarter, where the Maimonides Synagogue still exists (see box, p.80). Under colonialism, European Jews arrived, mainly merchants or professionals. A few families of this *haute Juiverie* – the Menasces, Rolos, Hararis and Cattauis – were financiers who moved in royal circles, and a number of businesses in the downtown district, such as the Cicurel and Chemla department stores (see p.67), were opened by Jewish entrepreneurs.

After the creation of **Israel** in 1948, Egypt's Jews found themselves in a tricky situation, and each war eroded their security further. By the time of the 1967 war their numbers had declined through emigration from 75,000 to just 2600, mostly living in Cairo. The city still had 26 working synagogues when mobs attacked them for the first time during the 1967 Six Day War. Thereafter, most of the remaining Jews emigrated, leaving the tiny community that remains today.

Books

Cairo is not so well covered in literary terms as other great cities. The best works on its history – such as Al-Maqrizi's *Khitat* – were written in the Middle Ages, and have never been translated into English. Still, there's plenty to keep you going, especially given that Egypt's finest novelists have always tended to focus on Cairo. Many of the books listed below are easiest to buy in Cairo's bookshops (see p.223), while a few classic Orientalist works of the nineteenth-century can be read for free online.

Architecture

Caroline Williams *Islamic Monuments in Cairo: the Practical Guide*. The subtitle pretty well sums up this thoroughgoing review of mosques, *madrassas*, *sabils* and *khanqahs* all over the old city, with lots of background and architectural explanation, though it could do with better maps and more illustrations.

Salah El Bahnasi *Mamluk Art: The Splendour and Magic of the Sultans*. A guide to Mamluke architecture in Cairo, Alexandria and Rosetta, with concise essays illustrated with colour photos, plans and walking routes.

Religion

Christian Cannuyer *Coptic Egypt – The Christians of the Nile*. A pocket-sized, easy-to-read study of Coptic history and culture, fully illustrated throughout.

The Koran (translated by Arthur J. Arberry, Oxford University Press; translated by J.M. Rodwell, out of print but available online at ⓦ www.gutenberg.org/etext/2800). The word of God as proclaimed by Mohammed is notoriously untranslatable. Arberry's version attempts to

preserve its poetic beauty and retains the traditional arrangement of suras (according to their length). Rodwell's 1861 translation is a little dated, but provides analytical footnotes, and was originally arranged, as far as possible, in the order in which the suras were composed, making it easier to follow the development of style and ideas; unfortunately most modern editions of Rodwell's translation revert to the traditional order.

Culture

Galal Amin *Whatever Happened to the Egyptians? Whatever Else Happened to the Egyptians?* Two insightful, wryly readable accounts of social changes in Egypt from the 1950s to the present. Subjects covered range from car ownership and Westernization in the first book, to TV, fashions and weddings in the second.

E. W. Lane *Manners and Customs of the Modern Egyptians* (online at ⓦ www.archive.org/details /accountofmanners00edwa). An encyclopedic study of life in Mohammed Ali's Cairo, which was first published in 1836. Highly browsable.

Maria Golia *Cairo: City of Sand*. An intriguing fly-on-the-wall look at the nitty-gritty of contemporary Cairo, including life in its satellite cities, the inanity of its prestige projects, and other subjects that defy easy generalization.

Nawal el-Saadawi *The Hidden Face of Eve*. Egypt's best-known woman writer; this is her major polemic, covering a wide range of topics – female circumcision, prostitution, divorce and sexual relationships. Her website (@www.nawalsaadawi.net) embraces literature, sociology and politics (see also p.272).

History

Said K. Aburish *Nasser: The Last Arab*. A new look at an old hero, who embodied the aspirations and contradictions of Arab nationalism. As the author of books on Saddam Hussein, Arafat and the House of Saud, Aburish mourns the lack of a new Nasser to inspire the Arabs today.

Andrew Beattie *Cairo: a Cultural History*. A wide-ranging history, covering everything from the city's monuments and religions to the writers who have described it and the conquerors to whom it has fallen, not to mention the really important questions, such as whether the pyramids really were built by Martians.

Desmond Stewart *Great Cairo: Mother of the World*. An informative summary of the city's history, concise and well put-together but decades out of date (it was last revised in the 1970s).

Max Rodenbeck *Cairo: the City Victorious*. This superb history of Cairo, by *The Economist*'s Cairo correspondent, is a very engaging read, full of anecdotes and observations on life in the great city from ancient times through to the end of the twentieth century.

Pyramidology

Guillemette Andreu *Egypt in the Age of the Pyramids*. Nicely illustrated study of the pyramids' evolution in the context of Ancient Egyptian life and culture, by a French Egyptologist.

Robert Bauval *The Orion Mystery*. Postulates a theory that the Giza Pyramids corresponded to the three stars in Orion's Belt as it was in 10,500 BC.

I. E. S. Edwards *The Pyramids of Egypt*. Lavishly illustrated, closely argued survey of all the major pyramids, though overdue for an update since it was last revised in 1991.

Graham Hancock *Fingerprints of the Gods*; *The Message of the Sphinx*; *Heaven's Mirror*. Asserts that the pyramids, Angkor Wat and the statues of Easter Island were all created by a lost civilization which disappeared around fourteen thousand years ago.

Peter Hodges *How the Pyramids were Built*. As a professional stonemason, Hodges has practical experience, rather than academic qualifications, on his side. An easy read and quite persuasive.

Mark Lehner *The Complete Pyramids*. Lavish but informative coffee-table book, whose colour photos of the pyramids – be it the famous ones at Giza or the less well-known ones further afield – are well supplemented with ground plans, maps, diagrams and detailed explanatory text.

Fiction

The Arabian Nights (translated by Malcolm and Ursula Lyons; three volumes). No translation – nor indeed any Arabic edition – of this famous, and rather adult, fairytale collection is entirely satisfactory, but this is the latest, the best, and certainly the most accessible (although Richard Burton's nineteenth-century version is available for free online at ⓦ www.burtonia.org. The *Nights* came together over centuries, but a large number of its tales were written and set in Mamluke Cairo. If you want to read about the *Nights*, the best introduction by far is Robert Irwin's *The Arabian Nights: a Companion*.

🏃 **Alaa Al-Aswany** *The Yacoubian Building*. Featuring such taboo subjects as gay sex, prostitution and police torture, Al-Aswany's first novel was an immediate – and controversial – bestseller across the Arab world. The tenants of a downtown apartment block are a microcosm of Egyptian society, with each character vividly drawn.

Salwa Bakr *The Golden Chariot*; *The Wiles of Men and Other Stories*. A novel set in a women's prison near Cairo; the inmates' tales highlight different facets of women's oppression in contemporary Egypt. Touching and disturbing.

Noel Barber *A Woman of Cairo*. Ill-starred love and destiny amongst the Brits and Westernized Egyptians of King Farouk's Cairo; from that perspective, a good insight into those times.

Len Deighton *City of Gold*. Hard-boiled thriller set in 1941, when vital information was being leaked to Rommel. The period detail of wartime Cairo is excellent.

Yusuf Idris *The Cheapest Nights*; *Rings of Burnished Brass*. Two superb collections by Egypt's finest writer

of short stories, who died in 1991. Uncompromisingly direct, yet ironic.

Robert Irwin *The Arabian Nightmare*. Paranoid fantasy set in the Cairo of Sultan Qaitbey, where a Christian spy contracts a mysterious affliction known as the Arabian Nightmare. As his madness deepens, reality and illusion spiral inwards like an opium-drugged walk through a medina of the mind. Irwin is an Arabist, whose non-fiction works include a companion to the *Arabian Nights* (see above).

🏃 **Khaled Al Khamissi** *Taxi*. Fifty-eight conversations with Cairo cabbies make up this brilliant portrait of daily life in the nation's capital, illustrating the joys, the frustrations and the resilience of its inhabitants as they negotiate the daily grind. After reading this, you'll never look the same way at a taxi diver again.

🏃 **Naguib Mahfouz** *Midaq Alley*; *The Beginning and the End*; *The Cairo Trilogy* (*Palace Walk*; *Palace of Desires*; *Sugar Street*); *Miramar*. The late Nobel laureate's novels have a nineteenth-century feel, reminiscent of Balzac or Victor Hugo. *Midaq Alley* (see p.79) and *The Beginning and the End* were both made into classic Egyptian films (well worth getting if you can find them on subtitled DVDs). *The Cairo Trilogy* is a tri-generational saga set during the British occupation, while *Miramar* looks back on the 1952 Revolution from the twilight of the Nasser era. Mahfouz muses on the discrepancy between ideology and human problems, and hypocrisy and injustice.

Dan Richardson *Gog – an End Time Mystery*. Set in a flood-ravaged Egypt after terrorists destroyed the Aswan High Dam, this near-future thriller, written by one of the authors of this guide, has some memorable Egyptian characters and savage plot twists, played out amid the ruins of Cairo, a Pre-Dynastic tomb on the Giza Plateau, and other dramatic locations.

Nawal el-Saadawi *Woman at Point Zero*; *The Fall of the Imam*; *God Dies by the Nile*. Saadawi's novels are informed by her work as a doctor and psychiatrist in Cairo, and by her feminist and socialist beliefs, on subjects that are virtually taboo in Egypt. Her best, *Woman at Point Zero*, is a powerful and moving story of a woman condemned to death for killing a pimp. You will find very few of her books on sale in Egypt, though *The Fall of the Imam* is the only one officially banned (see also p.270).

Language

Language

Arabic

Although Arabic is the common and official language of 23 countries, the spoken dialect of each can vary considerably. **Egyptian Arabic**, however, is the most widely understood in the Arab world, because of Egypt's vast film, television and music industry.

Cairenes are well used to tourists who speak only their own language, but an attempt to tackle at least a few words in Arabic is invariably greeted with great delight and encouragement. Most educated Cairenes will have been taught some English and are only too happy to practise it on you, but a little Arabic is a big help in *baladi* neighbourhoods or the remoter pyramid sites.

Transliteration from Arabic script into English presents some problems, since some letters have no equivalents and there is no set way of rendering vowel sounds either. This means that even where English signage is common (downtown, and major tourist sites), you can find the same Arabic names spelt in several different ways. The phonetic guide below should help with **pronunciation**:

ai as in eye	ey/ay as in day
aa as in bad but lengthened	ee as in feet
aw as in rose	gh like the French r (back of the throat)
' a glottal stop as in bottle	kh as in Scottish loch
' as when asked to say ah by the doctor	

Note that every letter should be pronounced, and that double consonants should always be pronounced separately. In the following vocabulary, **bold** type is used to indicate **stress**.

Vocabulary

Whatever else you do, at least make an effort to learn the Arabic numerals and polite greetings. The phrases and terms in this section represent only the most common bits of vocabulary you might need; for a comprehensive list, try the *Rough Guide Egyptian Arabic Phrasebook*.

Basics

Yes	**ai**wa or na'am	Come in, please	it**fad**dal (m)/
No	la (la-a for emphasis)	(to m/f)	itfad**dali** (f)
Thank you	**shok**ran	Excuse me	low sa**maht** (m)/
You're welcome	**af**wan		samahti (f)
Please (to m/f)	min fadlak (m)/	Sorry	aasif (m)/asfa (f)
	fadlik (f)	God willing	in**shal**lah

Greetings and farewells

Welcome/hello	**ah**lan w-**sah**lan
(response)	**ah**lan bik (m)/**bi**ki (f)/ bikum (pl)
Hello (formal)	assal**aam**u al**ei**kum
(response)	wa-al**ei**kum assal**aam**
Greetings	mar**haba**/sa'eeda
Nice to meet you	fursa sa'eeda
Good morning	sa**bah** il-kheer
(morning of goodness)	
(response: morning	sa**bah** in-nur
of light)	
Good evening	masa' il-kheer
(evening of goodness)	

(response–evening	masa' in-**nur**
of light)	
How are you (m/f) ?	iz**zay**ak (m)/iz**zay**ik (f)
[I'm] Fine (m/f)	kwayy**is** (m)/
	kwayy**isa** (f)
Thanks be to God	il-ham**du** lil**lah**
Good night	tis**bah** (m)/tis**bah**i (f)
	'ala kheer
And to you (m/f)	**wen**ta (m)/**wen**ti (f)
	bikheer
Goodbye	ma'a sal**aam**a

Directions

Where is…	**fey**n…
the hotel (name)?	il-**fun**duk (name)?
(name) restaurant?	mat'am (name)?
the airport?	il-mat**aar**?
the bus station?	ma**hat**tat il-autobees?
the hospital?	il-mu**stash**fa?
the service taxi depot?	el-**mo**gaf?
the toilet?	il-**twa**let?
the train station?	ma**hat**tat il-atr?
left/right/straight ahead	shim**aal**/yim**een**/ 'ala **tool**

near/far	areeb/ba'eed
here/there	**hi**na/**hi**nak
When does the bus leave?	il-autob**ees** yisafir imta?
When does the train leave?	il-atr yisafir imta?
…arrive?	…**yoo**sal?
What time (is it)?	is**sa'a** kam?
first/last/next	il-**aw**wil/il-**ak**hir/et-tani
nothing	walla**haaga**
not yet	**lis**sa

Shopping

Do you (m/f) have…?	fi '**an**dak (m)/ '**an**dik (f)…?
…cigarette(s)	…sig**aara**/sagayir
…matches	…kib**reet**
…newspaper	…gurnal
I (m/f) want something…	**ay**yiz (m)/**ay**yiza (f) haaga…
…else	…tani
…better than this	…ahsan min da
…cheaper	…arkhas min da
…like this	…zay da
(but)	(wa-laakin)

bigger/smaller	**ak**bar/asghar
How much (is it)?	bi-kam (da)?
It's too expensive	da ghaali **awi**
big	keb**eer**
small	sughayyar
That's fine	**maa**shi
There is/is there?	fi?
This/that	di/da
I (m/f) want my change	**ay**yiz/**ay**yiza fakka

Accommodation

Do you (m/f) have a room?	fi 'andak (m)/ '**an**dik (f) ouda?
Can I see the rooms?	mumkin ashuf il-owad?

Is there…?	fi…?
…hot water?	…mayya **sukh**na?
…a shower?	…doush?

| ...a balcony? | ...balcona? | ...a telephone? | ...telifoon? |
| ...air conditioning? | ...takyeef **hawa**? | How much is the bill? | kam il-his**ab**? |

Useful phrases

What is your (m/f) name?	**is**mak (m)/**is**mik (f) ey?	I (m/f) am hungry	ana gaw**'aan** (m)/ gaw**'aana** (f)
My name is...	**is**mi...	I (m/f) am thirsty	ana 'ats**haan** (m)/ 'ats**haana** (f)
Do you (m/f) speak...	tit**kall**im (m)/ titkall**imi**...(f)	I (m/f) (don't) want...	(mish) **ayy**iz (m)/ **ayy**iza (f)...
English?	ing**lee**zi?	I (m/f) am (not) married	ana (mish) mit**gaw**wiz (m)/ mitgaw**wiza** (f)
French?	fran**sawi**?		
I speak English	ana bat**kall**im ing**lee**zi	It's not your business	mish **shugh**lak
I don't speak Arabic	ana ma-bat**kall**im '**arabi**	Don't touch me!	sibni le wadi!
		Behave yourself	hatirim nassak
I understand (a little)	ana **fahem** (shwaiya)	Let's go	**ya**lla
What's that in English?	ya**'ani** ey bil-ing**lee**zi?	Slowly	ba**raahah**
I (m/f) don't understand	ana mish **fahem** (m)/ **fahma** (f)	Enough! Finished!	khalas
		Never mind	maalesh
I (m/f) don't know	ana mish '**aar**if (m)/ '**aar**fa (f)	It doesn't matter	mish muhim
		There's no problem	ma **fee**sh mush**kil**a
I (m/f) am tired/ unwell	ana ta'a**baan** (m)/ ta'a**baan**a (f)	May I/is it possible?	**mum**kin?
		It's not possible	mish **mum**kin

Calendar

day	youm	later	ba**'deen**
night	leyla	Monday	youm il-it**nayn**
week	us**boo**'a	Tuesday	youm it-talaata
month	shahr	Wednesday	youm il-arb'a
year	sana	Thursday	youm il-khamees
today	inna**har**da	Friday	youm il-gum'a
tomorrow	**buk**ra	Saturday	youm is-sabt
yesterday	im**baar**ih	Sunday	youm il-ahad

Money

Where's the bank?	feyn il-bank?	Egyptian pound	gi**ney**
I (m/f) want to change...	ayyiz/ayyiza a**ghayyar**...	half pound (50 piastres)	nuss gi**ney**
...money	...floos	quarter pound (25 piastres)	roba' gi**ney**
...British pounds	...gi**nay** sterlini	piastre	**ir**sh
...US dollars	...dolar am**rikani**		
...Euros	...euro		
...travellers' cheques	...shikaat siyahiyya		

Numbers and fractions

Though **Arabic numerals** may seem confusing at first, they are not hard to learn and with a little practice you should soon be able to read bus numbers without any problems. The one and the nine are easy enough; the confusing ones are the five, which looks like a Western zero, the six, which looks like a Western seven, and the four, which looks like a three written backwards. In practice, once you've got the hang of it, the trickiest are the two and the three, which are sufficiently similar to be easily confused. Note that unlike the rest of the Arabic language, the numerals are written from left to right.

0	٠	sifr	21	٢١	**wa**hid wa 'ashreen
1	١	**wa**hid	30	٣٠	talaa**teen**
2	٢	it**nayn**	40	٤٠	arb'aeen
3	٣	ta**laa**ta	50	٥٠	kham**seen**
4	٤	arb'a	60	٦٠	sit**teen**
5	٥	**kham**sa	70	٧٠	sab'aeen
6	٦	**sit**ta	80	٨٠	tama**neen**
7	٧	sab'a	90	٩٠	tis'**een**
8	٨	ta**maa**nya	100	١٠٠	**mi**yya
9	٩	**tes**'a	121	١٢١	**mi**yya wa-**wa**hid wa 'ashreen
10	١٠	'ashara	200	٢٠٠	mi**tayn**
11	١١	hi**dar**sha	300	٣٠٠	ta**laa**ta **mi**yya
12	١٢	it**nar**sha	400	٤٠٠	arb'at **mi**yya
13	١٣	tala**tar**sha	1000	١٠٠٠	alf
14	١٤	arb'a**tar**sha	2000	٢٠٠٠	al**fayn**
15	١٥	khamas**tar**sha	3000	٣٠٠٠	ta**laat** alaaf
16	١٦	sit**tar**sha	4000	٤٠٠٠	**arb**'at alaaf
17	١٧	sab'a**tar**sha	½ or 500g		nuss
18	١٨	**taman**tarsha	¼ or 250g		**ro**ba'
19	١٩	**tis**'atarsha	1/8 or 125g		**tum**na
20	٢٠	'ash**reen**			

Food and drink glossary

Useful words and phrases

Bottle	izaaza		Table	tarabeyza
Fork	showka		The bill, please	El-hisaab, min fadlak (m) /min fadlik (f)
Give me/us...	Iddini/iddina...			
...a napkin	...futa		This is not...	Da mish...
...a plate	...taba'		...cooked enough	...mistiwi kwayyis
Glass	kubbaaya		...fresh	...taaza
I can't/don't eat...	Ana makulsh...		...meat	...lahm
I didn't order this	Ma'alabtish da		This is very tasty	Da lazeez awi
Knife	sikkeena		We don't want this	Ihna mish ayyeeen da
Menu	lista/menoo		We'd like the menu please	Ayyeeen el-menu min fadlak
Spoon	mala'a			

| We'd like to have... | Ihna ayyzeen... | With little sugar | Sukkar aleel |
| What is this? | 'Ey da? | Without sugar | Bidoon sukkar |

Staples

'aish	bread	lahma	meat
'asal	honey	melh	salt
beyd	eggs	murabba	jam
fawaakih	fruit	samak	fish
filfil	pepper	sukkar	sugar
firakh	chicken	zabaadi	yoghurt
gibna	cheese	zeit	oil
gibna beyda	white cheese	zeitun	olives
gibna rumi	yellow cheese	zibda	butter
khudaar	vegetables		

Drinks

'aseer	juice	nibeet	wine
'aseer asab	sugar-cane juice	sahleb	milky drink made with ground orchid root
'aseer burtu'an	orange juice		
'aseer limoon	lemon juice	shai	tea
'aseer manga	mango juice	shai bi-laban	tea with milk
'er' sous	liquorice-water	shai bi-na'ana	tea with mint
ahwa fransawi	instant or filter coffee	shai kushari	tea made with loose-leaf
ahwa	coffee (usually Turkish)		
beera	beer	shai lipton	tea made with a tea bag
helba	fenugreek infusion		
irfa	cinnamon infusion	tamar hindi	tamarind (cordial)
karkaday	hibiscus	yansoon	aniseed infusion
laban	milk	zibiba	ouzo
mayya ma'adaniyya	mineral water	'ariha	little sugar
mayya	water	saada	no sugar
		ziyaada	very sweet

Soups, salads and vegetables

baamya	okra (ladies' fingers)	ruz	rice
basal	onion	salata	salad
bataatis	potatoes	salatit khadra	mixed green salad
bidingaan	eggplant (aubergine)	salatit khiyaar	cucumber salad
bisilla	peas	salatit tamatim	tomato salad
fasuliyya	beans	shurba	soup
gazar	carrots	shurbit 'ads	lentil soup
molukhiyya	Jew's mallow, a leafy vegetable stewed with meat or chicken broth and garlic to make a slimy, spinach-like soup	shurbit firakh	chicken soup
		shurbit khudaar	vegetable soup
		tarboola	salad of bulgur wheat, parsley and tomato
		torshi	pickled vegetables

Main dishes

bolti	Nile perch	kofta	minced meat flavoured with spices and onions, grilled on a skewer
bouri	mullet		
calamari	squid		
denis	sea bream		
dik rumi	turkey	lahm dani	lamb
fatta	mutton or chicken stew, cooked with bread	marqaan	snapper
		mokh	(sheep) brains
		samak mashwi	grilled fish served with salad, bread and dips
firakh	chicken grilled or stewed and served with vegetables	shish kebab	chunks of meat, usually lamb, grilled on a skewer with onions and tomatoes
gambari	prawns		
hamam mashwi	grilled pigeon		
kalewi	kidney		
kibda	liver, stewed with green peppers and chili	shish tawook	a kebab of marinated, spiced chicken
		soubeit	sole

Appetizers and fast food

babaghanoug	paste of aubergines mashed with tahina	mahshi	literally "stuffed", variety of vegetables (peppers, tomatoes, aubergines, courgettes) filled with minced meat and/or rice, herbs and pine nuts
fiteer	a sort of pancake made of layers of flaky filo pastry with sweet or savoury fillings		
fuul	boiled fava beans served with oil and lemon, sometimes also with onions, meat, eggs or tomato sauce	makarona	macaroni "cake" baked in a white sauce or minced meat gravy
		shakshouka	chopped meat and tomato sauce, cooked with an egg on top
hummus	chickpea paste mixed with tahini, garlic and lemon, sometimes served with pine nuts and/or meat (but also just the Arabic for chickpeas/garbanzo beans – more commonly used with that meaning in Egypt)	shawarma	slivers of pressed, spit-roasted lamb, served in pitta bread
		taamiya	falafel; balls of deep-fried mashed chickpeas and spices
		tahina	sesame seed paste mixed with spices, garlic and lemon, eaten with pitta bread
kushari	mixture of noodles, lentils and rice, topped with fried onions and a spicy tomato sauce	wara einab	vine leaves filled as mahshi are and flavoured with lemon juice

Desserts, sweets, fruits and nuts

'ishta	cream	mahalabiyya	sweet rice or cornflour pudding, topped with pistachios
baklava	flaky filo pastry, honey and nuts		
balah	dates	mawz	bananas
balila	milk dish with nuts, raisins and wheat	mishmish	apricots
		shammam	melon
basbousa	pastry of semolina, honey and nuts	teen	figs
		teen shawqi	prickly pear (cactus fruit)
battikh	watermelon		
farawla	strawberries	tuffah	apples
fuul sudaani	peanuts	umm (or om) ali	corn cake soaked in milk, sugar, raisins, coconut and cinnamon, usually served hot
gelati or ays krim	ice cream		
lawz	almonds		
lib batteekh	watermelon seeds		

Glossary

Common alternative spellings are given in brackets.

ablaq Striped. An effect achieved by painting, or laying courses of different coloured masonry; usually white with red or buff. A Bahri Mamluke innovation, possibly derived from the Roman technique of *opus mixtum* – an alternation of stone and brickwork.

ain (ayn, ein) Spring water.

amir (emir) Commander, prince.

ba The Ancient Egyptian equivalent of the soul or personality, often represented by a human-headed bird; also used to describe the physical manifestation of certain gods.

bab Gate or door, as in the medieval city walls.

bahr River, sea, canal.

baksheesh Alms or tips.

baraka Blessing.

beit (beyt) House. Segregated public and private quarters, the *malqaf*, *maq'ad* and *mashrabiya* are typical features of old Cairene mansions.

bey (bay) Lord or noble; an Ottoman title, now a respectful form of address to anyone in authority.

birka (birqa, birket) Lake.

burg (borg) Tower.

calèche Horse-drawn carriage.

caliph Successor to the Prophet Mohammed and spiritual and political leader of the Muslim empire. A struggle over this office caused the Sunni–Shia schism of 656 AD.

Canopic jar Sealed receptacle used in funerary rituals to preserve the viscera of the deceased after embalming. The stomach, intestines, liver and lungs each had a patron deity, sculpted on the jar's lid.

Central Security Force Riot-police, stationed on street corners downtown, and outside embassies, banks, etc.

cloisonné A multi-step enamelling process used to produce jewellery, vases and other decorative objects.

corniche Riverfront (or seafront) promenade.

darb Path or way; can apply to alleyways, thoroughfares, or desert caravan routes.

deir Monastery or convent.

felucca Nile sailing boat.

finial Ornamental crown of a dome or minaret, often topped by an Islamic crescent.

gadid/gadida "New" in Arabic; the ending depends on whether the subject of the adjective is masculine or feminine.

galabiyya Loose flowing robe worn by men.

gezira Island.

hagg/hagga One who has visited Mecca.

haikal Sanctuary of a Coptic church.

hajj (hadj) Pilgrimage to Mecca.

hammam Turkish bathhouse.

hara Alley, lane or quarter.

haramlik Literally the "forbidden" area, ie women's or private apartments in a house or palace.

Heb-Sed An Ancient Egyptian festival symbolizing the renewal of the king's physical and magical powers, celebrated in the thirtieth year of his reign and every three years thereafter.

Islamist(s) Groups aiming to replace secular with Sharia law and end Egypt's alignment with Israel – some by peaceful means, others violently.

ka Ancient Egyptians believed that an individual's life-force served as the "double" of his or her physical being and required sustenance after their death, through offerings to the deceased's *ka* statue, sometimes secluded in a *serdab*.

khalig Canal or gulf.

khan Place where goods were made, stored and sold, which also provided accommodation for travellers and merchants, like a *wikala*.

khedive Viceroy.

khirtiya Street-hustlers.

kufic The earliest style of Arabic script; Foliate *kufic* was a more elaborate form, superseded by *naskhi* script.

kuttab Koranic school, usually for boys or orphans.

leyla kebira "Big night": the climactic night of a popular religious festival.

liwan An arcade or vaulted space off a courtyard in mosques and *madrassas*; originally, the term meant a sitting room opening onto a covered court.

madrassa Literally a "place of study" but generally used to designate theological schools. Each *madrassa* propagates a particular school of Islamic jurisprudence.

malqaf Wind scoop for directing cool breezes into houses; in Egypt, they always face north, towards the prevailing wind.

mashrabiya An alcove in lattice windows where jars of water can be cooled by the wind; by extension, the projecting balcony and screened window itself, which enabled women to watch street-life or the *salamlik* without being observed.

Masr (Misr, Musr) Popular name for Egypt, and Cairo, dating back to antiquity.

mastaba Mud-brick benches outside buildings; Egyptologists use the word to describe the flat-roofed, multi-roomed tombs of the Old Kingdom, found at Saqqara and other sites.

midan An open space or square; in Tulunid Cairo most were originally polo grounds.

mihrab Niche indicating the direction of Mecca, to which all Muslims pray.

minaret Tower from which the call to prayer is given; derived from *minara*, the Arabic word for "beacon" or "lighthouse".

minbar Pulpit from which an address to the Friday congregation is given. Often superbly inlaid or carved in variegated marble or wood.

moulid Popular festival marking an event in the Koran or the birthday of a Muslim saint. The term also applies to the name-days of Coptic saints.

muezzin A prayer-crier (who nowadays is more likely to broadcast by loudspeaker than to climb up and shout from the minaret).

muqarnas Stalactites, pendants or honeycomb ornamentation of portals, domes or squinches.

naos The core and sanctuary of a Coptic or Byzantine church, where the liturgy is performed.

naskhi Form of Arabic script with joined-up letters, introduced by the Ayyubids.

ostracon (pl. ostraca) A Greek term used by archeologists to describe potsherds or flakes of limestone bearing texts and drawings, often consisting of personal jottings, letters or scribal exercises.

pasha (pacha) Originally a Turkish title for

the governors of provinces of the Ottoman Empire, it is nowadays a respectful term of address for anyone in authority, pronounced "basha".

pronaos Vestibule of a Greek or Roman temple, enclosed by side walls and a row of columns in front.

pylon A broad, majestic gateway that formed the entrance to temples from the XVIII Dynasty onwards, or a series of gateways within large complexes.

qadim/qadima (masc./fem.) "Old", as in Masr al-Qadima, or Old Cairo.

qalaa Fortress, citadel.

qasr Palace, fortress, mansion.

qibla The direction in which Muslims pray, indicated in mosques by the wall where the *mihrab* is located.

qubba Dome, and by extension any domed tomb or shrine.

repoussé A technique in which malleable metal is ornamented by hammering from the reverse side to form a raised design on the front, which is often combined with the opposite technique of chasing (hammering from the front) to form a finished piece.

riwaq Arcaded aisle around a mosque's *sahn*, originally used as residential quarters for theological students. Ordinary folk may take naps in these cool and quiet spaces.

sabil Public fountain or water cistern. During the nineteenth century it was often combined with a Koranic school to make a *sabil-kuttab*.

sahn Central courtyard of a mosque, frequently surrounded by *riwaqs* or *liwans*.

salamlik The "greeting" area of a house; ie the public and men's apartments.

sanctuary The *liwan* incorporating the *qibla* wall in a mosque, or the shrine of a deity in an Ancient Egyptian temple.

serdab The Arabic word for a cellar beneath a mosque. Also used by Egyptologists to describe the room in *mastaba* tombs where

statues of the deceased's *ka* were placed, often with eye-holes or a slit in the wall enabling the *ka* to leave the chamber, and offerings to be made to the statue from the tomb's chapel.

shabti (ushabti) Ancient funerary figurines, whose purpose was to spare their owner from having to perform menial tasks in the after-life.

sharia Street (literally "way"). Sharia also refers to laws based on Koranic precepts (in which case the word has an Arabic feminine ending, and is sometimes transliterated as Shariah).

squinch An arch spanning the right angle formed by two walls, so as to support a dome.

sufis Islamic mystics who seek to attain union with Allah through trance-inducing *zikrs* and dances. The name comes from the rough *suf* or woollen garments worn by early Sufis. Whirling Dervishes belong to one of the Sufi sects.

Supreme Council for Antiquities (SCA) The state organization responsible for Egypt's ancient monuments.

tariqa A Sufi order or dervish brotherhood.

Thuluth Script whose vertical strokes are three times larger than its horizontal ones; *Thuluth* literally means "third".

uraeus (pl. uraei) The rearing cobra symbol of the Delta goddess Wadjet, worn as part of the royal crown and often identified with the destructive "Eye of Horus".

Wadi Valley or watercourse (usually dry).

wikala Bonded warehouse with rooms for merchants upstairs, where they bought trading licences from the *muhtasib* and haggled over sales in the courtyard. *Okel* is another term for a *wikala*.

zebaleen Rubbish-pickers, who have their own settlement below the Muqattam Hills.

zikr Marathon session of chanting and swaying, intended to induce communion with Allah.

Small print and

Index

A Rough Guide to Rough Guides

Published in 1982, the first Rough Guide – to Greece – was a student scheme that became a publishing phenomenon. Mark Ellingham, a recent graduate in English from Bristol University, had been travelling in Greece the previous summer and couldn't find the right guidebook. With a small group of friends he wrote his own guide, combining a highly contemporary, journalistic style with a thoroughly practical approach to travellers' needs.

The immediate success of the book spawned a series that rapidly covered dozens of destinations. And, in addition to impecunious backpackers, Rough Guides soon acquired a much broader and older readership that relished the guides' wit and inquisitiveness as much as their enthusiastic, critical approach and value-for-money ethos.

These days, Rough Guides include recommendations from shoestring to luxury and cover more than 200 destinations around the globe, including almost every country in the Americas and Europe, more than half of Africa and most of Asia and Australasia. Our ever-growing team of authors and photographers is spread all over the world, particularly in Europe, the US and Australia.

In the early 1990s, Rough Guides branched out of travel, with the publication of Rough Guides to World Music, Classical Music and the Internet. All three have become benchmark titles in their fields, spearheading the publication of a wide range of books under the Rough Guide name.

Including the travel series, Rough Guides now number more than 350 titles, covering: phrasebooks, waterproof maps, music guides from Opera to Heavy Metal, reference works as diverse as Conspiracy Theories and Shakespeare, and popular culture books from iPods to Poker. Rough Guides also produce a series of more than 120 World Music CDs in partnership with World Music Network.

Visit www.roughguides.com to see our latest publications.

Rough Guide credits

Text editor: Emma Gibbs
Layout: Nikhil Agarwal
Cartography: Ashutosh Bharti
Picture editor: Nicole Newman
Production: Rebecca Short
Proofreader: Stewart Wild
Cover design: Dan May and Nicole Newman
Photographer: Roger d'Olivere Mapp
Editorial: **London** Andy Turner, Keith Drew,
Edward Aves, Alice Park, Lucy White, Jo Kirby,
James Smart, Natasha Foges, James Rice,
Emma Beatson, Kathryn Lane, Monica Woods,
Mani Ramaswamy, Harry Wilson, Lucy Cowie,
Alison Roberts, Lara Kavanagh, Eleanor Aldridge,
Ian Blenkinsop, Charlotte Melville, Joe Staines,
Matthew Milton, Tracy Hopkins; **Delhi** Madhavi
Singh, Jalpreen Kaur Chhatwal, Dipika Dasgupta
Design & Pictures: **London** Scott Stickland,
Dan May, Diana Jarvis, Mark Thomas,
Rhiannon Furbear; **Delhi** Umesh Aggarwal,
Ajay Verma, Jessica Subramanian, Ankur Guha,
Pradeep Thapliyal, Sachin Tanwar, Anita Singh,
Sachin Gupta
Production: Liz Cherry, Louise Minihane,
Erika Pepe
Cartography: **London** Ed Wright, Katie Lloyd-
Jones; **Delhi** Rajesh Chhibber, Rajesh Mishra,
Animesh Pathak, Jasbir Sandhu, Swati Handoo,
Deshpal Dabas, Lokamata Sahu
Marketing, Publicity & roughguides.com:
Liz Statham
Digital Travel Publisher: Peter Buckley
Reference Director: Andrew Lockett
Operations Coordinator: Becky Doyle
Operations Assistant: Johanna Wurm
Publishing Director (Travel): Clare Currie
Commercial Manager: Gino Magnotta
Managing Director: John Duhigg

Publishing information

This first edition published September 2011 by
Rough Guides Ltd,
80 Strand, London WC2R 0RL
11, Community Centre, Panchsheel Park,
New Delhi 110017, India

Distributed by the Penguin Group

Penguin Books Ltd,
80 Strand, London WC2R 0RL

Penguin Group (USA)
375 Hudson Street, NY 10014, USA

Penguin Group (Australia)
250 Camberwell Road, Camberwell,
Victoria 3124, Australia

Penguin Group (NZ)
67 Apollo Drive, Mairangi Bay, Auckland 1310,
New Zealand

Rough Guides is represented in Canada by
Tourmaline Editions Inc. 662 King Street West,
Suite 304, Toronto, Ontario M5V 1M7

Cover concept by Peter Dyer.

Typeset in Bembo and Helvetica to an original
design by Henry Iles.

Help us update

We've gone to a lot of effort to ensure that
the first edition of **The Rough Guide to Cairo
and the Pyramids** is accurate and up-to-
date. However, things change – places get
"discovered", opening hours are notoriously
fickle, restaurants and rooms raise prices or lower
standards. If you feel we've got it wrong or left
something out, we'd like to know, and if you can
remember the address, the price, the hours, the
phone number, so much the better.

Please send your comments with the subject
line "**Rough Guide Cairo and the Pyramids
Update**" to ©mail@uk.roughguides.com. We'll
credit all contributions and send a copy of the
next edition (or any other Rough Guide if you
prefer) for the very best emails.

Find more travel information, connect with
fellow travellers and book your trip on ⓦwww
.roughguides.com

Acknowledgements

Dan Richardson: Thanks to Bill Halsey for his insights into Cairo's theatres, and Stepan Kabele for the city's ethno-music scene.

Daniel Jacobs: Big thanks to Hisham Youssef (Berlin Hotel), Salah Mohammed, Hamdi Shora,

Humphrey Davies and Caroline Evanoff for their material help, their suggestions and their invaluable inside information.

Photo credits

Index

Map entries are in colour.

INDEX

T

U

V

W

Y

Z

Map symbols

maps are listed in the full index using coloured text

– – –	Chapter division boundary		✹	Shipwreck
═══	Main road		▣	Restaurant
═══	Minor road		◉	Hotel
:::::	Tunnel		⊙	Statue
�	Steps		★	Transport stop
- - - - -	Footpath/track		🝙	Garage/fuel station
———	River		ℂ	Telephone
— —	Ferry route		⊠	Post office
━━━	Railway		(i)	Information point
—Ⓜ—	Metro line & station		@	Internet access
———	Fortified Wall		Ⓟ	Parking
⊠	Gate		⋔	Monastery/convent
)(	Bridge/tunnel		✡	Synagogue
⚓	Ferry/boat stop		▬	Building
♦	Point of interest		⊞	Church
✈	Airport		◡	Mosque
ᶬᶬ	Cliff face/escarpment		⊡	Christian cemetery
🌴	Oasis/palm grove		⊡	Muslim cemetery
⋀ᶺ	Spring		▦	Park/national park
▲	Mountain peak		▨	Beach/dunes
△	Pyramid		⊟	Saltpan

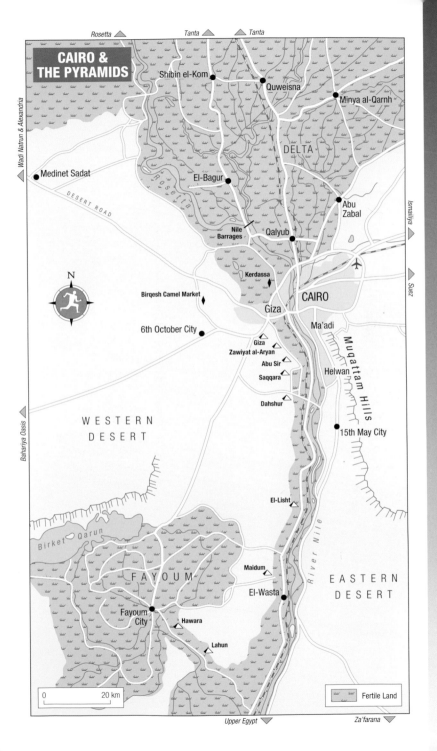

CAIRO & THE PYRAMIDS

Rosetta

Tanta

Tanta

Wadi Natrun & Alexandria

Shibin el-Kom

Quweisna

Minya al-Qarnh

DELTA

Medinet Sadat

El-Bagur

Abu Zabal

Ismailiya

DESERT ROAD

Nile Barrages

Qalyub

Kerdassa

Suez

N

Birqesh Camel Market

CAIRO

Giza

6th October City

Ma'adi

Giza

Zawiyat al-Aryan

Abu Sir

Saqqara

Helwan

Muqattam Hills

Dahshur

Bahariya Oasis

WESTERN DESERT

15th May City

EASTERN DESERT

El-Lisht

Birket Qarun

FAYOUM

Maidum

El-Wasta

River Nile

Fayoum City

Hawara

Lahun

0   20 km

Fertile Land

Upper Egypt

Za'farana

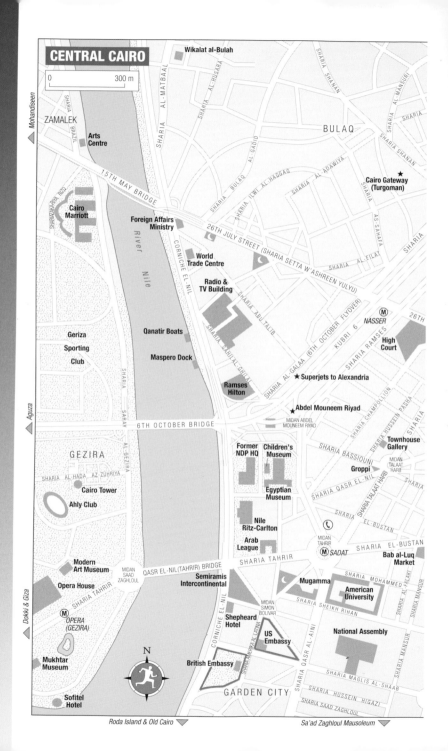

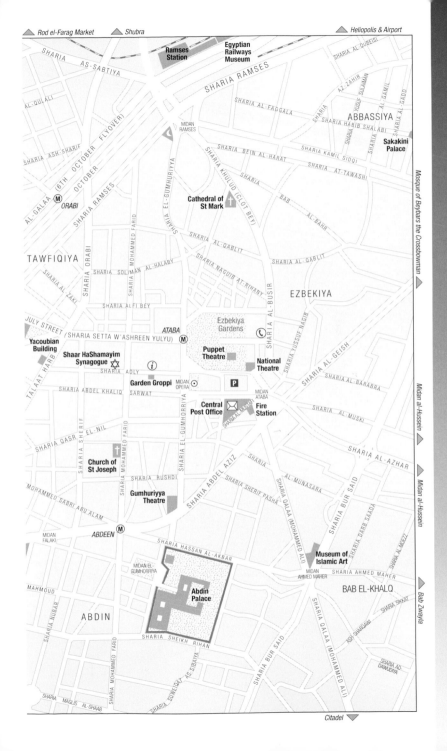

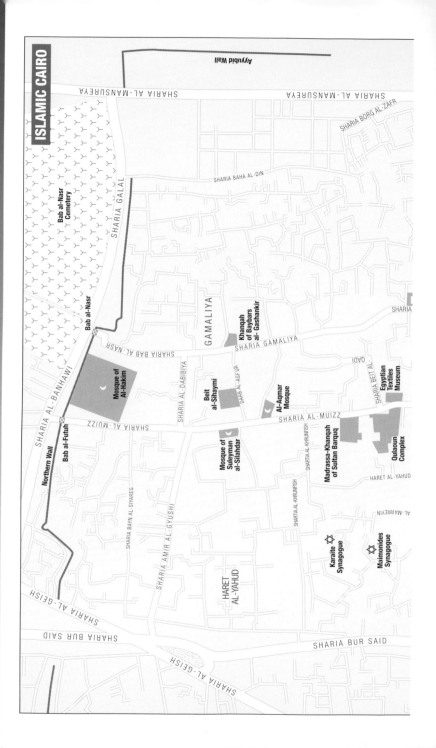

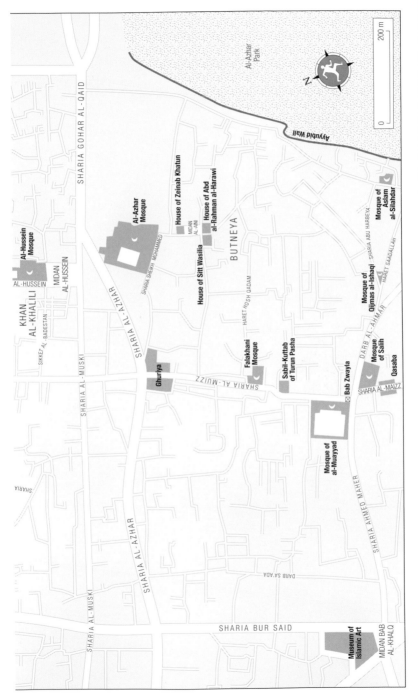

SHARIA AL-MUSKI

SHARIA

SHARIA AL-MUSKI

SHARIA GOHAR AL-QAID

Al-Hussein Mosque

KHAN AL-KHALILI

SIKKET AL-BADESTAN

MIDAN AL-HUSSEIN

AL-HUSSEIN

Al-Azhar Mosque

SHARIA SHEIKH MOHAMMED

SHARIA AL-AZHAR

House of Zeinab Khatun

House of Abd al-Rahman al-Harawi

MIDAN AL-AINI

House of Sitt Wasilia

BUTNEYA

HARET HOSH QADAM

Ghuriya

Falakhani Mosque

SHARIA AL-MUIZZ

Sabil-Kuttab of Turun Pasha

⊠ **Bab Zwayla**

Mosque of al-Muayyad

Mosque of Oljmas al-Ishaqi

SHARIA ABU HARBEYA

HARET SAADALLAH

DARB AL-AHMAR

Mosque of Salih

SHARIA AL-MAIZZ

Qasaba

Mosque of Aslam al-Silahdar

Ayyubid Wall

Al-Azhar Park

N

0   200 m

SHARIA BUR SAID

SHARIA AL-AZHAR

DARB SA'ADA

SHARIA AHMED MAHER

Museum of Islamic Art

MIDAN BAB AL-KHALQ

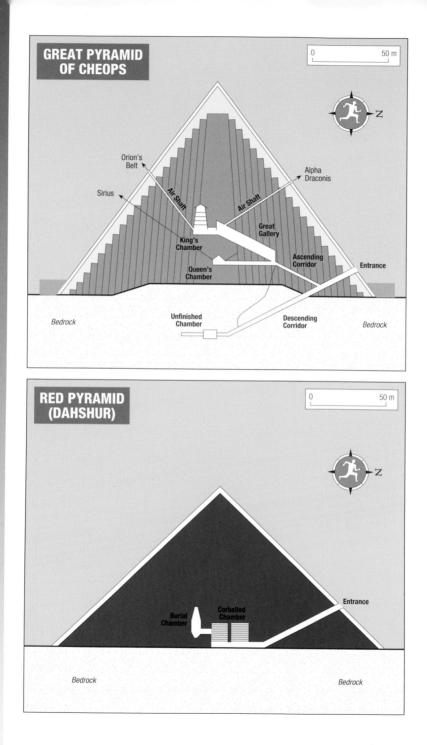

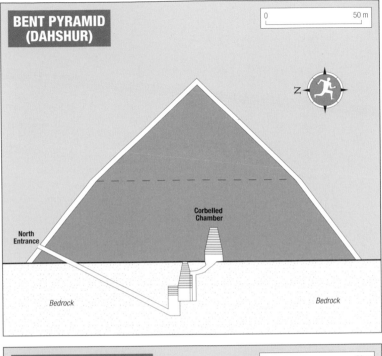

BENT PYRAMID (DAHSHUR)

0   50 m

Z

Corbelled
Chamber

North
Entrance

Bedrock   Bedrock

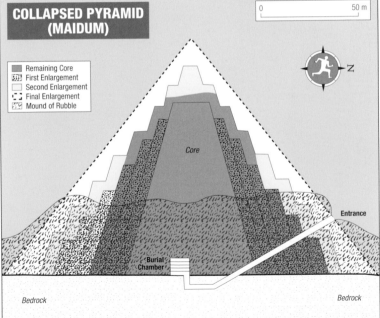

COLLAPSED PYRAMID (MAIDUM)

0   50 m

Z

Remaining Core
First Enlargement
Second Enlargement
Final Enlargement
Mound of Rubble

Core

Entrance

Burial
Chamber

Bedrock   Bedrock

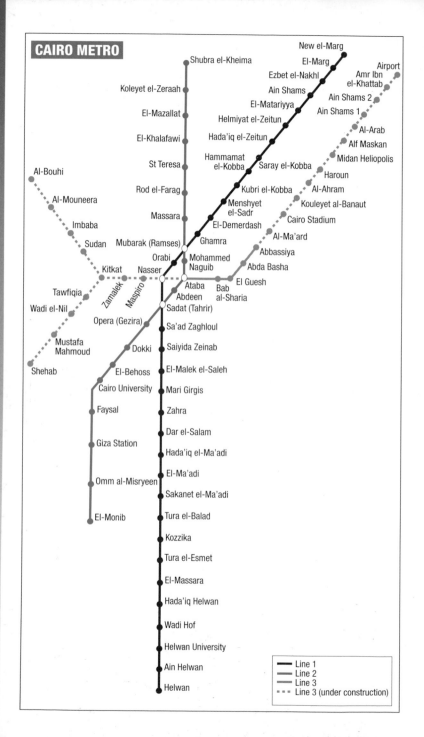

CAIRO METRO